In the Cockpit

Flying the World's Great Aircraft

Introduction by
Jeffrey Quill OBE, AFC

Edited by
Anthony Robinson

New Material Compiled and Edited by
Michael J H Taylor

USAF
00889

U.S. AIR FORCE

43

CHARTWELL BOOKS, INC.

Endpapers: a SEPECAT Jaguar GR Mark 1 of
the Royal Air Force (MoD)

Title page: the Northrop F-5F is the two-seat
trainer version of the Tiger II fighter (Northrop)

Half title: the unusual pusher configuration of the
J21A resulted from a desire to improve the pilot's
view, utilise a nosewheel undercarriage and concentrate a heavy armament in the nose of a single-
engined fighter. The type was employed in the
fighter and attack roles (Saab).

Contents

Antoinette 2
Mike Jerram

Avro Triplane 5
Mike Jerram

Bleriot Monoplane 8
Mike Jerram

Bristol Boxkite 13
Mike Jerram

Blackburn Monoplane 18
Mike Jerram

Curtiss Jenny 21
Peter Kilduff

Fokker Eindecker 26
Peter Kilduff

Sopwith Pup 32
Mike Jerram

Fokker Triplane 37
Peter Kilduff

Sopwith Camel 48
Mike Jerram

SPAD SXIII 56
Peter Kilduff

de Havilland DH4 and DH9 61
Peter Kilduff

Bristol Fighter 66
Mike Jerram

Handley Page O/400 72
Peter Kilduff

Avro 504K 76
Mike Jerram

de Havilland Moth 81
Mike Jerram

Ford Tri-Motor 85
Mike Jerram

Junkers Ju 52 89
Mike Jerram

Douglas DC-3 94
Mike Jerram

Bristol Bulldog 101
F.K. Mason

Hawker Hart 104
Duncan Simpson

Gloster Gladiador 109
Wg Cdr R.R. Stanford Tuck DSO DFC
RAF (Ret'd)

Hawker Fury 114
Mike Jerram

Boeing P-26 118
Lt Gen Ira C. Eaker USAF (Ret'd)

Hawker Hurricane 121
Wg Cdr R.R. Stanford Tuck DSO DFC
RAF (Ret'd)

Supermarine Spitfire 128
Air Vice-Marshal J.E. Johnson CB CBE
DSO DFC RAF (Ret'd)

Fairey Swordfish 141
Mike Jerram

Short Sunderland 148
Mike Jerram

Westland Lysander 152
Mike Jerram

North American B-25 Mitchell 157
Mike Jerram

de Havilland Mosquito 161
F.K. Mason

Avro Lancaster 170
F.K. Mason

Mitsubishi A6M Zero 181
Mike Jerram

Grumman F6F Hellcat 185
Peter Kilduff

Vought F4U Corsair 192
Vice Admiral William D. houser
USN (Ret'd)

Boeing B-17 Flying Fortress 201
Simon Clay

North American P-51 Mustang 213
Simon Clay

Yak-1 to Yak-9 221
General J.M. Risso

Lavochkin LA-5FN 225
Colonel František Fajtl DFC
and Ladislav Valoušek

Messerschmitt Bf 109 230
Frank Osman

Messerschmitt Me 262 238
Frank Osman

Grumman F8F Bearcat 241
Peter Kilduff

Douglas A-1 Skyraider 247
Peter Kilduff

Gloster Meteor 253
F.K. Mason

Grumman F9F Panther 258
Peter Kilduff

North American F-86 Sabre 261
F.K. Mason

Fiat G 91 265
Cesare Falessi

Douglas A-4 Skyhawk 269
Peter Kilduff

British Aerospace Harrier 277
Wg Cdr G.R. Profit RAF

McDonnell F-4 Phantom 283
Peter Kilduff

Lockheed SR-71 293
Mike Jerram

McDonnell Douglas F-15 Eagle 297
Anthony Robinson

Boeing 747 302
Anthony Robinson

**British Aerospace/Aérospatiale
Concorde** 305
Captain D.G. Ross

Panavia Tornado GR.1 309
Ken Delve

Lockheed F-117A Nighthawk 312
Bill Gunston

Mikoyan MiG-29 'Fulcrum' 314
Jon Lake

Picture Acknowledgments 317

Index 317

Introduction

'In the Cockpit' is aptly named. The book contains a series of well-informed, descriptive and extremely well-illustrated articles, written primarily from the pilot's point of view, about no fewer than 51 aeroplanes, many of which achieved in their day a most well-deserved fame; others of which have hitherto been remembered perhaps only somewhat vaguely as names appearing in aviation histories or in the memoirs of old aviators.

The selection is essentially international in character and has been wisely made. There are five aircraft from the pre-World War I pioneering era and, appropriately, two of these are French. Eleven aircraft have been chosen from World War I – that period during which aviation technology made its first huge leap forward under the stimulus of war – and these comprise six British, three German (counting Anthony Fokker's products as German), one French and one American.

The period between the wars when the aviation industries inevitably had to unscramble themselves from their wartime effort, drastically reduce themselves in size, pause to digest the rapid technological advances that had been made, regroup themselves commercially and set a new course for the future to include the application of aviation for civil purposes, is represented by eight aircraft, five from Britain and three from the United States. Here, perhaps, a greater representation from early inter-war civil aircraft might have been hoped for, but it does include the famous Ford Tri-Motor which was the real beginning of the explosive expansion of commercial aviation in the United States, and it includes the ubiquitous DC-3. On the British civil side, that little trailblazer the Gipsy Moth is very appropriately included and British inter-war military aviation is represented by the Tiger Moth, the Bulldog, the Hart, the Fury and the Gladiator. Some of us who flew in that era are perhaps a little sad to see no Gamecock nor Grebe nor Siskin.

It is perhaps to be expected (and by no means regretted) that the largest group of aircraft is drawn from the Second World War and these are British, American, German, Japanese and Russian. The 'greats' are there – the Hurricane, the Spitfire, Mosquito and Lancaster, as well as the Boeing B-17 – and Germany's classic technological achievement – the Me 262 – is extremely well described.

With the magnificent exception of the Anglo-French supersonic airliner Concorde, the post-World War II period is entirely military in character, containing the early jet aircraft, Meteor and F-86 (in

Opposite: Supermarine Spitfire Mark VC
fighters of No 417 Squadron fly over Italy
during World War II (IWM)

fact the Meteor did just see service in the war). It also contains the first Mach 3 aircraft to enter operational service in any country – the Lockheed SR-71 Blackbird.

So the book effectively spans a huge swathe of the history of aviation, which is no mean task in itself, in a very vivid and readable form. The contributions are professional and although written primarily from the viewpoint of the man in the cockpit, there is a wide variety of treatment and authorship which keeps the whole thing very much alive when it might all too easily have become a mere catalogue.

It really does put us into the cockpit and it makes fascinating reading for those of us who have lived or taken an active part in aviation during most of the period covered and have flown a good many of the aircraft described (the author of this foreword has flown nineteen of them), but it will surely have an equal appeal to those who were not pilots.

Above all the book must have a huge appeal to the younger reader to whom so many of these aircraft have hitherto been mere historical names, for they are splendidly described and, due to the now widespread existence of rebuilds or replicas and modern colour photography, the older aircraft are splendidly illustrated as well. There are also many beautiful drawings.

To see the superb colour photographs of the Fokker Triplane and DVII, Sopwith Pup, Camel and Bristol Fighter in flight is somewhat like coming suddenly face to face with the Baron himself or with McCudden or Ball or other legendary figures of the first Great War.

Whether a reader's interest in aviation is technical or historical or just stemming from general interest and enthusiasm, this book will be a most valuable source of knowledge, interest and pleasure.

JEFFREY QUILL OBE, AFC

In the
Cockpit

Antoinette

Few pioneering aeroplanes could truly be called attractive, but Léon Levavasseur's Antoinettes stood out among the boxkites and birdcages as elegant craft with long tapering wing, birdlike tails and triangular, boat-shaped fuselages. They were handsome machines, named after Levavasseur's financial backer's daughter, powered by advanced V-8 engines which had originally been developed as high-power/low-weight units for powerboats at the turn of the century.

The most popular Antoinette engine was a compact V-8 which developed 50 hp at 1,100 rpm with evaporation (steam) cooling and an advanced fuel injection system employing spring-loaded automatic inlet valves – quite revolutionary in 1909. The structure was primarily of wood, with the forward fuselage or 'hull' section composed of a number of fine aluminium tubes which formed a coolant radiator for the engine. The early Antoinettes, including that used by Hubert Latham for his first unsuccessful attempt at crossing the English Channel, employed ailerons for roll control which trailed at the tips of their 13 m (42 ft) span wing. Such large surfaces inevitably suffered considerable torsional

stress despite stiffening, and the ailerons proved ineffective, acting as servo tabs to bend the wing structure in the wrong direction.

Levavasseur substituted wing-warping, with conventional elevator and rudder controls. Contemporary literature described the cockpit thus: 'The driver's position has been selected to give the maximum security. It is a small cockpit level with the rear of the wingtips; in case of accident it would be necessary for the whole forepart of the apparatus to be demolished before the pilot could be reached.'

'To his right and left the pilot has an ordinary type of motor car steering wheel [mounted vertically on horizontal shafts from the cockpit sides]. The one on the right controls the rear horizontal plane forming the elevation rudder; thus if the wheel is turned ahead the plane is lowered and the aeroplane descends. A similar wheel on the left controls the wing-warping, giving lateral stability in winds. The vertical rudder at the rear is operated by a horizontal foot lever. The pilot has a smaller wheel mounted on the end of a horizontal shaft running forward, immediately in front of him. This controls both the petrol pump regulating the supply of fuel to the engine and the position of the spark when running on accumulators.'

With no fewer than three wheels to manage, an Antoinette pilot literally had his hands full, and the curious vertical wheels for roll and pitch required greater co-ordination than the single-stick controls employed on the Blériot, for example. However, the Antoinette did perform extremely well in windy conditions, as Latham – nicknamed 'Storm King' – proved during the Blackpool Aviation Meeting in October 1909. He flew his Antoinette in gusts up to 64 km/h (40 mph), amid cries of 'come down you splendid fool' from spectators. At one point he actually hovered at zero groundspeed above the field when the wind exactly equalled the machine's maximum speed.

Earlier in the same year Latham had demon-strated the Antoinette's inherent stability by flying with both hands off the controls, casually smoking a cigarette. All his Antoinettes were subsequently fitted with cockpit ashtrays.

The Antoinette engines, which were produced in 24 hp, 50 hp and, eventually, 100 hp versions powered many pre-1914 aircraft; they were – by the standards of those times – extremely reliable. It was all the more disappointing, therefore, that Latham's engines let him down on both attempts at crossing the Channel. Of the first, on 19 July 1909, a French journalist wrote: 'Down the hill sailed the Antoinette with the perfect precision and grace of a bird's flight... like a gigantic dragonfly skimming with iridescent wings through the summer air. Just as it took its flight the sun broke through and made the varnished canvas glisten in a golden haze.'

Below: the Antoinette II monoplane digs in a wingtip, a result of inadequate lateral control. Pilots were not only restricted by the inadequate degree of control over their aircraft, but also by the lack of satisfactory and standardised cockpit controls and instruments.
Right: Levavasseur (left foreground) pictured with an Antoinette IV, the world's first truly successful monoplane powered by the advanced and, for its day, reliable Antoinette V-8 engine. The undercarriage utilised wing-mounted skids to prevent such incidents as pictured below during take-off and while landing the aircraft

The Antoinette IV, the first of which flew in October 1908, underwent numerous modifications, notably to the undercarriage but most importantly to the ailerons. These were initially restricted to downwards movement only, and in order to bank, one aileron was lowered while the other remained level. In 1909, however, Levavasseur introduced differentially-operated ailerons, with which banking was achieved by lowering one aileron and raising the other. The Antoinette V also underwent modification, but the Antoinette VI reverted to wing-warping, utilising the wing's flexible structure

Latham himself commented: 'There came into my mind the idea that it would have been better had there been fewer spectators, in case of failure. My ear told me that the motor, which had been started a minute or so before, was working splendidly, and then I was away.

'There was a short, swift run down the slope towards the sea, and I launched myself into the air. My last thought was one of confidence that my motor would not leave me in the lurch. The start could not have been more auspicious. I left the ground in infinitely better style than was the case with my trial flight the previous Tuesday. Instead of wobbling on getting into the air, I went up with perfect steadiness. Indeed, I flew so well that I altered my plans. Instead of describing a circle, as I had meant to do, I went straight off over the edge of the cliff. First, however, so as to judge my height from the ground, I steered over the ruined Channel Tunnel workings. I estimated that I was six hundred feet above the level of the water.

'Everything was going beautifully. I ran up a flag to a masthead between the planes [wings] that I had decided should only be hoisted at the moment of leaving land. Then I took in my hand a little camera I had taken up with me. The cliffs had slipped away behind me; below, and in front, lay the torpedo boat. Smoke was pouring from her two short funnels, there was a foaming wake astern of her. I could see that she was being hard-pressed.

'I was preparing to take a picture when a disconcerting sound came to my ears. My motor was showing signs of breaking down. I could hear that more than one of the eight cylinders was misfiring. Instantly I gave up the idea of photography and did everything I could to remedy the defect. I examined all the electrical connections that were within my reach. I also tried to alter the carburation and ignition of the engine. But it was all in vain; in a few seconds my engine had stopped entirely. It was maddening, but I was helpless. Never before had the engine played me such a trick after so short a flight.

'The machine was under perfect control during the descent. Instead of diving into the sea at an angle I skimmed down so that I was able to make contact with the sea with the aeroplane practically in a horizontal position. It settled on the water and floated like a cork. I swung my feet up onto the cross-bar to prevent them getting wet, then I took out my cigarette case, lit up a cigarette, and waited for the torpedo-boat *Harpon* to come up... I did not even get wet; only a splash of water flew over me at the moment of impact with the sea, and the torpedo boat was alongside in less than five minutes.'

A week later another Antoinette engine failed and dumped him in the Channel once more. He was barely two miles from Dover, when his rival Blériot was already celebrating victory in London.

Those same 50 sq m (538 sq ft) wings which kept Latham afloat and dry in Channel waters lofted him to a world record altitude of 155 m (510 ft) at the 1909 Reims aviation meeting, where his daily demonstrations of mastery over the Antoinette earned him the admiration of the crowd and established Levavasseur's design as a firm favourite with the public. Indeed it was the only aeroplane which everyone could readily identify. Even the ladies were attracted to its glamorous lines and the sight of Latham manipulating the large control wheels as he thundered past brought on bouts of hero worship among the gentlemen, too. 'The biplane is a woman's machine,' one remarked, 'but the Antoinette is a man's aeroplane.'

'…one has the horrifying impression that the whole lot is about to turn turtle, like a small yacht in a gale.'

Avro Triplane

The Avro Mark IV Triplane of 1910 was the first fully and practically developed triplane. Roe had tested different systems of control on his previous three triplanes, with varying success. The Mark IV's system of rudder, tail-mounted elevators and ingenious wing-warping was the result of this process, and the aircraft was capable of sustained flight under – somewhat limited – control in all three axes. Control problems were exacerbated, however, by the Green engine's low power-to-weight ratio, which meant that it was wasting power lifting its own weight before providing power for flight. This was a critical factor in early engines, and inadequate power was a common problem

Alliott Verdon Roe made the first powered flight by an Englishman from Brooklands on 8 June 1908, though his achievement was never officially recognised. After abandoning his first machine, a Wright-style biplane with a front elevator, he built a triplane which was the first British-designed, British-engined aeroplane to fly, on 23 July 1909. He described it thus: 'The fuselage was of triangular section and carried a ten feet span triplane tail of half the area of the mainplanes. The propeller was geared down to about three-to-one, and various gear ratios were tried, both with chain and belt drive, the latter being more satisfactory.

'The mainplanes acted as the elevator, and arrangements were also provided for the tailplane to act as an elevator if desired, so that it would be possible to fly horizontally at the fastest or slowest speed. But this latter scheme was not tried out on the first machine [which made] many short flights in the summer of 1909. The tailplane being of large area it quickly left the ground; then, when sufficient speed was gained, the angle of the mainplanes was increased.'

The little 'Bulls-Eye Avroplane' which Roe flew from Lea Marshes in Essex spanned just 6·1 m (20 ft) and weighed, empty, a scant 90 kg (200 lb). The triangular fuselage frame was left completely open, with the pilot sitting amidships and entirely exposed to the elements. The engine was a 9 hp air-cooled JAP two-cylinder driving a seven-foot

diameter tractor propeller with four paddle-like blades, and was hard put to lift the combined weight of machine and aviator. The control system was unique, all pitch, roll and yaw commands coming from a single steering wheel. The angle of incidence of the triplane wings could be altered by upward or downward movement, while turning the wheel warped the wings and turned the rudder in a co-ordinated control movement.

Roe explained the handling of his little oil-paper-covered triplane thus: 'On the first two flights the machine heeled over and broke the left tip of the lowest plane on both occasions. I thought that this was due to propeller torque, but am glad to say that it was by bad steering, and should the machine lurch over, a slight twist of the planes brings it back instantly, but running against a wind of 12 mph or less the machine practically balances itself.

'It can be steered entirely by twisting the mainplanes in conjunction with the rear vertical rudder when running along the ground, and the front or back of the machine can be raised first according to the angle of the mainplanes. I usually run along with them at a slight angle, which allows the machine to gain speed and the tail to rise. On increasing the angle to about ten degrees the front comes off the ground, but owing to insufficient thrust it soon comes down again.'

The lower power of the JAP engine prevented this first machine from doing much more than hop off the ground. A larger motor improved matters, but here Roe ran into the familiar problem of poor lateral control. Wing-warping tended to be ineffective at low speeds, since the drag created in trying to lift a wing often succeeded in stalling it. The use of the rudder to increase the speed – and therefore lift – of the falling wing was a lesson Roe learned from bitter experience.

Roe built three more triplanes, the final 1910 model having a 35 hp Green engine and a conventional, single-surface tailplane with elevators for pitch control instead of the variable-incidence wings. Wing-warping was retained on the centre and upper wings, whose rear spars were cunningly hinged so that they could be warped without actually bending the wooden spars, resulting in much lighter control forces. Roe even plotted multiple load paths for the aircraft's bracing so that loss of one wire would not lead to complete structural collapse, as it often did with other aircraft of the period. He wrote: 'The patented system of bracing the twisting planes will, I believe, prove a valuable improvement, as it is applicable to biplanes, triplanes, or multiplanes. One plane is made rigid from tip to tip, the rest of the planes take their rigidity from this one by means of hinged struts; consequently all planes follow the movement of the rigid plane without any lateral or undue strains put upon them.

'Owing to the rigid plane being stiff from tip to tip, there is no need to have cables and pulleys from their tips; as a result, they are controlled from two points about five feet on either side of the centre line. Through levers and rods the planes are hinged to this point, and can be folded up for transportation without interfering with any part of the steering mechanism... I am confident the aeroplane has reached a stage well worth copying and building in numbers because it is so light and handy, and I feel justified in putting the machine through its paces before the most exacting financier, for at present it is obvious the machine will keep in the air under perfect control with a little more thrust.'

A little more thrust was what most of these pioneering craft needed, for they fought a constant battle of meagre power against monumental drag. Even so, the replica of Roe's 1910 Mark IV triplane built for the film *Those Magnificent Men in their Flying Machines* proved to be the best flier of all the film aircraft, though it did have an engine almost twice the power of the 35 hp Green. Like Roe at Wembley Park, the pilots who flew it soon discovered that the wing-warping, ingenious though it may have been, was barely capable of correcting a 20 degree bank, while the tiny rudder and open-frame fuselage provided little keel area for directional stability, so that balanced flight was difficult for a pilot to achieve.

An advantage of the forward-mounted engine was that it was possible to recognise balanced flight easily, despite the lack of instruments, for the Green blew a stream of hot, oily air into the pilot's face when all was straight and level; fresh air on a cheek meant side-slip and required urgent attention. 'A mild wing drop in the Avro,' test pilot Neil Williams reported, 'has all the making of an incipient disaster from the pilot's point of view as he winds the wheel with the energy of a London bus

driver taking a sharp corner. All to no avail as the wing continues to go down, and one has the horrifying impression that the whole lot is about to turn turtle, like a small yacht in a gale!' Williams also noted that 'old in design and delicate it may be, but it is much more demanding to fly than any modern aeroplane and there is a tremendous sense of satisfaction to be derived from flying it properly.'

Sir Alliott Verdon Roe recalled of his early flights: 'Soon after my flight at Brooklands on 8 June 1908, I had notice to leave. Although disappointed in some respects I was pleased at the opportunity of devoting my time to building another machine, which I thought would be an improvement on my first effort, especially as the only power available was a 9 hp JAP motor-cycle engine. This second machine was a tractor triplane with a main span

of 20 feet and three feet chord section.

'In September 1909 a move was made to Wembley Park. A 14 hp four-cylinder JAP engine replaced the 9 hp one. With this I managed to fly from the top of the hill, where the base of the old Wembley Tower still stood, round the buildings in the centre, and land on the hill again at the other side of a clump of trees which divided the alighting place from the starting point.

'It was while making one of these flights that I came to grief. In spite of warping the wing hard over to counteract the tilt, the machine fell over on its side and crashed. The cause of the accident was failure to use the rudder for increasing the speed of the falling wingtip. Up to this experience I had failed to appreciate the true worth of the rudder for this special purpose.'

Above: wing-warping on the Avro Mark IV was controlled by turning the wheel, and the elevators by pushing or pulling the wheel, which pivoted on a cross-bar. The rudder was controlled by a foot-bar. The throttle was mounted to the pilot's left, and its operation necessitated the awkard one-handed control of the wheel. In front of the wheel were mounted the magneto-switch and three basic flight instruments.

Left: in building the replica Avro Mark IV, now owned by the Shuttleworth Collection, for the film 'Those Magnificent Men in their Flying Machines' the ingenuity of the design was discovered. The wing-warping was achieved without bending the wing spars by hinging the trailing edges of the top and centre wings aft of the rear spar, thus producing light controls. The lower wing was rigid, providing the reaction against torsion on the top and upper wings. There were, however, directional and lateral stability problems and the pilot had constantly to struggle to achieve balanced flight

Left: the cockpit interior of the streamlined Type XXVII racing aeroplane was an improvement over that of the Type XI. Principal changes resulted from the use of a 50hp Gnome rotary engine, which necessitated mounting air and fuel fine adjustment levers on the control column and the throttle lever on the pilot's right. The Blériot system of controls comprised a control column which activated the wing-warping and elevator control wires via a chain and sprocket wheel, and a foot-operated rudder-bar

Right: the cockpit of the Blériot Type XI was sparsely equipped and awkwardly arranged. The example illustrated, preserved at the RAF Museum, Hendon, shows a variation of control column, having a simple 'stick' grip instead of a wheel-grip: in fact, the only function of the wheel atop the standard control column was to act as a hand-grip

Blériot Monoplane

While most of his contemporaries were flying bi-planes, Louis Blériot opted for the more stream-lined monoplane; with the now-conventional forward wing/aft tail assembly layout. His cross-Channel Type XI monoplane also featured the first modern-style control system with a single stick for pitch and roll commands and a foot-operated bar for yaw. The rear wing spar was flexible, permitting the tips to be warped differentially for roll control – a technique already perfected by the Wright brothers but still not widely understood in Europe in 1909 – while the outer portions of the tailplane rotated freely on a tubular spar to act as elevators.

Control wires from elevators and wings were connected via pulleys and pylons to Blériot's patented, bell-shaped housing at the base of a control stick on a universal joint, atop which was a fixed wheel forming a handgrip. This was pulled back to go up, pushed forward to go down and moved from side to side to dip or raise a wing.

The Blériot's engine was an air-cooled, three-cylinder Anzani, a melancholy device much prone to overheating and capable at best of producing about 22 to 25 hp at its maximum 1,400 rpm. The 'throttle' was a simple ignition advance/retard on the right side of the control stick. 'There were no instruments', one contemporary student pilot recal-

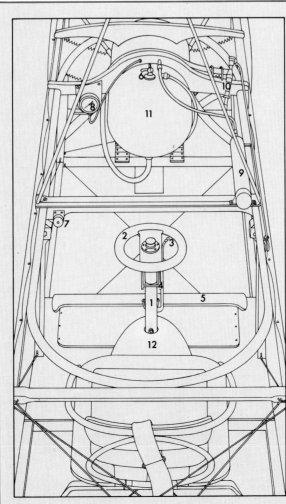

Blériot Type XI cockpit

1: *control column* **2**: *control column hand grip* **3**: *throttle lever* **4**: *throttle lever ratchet* **5**: *rudder bar* **6**: *fuel cock* **7**: *ignition switch* **8**: *oil tank pressure gauge* **9**: *oil tank pressure hand pump* **10**: *exhaust valve lifter (to stop engine)* **11**: *fuel tank* **12**: *'Cloche' control cover*

BLÉRIOT MONOPLANE

Right: the Blériot Type XI's fully-castoring undercarriage combined with the aircraft's lack of keel area to render ground handling unpredictable; assistance was invariably required prior to take-off. A Type XI is pictured at a Hendon air display.

Below: landing required a fair measure of skill and judgement as the pilot was provided with neither an air speed indicator nor an altimeter. The Type XI tended to be tail-heavy, facilitating technically-correct three-point landings.

Below right: the Blériot's unwilling Anzani engine is started by first flooding the carburettor, attaching the starter batteries and retarding the ignition. Once the propeller has been turned over to suck in the mixture, the ignition is turned on and the prop swung

led, 'not even an airspeed indicator nor a rev counter. We used to make a rough computation of engine revs by counting the throbs on the head of oil in the oil gauge.' Oil for the Anzani's lubrication system – visible in a glass tube which comprised the oil gauge – was supplied via a tank pressurised by a rubber hand bulb, and was thereafter thrown back over the pilot in a fine, aerosol-like spray.

Taxying the Blériot was never easy because all three wheels were free-castoring, and the tiny rudder provided little directional control. Clipped-wing Blériots appropriately called 'Penguins' were used to accustom trainees to the aircraft's feel, with no fear of becoming airborne. 'Round and round one would go like a dog chasing its tail', this student wrote. 'These ancient crates... were both so decrepit that the least rough spot on the field would upset their internal economy. Bolts were continually working loose, wires snapping, or their fan-shaped engines going wrong.'

The Anzani was a most unreliable power plant. When Louis Blériot made his Channel flight, the 37 minutes it took him to reach Dover was probably the longest period for which an Anzani had ever run. Half way through the flight the motor began overheating and losing what little power it had, and only a providential rain shower saved him from going into the sea. A loss of power with the drag-ridden aeroplanes of the day invariably resulted in a swift and involuntary return to earth, and Louis had only managed to put about 260 feet between his little monoplane and the sea. He later reported to the *Daily Mail* that having selected his landing spot, 'at once I stop my motor and instantly the machine falls upon the land from a height of twenty metres.'

Once a student had done his pre-flight ground hopping in a 'Penguin' he would graduate to a fully-fledged Type XI. Englishman Bertram Williams, who learned to fly at Blériot's Hendon School wrote: 'Its motor was quite new, certainly not more than five years old, and the wings were fairly well lined up, with not more than a four-inch list on one.'

Once airborne Williams reported the machine 'quite easy to handle'. In fact the Blériot was probably easier to fly than its contemporaries due to its now-conventional three-axis controls. However, the wing-warping provided very poor roll response, not more than ten per cent of that found on modern aeroplanes, and the tiny rudder was weak even with the full slipstream of the machine's 2m (6ft 10in) walnut propeller blowing over it.

The elevators, on the other hand, were quite powerful, though prone to adopt a slight 'up' attitude in level flight, requiring a constant forward stick force to prevent the nose pitching up and what little airspeed one had – usually 40-56 km/h (25-35 mph) – slackening off. Ross Browne, an American who trained under Roland Garros at Blériot's Pau school reported that the aircraft's centre of gravity

THE CHANNEL FLIGHT

On the occasion of the first English Channel Crossing on 25 July 1909, Blériot recalled: 'I begin my flight steady and sure, towards the coast of England. I have no apprehensions, no sensations. The [torpedo destroyer] *Escopette* has seen me. She is driving ahead at full speed. She makes perhaps forty-two kilometres an hour. What matters? I am making at least sixty-eight kilometres an hour. Rapidly I overtake her travelling at a height of eighty metres.

'The moment is supreme, yet I surprise myself by feeling no exultation. Below me is the sea, the surface disturbed by the wind, which is now freshening. The motion of the waves is not pleasant. I drive on. Ten minutes have gone. I have passed the destroyer and I turn my head to see whether I am proceeding in the right direction. I am amazed. There is nothing to be seen, neither the torpedo destroyer, nor France, nor England. I am alone. I can see nothing.

'For ten minutes I am lost. It is a strange position to be alone, unguided, without compass, in the air over the middle of the Channel. I touch nothing. My hands and feet rest lightly on the levers. I let the aeroplane take its own course, I care not whither it goes. For ten minutes I continue, neither rising, nor falling, nor turning. Then, twenty minutes after I have left the French coast, I see the cliffs of Dover away to the west the spot where I had intended to land.

'What can I do? It is evident that the wind has taken me out of my course. I am almost at St Margaret's Bay and going in the direction of Goodwin Sands. Now is the time to attend to my steering. I press the lever with my foot and turn easily towards the west, reversing the direction in which I am travelling. Now, indeed, I am in difficulties, for the wind here by the cliffs is much stronger and my speed is reduced as I fly against it. Yet my beautiful aeroplane responds.

'Still steadily I fly westwards, hoping to cross the harbour and reach Shakespeare Cliff. Again the wind blows. I see an opening in the cliff. Although I am confident that I can continue for an hour and a half, that I might indeed return to Calais, I cannot resist the opportunity to make a landing upon this green spot. Once more I turn my aeroplane and, describing a half-circle, I enter the opening and find myself again over dry land. Avoiding the red buildings on my right I attempt a landing, but the wind catches me and whirls me round two or three times. At once I stop my motor, and instantly the machine falls straight upon the land from a height of twenty metres. In two or three seconds I am safe upon your shore. Soldiers in khaki run up, and a policeman. Two of my compatriots are on the spot. They kiss my cheeks'.

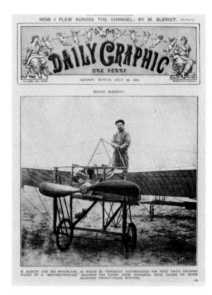

Above: Blériot's cross-Channel flight in July 1909 captured the public's imagination in a way that no previous flight had. The popular press were quick to cater for this interest, as the Daily Mail's first-hand account of the flight and the Daily Graphic's cover attest. Below: standard power plant of the Blériot Type XI was the three-cylinder Anzani, with a power rating of 25 hp. A measure of engine control was provided by an ignition retard and advance lever

'was so fine that working your wheel back and forth even an inch would make a big difference, and it would be very easy to turn on your nose.'

The Blériot's responsiveness in pitch was later to be exploited by the early aerobatics pilots such as Pégoud and Hucks, although this was not possible until the ponderous Anzanis had given way to more reliable Gnome rotary engines which more than doubled the power available. Pégoud managed to perform some advanced manoeuvres for his day, including the outside loops and the vertical 'S', but the poor lateral control of the machine was a limiting factor in the rolling plane, and the 'side-somersaults' he demonstrated were not rolls as such, but rather steep vertical banks or side-slips.

What was the most difficult part of flying a Blériot? 'Landing', said Ross Browne, 'was the hardest part of all, because that landing gear was a very tricky affair.' The 'volplane' or glide approach, with the ignition cut, was regarded as a stunt strictly for experts because the Blériot, though light at a mere 210 kg (464 lb) empty weight, was a high-drag machine like all its contemporaries. With power off it descended steeply at an angle of 30 degrees or more, losing height rapidly. The Englishman Williams confided that he 'never gained enough confidence to come down with the motor fully cut off.' Even so he ran into difficulties: 'several oldtimers commented on the remarkably steep angle of my landings, but it was not until many months later that I learned this was the result of keeping the stick rigidly fixed in the position I had pushed it in to descend. No one had ever told me you had to return it to the neutral position once the bus had started down!'

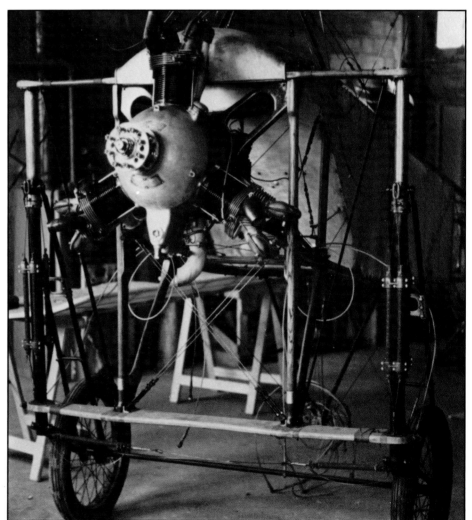

'On first acquaintance one is reluctant to believe that the contraption can actually fly.'

Bristol Boxkite

Below: the Bristol Boxkite's lateral control surfaces comprised ailerons on both upper and lower wings, which hinged down from the wing when the aeroplane was at rest and only became operable when the airflow had raised them into flying position. The tail unit mounted triple rudders and an elevator on the upper tailplane, which operated in concert with the foreplane elevator. Bottom: the pilot's position on the Boxkite was atop the lower wing leading edge, surrounded by bracing wires but otherwise open to the elements

'The control system of the Bristol biplane' ran an optimistic publicity brochure put out by the Bristol & Colonial Aeroplane Company in 1910, 'is simplicity itself. It can be mastered in a few minutes, and it requires so little physical effort that a child can manoeuvre one of these machines in flight.'

The 'Boxkite' was a pirated, but improved copy of the biplanes developed by Henri Farman from early Voisin designs, and was the first commercially-produced British aeroplane, selling in 1910 for about £1,100. Unlike the Voisin, the Boxkite had lateral controls in the form of ailerons on both upper and lower wings. A foreplane elevator was supplemented by a biplane tail surface/elevator, which was combined with triple rudders attached to rear outriggers. Pilot and passenger sat in the open on the lower wing centre-section ahead of the 50 hp Gnome rotary engine installed in 'pusher' configuration aft of the wing.

The controls consisted of a stick, the handgrip of which was directly level with the pilot's eyes. This controlled cables from the elevators and ailerons, which hung limply from the wingtips on slack wires when the Boxkite was stationary, assuming their 'flying' attitude when sufficient forward speed was attained to provide slipstream. Unlike modern ailerons, they worked only in the 'down' position, the opposite surface remaining neutral. The lowered aileron greatly increased the drag on that wing alone, creating an adverse yaw effect which opposed the attempted turn and correction with the rudder was necessary.

A young army captain named Sefton Brancker –later to become Director of Civil Aviation in Britain–flew as a passenger in a Boxkite during demonstrations at Aurangabad in India. He described the flight with Major Henri Jullerot thus: 'The Boxkite was not a particularly comfortable conveyance. The pilot sat on the leading edge of the lower plane with his feet on the rudder bar which was supported by an outrigger through which he looked between his knees into space. The observer sat close behind, and somewhat higher than the pilot with his legs wrapped round the latter's body. Our only instruments were an oil-pulsating gauge which did not work and an aneroid barometer which I think I wore around my neck. I also provided myself with field glasses and an ordinary artist's drawing block which I tied onto Jullerot's back for writing reports. I must admit that by the time we had the engine running and we were taxying across our improvised aerodrome followed by an immense cloud of dust I was thoroughly frightened. We climbed to 1,000 feet and flew round for half an hour . . . then headed for 1,100 feet, which was pretty near the ceiling of our old Boxkite, with its rather sketchy rigging.'

Rigging was a great problem, apparently, for Sefton Brancker reported: 'The Boxkite of 1910 was a mass of light spars, piano wire and fabric, which responded to every change of temperature; and as the nights were very cold with a heavy dew, while the sun by day was burning hot... the spars bowed, wires stretched and contracted, fabric sagged and

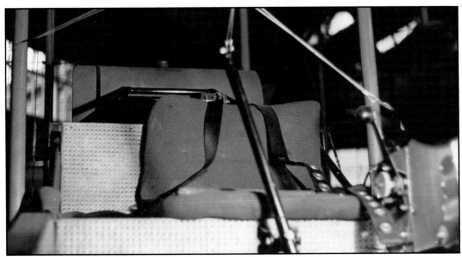

the whole structure creaked and cracked as if it were going to fall to pieces.'

Like most rotary engines of the era the Gnome was unthrottled in the traditional sense. Two levers – one for air, the other a fine-adjustment petrol tap– controlled carburation and it was left to the pilot to discover which combination provided the required power setting. This was not too difficult, since there were only two practical engine speeds with a rotary – full power, which was normally used throughout a flight, and slow running. A blip switch was provided which simply cut out the ignition as a crude means of throttling back.

Boxkites found ready application with the Bristol flying schools at Larkhill and Brooklands. Among many pilots who learned to fly on them was Robert Smith-Barry, the father of the 'Gosport' training system. Were they really so easy to fly as Bristol's contemporary publicity had claimed? Almost certainly not, at least by modern standards. The late Neil Williams, who flew the Shuttleworth Trust's Boxkite replica built for the movie *Those Magnificent Men in Their Flying Machines* reported 'The thing is a devil to fly.' He found it completely unstable in pitch because of centre of pressure travel on the foreplane elevator. Lateral control was extremely heavy and carefully-balanced flight absolutely critical, because any side-slip caused the airspeed – and the aircraft – to drop. Level flight could only be maintained at a speed of precisely 50 km/h (31 mph).

In the old days the side-slip problem caused many an accident, for the crude ailerons were unable to provide quick responses to departures from straight-and-level flight. Indeed, because of the gyroscopic action of the heavy, spinning rotary engine, it was all but impossible to persuade a Boxkite to make a left turn at all; there simply was not enough aileron power to counteract the aeroplane's right-turning tendency.

The Shuttleworth Trust replica has a rudimentary turn-and-slip indicator in the form of a piece of string tied to the foreplane. Because of the low airspeeds and absence of propeller slipstream, the pilot gets no sensory clues to unbalanced flight.

'When the engine stops,' Neil Williams observed of the Boxkite, 'the aeroplane stops soon afterwards.' With all the drag of an aerial galleon the machine practically stopped in its tracks with power off, hence the emphasis put on Edwardian aviators to get the nose down quickly in the event of an engine failure, which was not an uncommon event at that time.

One feature of the Boxkite upon which both old and modern pilots are agreed is that the open framework provides both an unsurpassed view and, on cold days, a chill reminder of the malevolence of the elements. When asked in 1910 what items of equipment might be needed for army observers flying above Salisbury Plain during manoeuvres, one Boxkite pilot replied through chattering teeth: 'layer after layer of clothing'.

Above and inset: the Shuttleworth Collection's Boxkite is a flying replica built for film work. It nonetheless faithfully reproduces the control difficulties of the original and one present-day pilot's impression of a flight was that he was a passenger carried by the Boxkite on sufferance with little control over the aeroplane. Left: a Boxkite flying at Hendon, the cradle of British aviation, in 1912. Two more Boxkites sit on the ground, with a Blériot monoplane to the left

Above: a Henri Farman biplane, from which the Bristol was evolved, flies over the water's edge at Nice in 1910. The principal refinements which were introduced on the Bristol aircraft were the addition of a centrally-mounted third rudder and the fitting of ailerons to the lower wing in addition to those carried on the top wing of the Farman. Above right: the Bristol Boxkite was widely used in Britain by private flying enthusiasts and flying schools, as well as by the Royal Flying Corps. Right: the first problem that the Boxkite pilot faces is reaching his seat from the ground. This is accomplished with the help of a ladder placed against the wing leading edge, but care is needed to avoid entanglement in the many bracing wires

A passenger describing flight in a Farman biplane, of which the Boxkite was a copy, at Reims in 1909: 'How I got up I do not know, and what I sat on I do not comprehend. I was only conscious that the pilot, when he scrambled in after me, was very close in front, wedging me tightly between himself and the extremely hot radiator of the engine behind. I was his first passenger, of either sex, and passenger flight had not been contemplated or arranged for. One word of warning he conveyed to me – not to touch his arms. The mechanic swung the propeller, the engine, already hot with recent flight, started with the first turn, and we were off across the track.

'The ground was very rough and hard, and as we tore along at an increasing pace that was very soon greater than any motor I had yet been in, I expected to be jerked and jolted. But the motion was wonderfully smooth – smoother yet – and then... suddenly there had come into it a new, indescribable quality – a lift – a lightness – a life! Very many there are now who know that feeling; that glorious, gliding sense that the sea-bird has known this million years, and which man has so long and so vainly envied, and which, even now, familiarity can never rob of its charm. But picture if you can what it meant for the first time: when all the world of aviation was young and fresh and untried; when to rise at all was a glorious adventure, and to find oneself flying swiftly in the air, the too-good-to-be-true realisation of a lifelong dream.'

The late Neil Williams commented on the Shuttleworth Boxkite replica thus: 'On first acquaintance one is reluctant to believe that the contraption can actually fly. It doesn't look like an aeroplane, with its forward booms and foreplane, balanced by the triple rudder and double tailplane surrounding the pusher propeller. It has a tangled forest of struts, spars, wires and turnbuckles. Common sense says it cannot fly.' Yet the same machine 'never fails to enthral spectators at a flying display as it sails through the air with the dignity of an old-time sailing ship.'

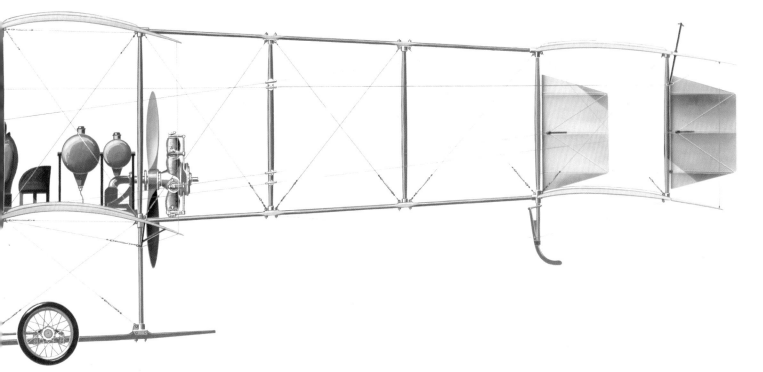

Blackburn Monoplane

Opposite: the cockpit of the 1912 Monoplane had only one instrument, an engine speed indicator. The wheel was pivoted upwards to lower and downwards to raise the elevators, and was turned to warp the wings. The rudder was controlled by foot-pedals mounted on a bar. Awkwardly mounted to the wheel's right were the air, fuel fine adjustment and throttle levers required by the 50hp Gnome rotary engine. The 'blip' switch was mounted on the control column. Below: the Shuttleworth Collection's original 1912 Monoplane takes off

Robert Blackburn became interested in aviation while working in France in 1908, when he saw Wilbur Wright fly at Le Mans. He returned to England and built his first monoplane, a well-engineered, immensely strong and heavy aeroplane powered by a water-cooled 35hp Green engine. The pilot sat in a box-shaped 'cage' beneath the wing, in a wicker garden chair set on sliding rails whereby the aircraft's centre of gravity could be altered.

Blackburn also devised and patented an all-in-one control or 'triple steering column'. This consisted of a motor car steering wheel which turned to operate the rudder, moved up and down for the elevator and from side to side for wing-warping. He also intended to fit an automatic stability device, in which a pendulum supplied compressed air to a cylinder and piston; this in turn would move the control surfaces to maintain level flight as a kind of rudimentary automatic pilot.

Blackburn took the completed aeroplane to a stretch of sandy beach at Marske in Yorkshire for test flying, sailing into the air into a light sea breeze. 'As soon as I started a turn, the low centre of gravity took charge and I got into a terrific wobble, came down in a nose dive from the great height of two feet, crashed the machine and landed on my head in the sand. However, this did not dim my faith in aeroplanes', he recalled later.

Work proceeded on a second monoplane, which bore a resemblance to Levavasseur's Antoinette and established Blackburn as one of the foremost British designers of the period. C. B. Hucks, who later became well-known for his aerobatic flying at Hendon, joined Blackburn and like his employer came to grief in a side-slip in the new monoplane at Filey Sands while attempting a turn.

There followed a succession of Blackburn Monoplanes, all employing the patented single wheel control, with triangular fuselages and tail surfaces. Perhaps the best-known of all – which still survives as the oldest original flying machine in Britain – is the Blackburn Single-Seat Monoplane built late in 1912 for Cyril Foggin and flown in exhibitions by him at Leeds the following year. The 1912 Mono was smaller and more compact than its predecessors, with a streamlined aluminium front fuselage partially cowling its 50 hp Gnome rotary engine. For the first time Blackburn abandoned his triple column and provided a foot-operated bar for rudder steering, with a wheel and column for roll and pitch control. This unique aeroplane now belongs to the Shuttleworth Collection at Old Warden.

The Blackburn's cockpit houses a solid-looking cross-bar, linking the ends of the rear wing spar in front of the seat, which served as a safety strap. The late Neil Williams, recalling his first flight in the machine, reported: 'To my horror one of the mechanics gave it a sharp tug, whereupon it hinged upwards giving access to the seat.' Williams was also disturbed to find that the control column had

to be moved upwards for down elevator and vice versa, and that application of full down elevator brought the wheel up until it completely blocked all forward vision. 'The instrument panel is painfully simple', he wrote. 'There in the centre, in solitary splendour, reposes a rev counter.' No airspeed indicator, altimeter or oil pressure gauge is supplied, though the latter is unnecessary with the Gnome engine, which throws oil back at the pilot who is exposed atop the fuselage without even a windscreen.

Though short on instrumentation, the old Blackburn has no lack of engine controls–five of them–levers for throttle, petrol and air, a large Victorian brass light switch for the ignition and a blip cutout button which delivers an electric shock when used. Neil Williams found that the throttle 'worked in theory only', and that full power was needed all the time, with judicious use of the painful blip switch.

With the Gnome turning at its maximum 1,240 rpm, the Blackburn can fly at 96 km/h (60 mph) and climb to 210 m (700 ft). Like its contemporaries it is sensitive to out-of-balance flight, shuddering and losing airspeed and altitude in a side-slip, but responsive to co-ordinated handling and remarkably stable in the right conditions. Perhaps the best tribute to Robert Blackburn's design is Neil Williams' memory of the machine: 'The modern aeroplane, with all its sophistication, is, of course, much easier to fly. But I personally would not exchange all the comforts in the world for the pleasure and sheer thrill of flying a real veteran machine.'

Harry Goodyear, apprentice with Robert Blackburn, remembers the 1911 trials of the Mercury Monoplane: 'I stayed at the Three Tuns that night and next morning walked along the sands, about a mile or so to join Mr Hucks, who was living alone in a small wooden bungalow, perched on the side of

a cliff. The machine was housed in a hangar close by, where a concrete slipway ran to the sands. A small hand-winch was fixed at the top for hauling the aeroplane up and down. I stayed with Mr Hucks until Easter, and the time was taken up in modifications to the machine, and Mr Isaacson working on his engine. I also had to do the chores at the bungalow and the time seemed to pass very quickly.

'I happened to be at Filey, after the Olympia Show, when Mr Hucks got his pilot's licence. As he was completing his last figure of eight the front bearing on the engine seized, the prop shaft sheered, and the propeller flew off. The machine suddenly twisted and side-slipped into the ground, doing a fair amount of damage, but Hucks was not seriously hurt and was back on the job after a few weeks, during which we had rebuilt the machine. But it was the end of the Isaacson engine, for Mr Blackburn bought a 50 hp Gnome, and from then on flying started in earnest.'

Above: Blackburn's first monoplane was of spruce, ash and steel tube. Weighing 360 kg (800 lb), it was nicknamed the 'heavy monoplane'. A metal structure below the wing carried the 35 hp Green engine, the pilot and the undercarriage, producing a low centre of gravity by thus concentrating the weight. As a result it was unstable and crashed after one brief flight. The cruciform empennage carried a tailplane, elevators and rudder. Lateral control was by wing-warping. A single wheel commanded all controls.

Below: Blackburn's tendency to heavy structures became exaggerated in the two-seat military Type E of 1912, which was too heavy to leave the ground. Powered by a large 70 hp Renault vee-engine, it was significant in being the first British-designed all-metal aircraft

'…I ducked down in the cockpit, waiting for the hand of death to touch me.'

Curtiss Jenny

More than 8,000 examples of the Curtiss Jenny were manufactured, making the type one of the most important training aircraft of World War I. Thousands of JN-4 aircraft were declared surplus to military requirements at the Armistice and began a new lease of life as the mounts of barnstormers. Selling for as little as 50 dollars, Jennies were regularly employed in such reckless manoeuvres as that performed below by ace barnstormer Earl Daugherty

The Curtiss JN trainer biplane series, which became an American aviation legend known as the 'Jenny', was designed by a Briton, B. Douglas Thomas, formerly associated with Avro and Sopwith. Following the tractor precepts standardised in Britain, Thomas produced a clean and functional design initially called the Model J. It was powered by a 90 hp water-cooled engine developed by Curtiss, the OX-5. Curtiss engineers married their own control system to the Thomas design. Consequently, a Deperdussin-type control column was installed and it allowed forward and aft motion of the column to operate the elevators, while a wheel on the column 'steered' the rudder in much the same way as one would drive an automobile. Further control of the aircraft was afforded by a yoke fitted to the pilot's shoulders; it provided aileron control, the pilot leaning in the direction he wanted to bank the aeroplane. A similar design, the Curtiss Model N, was also developed, but did not remain a separate production aircraft. Instead, Curtiss merged the two tractor designs to develop the JN series. That combination of initials eventually lent itself to the aircraft being referred to as the 'Jenny'.

When World War I began, Curtiss opened a production facility in Canada, as the United States was officially neutral for the first three years of the war. This facility was subsequently acquired by Canadian Aeroplanes Limited (CAL) and the JN-3s built there differed from the US-built variant by being fitted with stick-control to conform to Royal Flying Corps specifications. Much later, Curtiss abandoned the Deperdussin systems and followed CAL's lead, which included the addition of ailerons to the lower wing to improve lateral control. Improvements to the basic Curtiss JN-4 aircraft were incorporated into the Canadian-built variants. Officially designated JN-4 (Can) to denote their Canadian construction, these aircraft were more popularly referred to as 'Canucks'.

As aviation training facilities were expanded in Canada, the JN-4 came into greater prominence. The late Cecil Montgomery-Moore, who went from Bermuda to Canada in August 1917 to enlist in the Royal Flying Corps, recalls his aviation cadet training in the JN-4: 'While the "Canuck" was a fine aeroplane to fly, it was not totally unforgiving–as many student pilots learned. On 17 October 1917, for example, there were three crashes: one fellow tore off a tyre while making his first solo landing,

another chap (also solo) broke his undercarriage, longerons, four struts and both bottom wing sections –although he did not receive a scratch, and the third fellow among the solo aspirants made what we called a 'pancake' landing. At some point in the landing process, and not necessarily of his own choosing, he lost forward airspeed and the aircraft simply 'plopped' onto the ground. In this case, the 'pancake chef' broke his undercarriage, both bottom wing sections, his propeller and some struts. His own injuries consisted of a miniscule patch of skin ripped off his nose and a dent in his pride. He had recovered enough by lunchtime to play a few tunes on the piano in the mess hall.'

While with the 86th Canadian Reserve Squadron, one of two units flying JN-4s from Camp Rathbun in Ontario, Cecil Montgomery-Moore completed his primary flight training. On 26 October 1917, exactly two weeks after he had taken his first student 'ride' in the front seat of a JN-4, Montgomery-Moore's time came to make his first flight unaccompanied by his instructor, Lieutenant Morris.

'With slow, deliberate movements I climbed into the back seat and adjusted the safety belt, checked the instruments and got ready for the moment I'd been waiting for since I left Bermuda: to fly alone', he recalled. The engine turned over the first time the mechanic swung the propeller. I looked over the fuselage coaming to the empty front seat where, a few minutes before, I had sat as a student, secure in the knowledge that, no matter how badly I erred, Morris was in the back seat to get us down safely. Now it was up to me and a combination of fear and excitement ran through me.

'I gave it the gas and taxied across the field. By pulling back on the control column, increased ground speed soon became airspeed and the aerodrome drifted away beneath me. I went up to about 500 feet and made a few circuits around the aerodrome and came in for a landing. With some aircraft you can decrease power and simply let the plane "float" in for a landing and, as long as you keep the nose up, you will usually make it. But with the Canuck you had to maintain power or the plane would sink like a stone. So, I kept one hand on the throttle and the other on the joystick [control column], striving for that delicate balance of both needed to control the aircraft. Just as soon as I felt the wheels touch the ground and I could feel I was going to roll along the field and not bounce back into the air, I cut the power and pulled the stick back to let the tail settle on the ground.'

American military aviation was far below the level of its allies when the United States entered World War I. To make up for the deficiency and to make pilot training available to a large number of qualified young men, the United States and Canadian governments made an agreement. In return for training US Navy pilots in Canada during the pleasant Canadian summer, the US made available to the RFC a number of its bases in Texas during the winter of 1917–18.

However, the good flying weather almost proved to be the undoing of RFC cadet Cecil Montgomery-Moore. Assigned to the 81st Canadian Training Squadron for more advanced flying, the 18-year-old fledgling pilot concentrated on logging as much 'stick time' as possible. 'All of my flying in Texas

was solo and, with the aeroplane all to myself, I would let it drift across the miles of open prairie, making lazy turns, climbing and dipping as I pleased. I used to sing as loudly as I could in hopes of drowning out the engine noise, but it was a contest I never won', he reminisced.

'One morning in November 1917, I tried to out-shout the engine by turning it off while in flight. Usually the engine could be easily restarted as long as there was enough altitude. In this case I was at about 2,000 ft when I cut the power. I sailed along in tranquil silence for a minute or so and then, content that I had beaten the mechanical monster, I turned on the engine switch. The propeller was wind-milling in the slipstream, so it was a matter of a moment or two before it would kick over the engine for me. But moments passed and nothing happened. I flicked the switch off and let up on the throttle, thinking I had perhaps flooded the engine. Still with the throttle off, I switched on the engine in hopes the power of the air would turn over the engine and thereby vent any excess gasoline. Again nothing happened.

'In that moment it suddenly occurred to me that if my luck did not quickly improve, I could end up as a dead man. At that point I was really frightened and, despite all of the mental discipline I had acquired, I was finding it very hard to remain calm and logically to think out what to do. The "Canuck" was beginning to drop very fast and, as my airspeed decreased, my rate of descent increased. All I could do was pull back the joystick and keep the nose up.

'For a moment I thought of putting the crate

Above right: hailing from Long Beach, California, Earl Daugherty enlisted the aid of a partner, Wesley May, to devise ever more spectacular stunts.
Right: a former wartime flying instructor, Ormer Locklear was probably the most famous barnstormer. His upper wing handstand was facilitated by the JN-4D's projecting king-posts.
Below: the profile view of a Jenny on the strength of the Primary Training School of the US Army Air Service and based at Love Field, Texas in 1918

nose down, hoping that the strong rush of air would help me restart the engine. But I knew that if that failed, the old bird—as stable as it was—would get me into a hell of a dive that I'd never recover from. Hence, I abandoned all hope of restarting the engine. Now my salvation, if any, lay in bringing the plane back near the field to some flat landing spot, where, with any luck, I might make a fairly decent controlled crash.

'I was in such a nervous state that the perspiration around my eyes fogged the lenses of my goggles. In a grand gesture, I whipped the goggles up off my head and cavalierly threw them over the side. They would do me no good if I crashed. As I approached the ground, I could see that I had indeed almost made it back to the aerodrome and that I had room to land. Bless those seemingly endless miles of Texas prairie! For a moment I thought I might really make a perfect landing, as I maintained a delicate balance of stick control, holding the nose at just the right angle. But then I pulled back just a hair too much and the plane flared out and dropped to the ground. From my seat it sounded like the end of the world. First the cannon-like concussion with the ground, then the endless splintering sounds, as the undercarriage was jammed up through the bottom wings, and struts and wing panels all over the place came apart and tore into each other. Following the initial jolt, I ducked down into the cockpit, waiting for the hand of death to touch me.' A few moments later a hand did touch young Montgomery-Moore, but it was that of one of the RFC instructors, who had dashed out to the crash.

CURTISS JENNY

The Curtiss JN-4 series had, prior to the close of 1917, been regarded solely as primary trainers. With a 150 hp Hispano-Suiza engine replacing the JN-4D's standard OX-5 power plant, the resulting JN-4H was intended as a gunnery, bombing, observation and pursuit trainer and performed these roles with some success. A revised nose profile and radiator shape differentiated the 'Hisso'-engined aircraft from its Curtiss-powered predecessor

While certain hair-raising training incidents had their light moments, others did not. A tragic case in point was cited by the late Carl Dixon, who witnessed on 5 February 1918 the demise of the popular RFC instructor Captain Vernon Castle, who had served with distinction as a member of No 1 Squadron RFC in France before his assignment to the training command. 'He was a terrific pilot', Dixon recalled. 'Earlier in the war he had been a fighter pilot and had shot down several German aeroplanes over the Western Front. He used to say that any flying machine – even the Canadian-built Jennies we had – could be a combat aircraft. And to prove his point, he'd take one of those JN-4s up and do loops and stalls and turn it on one wing like nothing we had ever seen before.

'The day Vernon Castle went down I was on my way back to Benbrook when I saw two trainers in the air near the landing strip. I assumed they were doing some sort of close formation work until it suddenly dawned on me that they weren't working together – they were on a collision course. It turned out that as the two planes approached each other at right angles, Castle and his student were preparing to land at the same time the other JN-4 was lining up his final approach. I don't think the other student even saw Castle's plane because he just kept coming in.

'It was horrifying to watch because I knew damned well they were going to collide and, even though it did no good, I was screaming at them to pull away. We had no radios in those days, so my voice just got lost in the wind. Then I saw Castle drop his aeroplane to let the other man pass over him. It almost worked, but the other pilot either hit an air pocket and lost altitude or pushed the stick too far forward, because he came crashing down on Castle's plane and knocked the top wing right off. Castle's plane went into a crazy flat spin and hit the ground. The other pilot lost his undercarriage, but managed to "belly in" and get out in one piece. Vernon Castle was killed and the student with him was very badly injured.'

Following his discharge from the RAF in 1920, Carl Dixon subsequently flew with the Ivan R. Gates Air Circus, one of the more successful travelling

aviation exhibitions of the barnstorming period. He vividly recalled one of the highlights of the show, the wing walkers: 'When I first joined the air circus the chief stuntman asked me if I had ever walked out on the wing of an aeroplane. I said, "Hell, no, and I don't intend to, either." Then he asked if I would fly a plane in which a man would walk from its wings to a plane flying alongside. I told him, "if the guy is crazy enough to pull a stunt like that, I'll fly him anywhere he wants to go."

'As it turned out, the chief stuntman, a guy named Bartlett, was my passenger during the next air show. He explained that he would leave the cockpit, walk out on the bottom wing, climb up the struts to the top wing and then walk between the top bracing wires and the king-posts all along the length of the top wing and over to the bottom wing of another aeroplane.

'You could do a stunt like that in a Jenny, because it was big enough and a very stable aero-plane. The tricky part was in keeping the aeroplane on an even keel. As I felt Bartlett walk across the top wing, from left to right, I had to compensate gradually, tilting slightly to the right until he got to the middle of the wing. Then I'd tilt more to the left so he had an even platform as he continued his walk. Bartlett wore no parachute, so one bad move would have been the end of him. But the toughest part was when he got ready to go over to the other aeroplane. At exactly the right moment I had to be ready to turn into the other plane, since the loss of the wing walker's weight would naturally cause the wing to "lift" up and probably knock him off the other aeroplane. At the same time, the other pilot had to be prepared for the additional weight about to be on his left wingtip.

'The first time I tried to fly Bartlett, I pulled away a second too soon, to keep from hitting the other aeroplane, and poor Bartlett was hanging in mid-air, with only one hand on a strut of the other plane. Fortunately, he was a very muscular guy and could pull himself up. But, when we got back on the ground, he chewed my tail off for almost dumping him. It was a crazy way to earn a living and I was just as happy when I said goodbye to the old Jenny and got into serious commercial aviation'.

Fokker Eindecker

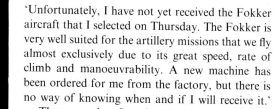

'Unfortunately, I have not yet received the Fokker aircraft that I selected on Thursday. The Fokker is very well suited for the artillery missions that we fly almost exclusively due to its great speed, rate of climb and manoeuvrability. A new machine has been ordered for me from the factory, but there is no way of knowing when and if I will receive it.'

Those words of praise for the new Fokker Eindecker (monoplane) were penned in a letter of 30 November 1914 by Oswald Boelcke, then a junior officer with Feldflieger-Abteilung 13 in France. Although he went on to score a number of his initial aerial victories in Fokker Eindeckers, at that early point in the war Boelcke was interested only in the superior flight characteristics of the then-unarmed monoplanes.

Oswald Boelcke notes his preference for the Eindecker, which he compares to the Taube monoplanes produced by Rumpler and others, in his letter of 9 December 1914. He wrote: 'Yesterday I picked up my Fokker, which had meanwhile arrived. It is a small Eindecker, with a forward-mounted French-built rotary engine, [the aeroplane

Fok. E III 210/15

Below left: in common with most scouts of the World War I period, the Fokker Eindecker's cockpit instrumentation was sparse. This is reflected in the pictured display of a British-built E III replica. Below right: the Eindecker's manoeuvrability was quickly exploited by such pilots as Oswald Boelcke and Max Immelmann. The latter evolved the celebrated Immelmann Turn – a roll off the top of a half-loop – while flying the E I, Fokker's first monoplane scout. Bottom: the aircraft depicted was captured intact by British servicemen in April 1916 and was subsequently flight-tested at the Central Flying School, Upavon, Wiltshire

is] about half as big as a Taube. It is the most modern machine. I have not yet been able to fly it. Until now I have flown the same types that we have in Germany. The Fokker was my greatest Christmas present.

'Now I have two aircraft: a big biplane for long flights and the small Fokker for artillery flights. The thing goes wonderfully well in the air and is very easy to handle. Now both of my "children" rest peacefully inside one tent hangar, the small one somewhat hidden, with its tail under the wings of the big one.'

During the early phase of World War I the Germans showed a clear lack of planning the best deployment of their military aircraft. For example, they virtually ignored the German patent granted in 1913 that proposed a very workable system to allow rounds from a forward-firing machine gun

to pass through a propeller arc. Instead, unarmed aircraft were sent up to perform visual reconnaissance and other non-combatant assignments.

The perils of the early unarmed reconnaissance flights can be seen in the experiences of Gustav Tweer, an Offizierstellvertreter (warrant officer) who was a pilot with Feldflieger-Abteilung 15 during the early campaign in Russia. A noted pre-World War I stunt pilot and exhibition flier, Tweer earned German pilot's license No 180 on 18 April 1912. His early experiences in a Blériot monoplane – including one of the first public displays of an outside loop – gave Tweer valuable experience in an aircraft with wing-warp controls. That experience was of particular value in flying the Eindecker.

'It is a beautiful bird', he wrote to an aviator friend, 'very solidly built and able to take much stress. That is important because in our daily flights over the enemy the Russkis fire madly at us. I always try to stay at several hundred metres altitude, but that is not always possible when one needs to go down to see what Ivan is doing. That is when the tremendous power of the engine is my saviour, as I skim along the treetops and swerve regularly to avoid being hit by rifle and small arms fire from the ground.

'Many times I have come back to our airfield and have been greeted in astonishment by the ground crewmen, who cannot believe that I have taken 15 or 20 hits during a single sortie and was still able to fly the aircraft. Quite simply, it is a very sturdy machine and the inferior Russki bullets cannot penetrate and break the steel tubing the way they would smash into the wooden frame of other aircraft. To be sure, the bullets have their effect and my comrades and I have suffered some structural damage – dents in the steel frame and an occasional break – but they are not as disastrous as they would be in other aircraft.'

Although aerial combat had been introduced on the Western Front as early as 5 October 1914 – when Sergent Joseph Frantz and Caporal Quenault in a French Voisin biplane used a rifle to shoot down a German Aviatik – aerial combat was slow to come to the Eastern Front. While supporting ground units of the XX Armee-Korps in its rapid drive through Poland in the early summer of 1915, Gustav Tweer had an unusual encounter with a Russian aircraft. He wrote: 'Often the only time we see the enemy is when long columns of his troops are marching back to Russia. Only rarely do we see the enemy's aircraft . . .

'The first time I saw such a machine approaching our lines, the pilot simply waved to me and veered away to head back to his own lines. It is like the spirit we experienced during air meets before the war. He waves to you and you wave to him and that is the end of it. But lately the Russkis have got very desperate. Our army is pushing them back at every turn and they know that our aeroplanes are reporting their movements and directing our heavy artillery. Hence, they are determined to bring us down at any cost.

'Not long ago, when the rear portion of my seat was occupied by my observer, Freiherr von Schorlemer, we saw just how desperate they are. We had completed our reconnaissance of Bialystock and were following the railway tracks back to Warsaw when von Schorlemer drew my attention to another aeroplane approaching us from the south-east. At first I thought it was another Fokker, because it was a monoplane like ours. But as the other aeroplane got closer to us, I could see the differences in its appearance. I was also suspicious of the dark colour, but I had one last thought that it might have come from the Austrian army to the south.

'Then von Schorlemer became quite excited and yelled into my ear that it was an enemy aeroplane. In approaching us, it had dipped one wing and my observer saw on it the red-blue-white cockade of the enemy. I told von Schorlemer that it would be all right and that the Russki probably just wanted to take a look at us, just as we had flown near some enemy birds to look at them.

'Yet I was suspicious of the way this Russki devil continued to close on us. What was his intent? He continued to change his approach, first dipping one black wing and then the other, as if he could not decide what to do. Meanwhile, I kept an eye on the railway tracks to make sure we did not become lost and von Schorlemer watched the Russki.

'Some minutes passed and our opponent drew closer and closer. Then, when he was perhaps 50 metres away, he dipped one wing and started to

turn in to us, heading straight for our tail. I thought it was a bluff to throw us off course and foolishly pulled up, which caused me to slow down and allowed the Russki to close in faster.

'I suddenly discerned what he wanted to do. He was heading for our tail because he wanted to chew it up with his propeller! This crazy fool was going to risk his own neck just to bring us down; for, unless he had a metal propeller, he would smash his own propeller and have to crash. More important to us, if he smashed our rudder or other control surfaces, we would flutter to the ground like a crumpled leaf.

'I pushed the stick forward and dived for speed to get away from this madman. He barely missed us and made a wide swinging turn above us. Now of course he had the advantage of altitude and could swoop right down on us and there would be no way to stop him. I had no gun – not even a service revolver or a flare pistol – so we were at the mercy of this suicidal fool.

'He made several further attempts to strike us and each time I barely escaped him. The added weight of my observer made it more difficult than usual quickly to manoeuvre my Fokker away from him. Worst of all, with each evasive manoeuvre, I lost altitude and was in great danger of striking a chimney or some other large object protruding from the ground.

'Then, thank heaven, some of our ground troops

Inset top: the operational assessment of Fokker's first Eindecker, the E I, commenced in mid-1915. The promising results obtained led to production of the E II later in the same year. An E I is pictured over France.
Left: Fokker's monoplane scouts successfully utilised an interruptor gear, enabling a fixed Spandau machine gun to fire through the aircraft's spinning propeller.
Below: the Eindecker's mastery of the air during the winter of 1915-16 was ended by the appearance of Sopwith and Nieuport scouts

must have realised my difficulty and assisted me by opening fire on him. By this time we were low enough for our national insignia to be recognised. We had just turned back to the railway tracks when a fatal shot found its mark on our adversary. Freiherr von Schorlemer and I watched in horror as the Russki bucked up, then dropped nose first into the roadway alongside the railway tracks. The wreckage burst into flames.'

Gustav Tweer's encounter with the would-be aircraft destroyer was only one example of the desperate measures taken by some military pilots to bring down their adversaries. Another Russian pilot, Staff-Captain Alexander Kazakov, tied a grappling hook to his Morane-Saulnier monoplane and ripped apart the wings of German aircraft that he was able to fly over.

In France the pre-war stunt pilot Roland Garros had metal plates fitted to the propeller blades of the Morane so that he could direct a forward-firing machine gun through the propeller arc without destroying the propeller. Shots that did not pass freely through the arc would be deflected by the plates. Through this crude but effective method Garros shot down five German aircraft within a three week period. His unequalled threat to the Germans came to an end on 19 April 1915 when Garros' Morane-Saulnier Type L was brought down by ground fire near Courtrai.

Garros was taken prisoner and the undestroyed wreckage of his parasol fighter was closely studied by the Germans. Anthony Fokker was given the challenge of replicating the device. Garros' deflector equipment was in turn handed over to Heinrich Lübbe and Fritz Heber, two Fokker engineers who were quite familiar with the interruptor gear patented in 1913 by Franz Schneider, technical director of the Luftverkehrsgesellschaft (LVG) factory. Inspired by Garros' audacity and the feasibility of the Schneider patent, the Fokker engineers successfully married the concept of an interruptor gear to an M5K Eindecker. Thus was born the first of the Fokker fighters, the E I type.

FOKKER EINDECKER

Among the air units to receive the improved Eindeckers was Flieger-Abteilung 62, which subsequently produced the two early fighter aces Oswald Boelcke and Max Immelmann. Although the encounter did not result in an aerial victory, Boelcke described a fight that took place in September 1915 in which he used elements of his famed dicta, or code of air fighting. In telling his interception of a flight of French aircraft that bombed a nearby city, Boelcke wrote: 'After they dropped their bombs, they flew homeward. I gradually reached the altitude of the enemy aircraft and closed in on them. Then I saw one of their big aeroplanes, which appeared to be the escort for the others, start to attack me. It is very difficult if not impossible to fire upwards. [Therefore] I exchanged a few shots with my opponent and then pulled away. That move satisfied the Frenchman and he flew away with the others.

'I hung along behind the enemy squadron and, since I had the faster aircraft, I soon succeeded in getting close enough to the rearmost aircraft to open fire. But I did not open fire straight away, so as not to draw the attention of the other aircraft too soon. It was not until I was 100 metres away that I began firing. My opponent became frightened and tried to get away. My trouble then was with the others, who had heard my shots and came to help their comrade. Therefore I had to hurry.

'I noticed that I was successful, as the Frenchman went into a steep dive to escape from me. Eventually, we both went down from 2,500 to 1,200 meters. I fired at his rear as well as I could. But meanwhile two of his comrades came down and sent me friendly greetings', the future ace noted as a lighthearted way of offering an excuse for breaking off the engagement and returning to his own airfield.

The Fokker E I was admittedly rushed into service to provide German air units with an aggressive weapon. The E II which soon followed it showed a sense of further development, fitted with a 100-horsepower engine and a slightly increased wingspan. The E III was introduced soon thereafter and for a time in 1915 all three Eindeckers – E I, E II and E III – were in service.

The improvements in the Eindecker series, which led to their being called 'the Fokker scourge' by their opponents, gave German fighter pilots great advantages. These advantages held true even under the most trying conditions, as noted by Leutnant Gustav Leffers, a pilot with Flieger-Abteilung 32 who subsequently won the coveted Pour le Mérite, the highest Prussian bravery award.

In describing the first of his nine aerial victories, Leffers noted that on the afternoon of 5 December 1915 he took off from the airfield at Vélu in a Fokker E II on an air defence mission. 'At almost 3 o'clock', he continued, 'I found myself over Bapaume and puffs of smoke from our artillery drew my attention to an enemy aeroplane almost over Martinpuich at about 1,500 metres, flying northward. I immediately took up the chase. Between Grévillers and Aichet-la-Grand, I came down to 600 metres and opened fire, which was immediately returned.

'I found myself 200 metres higher than the enemy aeroplane and went into a long dive, firing my machine gun until I was an aeroplane's length away.

Now I noticed that the pilot was hit and the aeroplane began to flutter. In an instant I was firing furiously with my machine gun at my opponent.

'I was suddenly caught in a strong blast of wind from the strong propwash of the enemy aeroplane and my own aeroplane was thrown into a side-slip for about 150 metres. However, I immediately started after him again to cut off my opponent's escape to the front lines. But he went into a steep dive and from an altitude of 300 metres plunged straight down and smashed into the ground. Both crewmen were immediately killed.'

Leffers' victim was most probably one of two BE2c aircraft from No 13 Squadron RFC, that were lost due to enemy action that day. The slow BE, with the observer's field of fire severely limited by his front seat location, was no match for the fast and nimble Fokker Eindecker. The point is driven home by the ease with which Leffers scored his second victory, a BE2c of No 8 Squadron RFC, on 29 December 1915.

The entry for that day in *The Royal Flying Corps War Diary* notes that Lieutenants Douglas and Child in one BE2c were escorting Second Lieutenant Glen and Sergeant Jones in a similar No 8 Squadron machine when 'about three miles west of Cambrai, Lt Glen and Sgt Jones, flying at

Below: Fokker monoplane scouts were also flown by the Austro-Hungarian Luftfahrtruppen, whose units were initially equipped with a mixture of single and two-seat types. The pilot pictured in the cockpit of his Fokker is Hauptmann Kostrba, a leading flier with Fliegerkompanie (Flik) 4 in 1916.
Bottom: the Eindecker's steel-tube undercarriage incorporated elastic cord shock absorbers at the top of the main members to cushion the impact on landing. The lack of a fixed fin or tailplane – both vertical and horizontal surfaces pivoted for control purposes – demanded a high degree of competence from the pilot, particularly on landing

Top: a flying replica of the Fokker E III was constructed at Booker, Buckinghamshire by Personal Plane Services in the late 1960s. For ease of maintenance and operation, an 82 hp Continental power plant was substituted for the original aircraft's 100 hp Oberursel rotary engine. Above: with a rudimentary row of hangars in the background, German pilots pose with one of the earlier E III aircraft to reach the Front in 1915. The Eindeckers were at first employed to protect two-seaters from enemy attack

about 6,400 feet, were attacked by two Fokkers. Almost immediately the BE2c descended in a very steep spiral to 2,000 feet and then flattened out. The BE2c was seen to land and then the machine was smashed. The impression which Lt Douglas received was that Lt Glen was wounded with the first burst, and on landing intentionally smashed his machine.' Douglas and Child were then attacked by three Eindeckers, one of which they hit and forced out of the fight. They fought a running gun battle with the remaining Fokkers and managed to reach the safety of their own lines.

The tenacity of the No 8 Squadron crews was described by Leffers: 'At 12 noon I was informed by telephone that three enemy aircraft were heading for the airfield at Vélu. I immediately took off in my Fokker. Shortly thereafter I saw that two British BE biplanes were being fired at by the guns protecting the observation balloons at Bertincourt. The enemy aircraft flew toward Cambrai. I pursued them

and caught up with them near Marquain, along the road from Cambrai to Arras.

'Both aircraft, which flew close together, fired at me with (a combination of) four machine guns. When I got within 400 metres I likewise opened fire with my single machine gun on one of the enemy aircraft, while the other came at me from the side with both machine guns firing. When I was just a short distance away, my gun suddenly jammed. But my last shots had hit so well that at the last moment the enemy aeroplane went down in a steep spiral and from an altitude of 300 metres plunged straight down. The second aeroplane immediately turned away and soon thereafter disappeared from my field of vision as I followed the other until just before it hit the ground.'

Although the advent of the machine gun-equipped Fokkers led to the development of specialised fighter units called Kampfeinsitzer-Kommandos, the Eindeckers themselves soon lost their superior edge. New Allied aircraft – such as the de Havilland DH2 'pusher' fighter and the Nieuport 11 – provided the same armament advantage. Even the special three-gun Fokker E IV furnished to Max Immelmann did not regain that advantage. Indeed, when Immelmann himself was killed in an Eindecker on 12 January 1916, many questions were raised about the Fokker Eindecker's effectiveness.

But it was Oswalde Boelcke, one of the first admirers of the Fokker Eindeckers, who aided in nudging them aside as the premier front line fighter. His 24 March 1916 evaluation of the improved E IV concluded that earlier aircraft in the Eindecker series were better in many respects than the 160-horsepower E IV monoplane. The Eindeckers were soon retired in favour of the new Albatros biplane fighters and the vaunted Fokker fighter 'scourge' went into an eclipse that did not end until nearly a year later, when the Fokker Dr I triplane emerged.

Right: the cockpit of a Pup preserved at the Museum of Science and Technology in Ottawa, Canada, exhibits several differences to the artwork above, which is based on the Shuttleworth Collection's aircraft. A compass is positioned in the centre of the former's instrument panel – the Shuttleworth Pup is rarely flown outside the environs of its home airfield – while a number of engine controls appear to be lacking from the purely static exhibit. The Canadian machine retains the Pup's 0·303 in Vickers gun, however, whereas the unarmed machine was converted from a postwar civil variant, the Sopwith Dove

Sopwith Pup

'The Pup', wrote James McCudden VC, 'could out-manoeuvre any Albatros no matter how good the German pilot was… and when it came to manoeuvring, the Sopwith Scout could turn twice to the Albatros' once. In fact, very many Pup pilots have blessed their machine for its handiness when they have been a long way behind the Hun lines and have been at a disadvantage in other ways.' He was certainly right about the abilities of the German pilots not counting for much, for even Manfred von Richthofen commented 'we saw at once that the enemy aeroplane was superior to ours' after his flight of Albatroses had been attacked by a Pup in January 1917. The Pup was shot down but only 'because we were three against one', the German ace admitted.

Thomas Sopwith's Pup, which was officially called the Sopwith Scout, was that company's first single-seat fighter, entering service late in 1916 with No 8 Squadron, Royal Naval Air Service. The Pup differed from its predecessors in being extremely compact and light. It weighed just 358 kg (790 lb)

empty and despite the relatively low power of its 80 hp Le Rhône rotary engine, could manage a maximum speed of 179 km/h (111 mph)–certainly the fastest aeroplane using that engine.

The Pup's manoeuvrability and tractability won it instant affection from everyone who flew it. One contemporary test pilot for the Royal Flying Corps stationed at Upavon described it unequivocally as 'the prettiest to look at and the sweetest on the controls of all the aeroplanes of World War I.' Coming from a pilot who had access to all the British and German aircraft of the period that was no mean compliment.

The Pup's lightness, generous wing area and–even with the Le Rhône–good power-to-weight ratio, gave it fine high-altitude performance, with adequate combat manoeuvrability even after an hour-long climb to its maximum service ceiling of 5,330 m (17,500 ft). At that altitude many contemporary scouts became sluggish, their controls unresponsive and performance marginal, at a time when pilots, icy cold and suffering from oxygen

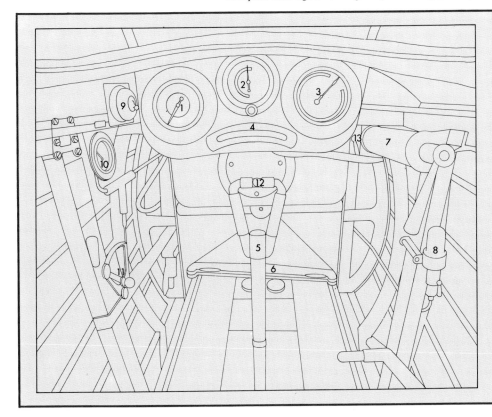

Sopwith Pup cockpit

1: *Engine speed indicator* 2: *Altimeter* 3: *Airspeed indicator* 4: *Inclinometer* 5: *Control column* 6: *Rudder bar* 7: *Fuselage fuel tank pressure hand-pump* 8: *Oil flow sight-glass* 9: *Magneto switch* 10: *Fuel tank pressure gauge* 11: *Engine controls* 12: *Ignition cut-out button* 13: *Fuel tank pressure control*

SOPWITH PUP

starvation, least needed recalcitrant aeroplanes.

The Pup's structure was conventional wood frame with strut-and-wire bracing and fabric covering. To improve the aircraft's roll rate ailerons were fitted on both upper and lower wings. The cockpit was roomy, with a fixed basketwork seat which was hard and not especially comfortable, and a tall pilot projected a long way out into the slipstream, shielded only by a small, heavy glass windscreen around the butt end of the single Vickers 0·303 in machine gun. This weapon was synchronised to fire between the propeller blades by means of a Sopwith-Kauper interruptor gear.

As with all rotary-engined aeroplanes, the key to successful Pup operation lay in good engine management. The rotary engine was designed primarily to give good cooling, as the cylinders and propeller rotated about a fixed crankshaft through which were fed oil and fuel. Castor oil was used because it did not mix with petrol, and since the oil system operated on a 'total loss' basis, much of it eventually found its way on to the pilot.

Engine controls comprised a hand pump and blow-off valve on the right side of the cockpit for raising pressure in the fuselage tank, a petrol fine adjustment lever and an air lever which was effectively a crude throttle used in conjunction with the fine adjustment. There was also a magneto switch, and an ignition cut-out or 'blipper' button on top of the control column's spade grip.

For starting, pressure was pumped up in the tank until the blow-off valve started to hiss. The ground-crew would prime each of the Le Rhône's nine cylinders with a big brass syringe full of petrol and turn the propeller/engine combination over by hand to 'suck in' the mixture. With the air lever set about half-way on the calibrated quadrant and the petrol fine adjustment almost closed the crewman would swing the propeller while the pilot threw on the magneto switch. If the priming ritual and the vital air/fuel settings had been carried out correctly the engine would fire in a cloud of blue smoke and a waft of tangy castor oil. The pilot would then carefully lean the mixture to avoid a rich cut, which, with attendant plug fouling, meant that any further thoughts of starting could be abandoned for the time being.

The Pilot's Notes for the Pup offered the following advice: 'Theoretically, the position of the fine adjustment can be found once and for all for every position of the throttle, so that having set the fine adjustment once, it need not be moved again, the throttle lever then being worked as on a stationary engine. Practically, the engine will run if worked this way, but better results are obtained by varying the position of the fine adjustment lever with varying positions of throttle… When the engine starts, the throttle lever should be closed until the engine is giving a few hundred rpm smoothly, then cut down petrol supply until the engine begins to miss. This determines a position beyond which the lever cannot be used. The throttle is then pushed forward well open and the petrol lever advanced until maximum rpm are obtained. Black smoke means too much petrol, white smoke, too much oil.'

Once running smoothly the Le Rhône would open up to about 1,100 rpm on the ground, with oil flow showing on a glass-bowl pulsometer. Throt-

Right: the Sopwith Pup's Le Rhône rotary engine developed 80 hp. Its nine cylinders rotated, as did the propeller, which was fixed to the crankcase. The crankshaft was attached to the aircraft. Starting the Pup required careful priming of each cylinder by the ground-crew before the propeller was swung. Rocking on its narrow undercarriage, the aircraft would remain on the chocks until the motor ran smoothly.
Below: once the brakeless Pup had been taxied to its take-off point by dint of much use of the engine blipper switch, the machine could enter its element – the air. As with all rotary-engined types, the Pup had a tendency to swing on take-off if not corrected. Rate of climb was particularly good and the aircraft could maintain height at altitude, an attribute rare in contemporary scouts

tling back using the fuel lever had only limited effect, reducing revs to 750-800 rpm, which was excessive for taxying the brakeless aircraft, so pilots used the blipper switch to cut the ignition, thus further reducing power. Once underway on the ground there was little to check before take-off.

The engine warmed quickly and the only instruments apart from the pulsometer were an airspeed indicator, altimeter, tachometer, compass and a bubble-type inclinometer or slip indicator. An adjustable-incidence tailplane for trimming – rare in its day – caused noticeable changes in elevator cable tension, which is probably why the Pilot's Notes advised that there was 'no necessity to use this at all'. Once rolling for take-off, pilot visibility was severely restricted, not just by the nose and upper wing but by the haze of castor oil. Plenty of right rudder was needed to keep it from swinging to the left, and acceleration was so brisk that the Pup invariably left the ground before an inexperienced pilot was ready for it, despite the caution in his Notes.

At this point, climbing fast at around 80 km/h (50 mph), the newcomer to the Pup discovered one of its failings. Despite the windshield, the cockpit was exceedingly draughty, windy enough to whip away a loosely-fastened pair of goggles. The climb rate was brisk, topping 3,000 m (10,000 ft) in under twenty minutes; the next 1,500 m (5,000 ft) took much longer, and it was during these protracted climbs to altitude, or subsequent descents, that Pup pilots were at greatest risk from an attacker.

In 1936, Major Oliver Stewart wrote of the Pup: 'In the Sopwith pilots found that their speed was not high enough to be a predominant factor in combat. But the way the Pup climbed from, say, 8,000 feet upwards and the way it could cling to its height proved to be of enormous value. The Pup could engage in circular chase tactics at 15,000 feet and keep circling without losing height, a thing of which no contemporary German aeroplanes were capable. It was this power to hold height during a dogfight that made the Pup a useful aeroplane, and it was this quality that pilots sought to amplify... And these were the powers that made the aeroplane a formidable opponent to the Germans and that enabled it to defend itself against superior odds when flying high.'

Pilots weaned on less nimble machines found the Pup's controls delightfully light and precise – at least by the standards of their day – with powerful and effective ailerons and elevators. Modern pilots who have flown the type are less enthusiastic. Neil Williams recalled of the Shuttleworth Collection's Pup that 'turning to the right she is pleasant and well-harmonised, but to the left she feels clumsy and needs a lot of rudder. Certainly she is not "sweet on the controls", nor particularly sensitive either, unless one considers the deterioration in pitch stability with power "sensitive". It is only in turns to the right that she begins to approach the sort of handling that one has come to expect in a classical modern type.'

John Lewis, who regularly flies the same Pup, agrees: 'In the climb the strong airflow from the big, efficient propeller is evident from the marked rudder deflection needed, and the gyroscopic effect of the motor is powerfully evident if turns are made. Go one way and the nose drops, the other and it rises. The higher the rate of turn used, the worse this becomes. It must have been the very devil of a nuisance in a fight.'

Perhaps this was so, although few World War I pilots make mention of it, probably because they were well used to the idiosyncrasies of rotary-engined flight. In combat the Pup's manoeuvrability, as we have seen, was its greatest asset. It lacked firepower, having only the single Vickers, so that the gun jamming – an all too common occurrence – meant a swift dive for the safety of the British lines.

Oliver Stewart was forced to dive for cover when his Pup was attacked by five German aeroplanes after he had become separated from his patrol far beyond enemy lines: 'I was forced to abandon heroics and to run for the lines, turning every time I was attacked to bring answering fire to bear. On that occasion the 80 hp Le Rhône was frequently forced up, by means of what are now given the grandiose title of "power dives", but which were then called "shoving the nose down", to fantastic revolutions per minute. But the engine did not falter or give up, and when the aeroplane reached home it was running just as well as when it set out'.

Despite its light construction, the little Pup was a sturdy machine, capable of absorbing substantial combat damage and still returning safely. Oliver Sutton—inventor of the Sutton Harness which replaced the lap-strap in British aircraft—was attached to a Pup squadron when his formation was attacked by a number of Albatros DVs, one of which made a head-on attack on his machine. Neither pilot would give way until, with a closing speed around 400 km/h (250 mph), Sutton pulled up in an attempted Immelmann turn. It was too late, however: his left wingtip struck the Albatros' starboard upper wing at mid-span, and although the German scout immediately spun to the ground, the badly-damaged Sopwith returned home.

Once back at home base a Pup pilot's problems were not over. Even throttled back to 800 rpm, the aircraft was so light and such a good glider that its rate of descent was inadequate for landing. The 'blip' switch had to be used judiciously, for the abrupt on-off-on motion of the Le Rhône unsettled directional control and lateral stability. 'The whole trouble with landing', cautioned the RFC's Pilot's Notes, 'is caused by the machine being sensitive fore-and-aft even at slow speeds.

'Glide down at 65 mph, flatten out and float along as close to the ground as possible, just holding the machine off as long as possible. Avoid letting it float into the air again, for if it pancakes at six feet it is certain to crash, and it may crash from a two foot pancake. If you hold the machine off as long as possible, the tail will come down, and, for a first landing, wheels first is quite safe, though not the best landing possible, which is wheels and tail together, when the machine will hardly run any distance. It is essential to land into wind. The undercarriage will not stand the slightest amount of drift when landing and a common fault on this particular machine is that it will finish up on its back or on its nose.

'Ascertain very definitely the absolute direction of the wind and, if no smoke is to be seen, do it by seeing your drift across the ground when still high up. Counteract all drift and if not sure of your ground, pancake from two feet, when the machine will stop at once and not run more than its own length. It is essential to counteract all drift. When 'S'-turning to land, avoid hurrying the landing and getting the speed up unnecessarily. On a strange ground, the slower the landing the better. When landing on a windy day, the wind tends to keep the machine head into wind as it slows up on the ground, and does this by blowing the tail round. On a calm day there is a great tendency for the machine to swing violently as it comes to a stop. This must be counteracted by suitable (generally left) rudder at once. Failure to do this causes burst tyres, if not more serious trouble.'

For all the daunting warnings of the Pilot's Notes, a flier who knew the Pup well could put it down safely almost anywhere, thanks to its fine handling qualities and light wing-loading. What better tribute to the aeroplane than these words from Oliver Stewart: 'The perfect flying machine. This

is the term which the Sopwith Triplane nearly fulfilled and which the Sopwith Pup did fulfil. As a military aircraft it had certain shortcomings, but as a flying machine—a machine which gave a high return in speed and climb for a given expenditure of horse-power, which had well-balanced, powerful controls, which was stable enough but not too stable, which was sensitive without being over-sensitive, and which obeyed its pilot in a way that eventually secured his lasting admiration and affection—the Sopwith Pup was and still is without superior.'

In his book *No Parachute* Arthur Gould Lee pays tribute to the Pup's dogfighting qualities: 'A few minutes later, at 17,000, Scott dived on a group of five Albatros D Vs about 1,000 feet below, and

eight of us might have knocked them into a cocked hat but for one small thing. Fourteen—yes, 14!—more Albatroses rushed along and joined in, we learned afterwards from Armitage, whose engine cut out in a dive, and who watched them swooping on us as he glided westwards.

'When we dived, I picked out a red-and-grey Hun, but kept above him while waiting my chance for a burst. It was a free-for-all as usual, with planes flashing like fireworks, and I was concentrating on getting a bead [centring in the gunsight] on my Hun while in a very tight vertical turn, and had just sent in one burst, which went in half-way up his fuselage, when—rak-ak-ak-ak! Tracers spitting past my head. Joystick right back, full right rudder, a twist of a spin, dive and zoom, and suddenly I realised the sky was crowded with aeroplanes, all Albatroses, all thirsting for our blood.

'I had a maniacal two minutes, skidding to the left, to right, diving, zooming, and generally throwing the poor old Pup around like a drunk on skates. I must admit I began to quake, as we didn't seem to have a hope in hell, but I managed to find a spare second to touch wood, and I also put in a snatch burst whenever a Hun whizzed past my nose. We Pups all lost height quickly, with D Vs buzzing over and among us like a swarm of wasps, to the tune of a continuous rattle of guns, with tracer criss-crossing all over the sky.

'It was incredible that we escaped, and the main reason was that there were so many of them they got in each other's way, but somehow it all ended and we weren't even badly shot about, thanks to the Pup's amazing manoeuvrability.

The torque created by the Sopwith Pup's Le Rhône rotary engine was considered by many modern pilots to mar its otherwise delightful handling characteristics. By the standards of the time, however, the Pup was considered an effective and relatively easily-controlled scout. The engine's gyroscopic effect could be utilised to effect rapid turns to the right which, if performed judiciously, could bring the Pup behind its adversary

'…the Triplane is extremely manoeuvrable and equal to any of the British fighters.'

Fokker Triplane

After the Fokker Eindecker series of rotary engine-powered monoplane fighters was withdrawn from front-line service in 1916, the manufacturer was unable to follow up with another singularly successful fighter aircraft design. Fokker's attempts at a series of biplane fighters evolved from the Eindecker design were not impressive. The newly-newly-emerging German *jagdstaffeln* were being equipped with inline-engined Albatros fighters which quickly earned a reputation for dogfighting superiority. The fact that the month of 'Bloody April' 1917, so-named due to very high losses suffered by Allied air units, favoured the Germans was due largely to Albatros fighters.

Fokker was therefore receptive to the idea of trying a new concept when the Germans managed to obtain examples of the successful Sopwith Triplane fighter. German air authorities were highly impressed by the triplane's incredible rate of climb and manoeuvrability, and considered that the three-wing configuration had much to do with the aircraft's performance. Thus a number of German aircraft firms were invited to inspect a captured Sopwith Triplane–just as they had earlier been invited to copy the Nieuport design–and to copy or adapt the design as they saw fit.

While the Fokker triplane was certainly inspired by the Sopwith Triplane, it was not a direct copy. The Fokker-produced triplane's cantilever wings needed little of the bracing found on other aircraft and its welded tubular steel frame provided great structural integrity. It was of nececessity powered by a rotary engine, as Fokker himself was out of favour with the high command at the time and simply did not have access to the supply of inline engines being provided to Albatros, Pfalz and other favoured manufacturers. Moreover, there seems to have been a surfeit of rotary engines, which, coincidentally, were the type of power plant found in the successful Sopwith Triplane.

Initially, the triplane designs solicited by the German Army were to be given their own class designation. Hence, the Fokker V4 became the F I production aircraft under a system in which the letters D and E were applied to single-seat biplane and monoplane fighters, respectively. The designation was subsequently changed to Dr I to denote

The Fokker Triplane is associated by many with Manfred von Richthofen, the so-called 'Red Baron', who flew it from August 1917 until his death

it as the first *dreidecker* (triplane). For operational evaluation purposes, two aircraft were sent to Jagdgeschwader I, the first fighter wing, commanded by Manfred von Richthofen. The first aircraft was assigned to von Richthofen and the second to Leutnant Werner Voss, commanding officer of Jagdstaffel 10.

At 0750 hours on 1 September 1917, von Richthofen approached an RE8 two-seat reconnaissance aircraft from No 6 Squadron, Royal Flying Corps, which was on a mission near Zonnebeke, within the German lines. In his combat report, von Richthofen described the encounter: 'Flying my triplane for the first time, I and four of my gentlemen attacked a very courageously-flown British artillery aircraft. I approached and fired 20 rounds from a distance of 50 metres, after which the Englishman plunged to the ground and crashed near Zonnebeke. It is most likely that the British pilot mistook me for a British triplane, because the observer was standing upright in his aeroplane and watched my approach without using his machine gun.'

Two days later von Richthofen found a more spirited opponent in Lieutenant A. F. Bird of No 46 Squadron, whose unit had just returned to France after a month's tour as a home defence unit outside London. While von Richthofen mistook Bird's Sopwith Pup for a single-seat SPAD, there is no doubt that, even in the early morning, Bird spotted the triplane as an enemy aircraft. Von Richthofen's combat report supplies the details of his 61st aerial victory and second kill in his Fokker Triplane.

'Being engaged with five aircraft of Jagdstaffel 11 in a fight with a Sopwith single-seater SPAD (sic), I attacked the enemy machine at an altitude of 3,000 metres. After considerable manoeuvring, I succeeded in forcing it to land near Bousbecque. I was convinced that I had a very capable adversary, because he refused to surrender, even after I had

forced him down as low as 50 metres above the ground. Even then he continued to fire. Before he landed, he emptied his machine gun into one of our infantry columns and then, once on the ground, he deliberately steered his aeroplane into a tree and smashed it. The Fokker triplane was undoubtedly better and more reliable than the British machine.'

The Allies had no way of knowing just what it was like to fly the Fokker triplane or to perform one of its most interesting tactics – that of seeming to 'hang' on its propeller with the nose raised to pour machine gun fire into the undersides of an adversary. Instead, newer pilots learned about the Dr I from the exploits of their comrades who had tangled with the German triplanes and survived. A case in point was described by Thomas B. Buffum, an

American who flew with the French SPAD fighter squadron Escadrille SPA 77: 'The new Fokker Triplanes . . . seemed strange to us, but apparently had marvellous manoeuvrability, especially in standing on their tails and shooting straight up. They could also go into a vertical dive with surprising quickness.

'My first acquaintance with them was over Amiens on a high patrol. We attacked three of them from above. They immediately went into a vertical dive. The one I had picked out went even beyond the vertical [and] I thought he was never going to pull out of it as I followed with [my] motor wide open and the wires and struts screaming in our mad descent. While I worked the hand pump frantically to keep up the air pressure in the gas tank, he turned

under completely and, after making half a barrel-roll, he disappeared into the clouds.'

Another celebrated German fighter pilot who preferred the Dr I was the 48-victory ace Josef Jacobs, commanding officer of Jagdstaffel 7. Jacobs picked up a new Fokker triplane on 28 February 1918 and flew it continually until it was destroyed in a crash during the last month of World War I. Under Jacobs' command, Jagdstaffel 7 was composed of Fokker Triplane, Albatros DV and Pfalz DIII aircraft. He noted that the triplane was 'slower than the Albatros DV and therefore of little use in sneaking up on the enemy at higher altitudes. Down low, however, the Triplane is extremely manoeuvrable and equal to any of the British fighters.'

Jacobs' tenacious use of the Fokker Dr I is evident in the combat report he filed after a late afternoon aerial combat on 11 April 1918: 'At about 5.45 pm, I started to fly home when I saw some anti-aircraft bursts to the north. I soon spotted a British RE8 in front of and below me. I immediately dived after him. As we approached Dixmude, I opened fire with my machine guns from the left side and behind him, and the observer returned the fire as the enemy aircraft turned to the right, crossing Dixmude.

'There were two bursts of anti-aircraft fire to one side of me and then no further firing from the ground. I then pursued the Englishman across Ichteghem, towards Aartryke, firing short salvoes and noticing my hits with rounds of tracer ammunition. Meanwhile, we had come down to about 200 metres and the RE8 pilot apparently applied full throttle to his aeroplane and flew north between 100 and 150 metres above the ground. He tried to slip and dive each time I opened fire with my guns. It was obvious that the enemy pilot had lost his way while manoeuvring to avoid my guns, as we now

Above left: an imposing line-up of Fokker Triplanes flown by Jagdstaffel 11 is pictured prior to an operational sortie in the spring of 1918.
Left: the Triplane was famed for its manoeuvrability, a reduction in wingspan being made possible without lack of wing area. The cantilever wings were identical in chord.
Above: one of two Triplane replicas from Cole Palen's collection at Old Rhinebeck, New York. Only 320 original machines were built, the type achieving renown far beyond its operational strength.
Right: the Fokker Dr I's twin Spandau machine guns were synchronised to fire through the airscrew and each gun could be operated independently

flew over the airfield near Ghistelles. Ostende suddenly rose up before us and the RE8 flew very low over the first row of houses and then turned back toward Nieuport, just south of the beach.

'Since I had only a few rounds of ammunition left, I decided to hit him with the next burst and fired a deflection shot just ahead of his nose. He immediately hit the ground and turned over on his back. I believe that my last burst destroyed his propeller and, as a result, he was forced to land immediately, as he no longer had any altitude. During the time that we were hedge-hopping a few metres above the ground, there was no sign of anti-aircraft fire. The RE8 came down at the first row of houses, just east of Ostende.'

Jacobs' aircraft was painted all black, with a white rudder, and decorated with a red and gold devil's head on both sides of the fuselage just aft of the cockpit. He scored most of his aerial victories in that one Triplane and, as his combat report for 14 May 1918 notes, he also used it to shoot down Allied observation balloons.

The combat report states: 'My Staffel and I took off for a mission at 4.10 pm, but we found little enemy air activity. Several British balloons were observed through the clouds and, with my entire Staffel following me, I dived downward and fired a burst at the first balloon, which immediately caught fire and went down blazing. I then attacked a second balloon while Unteroffizier Mertens in a Pfalz DIII fired at a third one. Both balloons immediately exploded in flames. Meanwhile, I turned my guns on a fourth balloon, but I had to pull away quickly due to heavy machine gun and anti-aircraft fire from the ground. We noticed that the last balloon had been hauled down rather quickly and that perhaps eight or ten observers had to jump out of the balloons when we attacked.'

Although the Fokker Dr I was matched and often outclassed by Sopwith Camel and SE5 pilots, the triplane remained in front-line service right up to the Armistice on 11 November 1918. When top-rated *jagdstaffeln* received new Fokker D VII and Pfalz DXII fighters, their Dr I aircraft were handed down to units of lesser standing. However, Josef Jacobs intentionally kept his black Dr I and a spare machine for use when the former was being serviced. Jacobs' faith in the nimble and manoeuvrable Fokker triplane is proven by the narrative for his 24th aerial victory, scored on the morning of 19 July 1918.

'We spotted some enemy one and two-seaters below the clouds at 1,500 metres altitude, where they were being fired at by our anti-aircraft units. I immediately armed my guns and scarcely had time to fire a red warning signal from my flare pistol when several SE5s hurtled out of the clouds at me, their guns rattling incessantly. I kicked left rudder and immediately swung toward one of the fighters when I was "jumped" from behind by three other SE5s, as well as three Bristol Fighters that came in shooting at me. At this warm welcome, I stood my triplane on its tail and got out of there to gain some altitude from which to engage the enemy again. Meanwhile, a second SE5 squadron and two German *jagdstaffeln* joined the fray.

'I was all over the sky, banging away at enemy fighters to make them break away from their intended victims. I saw an SE5 on the tail of a Fokker

D VII, which seemed to be doomed, and I banked and fired a burst into the enemy's centre section. He pulled off to one side and then a second fighter came into my gunsight. From my point only 15 metres behind him, I raked his aeroplane with machine gun fire. He turned toward our lines and prepared to land with his propeller turning slowly with no power. He glided slowly down and, as he passed over a road, he pulled up slightly and finally nosed his aircraft over. The pilot jumped out of the cockpit and attempted to escape, but he was captured by German soldiers.

'After returning to our airfield, I drove to the site of the enemy aircraft, where we discovered the SE5 to be very new. The pilot, an American, First Lieutenant Roberts, had been at the front for three months and expressed astonishment at the speed of my Fokker Triplane.'

*Above: although his unit, Jagdstaffel 7, possessed examples of the faster Albatros DV and Pfalz DIII scouts, Josef Jacobs preferred to fly the Fokker Triplane. He is pictured with fellow pilots in front of his Triplane, serial number 450/17, which he flew during most of 1918 before writing it off.
Below: the Triplane's initial designation was F I which, together with the machine's serial and maximum allowable weights, was stencilled on the fuselage side. The pictured aircraft has been painted to represent the first Triplane evaluated in combat by Manfred von Richthofen, Germany's most famous ace of World War I, who subsequently flew six further machines*

Fokker DVII

Nearly 800 examples of the Fokker D VII biplane scout were in service by the Armistice of November 1918, reflecting the regard in which it had been held since its appearance early in the same year. This evaluation was shared by the Allies, who made special mention of the type when designating material to be handed over at the war's end. A number of aircraft escaped to Holland, where limited production continued

Quick to follow up on the success of the Dr I triplane, Anthony Fokker ordered his design staff to improve further his single-seat fighter. The first result was *versuchsmaschine* (experimental type) V8, a triplane with two additional wings aft of the cockpit. That design was discarded, but followed by the V9, a rotary engine-powered biplane, which, except for its 'V' interplane struts, was quite similar to the Dr I type.

Further experimentation led to the V13/1 fitted with 'N'-shaped interplane struts. Limited production of 59 aircraft, designated Fokker D VI, followed and led to continued development of a biplane fighter powered by an inline engine. The impressive performance of the Dr I at a time when Albatros DVa fighters were suffering structural accidents meant that inline engines were available for the Fokker Works. Reinhold Platz, Fokker's

chief welder-turned-designer, employed the inline engines in a series of experimental models from the V11 through the V24 types. The V11 won the January 1918 single-seat fighter competition and virtually assured Fokker of a large production contract for the aircraft.

Fokker himself admitted that other aircraft in the competition might have been better than his biplane fighter with typically Fokker cantilever wings, but the Dutchman won the day through a good measure of salesmanship. He recognised that the aircraft's tail had a tendency to swing quickly, but turned it into an advantage. He approached Oberleutnant Bruno Loerzer, a leading fighter ace called back from the front to test some of the new machines, and said: 'You will notice a special feature of my ship, Herr Leutnant, its quickness in turns. Let the others in on it so they can show it off

Top: a design feature shared by both the Fokker D VII and its predecessor, the Triplane, was a 'one piece' lower wing, with the spars passing through the fuselage. Although the top wing tapered at the tips, the distinctively-shaped horn-balanced ailerons restored the parallel planform apparent in this view. Above: the Fokker D VII possessed a creditable rate of climb which, combined with its manoeuvrability, made it one of World War I's most successful scouts. Designed by Anthony Fokker and Reinhold Platz, the D VII replaced earlier combat types with the majority of jagdstaffeln during the summer and autumn of 1918. The aircraft arrived too late, however, to win the air war

to best advantage.' Unwittingly tipped off to a potential weakness in the aircraft, the pilots who tested the Fokker biplane soon learned how to use the fast turn to their advantage. That aspect, plus the aircraft's much admired ability to 'hang on its propeller' beneath an opponent and overall manoeuvrability led to Fokker being awarded a production contract for what was to be one of the most celebrated aircraft of World War I.

Interestingly enough, when the Fokker works in Schwerin could not meet the production demands of the German government, Fokker's old rival, Albatros, was ordered to produce additional Fokker D VII types under licence. To add insult to injury, Albatros received less money for each aircraft produced than did Fokker. The additional fee paid to Fokker was to cover his development expenses. The Albatros-produced Fokker D VIIs were nearly

identical to the Fokker-produced machines, although Albatros never received a set of plans. Instead, the aircraft produced at Schneidemühl and Johannisthal were based on one Fokker D VII provided to Albatros for copying.

There is general agreement, however, that all of the Fokker D VIIs were fast and manoeuvrable. They began to arrive at the Front during the early summer of 1918, a time when the German army's unsuccessful spring offensive was meeting with stiff resistance and Allied air units were proving their superiority over existing German fighters.

Carl Dixon, an American who enlisted in the Royal Flying Corps in 1917 and subsequently remained in the RAF until 1920, recalled the finer points of the Fokker D VII which he flew after the war: 'We were based at Nivelles, Belgium, after the war and one of the first things I noticed when we got there was the large collection of German aeroplanes there. Apparently, Nivelles was one of the central points where German aircraft were supposed to be turned over to the Allies under the terms of the Armistice. I was just a flying fool in those days and would go up in anything that had wings, so I made up my mind that, one way or another, I was going to take a spin in some of the captured German aircraft.'

Dixon, then a Handley Page 0/400 pilot with No 58 Squadron RAF, had a special interest in the Fokker D VII, a type that had 'chewed up the Handley Page bombers of the Independent Force that had carried out raids over German cities. We didn't get into combat with the Handley Page, but I did talk to some people who had flown missions over Germany and they told me that their worst problem was with the German home defence squadrons equipped with Fokker D VIIs – or, as we used to call them "square-nose Fokkers", because of the squared-off appearance of the radiator. While we were at Nivelles, I flew the Albatros DVa, the Pfalz D III and D XII, and the Fokker D VII. Of the four, I definitely preferred the Fokker D VII. It was much faster, more manoeuvrable and responsive than the Pfalz D III, which was a beautiful-looking aeroplane, but which was badly underpowered and did not manoeuvre very well; it was very good in a dive, but that was all.

'The Albatros, too, was not as fast or manoeuvrable as the Fokker D VII. Even though the Germans added extra bracing to the aeroplane, the Albatros DVa still suffered from wing flutter and the first time I saw those wings begin to quiver, it scared the hell out of me. The Fokker D VII, on the other hand, was a really good, stable aeroplane. It climbed very well and at a good rate of speed, it turned very well and very tightly when you needed it. A Belgian pilot and I were horsing around one afternoon and staged a mock dogfight – he in a SPAD and I in the Fokker. At one point he got on my tail and, if this had been combat, he would have blasted me to kingdom come. But just as he started to close in, I put that Fokker into a tight climbing turn and just pulled right away from the SPAD. He just couldn't keep up with me. Then, once I got on top, I knew I had him. The top man usually wins in a dogfight because he can get behind his opponent easier. Sure enough, at the top of my climbing turn, I just sort of fell over on one wing and

HITTING THE SILK

During the last year of World War I, a number of German fighter pilots made miraculous escapes from their stricken aircraft by using parachutes. Probably the first Fokker D VII pilot to parachute successfully from his aircraft was Leutnant Ernst Udet of Jagdstaffel 4, who 'hit the silk' on the morning of 29 June 1918 and landed safely at Cutry. Not so lucky, however, was Leutnant Fritz Friedrichs of Jagdstaffel 10, who bailed out of a Fokker D VII on 15 July 1918 and whose parachute became fouled in the tail of his plunging aircraft.

Ten days after that incident Leutnant Josef Raesch of Jagdstaffel 43 was flying a Fokker D VII at 4,500 metres over La Bassée when he and his four comrades were 'jumped' by five SE5s. One of the British fighters got behind Raesch, as he noted: 'I glanced over my shoulder, then kicked rudder and stick to my left as there was an Englishman on my tail. My manoeuvre led me into the path of his deflection shots because tracer ammunition passed by my head, centring into my machine. Then my machine was burning. A blazing fire hit my face, and I could not see anything because of the smoke and flames, and I felt my flight boots begin to shrink.

'I had a feeling that I was lost and, im-mediately, my parachute came to mind. I had carried one for the past two weeks. Now, hoping to live, I looked for the release pin, but could not find it in the excitement. At last I had it and pulled it out, then I dropped over the side, hoping that I would not foul the tail planes.

'At about 3,700 metres and free of the aircraft, I fell through the air. My goggles were black with smoke, so I pulled them off and saw for the first time that my parachute had not opened. The container that was normally fastened within the aeroplane still surrounded all of the shroud lines and only a portion of the silk parachute had been pulled out.

'I fell like a stone and, fighting for my life, I reached behind me and began stripping the 'chute out of the container when it popped into a full canopy with the sound of a cannon shot. With a jerk, the shroud lines pulled taut and I saw a hole at the top of the canopy that was almost two metres [six feet] in diameter. The hole did not enlarge and I floated down to earth. About this time the SE5 began to make a pass at me with his machine guns. Oberleutnant Gut-knecht [the commanding officer] saw my predicament and made a frontal attack on this aircraft until it broke off. My burning D VII curved above me and then fell away into oblivion.'

Below: Leutnant Schmidt of Jasta 43 was one of the first pilots to save his life by parachute when shot down in combat. Centre: Schmidt's comrade, Leutnant Raesch, lands his damaged parachute after falling victim to an enemy scout. This parachute was later repaired and used by Schmidt to depart his aircraft. Bottom: although flown by many noted aces, the Fokker D VII could make a good pilot from mediocre material

made a screaming dive right on top of my Belgian friend. He raised both hands to signify that I had 'got' him.

'Of the three other German aeroplanes I flew, the one that came closest to the Fokker D VII was the Pfalz D XII. In fact, it was very much like the Fokker. It had the same type of six-cylinder Mercedes engine, but was a little bit lighter than the Fokker and I think that made a critical difference in the way the Pfalz seemed to zip right up easier than the Fokker. Both the Fokker and the Pfalz were fast-turning aeroplanes. But the Pfalz had a bigger rudder area and you seemed to have more control over your turns; you sort of 'slid' into them and by going neutral on the rudder and applying power, you could straighten out. But with that damned Fokker, you had to have a very light foot on the rudder bar, because if you really kicked the rudder and gave it power, it would throw you into a spin. I did that once and I thought I was going to crash. I pulled out just above the treetops and when I got back on the ground an intelligence officer came over and chewed me out for almost wrecking his best captured Fokker.

'In fact, after that they were very careful of who they allowed to fly the captured aircraft–especially the fighters. I still flew some of the German birds, but mainly two-seaters. I also flew some of the better RAF fighters and, in my opinion, the best of the bunch was the SE5, which was easily as sturdy and manoeuvrable as the Fokker D VII and quite a bit faster.'

The superiority of the SE5A over the Fokker D VII was amply seen in a 45-minute air fight on the morning of 16 September 1918, when seven SE5A aircraft from No 29 Squadron RAF, shot down five Fokker D VIIs, two Fokker Dr Is and a captive

observation balloon. According to the combat report: 'At 8.30 am 'B' and 'C' Flights of No 29 Squadron saw eight Fokker biplanes and one Fokker triplane at 7,000 feet, flying from Armentieres in the direction of Menin. OP [offensive patrol], who were about the same height, engaged EA [enemy aircraft] and a general dogfight ensued. When over Deulemont, six more Fokker biplanes came out of the sun and joined in the fight, and a little later three more Fokker biplanes dived from about 13,000 feet, and also took part.

'Captain C. H. R. Lagesse fought one Fokker biplane down to 6,000 feet and shot it down completely out of control, EA crashing in the yard of a house south of Linselles at 8.35 am. Captain E. C. Hoy got very close to another EA and fired a burst of 50 rounds, upon which the EA went down vertically and crashed on railway lines north of

Quenoy at 8.40 am. Captain Hoy then drove another Fokker biplane off Captain Lagesse's tail and chased the EA down to 2,000 feet, firing 75 rounds at very close range. EA fell completely out of control and Captain Hoy saw it crash just east of Becelaere at 8.45 am.

'Meanwhile, Lieutenant E. O. Amm and 2nd Lt W. L. Dougan each engaged another EA. Lieutenant Amm drove one to 1,500 feet, firing over 200 rounds at close range, and crashed it at Bas Warneton. 2nd Lt Dougan fought another EA down to 3,000 feet, firing 200 rounds at close range, and EA crashed south of Wervicq at 8.35 am. Other squadron aircraft shot down the two triplanes and the balloon. Only one No 29 Squadron pilot failed to return from the mission.'

Presumably, the German pilots who encountered No 29 Squadron were either new to the Fokker

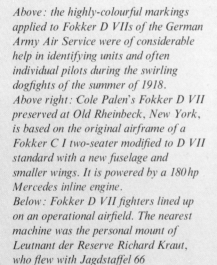

Above: the highly-colourful markings applied to Fokker D VIIs of the German Army Air Service were of considerable help in identifying units and often individual pilots during the swirling dogfights of the summer of 1918.

Above right: Cole Palen's Fokker D VII preserved at Old Rheinbeck, New York, is based on the original airframe of a Fokker C I two-seater modified to D VII standard with a new fuselage and smaller wings. It is powered by a 180 hp Mercedes inline engine.

Below: Fokker D VII fighters lined up on an operational airfield. The nearest machine was the personal mount of Leutnant der Reserve Richard Kraut, who flew with Jagdstaffel 66

D VII or new to combat flying; in the hands of an experienced pilot, the D VII was a formidable opponent. The 30-victory ace Leutnant Carl Degelow, commander of Jagdstaffel 40, attained over 20 of his victories in a Fokker D VII – and within a five-month period. Other German aces also performed well with this aircraft. One of them, Paul Strähle, a 13-victory ace and commander of Jagdstaffel 57, recalls the Fokker D VII as 'the best fighter aircraft provided to German pilots during World War I.'

Herr Strähle further notes: 'I greatly preferred the Fokker D VII to any other aircraft I flew during World War I. Earlier in my career, when I was assigned to Jagdstaffel 18, commanded by the famed Hauptmann Rudolf Berthold, I flew the Albatros DIII and DV. The latter was plagued with structural problems, most notably the tendency of the wings to break away from the fuselage in a dive. However, the Fokker D VII was wonderfully sound and a pilot could confidently put great stress on the aircraft and be sure he would return home in one piece.

'In my *staffel* the Fokkers were not decorated with different symbols, as used by some units to distinguish each other in the air. Rather, in Jagdstaffel 57 we painted the nose of each aircraft a different colour, covering the area from the radiator back to the cockpit. All aircraft had the same pale blue fuselages and white rudders, but the different nose colours allowed me to tell at a glance just who was where. After take-off, all my comrades followed me in a staggered line – not in a 'V' formation – drifting back at intervals of 30 to 50 metres. When I looked along this line, it appeared as a many-coloured palette. The nose of my Fokker was painted red and

Right: a Fokker D VII pictured during a climbing turn. This was a favourite manoeuvre of German fighter pilots to position themselves in the blind spot beneath an adversary, as it exploited the D VII's excellent rate of climb. Below: a replica Fokker D VII carries the personal marking of Ernst Udet, the most famous pilot to fly the type and Germany's second-ranking ace of World War I

my comrades used every other colour in the rainbow.'

During his time with Jagdstaffel 57, Paul Strähle most often flew in a licence-built variant produced by the Ost-Deutsche Albatros-Werke (East German Albatros Works) at Schneidemühl. Typical of the Fokker D VII tactics used by Strähle and other German fighter pilots is the evening encounter of 23 August 1918. Patrolling at 2,500 m (8,200 ft) beginning at shortly after 7.00 pm, Strähle noted in his combat report: 'An enemy squadron of approximately 15 aircraft fled as my *staffel* and I approached them, especially after I fired a red flare . . . Several times we were under heavy enemy anti-aircraft fire. We turned around and flew for home.

'Above our airfield at Erchin, I observed an enemy squadron . . . We approached the enemy formation, which turned out to be seven DH9 two-seaters, and we caught up with them just west of Douai. We

chased them as far as Lens, but we had to abandon further pursuit because we were all having trouble with our machine guns! What a shame! It would have been so easy to shoot down a few of the British two-seaters without endangering ourselves because with the Fokker we can attack from behind and below.'

Strähle had a more successful encounter six days later, on the morning of 29 August. East of Douai, Strähle and his pilots attacked a flight of 16 British two-seaters escorted by nine Sopwith Camels. At the outset, Strähle reported, his group 'approached them at the same altitude and I singled out a single-seater, which immediately gave up and tried to save himself by spinning down. It would have been easy enough for some of my young pilots, who were just coming up from below, to force those single-seaters to land, but my boys were not fast enough.

'I chased a flight leader with red pennants waving from his struts and I opened fire on him at

close range. He went down, trailing heavy smoke behind him before he crashed. I immediately attacked the second Sopwith Camel, who tried to escape by spinning away. Near Cantin he flew very close to the ground and I thought he was going to land, but then I realised that he was continuing to fly just above the treetops and rooftops. It developed into a wild chase at an altitude of five to ten metres until I placed a shot in his fuel tank as he approached one of our captive balloons. Leaving a heavy banner of smoke behind him, he landed south of Brebieres.'

After the war, Anthony Fokker successfully smuggled a number of Fokker D VIIs to Holland to continue his business there and eventually sold examples to the Dutch armed forces. The Fokker D VII was so highly regarded by its former enemies that it was evaluated by both the US Army and Marine Corps with a serious view toward producing examples in the United States—a fitting tribute to what was probably the best of the Fokker fighters.

SOPWITH CAMEL

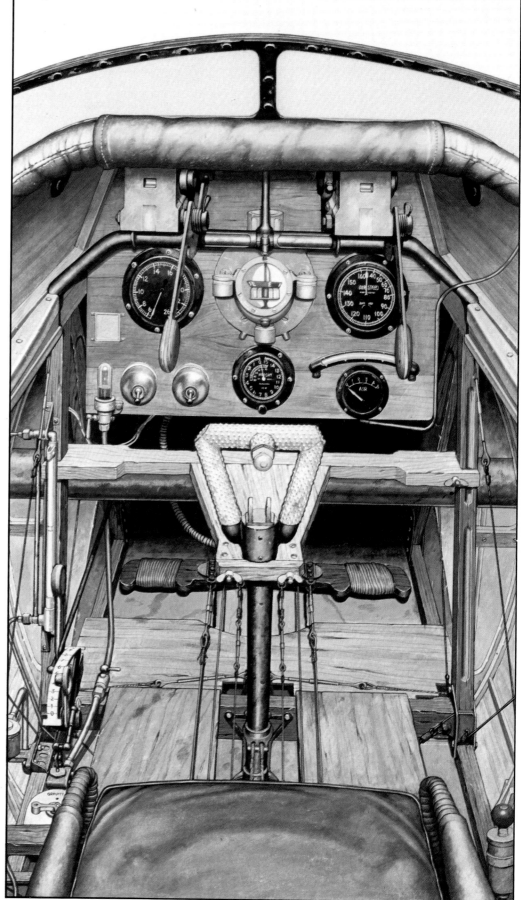

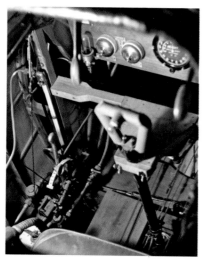

Rotary engines appearing after 1916, such as the Clerget and Bentley fitted to the Camel, had carburettors which allowed some measure of control over engine speed and power. The Camel pilot had four basic engine controls. The first, the petrol main tap, turned the petrol supply on and off. Located in a quadrant to the pilot's left were the petrol fine adjustment lever – which allowed a very fine regulation of the petrol supply flow – and the throttle lever, which regulated the proportions of air and petrol in the combustible mixture fed to the engine. The ignition cut-out button, on the hand-grip, cut the engine briefly to control power for landing and taxying. Later rotaries had dual ignition, thus two magneto switches

'A skilled pilot could not wish for a better mount ... it was like having a pair of wings strapped onto his shoulder blades.'

Sopwith Camel

Like its predecessor, the Sopwith Camel also earned the affection of those who flew it, although this was tempered with a healthy, cautious respect, for it was no docile Pup to handle. The Camel–so-named because of its hump-backed appearance–was the most successful combat aircraft of World War I, destroying no fewer than 1,294 enemy aircraft in less than two years' service, a record not even approached by any other fighter of the period. Less happily, no other type terrified or killed so many inexperienced pilots, either, for the Camel could be just as lethal to those who mishandled it as its twin Vickers 0.303 in machine guns could be to the enemy.

Both the Camel's superiority in combat and its unenviable reputation as a biter of the unwary stemmed from its manoeuvrability. This was due mainly to the concentration of the main fuselage masses–engine, guns, ammunition, pilot and fuel–in the forward seven feet of the aircraft.

The Camel was powered by a 100 hp Gnome Monosoupape, a 110 hp Le Rhône, a 150 hp Bentley or, most commonly, a 130 hp Clerget rotary engine. The strong gyroscopic forces of these powerful rotary engines combined with the built-in mass concentration to make the aeroplane uniquely responsive in turns, but also highly sensitive.

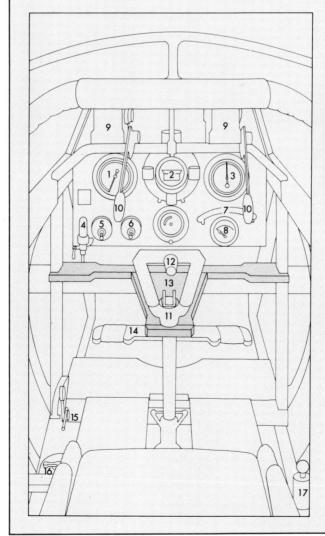

Sopwith Camel cockpit

1: *Engine speed indicator* **2:** *Compass* **3:** *Airspeed indicator* **4:** *Oil flow sight-glass* **5:** *Magneto switches* **6:** *Altimeter* **7:** *Inclinometer* **8:** *Fuel tank pressure gauge* **9:** *0·303 in Vickers machine guns* **10:** *Machine gun cocking levers* **11:** *Control column* **12:** *Ignition cut-out button* **13:** *Control column lock (for ground use only)* **14:** *Rudder bar* **15:** *Engine controls* **16:** *Fuel tank selection controls* **17:** *Fuel tank pressure hand-pump*

SOPWITH CAMEL

Unlike the Pup's Le Rhône and Gnome engines, which offered only 'on' and 'off' control via a blip switch, the Clergets and Bentleys were throttled in the conventional way, but with the blip switch ignition cut-out button retained on the control column's spade grip. Even so the powerful gyroscopic forces generated by the rotating engine and propeller were sometimes more than the aircraft's controls could compensate for. The Clerget in particular was sensitive to careful mixture control after take-off. The incorrect mixture for take-off caused the engine to choke and cut-out during the climb-out, and many inexperienced Camel pilots died in take-off accidents when they failed to lean the mixture correctly, or too late.

Arthur Gould Lee recalled: 'I flew in a wool-lined leather coat, a red knitted scarf – important to keep out the draught – mask, goggles and mittens, plus long sheepskin thigh boots. We would belt ourselves in, though there was, of course, a fitter and a rigger, check the altimeter, Very pistol on the right for emergency signalling, and be sure we had a map on board at the left of the cockpit. We checked the fine adjustment, a little aluminium lever on the left, and the petrol gauge on the dash, an ancient automobile-type gauge. Then we would push down the brown wooden pump handle on the right to get sufficient pressure for starting. We had it practised to the point where we could dash out of the mess and be airborne in one minute.

'Take off went like this. When the pressure was sufficient I would shout "Ready". The crewman

The Camel had few instruments and pilots had to rely in great measure on their senses. The most useful instrument was the engine speed indicator. The pilot had control only over the slowest and the fastest engine speeds. Full engine speed, about 1,100 rpm, was used to climb but for normal flight this was lowered by 100-200 rpm by decreasing the fuel supply. Very low engine speed was needed for landing and taxying, but the lowest fuel supply adjustment only reduced engine speed to 750 rpm; the ignition cutout button was used in short bursts to give the required power for such low-speed manoeuvres

would reply "Switch off, Sir". I would confirm it was off and call "Suck in". He turned the prop three or four times and shouted "Contact, Sir", and I replied "Contact", and turned on the ignition switch. He gave the prop a jerk downward and it caught and I revved up the engine. It wasn't too loud and usually started with a puff of white smoke.

'After I saw the revs were right I throttled back and pushed the first shell in the chamber of each Vickers by moving metal levers in front of me. That pushed the first 0.303 bullet into the chamber of each. Our aluminium gun belts were unlike those used in ground guns. The links broke apart as each bullet was withdrawn and slid away down a chute. When you had fired all 600 bullets there was nothing left of the belt. Having two guns was a vast improve-

ment over the one in the Pup. And by this time we had the new Constantinesco hydraulic interruptor mechanism which gave a quicker rate of fire. I seldom lost both guns at the same time in a Camel, which was a great advantage over the Pup.'

The Camel set new standards for manoeuvrability in its day, notably in its ability to turn seemingly within its own length. Such was the gyroscopic action of the engine that left or right turns both required full left rudder, and the rate of turn to the left was so slow against the gyroscopic force–and that to the right so fast–that many pilots made 90-degree left turns by flying through 270 degrees to the right. The need for firm rudder control, often in the opposite direction to that expected, caused many a Camel novice to end up in a spin, particularly if he misused power close to a stall. Little was known in World War I about spinning or the corrective measures to be taken, and the Camel became notorious as a killer.

The Camel's tendency to unintentional spins was equalled by its apparent inability to recover from inverted flight. A number of fatalities occurred after an inverted Camel dived into the ground, and rumours abounded among pilots that the aeroplane became stabilised upside-down and could not be recovered. Such was the hysteria surrounding losses of Camel fliers that all 'stunting' was summarily banned and questions were asked in the House of Commons about the aircraft's safety. However, many of the rumours which flew around RNAS and RFC messes were unfounded. Major Oliver Stewart recalled of the inverted stability problem that 'many of the upside-down Camel crashes had been due to the suddenness of the machine's responses throwing the pilot out of his seat, and to his inability to get back in time. A slight touch forward on the stick did tend to hurl the pilot bodily out of the seat . . .'

Captain Ronald Sykes DFC, who flew Camels with No 9 Squadron RNAS, noted that 'the long metal spade-handled stick [was] strong enough to

hang on to if the aeroplane got inverted', while the RFC's Pilot's Notes for Camel students cautioned them to 'always wear a belt or harness as there is a tendency to leave the seat when diving vertically.' That problem was finally solved when Oliver Sutton introduced his famous four-piece Sutton Harness, but investigation into the Camel's inverted and spinning characteristics lasted until well after World War I, when Squadron Leader Roderick Hill, the pioneer test pilot, conducted trials at RAE Farnborough, Hampshire.

Those who mastered the Camel–'that gyroscope with wings' as one RFC veteran called it–quickly learned to employ its fine aerobatic qualities to good effect, both in combat and for private amusement. The two masters of 'Camelbatics' were Major Oliver Stewart MC AFC and Captain D. V. Armstrong DFC. Stewart described Armstrong, who flew with No 78 Squadron from Suttons Farm, near London, as the supreme exponent of low-level aerobatics.

'He specialised in loops from a relatively low speed from ground level. It seemed there was no possibility of escaping from a crash if the engine failed or faltered, although Armstrong himself always held that he had means of side-slipping out safely. His flick rolls were started at less than the height of the sheds, and it is recorded that on one occasion a wingtip brushed the grass as the aeroplane went round . . . Armstrong succeeded in

doing these flick rolls without losing height by starting them at about 80 mph and bringing the engine in fully as the machine went over. There was just enough thrust to hold the machine up as it came out in a stalled condition and at a big angle of incidence.'

Armstrong was eventually killed in a Camel stunting accident, just two weeks before the war's end. Captain Ronald Sykes offered the following advice on looping and rolling the Camel: 'Loop: nose down, speed up to 150; pull up, then over the top . . . and now the trouble starts! The Camel gives a sudden flick to the right, and as you throttle back it does something like an inverted stall; you feel that you are slipping through your belt, although it is very tightly fastened; you draw your feet out from under the rudder bar-straps and bring your knees up to your chin; this stops you from slipping out, but the subsequent antics of the Camel seem even more confusing. At last, however, the use of full aileron will set it right side up, and then into level flight again. Needless to say, you need plenty of height when you try this trick.'

To roll, Sykes suggested, 'use the stick as if you were stirring a pudding and kick on some appropriate rudder. The results, in my view, are not pleasant; you will probably be thrown against the cockpit side and subjected to a violent air blast on one side of your head. By the time you get the Camel under control again you will probably have done two gyrations about a horizontal axis!' Sykes' description of roll technique is unfamiliar to modern pilots, but supported by notes issued to students in 1918, which advised: 'Get the machine going at about 70 mph, nose-up slightly at an angle of about 30 degrees to the ground. Shut off engine. Pull stick back sharply and almost simultaneously kick on full rudder. Take off rudder when upside down and you will come butter-side up in normal flying position.' That is a text-book description for a snap- or flick-roll, which is really a horizontal spin. Apparently, the lateral control of the Camel, like that of its contemporaries, was not good, and it was the flick-roll which was known simply as a 'roll'. Small wonder so many inexperienced recruits fell foul of aerobatics in the Camel.

In combat, particularly at middle altitudes, the Camel was supreme. Norman Macmillan OBE MC AFC said of the aeroplane: 'In No 45 Squadron we used to estimate that the Camel could complete three turns to the right to the Albatros DV's two', while Henry Woollett, a 36-victory ace who flew with No 43 Squadron in France declared: 'The Camel could dictate a fight and turn inside any scout the enemy used . . . Most of my patrols were carried out at about 12,000 feet, because at that height I knew what we could do. We could, of course, climb to 18,000 feet, but at this height the machine became less manoeuvrable and gave advantage to the Hun, so I worked on the principle of letting him come to me if he wanted a fight.'

Air Vice-Marshal Arthur Gould Lee described a ground-attack mission in a Camel thus: 'My specified target was a house on the edge of Bourlon village, a headquarters of some kind. I tried to sneak across the lines to get there no fewer than seven times, but each time V-Strutters and Triplanes came rushing towards us, and we had to turn away. Some had red colourings, which meant Richthofen's Circus, and it was no good trying to fight them with bombs on . . .

'At last, fed up with not being able to penetrate the screen of Hun planes, I went westwards . . . climbed to 4,000 and flew five miles northwards in the base of the cloud, then approached Bourlon from the north-west. I saw the target and gave the signal to dive . . . We dived steeply, and I let go at 200 feet . . . then I climbed up to the cloud base, at 4,000 and made south . . . Suddenly a DV passed across my front from the west, about 200 feet below. As it slid by, I saw the pilot looking out of

The Camel was armed with two synchronised 0·303 in Vickers machine guns mounted on the forward fuselage. The cowling over the guns gave the aircraft a 'humped' appearance and thus its name. In having two machine guns the Camel had an advantage over the Pup, Triplane and many contemporary fighters because it was rare to lose both guns in action through jammed rounds. Machine guns had to be mounted with the breeches within the pilot's reach to enable him to try to clear blockages

the further side of his cockpit at the smoke of battle below. He hadn't seen me.

'I swung steeply down on his tail, and caught him up so quickly he seemed to be coming towards me. At twenty yards' range I pressed the triggers. The tracers flashed into his back. The machine suddenly reared up vertically in front of me, and I banked to the right to avoid him. He fell over sideways, and went down in a vertical dive. I swung over and followed him down for a thousand feet, but he was going too fast. He didn't pull out, and crashed west of Bourlon village.'

Evidently the young Gould Lee had taken note of the student combat pilot's notes *Fighting the*

Sopwith Camel issued by the RFC which advised: 'Learn to manoeuvre with purpose – that of bringing your guns to bear on the hostile machine without him being able to fire on you. Practise the following: a quick change to an entirely opposite direction by vertically-banked or stall turns; a spin; vertical dives. Learn to shoot whilst diving as steeply as possible. Take every opportunity to practise scrapping with another machine. Remember, it is no good being able to out-manoeuvre a Hun unless you can shoot him down when your guns are brought to bear on him . . . Surprise is the first factor of success in aerial fighting and ability to out-manoeuvre your opponent the second . . . You are vulnerable from the

Above: Michael Turner's painting depicts a brace of Camels on a balloon-busting sortie. Such missions were not undertaken lightly, as pilots had to run the gauntlet of 'Archie', 'flaming onions' and other ground-to-air deterrents, in addition to the attentions of enemy scouts. Special authorisation was needed to carry the Buckingham incendiary ammunition required to ignite the contents of the gas-bag, although tracer bullets were interspersed for sighting purposes. The German observer may be seen leaving his basket

rear. Keep looking over your shoulder . . .'

Pilots who remembered those cardinal rules found the Camel a willing and most able weapon. 'Once a Camel pilot, always a Camel pilot', wrote Oliver Stewart, while Major W. G. Moore OBE DSC, who flew the type with the RNAS, paid this tribute: 'The Camel, being totally unstable in all directions and very sensitive fore and aft, and much influenced by engine torque, was a death-trap for the inexperienced pilot. A skilled pilot could not wish for a better mount. To him it was like having a pair of wings strapped onto his shoulder blades. Once you knew them, you could do anything you liked with them and turn their peculiarities to advantage. They were wonderful in a dogfight because they could make the quickest change in direction of any machine that flew in that war. Its peculiarities made it the most manoeuvrable fighter ever built and the best all-round performer.'

Arthur Gould Lee recalls in his book *No Parachute* 'I've done five flights today, including two short ones on the Camel. First impressions – more room in the cockpit, so you can take a deep breath without feeling you're going to burst the fuselage at the seams. (But why on earth didn't they fit it with a parachute?) Second, the exciting pull of the 130 hp Clerget, and the surge of power at full throttle. Third, her amazing lightness on the controls, lighter even than a Pup which is gentle-sensitive, while the Camel is fierce, razor sharp. She turns with lightning quickness to the right. You have to be careful taking off, as the engine torque veers her to the left, and you have to apply full right rudder, but it's easy enough once you get the knack. I've not fired the guns yet, that's a pleasure to come.

'Two more Camels have arrived, and everybody is having short practice trips. I did twenty minutes, which brought me up to 300 hours solo. I tried a few stunts. She loops practically automatically, as she is tail heavy, so much so that in level flying you have to press against the joystick the whole time. Result, if you don't press, she just goes up and over. But you have to watch your rudder. She does a very fast flick-roll – on the Pup this calls for a certain knack, but the Camel goes round effortlessly and instantly. I've not tried the upward spin yet – I'll wait for that until I've got the feel of the machine.'

Gould Lee remembers another occasion, flying over the Front. 'I spotted a bunch of black specks, well below us. I made for them, and found they were coming towards us, and also that they were being chased by another group, and that tracers were flashing between them. These I recognised as V-Strutters, but I couldn't identify the nearer ones, two-seaters. Then, as they passed underneath, I saw the roundel. They were an escadrille of five French Bréguets. The Huns, four Albatroses, now spotted us, and turned back east, but we had 2,000 feet advantage in height, and I led the patrol into a 70-degree dive after them.

'It was the first time I'd really dived the Camel, and the shrieking wires gave me a thrill, at 140 mph she cuts through the air like a knife, in fact our downward swoop put me in mind of hawks dropping on their prey. But the Albatros dives fast too, and we couldn't catch them up. We opened fire at long range, 400 yards, but nothing happened, and suddenly I realised we'd come down to 1,000 and were miles over [the Lines]. I turned back and climbed west by compass until I regained my bearings, and made for home.

'I find the Camel tiring to fly in formation for a long patrol. She's so sensitive you can't relax for a second, and you have the constant pressure on the joystick, which in two hours' flying makes your right arm ache. But she's such a marvellous plane these handicaps are unimportant'.

Right: a Camel is captured at the apex of an aerobatic loop by a contemporary air-to-air cameraman. The type's tail-heavy trim made it responsive to the slightest backward pressure on the control column; indeed, straight-and-level flight necessitated a constant forward inclination. Rolling was also easily accomplished, thanks largely to the torque of the Camel's powerful rotary engine. As with many scouts of the period, the Camel's performance at high altitude was undistinguished, a height of 3,660 m (12,000 ft) being optimal

Spad SXIII

*Right: the SPAD's cockpit, situated
forward of the characteristic dorsal
fuselage coaming, was devoid of
elaborate instrumentation. The pictured
aircraft is a SPAD SVII, the SXIII's
immediate predecessor, and carries only
a single 0·303 in Vickers machine gun in
place of the latter's twin-gun armament.
Below: bearing a flamboyant unit
marking on the fuselage side, this
SPAD SXIII served with the 22nd
Aero Squadron, US Army Air Service in
France in 1918. American airmen fought
prior to April 1917 as the Escadrille
Lafayette, which had been equipped
almost entirely with the SPAD SVII.
The SXIII continued to fly with the US
Army postwar*

Building on the success of its SPAD SVII single-seat fighter, in the late summer of 1917 the Société pour Aviation et ses Dérivés introduced a much-improved model, the SPAD SXIII type. Within a year of the SXIII's first flight it became one of the most effective Allied fighter aircraft and the best-known product of the SPAD works whose initials provided its popular name.

Like the SVII, the SPAD SXIII had interposing tie struts mid-way on each wing to maintain the integrity of the bracing wires; these gave the appearance of a two-bay biplane. The newer SPAD fighter also had an uprated Hispano-Suiza engine and the same rugged construction which had given the SVII an edge over the fine Albatros fighters produced by the Germans. Demand for the SXIII became so high that, of the 8,472 machines finally built, only 1,141 were produced by SPAD; the

remainder was produced under licence by Blériot, Bernard, Kellner, Nieuport, Borel, Levasseur, SCAP and ACM. First and foremost customer of the new fighter was the existing French *escadrilles de chasse* (fighter squadrons), which replaced their SVII types with SXIII machines.

However, Royal Flying Corps squadrons equipped with SVIIs did not re-equip with the newer aircraft and its two forward-firing machine gun capability. Instead, units such as No 19 Squadron opted for the Sopwith 5F1 Dolphin, also powered by the Hispano-Suiza engine. Nevertheless, the loss of RAF orders was more than compensated for by the SXIIIs which were provided for 11 *squadriglie* of the Italian air arm, one Belgian unit and, ultimately, 16 squadrons of the US Army Air Service.

The SXIII was fast. When powered by the 220hp Hispano-Suiza 8BA engine, the aircraft could reach

a maximum speed of 215 km/h (133 mph) at 2,000 m (6,560 ft). Even at an altitude of 5,000 m (16,400 ft), the same SPAD could attain the respectable top speed of 203 km/h (126 mph). It was also quite manoeuvrable, although pilots did complain that its thin aerofoil and wing arrangement did not give it very good gliding characteristics. Therefore, the aircraft had to be landed 'hot' (with power on) and, unlike the nimble Nieuports, was not known to glide any great distance if the engine was to malfunction or stop altogether.

It has been over half a century since the SPAD SXIII was in squadron service, but the pilot with the most recent experience in the type is Cole Palen, founder of the Old Rhinebeck Aerodrome in the United States. Palen, a collector and restorer of

classic aircraft, began with a SPAD SXIII which he acquired from the old Roosevelt Field collection in New York. Palen's SPAD was one of a number of aircraft shipped to the US after World War I and, when the 220 hp Hispano-Suiza engine proved troublesome, it was replaced by the ungeared 180 hp Wright-Hispano E, which provided good performance for the new American air arm. 'Sitting in the cockpit of the SPAD,' Palen notes, 'is like sitting on a sled, with your feet out ahead of you on a rudder bar. You have to sit that way because the engine mount comes back almost to the pilot's seat, and you are sitting [both to the rear of and] under the engine mount.'

Although Cole Palen was a licensed pilot at the time he acquired his SPAD SXIII, he had no previous experience in open-cockpit biplanes. He therefore had literally to teach himself how to fly the unique machine which, despite its age, was in very good structural condition. After removing the SPAD to a private field and performing some routine maintenance on it, he says he became acquainted with the type by taxying it. 'I taxied it back and forth a few times, just to get the feel of the controls and how they acted with various degrees of engine power. Then I flew it the length of the field, getting up about 20 feet in the air and landed on the other side of the field. I flew it back and made another trip, as well.

'On the third trip, at the end of the landing roll, it ground looped and swung toward the hangar. Fortunately, it stopped about 20 feet from the

hangar doors, which were closed. At that point I decided that if there was a chance I might ground loop or damage the aeroplane, I might just as well fly it. So, on the next trip I just took it up. And it really went. Within five minutes I was at 4,500 feet and soaring just grandly. Of course I was scared to death the whole time, but the SPAD climbed very fast and flew well. I flew it for a half hour and then came back and landed – and ground looped.

'As I became more experienced with the SPAD, I did find that it was prone to ground looping – to making an out of control turn on the ground. I I didn't do any damage, but there was always the chance that, with no brakes on the aeroplane, I could run into something. The danger of ground looping is that the higher the speed at which you lose control – or enter the ground loop – the more the aeroplane will turn. The ultimate ground loop, of course, is to turn the aeroplane upside-down, usually with considerable damage to the aeroplane. But the SPAD wouldn't do that very much because it is so heavy in the tail. I learned that to counter the ground loop you have to throw the ailerons into the direction you are turning, to create drag on the fast moving wing, on the outside, and relieve drag on the other wing – and that tends to straighten out the aeroplane.'

Cole Palen subsequently added other original World War I aircraft to his collection and put on aerial exhibitions which included mock dogfights between the former belligerents of the Western Front. The SPAD was a sturdy performer until it was eventually retired to the museum adjacent to Palen's air display facilities.

There was no pretence in the engagements experienced by Thomas B. Buffum, an American who trained with the French and who elected to remain in French service. In the spring of 1918 he flew SPAD SXIII aircraft with Escadrille SPA77. The first rule of aerial combat he learned was that 'no straight flying was ever done on any patrol over the lines. There are too many blind areas from the seat of the plane, which can hide the approach of enemy aircraft. Accordingly, a kind of weaving flight was maintained so that one can see in all directions without continually twisting the neck. Watching out for enemy machines, keeping up with my patrol, following the map and at the same time noting that all the instruments on the dashboard were functioning properly was very bewildering . . .

'On 4 May, some new 180 hp SPADs arrived for our *escadrille*. I had been without a ship for a couple of days, as mine had been put out of commission by anti-aircraft shells. Late in the afternoon I decided to try out one of the new planes. As two others were starting out on a patrol, I received permission to join them. Our objective was an enemy observation balloon behind the salient at Montdidier, where the French were preparing an attack. The ceiling of clouds was fairly low, about 3,000 feet, and with this to help us, we arrived at our objective without much opposition. The day was murky and, as the sun had almost set, the visibility was very poor. The battle-front seemed to be enveloped in a haze of dust and smoke.

'The ground crew of the balloon began to haul it down as soon as they sighted us. We were immediately surrounded by ''Archie'', ''flaming

onions" and what seemed like every anti-aircraft device known to warfare. Machine gun tracer bullets streamed up to our level and then curved gracefully over like fireworks. While two planes stayed above for protection, we each took turns attacking the balloon. Suddenly I heard the familiar and unmistakable crackle of machine gun bullets from another plane. I looked up and the ceiling of clouds just above appeared to be raining black Fokker Triplanes. Instinctively, I pulled my SPAD into a tight climbing spiral and opened up on the first one that came into my machine gun sights.

'While making an Immelmann turn to shake off one very persistent fellow on my tail, I saw one of the other German planes burst into flames – one victory for our side, but the odds were still four-to-one against us. The next second I heard a crash followed by a loud roaring, as if huge seas were closing over my head. For what seemed like a long period of time I was paralysed. I realised that I was on fire. A great feeling of rage filled me. Then my mind suddenly became clear and I could think with

extraordinary speed. The pressure gauge for my fuel tank read zero. I switched on the gravity feed emergency tank in the top wing and, as the sputtering engine picked up again, I threw the plane into a side-slip. This helped to keep the flames away from the cockpit.

'The SPAD that I was flying had an emergency procedure for ripping out the bottom of the fuel tank. It worked by pulling up a ring in the floor of the cockpit. The ring and wire came off in my hand from the tremendous pull I gave it. But it evidently must have worked [and dumped the excess fuel]. My troubles were only beginning, however, for another bullet exploded the emergency tank practically in my face. It looked as if everything was all over as I ducked down into the cockpit and a sheet of flames swept over my head. My engine went dead, but by keeping in a sort of combined spiral and vertical wing slip, the flames stayed fairly well to one side and did not set fire to the cockpit. As it was impossible to see the ground from my position, the altimeter was my only hope. When it registered 50

Above: the SPAD's high-aspect-ratio wing, which promoted its favourable rate of climb, could present problems at low speeds. Unlike the British SE5A, the SPAD had to touch down with engine on, as a glide approach often proved hazardous. A SPAD SVII is pictured

metres, I decided to take a quick look at what was below me. The flames still roared overhead, but my wing-slipping had spread them well out on the upper wing.

'My plane was less than a hundred feet above a large grove of trees, but–oh, what luck!–on my right was a nice open field, full of shell holes, to be sure, but with no trenches or barbed wire entanglements. A quick push on the right rudder bar and I came out of the wing slip and straightened out over the field as the flames roared back over the cockpit. My seatbelt was already undone and as the machine lost its speed, I pulled the stick back into my stomach. With the first thud of the wheels on the ground, I was out of the cockpit and landed on my feet. The tail plane struck me as it swept by and sent me spinning. The machine rolled on for a distance and, already a mass of flames, came to rest between the shell holes. By a tremendous piece of luck I had made what was practically a blind three-point landing in what was far from an ideal landing field. My helmet and forehead were singed, but otherwise I appeared to be unhurt.' Corporal Thomas Buffum's fiery landing was testimony to the ruggedness of the SPAD SXIII type. His aircraft was totally destroyed and Buffum was taken prisoner by German ground troops. He was the 12th of 22 aerial victories scored by Leutnant Hans Pippart, commander of Jagdstaffel 19.

Because of its speed and durability, the SPAD SXIII was the natural choice of Allied fighter pilots who specialised in 'balloon busting'. Second Lieutenant Frank Luke, Jnr of the 27th Aero Squadron, USAAS, flew SPAD SXIII aircraft to score 21 aerial victories in 17 days. Small wonder, therefore, that virtually any SPAD in the vicinity of a German observation balloon was the object of considerable defensive measures. In most cases the defences were entirely justified. In the case of Lieutenant William S. Cousins of the 13th Aero Squadron, however, circumstances made him the victim of the SPAD's notoriety among German forces.

On 31 October 1918, Lieutenant Cousins was sent to Colombey to ferry a new SPAD back to his squadron. In a standard postwar interview with returning prisoners of war, Cousins reported: 'I had never been over that territory before, but was quite sure I knew the route. In going over Toul I picked up the Moselle instead of the Meuse. I floundered along for a few minutes, waiting to pick up St Mihiel, and suddenly "Archie" began bursting all around me, mostly in front. I pulled up and looked around and saw quite a large city, which I determined was Metz. I turned around and started back in the direction I had come from.

'I had probably gone along a minute or so when suddenly there was a shower of tracers off my right wing, another one right under me, and some above. I looked back and saw a red-nosed Fokker sitting back on my left at a distance of 40 metres, and another one on my right at about 60 metres. I stuck the SPAD's nose down and started kicking on the rudder. They followed, firing occasional bursts, which were going wide. Suddenly I noticed great "Archie" activity all around. I looked ahead and saw a German balloon just in front of me and a little below which seemed to be being hauled down rapidly. The Germans probably thought I was going to attack the balloon and put up a most terrific barrage of all sorts of shrapnel, "flaming onions" and machine gun fire.

'Just before I saw the balloon I managed to draw away from the Fokkers to about 400 metres' distance, but I could not turn around in this barrage because they would have cut me off. I could not fly straight through the barrage for fear of getting a direct hit, so I started zig-zagging. The Fokkers closed in on me, actually coming into their own barrage fire, and began firing bursts at me, with their tracers coming awfully close. I decided that my one chance was to spin down and hedge-hop home. My altitude then was about 1,200 metres. I spun down partly to the ground, came out in a dive and pulled up. When I pulled up my motor seemed to freeze, the prop made a few turns and then stopped dead. Below me I saw a little village in a sort of valley toward our lines. I slipped down into this valley and made a landing, damaging the landing gear in some shell holes. As soon as I hit the ground, some ground machine guns on a hillside about 400 metres

Right: the US Army's 28th Aero Squadron was one of four American units to use an Indian head insignia, just visible on the fuselage of this SXIII. Other air arms to fly the type included those of Italy and Belgium, while the SXIII had become France's first-line scout by 1918

away began to fire. They fired all around me, but apparently could not get the range. I sat in the machine, trying to find some matches to set it on fire.' Cousins went on to report that his attempts to destroy the SPAD were unsuccessful, as were the efforts of the German ground troops, who subsequently stopped firing at him and, at length, took him prisoner.

Equally fortunate was Lieutenant Ben E. Brown, a pilot assigned to the 28th Aero Squadron, USAAS. He was the pilot of one of eight SPAD SXIIIs scheduled for a morning patrol on 6 November 1918 and one of only three to actually reach the front lines. Engine and other equipment problems caused Brown's five squadron-mates to turn back. Brown reported that 'while flying at about 1,500 metres, we sighted an enemy two-seater. Lieutenant Stenthes dived on the plane and then pulled up again. Lieutenant McClung went on down after the plane and I followed him. The plane dived towards its own side of the lines. When Lieutenant McClung pulled off, the enemy aircraft was evidently still under control and I followed it down. I was diving straight down and began to manoeuvre to get behind the enemy plane. The German plane continued diving and as I came behind it, it landed and turned over on its back.

'I pulled up with the intention of going back toward our lines when I was suddenly attacked from the rear by a Fokker. I did a quick turn and flew back under him and was attacked by a second Fokker. I had been surprised by a formation of four enemy planes. I succeeded in getting into position to attack one of the planes, but was forced to cease the attack by other Fokkers behind me. We were fighting so close to the ground that I was unable to shake the Fokker from my tail. My machine was being shot up badly and I was shot in one finger. While trying to get out of the machine gun fire, my machine started into a flat spin. I throttled back on the engine, straightened up as much as possible and crashed.' Again, the sturdy construction of the SPAD kept the pilot from serious harm and, although badly shaken by the crash, Lieutenant Brown went off for a brief period of captivity. The war ended five days later, on 11 November 1918.

The literature of aviation history abounds with the exploits of fighter aces who achieved some of their greatest aerial victories in SPAD SXIII aircraft. Captain Eddie Rickenbacker of the 94th Aero Squadron bagged most of his 26 kills in a SPAD, as did the Italian ace of aces, Major Francesco Barraca. Captain René Fonck, the leading French ace, used the SPAD SXIII to such good advantage that on two occasions—9 May and 26 September 1918—he brought down six German aircraft per day. Fonck himself, incidentally, was one of the few top aces who was never shot down by his opponents. He was as sturdy and remarkable as the most illustrious of the SPAD fighters.

Despite their deceptive appearance, both the SPAD SVII and SXIII were single-bay biplanes. The inner pair of wing struts was deemed necessary to prevent the flying and landing brace wires from excessive and violent movement in flight. Louis Bechereau, who designed the aircraft, granted SPAD scouts a robust construction which, although differing in several respects to British practice, enabled pilots to dive their machines with little fear of structural failure or control malfunction

De Havilland DH4 and DH9

The pilot's and observer's cockpits in the DH9 were close together. This was an improvement over the DH4, in which the pilot's cockpit was under the wing, separated from the observer's by the fuel tank, which was vulnerable to enemy fire. In the DH9 the pilot was behind the tank, thus increasing his chance of survival in a crash, while improving his view and crew communication. The pilot had a 0·303 in Vickers machine gun and the observer a 0·303 in Lewis machine gun

A successful designer for both the Royal Aircraft Factory and the Aircraft Manufacturing Company (Airco), Geoffrey de Havilland was called on to develop Britain's first aircraft specifically intended to be used as a day bomber. The resulting two-seat DH4, introduced by Airco in 1916, was the first of several promising day bombers which never quite lived up to expectations.

Equipped with a variety of engines from the 230 hp BHP to the 375 hp Rolls-Royce Eagle VIII, the DH4 was a two-bay biplane with equal-span wings. The traditional wood and fabric construction was augmented by the extensive use of plywood for

the forward fuselage section. A synchronised 0·303 in Vickers machine gun was available to the pilot, while the observer had one or two Lewis machine guns mounted on a movable Scarff ring.

The DH4 was used by both the Royal Naval Air Service and the Royal Flying Corps, as well as the Royal Air Force which was created on 1 April 1918 from those two air arms. The big two-seater served on the Western Front, as well as in the Aegean theatre, Italy, Macedonia, Mesopotamia and Palestine. While it had its grander moments – such as the destruction of the German Zeppelin L70 in August 1918 – it also had its drawbacks. The most notorious

DE HAVILLAND DH4 AND DH9

Right: a DH9 brought down behind German lines in France. The DH9 was used extensively for bombing and reconnaissance, but its six-cylinder 230 hp BHP engine was very unreliable and was the cause of many DH9s aborting missions or being lost. Below: the pilot's cockpit of a DH9 which served with No 206 Squadron RAF in France. At the lower centre of the panel is the compass; to its right is the altimeter, immediately above which is the oil-flow sight glass and, at the top, the airspeed indicator. On the right is the engine speed indicator. On the left is the 0·303 in Vickers machine gun, and on the right is the Aldis gun-sight; early DH9s had ring-and-bead sights. The board with the Allied cockade, German cross and question mark enabled the pilot and observer to non-verbally identify the nationality of distant aircraft

shortcoming of the DH4 was the positioning of the fuel tank in the considerable space between the pilot and the observer. That particular vulnerability caused the aircraft to be called the 'flaming coffin'.

After the United States entered World War I on 6 April 1917, the DH4 was one of four European-produced aircraft which the American Government contracted to manufacture for its own air arm. Impressed by the aircraft's good qualities and mindful of the availability of the 400 hp Liberty V-12 engine, US authorities considered the DH4 to be a good choice for fledgling American bombing crews training for service overseas.

In US Army Air Service markings the DH4 was simply called the 'Liberty Plane'. It served with 13 front-line units and a number of advanced training squadrons in France. One of the latter was the 89th Aero Squadron, attached to the Second Corps Aeronautical School at Chatillon-sur-Seine, France. There the American-built DH4s were considered anything but the lumbering, slow 'easy meat' that German fighter pilots of 1918 greeted with visions of adding to their victory scores.

As former 89th Aero Squadron pilot Hyman C. Block pointed out, the arrival of the Liberty air-craft in France was an event to be celebrated. 'After our arrival in France,' he recalls, 'we were provided with a number of tired old [Dorand] AR 1 aircraft that had been discarded by French squadrons when

they received new Breguets. We found the AR 1s to be very heavy, cumbersome aircraft that were not at all manoeuvrable. They climbed slowly, but had to be landed fast on two wheels before slowing down. Otherwise, they would stall and nose-dive into the ground. You also had to have a very smooth field to land an AR 1, as they had a tendency to turn over on landing if the terrain was at all rough or uneven.

'Then in September 1918 we received our first American-made DH4s and that to us was the height of glory. The DH4 with the Liberty engine was a very sturdy, substantial aeroplane. I used to enjoy sailing along, idling the engine and holding the aeroplane level until it stalled and then let it fall into a nose dive. I got a thrill out of the trick, like going down a roller coaster. I don't know if my student observer in the back seat enjoyed it as much as I did, but I used to love doing that.

'We used to be scared stiff of the AR 1s, but we felt very confident in the DH4. Like most aircraft of the time, you had constantly to apply a little right rudder to offset the torque of the engine and keep the aircraft on a true heading, but we had no problems with our DH4s. In fact, it was the nicest landing aeroplane that I ever flew. Unlike the AR 1, which had to be landed 'hot', you could ease the DH4 in–

Above: pilots and observers of the 135th Aero Squadron, American Expeditionary Force in France inspect a newly-arrived American-built DH4 in the summer of 1918. A total of 4,846 DH4s was built in the USA. Powered by the American-developed 400 hp Liberty V-12 engine, one of the war's most powerful aero-engines, they were known as 'Liberty Planes'. The DH4 equipped 13 American squadrons in France. Below: several engines were installed in the DH4, including the 230 hp Siddeley Puma, the 200 hp RAF 3a and the 260 hp Fiat A 12. The best production model was powered by the 375 hp Rolls-Royce Eagle VIII, which gave the DH4 a maximum speed of 230 km/h (143 mph) at sea level

even if the terrain was a little rough – make a nice slow approach without stalling and then let it settle into a nice three-point landing; the wheels and the tail skid would all seem to touch down at the same time and you just taxied over to your hangar.'

Captain Merian C. Cooper, who later gained fame as the producer of such Hollywood film classics as *King Kong*, was the pilot of one of the seven Liberty-engined DH4s from the 20th Aero Squadron and one from the 11th Aero Squadron assigned to bomb Dun-sur-Meuse on the morning of 26 September 1918. Cooper noted in the report he filed after the war: 'We had already been in one fight during the same raid and, according to the story which the flight leader told when he returned home, his observer was killed during that fight and, falling forward, jammed the controls so that the pilot was unable to turn the aircraft. We had therefore continued almost straight on into German-held territory and were just gradually beginning to turn when we were attacked a second time. Five of our planes were shot down during this second fight.

'My observer, First Lieutenant Edmond C. Leonard Jnr, was shot through the neck, the shot coming out through his shoulder, and knocked down into his cockpit during the second fight. I received a graze across the head, stunning me. My observer, although severely wounded and bleeding, endeavoured to carry on the fight, but collapsed.

'As my engine was hit and I was unable to keep up with the formation, I became surrounded by enemy planes. Just at the instant of kicking into a spin in order to make myself as poor a target as possible, my engine caught fire, due I believe to the fuel line or carburettor being hit and the petrol spurting out onto the hot exhaust pipe. On fire, I fell one or two turns in a spin, during which time my hands and face were burned. By putting the plane into a nose-dive and opening the throttle wide, I was able to burn out the petrol in the engine and extinguish the fire.

'When I pulled out of the dive, however, I had absolutely no engine power and was forced to glide down the rest of the way to the ground. My control of the plane was very poor at this time, as my hands were in such a condition as to render them practically useless. I crashed the plane on landing, wiping out the landing gear and breaking the propeller,

even though I had made it to a fairly good field.'

Captain Cooper and his observer, Lieutenant Leonard, made their final landing near La Mourtiere, south-east of Longuyon. The Fokker D VII which had shot them down remained with them and, indeed, landed alongside the wreckage of the DH4. Cooper and Leonard both reported that their opponent spoke to them in English, inquiring about their wounds and criticising the DH4 as 'an easy type to shoot down'.

Even as the early DH4s were in production it became clear that much improvement was needed on the basic design. The location of the landing gear placed the wheels too far aft, thereby making the DH4 nose-heavy on the ground and prone to pitch forward and break the propeller. Furthermore, the large space between the pilot and observer made any meaningful communication impossible and, of course, using that space for fuel storage virtually sealed the doom of the pilot if a crash should occur.

A replacement for the DH4 was in the works when stepped-up German daylight bombing raids on London in 1917 hastened the advent of DH9 production before the type could really be proven effective. The overall dimensions of the DH9 were similar to the DH4, although the 'Nine' was equipped with the 230hp BHP or 250hp Fiat engines. The 'Four' went on to offer much-improved performance with the 375hp Rolls-Royce Eagle VIII and, in the US-built version, with the 400hp Liberty engine. On balance, the DH9 was probably a backward step in the evolution of Airco's two-seat bombers. To its credit, however, the DH9 did have a better arrangement for the pilot, placing him aft of the wings and back-to-back with his observer.

Despite technical problems in producing the engines and the subsequent hazards of operating with such engines, the DH9 went into full production. In April 1918 – the month in which the RFC and RNAS combined to form the Royal Air Force – DH9s were delivered to Nos 98, 206 and 211 Squadrons, RAF. A month later, Nos 99 and 104 Squadrons received the type.

While the DH9s were being introduced to front-line service, a group of over 200 American aviation

Above: a DH9A pictured in flight. The DH9A was developed from the DH9 to take advantage of the American-built Liberty engine, which developed 400 hp at 1,750 rpm. The DH9 had been plagued by engine trouble, and the DH9A's performance and reliability showed an overall improvement. The DH9A had wings of increased span and a strengthened fuselage, but carried the same bomb-load and armament as the DH9. Known as the 'Ninak', the type entered combat in France in August 1918 but by the Armistice only one RAF squadron, No 110, was fully equipped with the DH9A. However, the type was the RAF's standard day bomber in the 1920s at home and overseas

officers was being phased into British squadrons due to the lack of organised US Army Air Service units in France during early 1918. Some 35 of the Americans were posted to RAF DH4 and DH9 squadrons. One of that number, Clayton Knight – later a leading American aviation artist and author – qualified to fly the DH9 in England and, on 18 August 1918, reported for duty with No 206 Squadron based at Alquines, France.

'On my first take-off, I very nearly came a cropper,' Knight recalled, 'because the aircraft at the Front were rigged differently than the ones I had flown in England. There was a lever on the side by the throttle, which in the front-line machines was used to open up for extra air so that when you got to altitude you could thin-out the fuel and air mixture even more and thereby extend your range. But in the DH9s I had flown in training, we always opened

that up when we pushed the throttle forward during the take-off run. So I pushed it full open, got a run down the field and suddenly found the engine sputtering. We had no brakes in those days, so it was "nip 'n' tuck" whether I'd stop in time, but I did, and turned around and took off smoothly – using the proper throttle.'

Clayton Knight considered himself fortunate that the DH9 he was assigned had a good strong engine. The aircraft performed very well until one day in September, when the squadron commander ordered a flight to take off in formation. He recalled: 'Unfortunately, the morning he picked for this particular stunt there was a cross-wind blowing and we had to take off in the direction of a line of hangars and trees. I was flying first right, behind my flight leader. The leader got off the ground and I gave my engine full throttle, but nothing happened. I just stayed on the ground. Later I figured that he had slid in front of me and that his propwash was holding me down. I was getting so close to the hangars that something had to be done. I couldn't stop, so I pulled back on the stick and hoicked the plane up, just clearing the hangar. I felt the controls go floppy and I knew I was in a stall, so I switched off the engine. In the next instant we crashed beside a huge canvas hangar filled with Handley Page bombers being loaded for a night-time mission. As we hit the ground, the engine went flying off to one side, the bombs we were carrying whipped off . . . but there was no great damage to us.'

Lieutenant Knight was given a replacement aircraft, an Airco-produced machine; the new aircraft was beset with engine problems and Knight's logbook contains several entries noting missions that were shortened due to 'dud engine'. On 1 October 1918, the aircraft went in for an engine change and the following day Clayton Knight flew two missions in a DH9 built under licence by Bar-

wick & Co. He got two more days out of his regularly-assigned DH9 until, on the afternoon of 4 October, a broken piston forced him to land at an emergency airfield. Thus, on 5 October 1918, Lieutenant Clayton Knight and his RAF observer, Second Lieutenant J. H. 'Bert' Perring, were assigned another newly-arrived and untried aircraft produced by Cubitt Ltd of Croydon, one of almost a dozen firms manufacturing DH9s.

That day No 206 Squadron's 'B' Flight was assigned to bomb Courtrai, an important German railhead. As the flight approached the target, however, they were attacked by a swarm of Fokker D VII fighters led by Oberleutnant Harald Auffarth, commander of Jagdstaffel 29 and a 22-victory ace. Despite all of the pilot's coaxing, Knight's DH9 did not produce sufficient power to allow the machine to keep up with the rest of 'B' Flight. Consequently, Knight and Perring drifted to the rear and below the rest of the formation, an ideal target for the enemy fighters which quickly descended.

Clayton Knight recalled: 'The first Fokker that came down got a shot underneath my aeroplane, along the floorboards. The bullets must have set fire to the spattered grease and oil there, because I suddenly looked down and noticed that, instead of being dark in the cockpit, it was bright red. The horrible thought of going down burning was a fear

from the front until they were sure that they had you. I thought to myself, "This is the end – but I'm going to get this one anyway, even if I have to crash into him." I was looking through the Aldis gunsight and I could see him gradually getting bigger and bigger, filling the sight; it seemed like a slow-motion picture. I had a very clear view of the pilot in the cockpit and the yellow comet design painted on the side of his Fokker. Firing at him, I could see my bullets stitching right up to where he was sitting and yet he wouldn't fall. I closed my eyes and thought, "This is the end, but I'll crash into him." The German went underneath me and, as he did, I was hit in the leg. The bullet went in beside my knee, exploded, and went out at the hip. I didn't know how bad it was – it didn't hurt at the time – but it jammed me back in the seat and felt like a hot iron scorching me.

'As I looked over the side, the Fokker seemed to be going down out of control. Another Fokker fired at me from the other side and I turned and sprayed him. I had been trying to find which way was home, but low clouds blotted out the rising sun and the compass was whirling madly in the spin. Every time I'd fly straight – just for a few seconds to let the compass settle – another Fokker attacked. I might have been flying into Germany for all I knew! After I'd flown straight to get my bearings, and got sprayed every time, I became more and more des-

Above: an American-built DH4 'Liberty Plane' serving in France in 1918 with the 50th Aero Squadron, American Expeditionary Force. American flyers criticised the DH4's tendency to nose over when landing on soft ground and the separation of the observer and pilot. An extensive redesign in the USA produced the DH4B, in which the undercarriage was repositioned and the pilot's cockpit located behind the fuel tank as in the DH9. The DH4 was retired from US service in 1932. Right: two passengers boarding a DH9 leased from Aircraft Transport and Travel Ltd by the Dutch airline KLM in 1920 for its first passenger service. Many ex-RAF DH4s and DH9s were used for commercial work or by private pilots for pleasure and racing

we all had, naturally, because we had no parachutes in those days.

'Some of the fabric on the fuselage side was burning. I beat that out with my glove, then I stamped out the flames on the floorboards and finally stopped the fire. In the meantime I was spinning down, smoking and out of control. We had started at about 15,000 feet and, when I pulled out of the spin, we weren't more than 1,500 feet. Two or three of the Fokkers that had spun down with us now began to pepper us. Perring was very good. He fired as long as his guns worked and then suddenly stopped. I looked back and couldn't see him, as he had been hit and dropped to the floor of his cockpit.

'I turned on two of the Fokkers and sprayed them. They swerved off to one side. Then another Fokker came down ahead of me. In my mind I thought this was the end, because they never attack

perate. I had never heard the bullets so close – it was like cracking whips on the wings – and a stream of tracers zipped past my head. Suddenly the racket stopped and there was absolute silence. The engine had quit and for the moment nobody was firing at me. There was a field of new wheat below and I headed for it.'

Upon touching down, Knight's DH9 sunk into the soft earth and nosed over. Knight and Perring were subsequently captured and taken to a German field hospital. The DH9 was officially recorded as the 23rd aerial victory of Oberleutnant Auffarth, but it should be noted that his aircraft was also disabled and forced to land by Clayton Knight's return fire. It was an unusual occasion when one of the trouble-plagued de Havilland two-seaters managed to sting its attacker before meeting its end in a Flanders field.

Above: the Bristol Fighter was the finest two-seat fighter of World War I, entering service in the spring of 1917 and undertaking the fighter, reconnaissance and army co-operation roles. After the war the type became the RAF's standard army co-operation aircraft and served until the 1930s

Bristol Fighter

'The Bristol Fighter', wrote Major Oliver Stewart, 'should be spoken of in terms of the heroes of classical mythology. It was, in the fullest sense, a hero after their pattern–a fighter by name, inclination and aptitude.' The 'Brisfit', as the aircraft was affectionately known, was the first British two-seat fighter to enter service in World War I, although its début was hardly auspicious.

By using the aircraft's armament purely defensively, the first Brisfits to cross the German lines in April 1917 were decimated by Manfred von Richthofen's 'Circus'. It was not until Brisfit crews realised that their big and seemingly unwieldy aircraft had all the speed and manoeuvrability of the German single-seat scouts, and greater firepower, that the machines became the superb, heroic weapon which Major Stewart eulogised.

In its most familiar F2B form the Brisfit was powered by no fewer than 17 different engine types, of which the commonest was the 275 hp Rolls-Royce Falcon III water-cooled V-12. After struggling to master recalcitrant, idiosyncratic rotary engines, RFC pilots found the Rolls-Royce a positive delight. Until the Hucks Starter came into general use, however, the Falcon's big propeller had to be hand swung–a method known colloquially as 'armstrong' starting–and it was usual for two or three groundcrewmen to do the swinging, linking

hands with the one nearest the propeller putting his hand on the lower blade. Upon the call of 'contact', they would all pull together while another crewman wound the starting magneto handle.

Compared to the single-seat scout fighters such as the Pup and Camel, the Bristol Fighter was immense, with a wingspan of 12 m (39 ft) and a loaded weight of 1,270 kg (2,800 lb). Its cockpit accommodation was compact, with pilot and observer crammed together, back-to-back atop the lower mainplane's trailing edge, so that both had a good field of vision, except for the observer's blind spot below the rear fuselage. Early losses invariably resulted from attacks from below and directly astern. The armament consisted of a single 0·303 in Vickers machine gun fixed in a trough forward of the cockpit between the two banks of 'V' engine cylinders, firing forwards through the geared, slow-revving propeller by means of a Constantinesco interruptor gear, and single or twin 0·303 in Lewis guns mounted on a Scarff ring on the rear cockpit.

With three guns, the Brisfit represented a radical departure from previous tactical thinking. Here was an aeroplane being used for the first time as a platform for gun positions and, as Oliver Stewart wrote, 'The method of fighting a Bristol Fighter was the subject of a good deal of discussion when it first appeared. The chief question was whether the pilot

Above: rearward defence for the Bristol Fighter was provided by a 0·303 in Lewis gun mounted on a Scarff ring and operated by the observer. Six replacement ammunition drums for the Lewis were stowed in racks in the rear cockpit. Offensive armament was the pilot's forward-firing Vickers gun

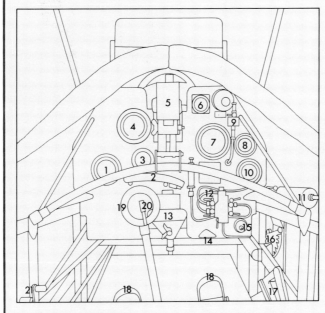

Bristol F2B Fighter cockpit
1: *Altimeter* **2**: *Inclinometer*
3: *Clock* **4**: *Airspeed indicator*
5: *0·303 in Vickers machine gun*
6: *Radiator coolant temperature gauge* **7**: *Engine speed indicator*
8: *Oil pressure gauge* **9**: *Fuel tank pressure release valve* **10**: *Fuel tank pressure gauge* **11**: *Fuel tank pressure hand-pump* **12**: *Fuel system pressurisation controls* **13**: *Fuel tank selector cock* **14**: *Starter magneto hand-crank location*
15: *Magneto switch* **16**: *Radiator shutter control* **17**: *Tailplane incidence adjustment lever*
18: *Rudder pedals* **19**: *Control column* **20**: *Machine gun firing lever*
21: *Engine control levers*

should seek to place his aeroplane so as to give his observer an opportunity for shooting and reserve the front gun for emergency purposes, or whether he should fight the machine as a single-seater, seeking always to attack with his front gun and leave to the observer the task of beating off any machines that might attack from the rear with his flexibly-mounted Lewis gun.

The problem was wrapped up with the comparative performance of the Bristol Fighter and the enemy aeroplanes with which it came in contact. Had the performance been less good, the observer's guns might have been used for the attack; but, as it was, the method generally adopted was that of using the front gun, fighting the machine always as a single-seater, and regarding the observer as a sort of armour against attack from the rear. The high speed – for the time – the powers of manoeuvre, and the immense strength of the Bristol Fighter ministered to this form of tactics.'

The Bristol's handling was thus the key to its success. Air Commodore Allen Wheeler found the machine 'very stable with rather heavy controls all round. We were told that the elevators were made specially heavy since the specification called for a maximum diving speed [of] 400 mph, and light elevators at that speed could have been embarrassing. I doubt if the Bristol could have reached such a figure even in a vertical dive, but it certainly picked up speed very quickly in a shallow dive at full power – as for a loop, which one entered at speeds between 120 and 140 mph.

'Its spin characteristics were normal, but a lot of height was lost during recovery owing to the steep angle of spinning and the aircraft's relatively heavy weight. One of the most impressive aerobatic manoeuvres practised in the Bristol was the flick roll, induced by adjusting the speed to approximately 85 mph in level flight and pulling the stick hard back with full rudder; it then did an impressive turn of a spin horizontally, following which the pilot quickly normalised the controls to prevent it started another. A "falling leaf" was also possible, and quite neat, but one had to use a little engine power during the change-over to keep the manoeuvre symmetrical. As in the Avro, a slow roll was virtually impossible owing to very heavy ailerons. Furthermore, we only had lap straps in the Bristol Fighter.'

Despite a few opinions to the contrary, most pilots who have flown Bristol Fighters agree that it was very heavy on the controls, particularly on the ailerons, and it was often said, not without cause, that one could tell a Brisfit man by his bulging biceps. Nevertheless, performance was excellent, even at an all-up weight of nearly 1,360 kg (3,000 lb). With the Eagle III engine, a Brisfit's top speed in level flight was about 200 km/h (125 mph), its rate of climb in excess of 244 m (800 ft) per minute, and its service ceiling 6,000 m (20,000 ft). It could also dive faster than any other fighter on the Western Front.

'The pilot could enter a dogfight and turn almost

Left: although large and somewhat heavy on the controls, the Bristol Fighter was both strong and fast. It was normally flown as a single-seat scout, with the pilot utilising his forward-firing gun in combat, while the observer guarded the tail. Michael Turner's painting shows a pair of Albatros scouts falling victim to the Lewis gun of a Bristol's observer. Below: a factory-fresh Bristol Fighter awaits a pilot. Over 3,000 examples of the Rolls-Royce Falcon-engined scout had been built by the close of 1918, while production continued postwar. One of the less-numerous Sunbeam Arab engined variants is pictured

Above: a Bristol Fighter of No 22 Squadron RAF exhibits an improvised Lewis gun mounting atop the wing. It was based in France in 1918. Left: the last airworthy 'Brisfit' is flown by the Shuttleworth Collection Old Warden, Beds

as quickly and on almost as small a radius as the best single-seater', wrote Oliver Stewart. 'He could fling his machine about, go into vertical dives, pull it out quickly, turn it on its back, spin it, roll it and generally do every sort of manoeuvre if the need arose. And all the time there was the comfortable feeling that the observer was there with his pair of Lewis guns, watching and protecting.'

Quite how comfortable the poor observer himself felt during all that gyrating Major Stewart does not say, though he does allow that 'the thing which ought to be remembered about Bristol Fighters above all else was the heroism of the observers. Machines came back from patrol again and again with their observers dead in the rear cockpit, and the casualties among observers were exceptionally high. The reason is to be found in the tactics used . . . the pilots fought their machines as single-seaters and left the rear defence to the observer. Acts of prodigious courage were entailed in this defence work, for the observer, with no engine to protect him, had often to stand up in his narrow cockpit and face the fire of diving fighters and, at the same time, to attempt to bring effective fire to bear upon them. At such moments the observer's twin Lewis guns must have seemed a poor counter to the fixed guns of the German machines.

'Yet, in spite of the difficulties and dangers of the observer's task, in spite of the heavy casualties, there was never any lack of volunteers for work with Bristol Fighters. It happened, too, on more than one occasion, that the observer found himself in an aeroplane whose pilot had been killed or disabled by enemy fire. He then had to strive to regain control by whatever means he could to bring the machine safely to the ground.'

Landing the Bristol, even from the front cockpit, was not always easy, as Air Commodore Allen Wheeler recalls of his first solo in the aeroplane: 'I was much more confident on this one than I had been on the Avro. All went well until I came in to land with what seemed to me to be a perfectly normal approach in speed and height; but the Bristol floated right across the aerodrome and showed no sign of wanting to land. I put the engine on and went round again, deciding that I must have come in too fast.

'On my second approach I paid particular attention to my speed, and, if anything, was on the slow side. Again the Bristol floated right across the aerodrome and again I put the engine on and went round again wondering whether the airspeed indicator and my own sense of feel were both at fault . . . I was not unduly worried myself since I had made up my mind that if I simply could not land within the aerodrome at Digby–which was big enough in all conscience–then I would fly over to Cranwell only six miles away where the aerodrome provided a mile or more of clear landing space.

'On my third attempt, again with considerable attention to the speed of approach, I could sense that the same thing was going to happen again and as I passed in front of the hangars I glanced apprehensively towards the Flight Commander's office to see whether he was, as I suspected, jumping up and down with fury and anxiety. In glancing towards the hangars I inadvertently let the Bristol's wheels touch the ground and the Bristol bounced several feet into the air: fearing that I would then stall and drop with a bump I gave a burst of engine and then shut the throttle again smartly. The Bristol settled down for a perfect landing and the mystery was solved.

'As one closed the throttle on the Bristol there was a stiff point just above the idling position where the throttle movement also retarded the ignition; on my first solo I had been particularly light-handed on all the controls, including the throttle; thus when I thought I had closed the throttle the engine was still giving about 20 per cent of its power, but the Falcon engine was so quiet that one did not notice it and this 20 per cent power was quite sufficient to keep the Bristol floating right across the aerodrome.'

The Bristol Fighter, which first entered service in April 1917, equipped 14 full squadrons at the end of World War I, and soldiered on long after the Armistice to become a mainstay of the embryo Royal Air Force. It remained in production until 1926, having been built in ten British factories and three in America, and in RAF service until 1932, when No 6 Squadron in Iraq finally re-equipped with Fairey Gordons.

Handley Page 0/400

Right: flown in December 1915, the Handley Page 0/100 was Britain's first heavy bomber and the precursor of the 0/400. The pictured aircraft, flanked by a Sopwith Triplane and a Nieuport Scout, was the first to arrive at Coudekerque, France, in early 1917 to fly armed day reconnaissance patrols. The type was later restricted to night operation due to its vulnerability. Below: the Handley Page 0/400 introduced more powerful Rolls-Royce Eagle engines, an increased bomb-load and other improvements in late 1917. An aircraft of No 207 Squadron RAF is pictured with a 1,650 lb SN bomb, the largest weapon to be dropped in anger by the Allies in World War I

The largest British bomber to reach production during World War I traced its beginning to pre-war interest in flying the Atlantic Ocean. A development of the Handley Page 0/100, the HP 0/400 was evolved from the earlier bomber in September 1917 by the installation of more powerful 360 hp Rolls-Royce Eagle VIII engines. With the amalgamation of the Royal Flying Corps and the Royal Naval Air Service to form the Royal Air Force in April 1918, former naval units were renumbered; for example, No 7 Squadron RNAS–the original so-called 'Handley Page Bombing Squadron'–simply became No 207 Squadron RAF. By August, eight squadrons of 0/400 aircraft were on the continent. Handley Page 0/400 bombers served right up to the final evening of the war and carried tremendous bomb-loads to important German targets well behind the front lines.

The late Carl Dixon, an American who left his home in New Britain, Connecticut in 1917 to enlist in the Royal Flying Corps in Canada, became a Handley Page 0/400 pilot late in the war. Following flight training in Canada and Texas, Dixon was posted to No 8 Training Squadron at Netheravon, Wiltshire, where he was supposed to receive final preparation for service with a squadron at the Front. Dixon, who had been frustrated at not obtaining a posting, recalled: 'While I was sitting on a hard wooden bench trying to figure out a way to get a decent posting, a Captain poked his head into our ready room and asked if anyone there had experience in twin-engined aircraft. Nobody answered and I was bored stiff, so I raised my hand and nodded.

'I followed the Captain out onto the flight line and, since he wasn't a pilot, I figured I could [play] him along. I told him I had flown "twin-engined

Jennies'' back in Texas and, since he didn't know that I was kidding him, he was very impressed. But as we got out onto the flight line, I wasn't so sure my trick was such a good idea. Out at the end of the flight line, away from the hangars, was the biggest damned aeroplane I'd ever seen. I had heard about and seen pictures of the big Handley Page bombers, but I had never actually seen one. I couldn't get over the size of it. The groundcrewmen working on it looked like ants crawling all over an apple.

'I was really scared witless at the thought of flying that monster by myself. But I felt better when the Captain told me I was going along as a relief pilot. He had a pilot and an observer, but couldn't find anyone to spell the pilot during the long flight to France. When he told me the Handley Page was

going to France, I really got excited. I thought this would be my big opportunity to see some action. If nothing else, I hoped I could get qualified on this big buzzard and use that qualification as a way to get out of Netheravon.

'The Captain introduced me to the pilot of the Handley Page, a fellow named Stevenson and then left us. I knew I couldn't lie to Stevenson and get away with it, so I told him that there were no pilots in our pool with twin-engined time, but that I had volunteered to get some experience. He wasn't too happy about that, but he took some comfort in the fact that I was at least enthusiastic about the idea. He also felt better when I told him I had logged a lot of time in FE2b and FE2d machines, which was true. He said that a lot of Handley Page pilots– especially those assigned to night-bombing missions –had started out in FEs, which were like 0/400s in some ways. In both planes the pilot was placed out ahead of the wings, with the engine behind him, which gives you a different relationship with the ground when you take off and land.

'While I waited for my batman to bring my overnight kit and my flight suit, Lieutenant Stevenson familiarised me with the aeroplane. To get into the Handley Page, there was a trap door in the floor of the forward fuselage and a ladder leading up to it. We made our way up the ladder and then forward to the cockpit area. He sat in the pilot's seat, on the right, and I sat in the left-side seat, normally occupied by the observer. That way I could watch Stevenson work the controls. The groundcrew people finished packing in all our gear and we got into our flight suits. I was curious as to how they were going to start the engines of this bird, because the propeller tips were easily five feet or so above the ground and we didn't have self-starters in those days. The way they started each engine was to have two men climb up on the wing, one on each side of an engine nacelle, and use starting handles to crank over the engine. First they would do the port engine, then the starboard engine.

'Once both engines were started, the pilot would move the throttle forward to get them warm enough for take-off. There was a big metal knob on top of the throttle lever and you could increase the rpm of either engine by turning it–clockwise for the port engine and counter-clockwise for the starboard engine. Of course, simply pushing the throttle lever forward [brought] both engines to full power. Since we were flying to France, this Handley Page was fully armed. The twin Lewis machine guns in the forward gunner's cockpit were loaded with fresh drums of ammunition. And the single Lewis gun for the rear gunner, who sat behind the fuel tanks with a clear view upward, was also ready for action. The only problem was there were only three of us. I guess if we were attacked, the observer would man one of the gunner's positions and I would take the other one–and hope that the pilot wasn't hit.

'When we were ready to go, Stevenson tried the controls and then waved away the chocks. Up to that point I was used to smaller aircraft that took off within a short space–just a fast run down the grass and into the air. But the big Handley Page seemed to roll on forever before it finally started to get into the air. And, at that, it was a few minutes before we reached any sort of altitude. We circled the aerodrome and then headed east for France. Once we were in the air, it was a very nice ride. The aeroplane was very stable and it was more like being on a ship than in an aeroplane, because the Handley Page seemed to "cruise" through the air.

'We were going along at about 80 miles per hour and once we got up to 6,000 feet and had set our course, Stevenson changed seats with me, so I could get the feel of the aeroplane. The Handley Page 0/400 used a Deperdussin-type wheel control column, instead of the simple "stick control" I was used to, but I had flown wheel-control Jennies in Texas, so it was easy enough to figure out what I had to do. With the wheel control, you just turned the wheel to activate the ailerons, instead of moving the stick from side to side. Of course, the rudder bar worked on the Handley Page the way it worked on other aircraft. The most surprising thing about the Handley Page was that the controls were sort of "slow". I didn't expect such a big plane to be as quick to respond as a fighter, but this buzzard took its own sweet time in doing what you wanted it to do. Sitting up ahead of the engines, Stevenson and I could get a few words to each other over the noise of the wind, so when I told him I thought the plane was very sluggish, he agreed and said you had to anticipate your moves and make them a second or two before you expected them to happen. Sometimes it was more than a second or two, but I finally got used to the delayed reaction of the controls and then it wasn't too bad.

'By this time the Germans were really on the run, so when we got to France later that day, it was pretty quiet. Stevenson brought the plane down at an aerodrome near Alquines, behind the Flanders Front. Again, it seemed to take the Handley Page a long time to settle down. We made what seemed to me like an awfully long final approach, gradually losing altitude, then clearing some trees at the edge of the aerodrome and then touching down to begin a long taxi run. Stevenson had the throttle way out, so the propellers were turning very slowly as we taxied.

'The nice part about the Handley Page – or any twin-engine aircraft of that time – was that you could really manoeuvre the aeroplane on the ground. Using the control knob on the throttle, you could give one engine more rpm than the other to get the aeroplane to turn. If you wanted to turn to the right, you increased the revs of the port engine and the aeroplane would pivot on the axis of the slower engine. Of course, you had to be careful that you didn't overdo it and give one engine too much power; there were no brakes on the aeroplane, so it would just spin around like crazy.

'I spent the night at Alquines, which was then the home base for No 58 Squadron. The next morning they sent me back to England in a beat-up old Armstrong Whitworth FK8 reconnaissance plane. I was mad as hell about that because I wanted another Handley Page "ride", but one of the flight leaders, Lieutenant Stanley Martindale, said he would see what he could do to get me some more experience in the Handley Page and perhaps a posting in his Squadron.'

In view of his recently-acquired Handley Page bomber experience, Dixon went back to Netheravon

with an 0/400 crew preparing to take the aeroplane overseas. He made several other 0/400 flights from either Netheravon or Stonehenge to France. In the process of these ferry flights, Lieutenant Carl Dixon gained experience in taking off and landing in the big bombers. In mid-October he finally received his much-sought posting to a front-line unit. Dixon was very pleased that the assignment was to No 58 Squadron in France. When he arrived in France – little more than two weeks before the Armistice – Carl Dixon did not start to fly as a pilot immediately. True, he did have only limited flight experience in the Handley Page 0/400, but he was disappointed by the 'pecking order' he had to endure before he was able to climb into the pilot's seat.

'After I got set up with a good bunk and was introduced to the Mess Steward', he recalled, 'I was given a pile of maps to study, to familiarise myself with the Front. Then, when I was finally

Above left: the immense size of the 0/400 is confirmed by reference to the figure standing in the shadow of the port engine. Seven squadrons of the Royal Air Force had been equipped with the type by the Armistice of November 1918, being re-equipped postwar with the Vickers Vimy and de Havilland DH10. Left: following the manufacture of over 100 sets of 0/400 components by the Standard Aircraft Corporation in the United States, eight further aircraft were assembled for the US Army. Powered by the ubiquitous Liberty engine developed for the DH4, one such example is pictured after the Armistice. Above: arriving in Palestine in September 1918, a single 0/400 was taken on the strength of No 1 Squadron Australian Flying Corps. This painting by Stuart Reid depicts the aircraft during its bombing of Nablus by night

assigned a mission, I wasn't even placed close to the cockpit. Their routine was to have the new pilots spend some time in each of the gunners' positions before doing any actual flying. So, my first few flights were made in the rear gunner's position—separated from the rest of the crew by the fuel tanks and, if we carried them, our bomb-load. Then I worked my way up to the forward gunner's position and, finally, to the observer's seat. I celebrated the signing of the Armistice by making my first flight as a squadron pilot.'

The cessation of hostilities did not bring an end to No 58 Squadron's flight operations, however. As Carl Dixon reminisced: 'We maintained a full schedule of flights, because we were told the Germans might start fighting again. That didn't make much sense to me, because we had most of their aeroplanes, guns and supplies. Anyhow, we kept up a pretty strict schedule and flew a lot of night missions—mostly to carry mail and supplies to British forces in Coblenz—but always at night to keep us accustomed to night-time operations.'

In the late spring of 1919, the Air Ministry decided to send three squadrons of Handley Page 0/400s to Egypt to serve as reinforcements for British forces involved in the administration of Palestine. Nos 58, 214 and 216 Squadrons were ordered to make the flight both a navigational experience exercise and a goodwill tour. The three squadrons were to fly from France to Italy, thence to Greece and Crete before making the long over-water journey to Egypt. Just before departure, however, an unusual visitor joined the flight. Colonel T. E. Lawrence, the legendary desert fighter, had become disenchanted with the proceedings of the Versailles Peace Conference and requested permission to return to the Middle East. He literally "thumbed a lift" to Egypt with the Handley Page bomber group.

Carl Dixon and a mechanic were conducting a pre-flight check of his Handley Page 0/400 at Provin, France on the morning of 3 May 1919 when a small, slender man stepped up to them and said, 'Hello, I'm Lawrence'.

'I almost fell over', Dixon recalled. 'Here was one of the most famous figures of the war—a lieutenant-colonel in the British Army—standing in front of us wearing a jacket with lieutenant's pips, civilian slacks and sandals. He was the most unlikely-looking hero I ever saw.'

For the first leg of the trip Captain Martindale, leader of 'B' Flight, took command of Dixon's aircraft and invited Colonel Lawrence to join him. 'We had each stowed our kit in the deep space in the fuselage where we used to store bombs during the war', Dixon said. 'Lawrence fastened himself in amongst the baggage during take-off, but once we were in the air he came up forward for a look around. While Captain Martindale and Lieutenant L'Holliers manned the controls, I sat in the forward gunner's seat. Lawrence made his way past the pilot and co-pilot and came up alongside of me. I started to salute—I was still impressed by the fact that he was a colonel, even though he didn't act the part. He just smiled and looked over the side. We were only up about 2,000 feet, so we still had a good view of the ground. It took us about a half hour to get up to 6,000 feet and longer still to get up to our ceiling of 8,500 feet. I had seen this view of the ground many times before, so I offered him the gunner's seat and went back into the fuselage to take a nap.' The flight stopped at Pisa, Italy to refuel and then continued on to Centocelle, outside Rome. During the stop-over in Pisa, however, Colonel Lawrence changed aeroplanes and continued on in another Handley Page piloted by Lieutenants Prince and Spratt. Coming into Centocelle, however, disaster struck.

'In France we used to lay out a big white 'T' to indicate wind direction, the horizontal bar being the head', Carl Dixon remembered. 'In Italy, however, they did it just the opposite. Not realising this, Spratt and Prince brought the aeroplane in from the wrong side, landing with the wind instead of into it. They came in too short and hit some trees on the edge of the field. The whole flight was watching from the air, waiting for them to land. We could see the plane start to nose over as it snagged the trees. Up and over like a big wounded bird. It must have hit with an awful impact. A lot of dust was flying around as Martindale and I made a low pass over the crash site. Some men on the ground—they must have been pilots—pointed in the other direction, which we assumed was the direction to come in from. By the time we got on the ground, there were a lot of Italian soldiers at the scene. Prince was already dead and Spratt died in an Italian hospital. Lawrence broke his collar-bone, but it was a miracle that he survived the crash. He must have been in the fuselage section, cushioned by the baggage, or knocked back there when the plane first hit the trees.'

T. E. Lawrence subsequently completed his journey in a Handley Page 0/400 of a communications unit after No 58 and the other squadrons had moved on. Carl Dixon was discharged from the RAF the following year and pursued a long and fruitful career in American civil aviation. He never forgot 'those big buzzards', the Handley Page 0/400 bombers which remained in RAF service until the early 1920s.

The instrument panel of the *Avro 504K trainer comprises four basic instruments: airspeed indicator, altimeter, inclinometer and engine speed indicator. This simple layout could be mastered by the trainee pilot without undue difficulty*

Avro 504K

For nearly three decades, no British aerodrome, air meeting nor touring airshow was without an Avro 504. Few pilots were without one in their logbooks either, for tens of thousands of service fliers took their first faltering steps in this archetypal training aeroplane. The 504 first entered service with the Royal Flying Corps and Royal Naval Air Service in the earliest years of World War I.

By far the most numerous of the many Avro variants, the Avro 504K was powered variously by the 110hp Le Rhône, the 130hp Clerget or, most commonly, the 110hp Gnome Monosoupape rotary engine. Although the Pilot's Notes opined optimistically that 'running the engine is simple', raw recruits found engine handling the most difficult part of their training. It was the most important too, for it was essential for the student to master the Monosoupape's idiosyncrasies before taking to the air or even attempting to taxi the Avro.

The Avro 504 had tandem open cockpits with minimal instrumentation, the few that it had being in the rear position where the instructor sat. These were airspeed indicator, tachometer, compass, altimeter, a spirit-level inclinometer, oil pulsometer and air pressure gauge. In the earliest days there was no form of communication between instructor and pupil – a waggle of the stick or, as a last resort, a hastily-scribbled note, had to suffice. However, when Colonel Smith-Barry established his School of Special Flying at Gosport in Hampshire, the 'Gosport' speaking tube became the standard method of inter-cockpit communication in Avros.

On take-off the Avro 504K was prone to swing sharply to the left when the engine was opened up. Due to its light, finless, balanced rudder, which was powerfully effective, many a student overcorrected with right rudder, causing the aeroplane to change direction in a 180 degree turn. In those early days

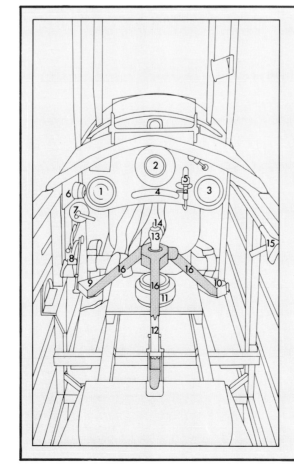

Avro 504K cockpit
1: *Airspeed indicator* 2: *Altimeter* 3: *Engine speed indicator* 4: *Inclinometer* 5: *Oil flow sight-glass* 6: *Magneto switch* 7: *Fuel tank selection control* 8: *Engine controls* 9: *Left rudder pedal* 10: *Right rudder pedal* 11: *Compass* 12: *Control column* 13: *Control column handgrip* 14: *Ignition cut-out button* 15: *Gosport tube* 16: *Control column and rudder pedal locking bars (for ground use only)*

instructors often left take-off technique until late in the student's training, when they had mastered the aeroplane's control responses and developed their own reflexes accordingly.

In a 32 km/h (20 mph) wind the Avro, weighing just 750 kg (1,660 lb) loaded, would be off the ground in 15 m (50 feet), and climb at 88 km/h (55 mph) with the Monosoupape turning at 1,150-1,200 rpm. With two aboard, the climb to 1,000 m (3,500 ft) took five minutes, and the level cruise speed was 105 km/h (65 mph), 113 km/h (70 mph) if the aeroplane was new and not suffering the oil-soaking and mis-rigging which beset most hard-used training school Avros.

By contemporary standards the Avro 504K was easy and forgiving to fly, but engine control was the bane of students' lives. In essence there was no 'control'; the engine was either on or off, although some small measure of intermediate throttling could be obtained using a blip switch. The Mono Avro was especially sensitive to over-rich mixture, as Air Commodore Allen Wheeler recalls: 'If it did get too rich the engine slowly lost power and black smoke would trail behind the Avro, although the pilot could not see it. Very soon the engine would give a despairing cough and cut out.

'Thereafter the immediate corrective action was to close the fuel lever down completely and wait. After perhaps eight seconds, which seemed like ten

minutes with the Avro necessarily in a steep glide towards the ground to maintain flying speed, the engine might come on again but, in the pupil's mind, there was the worrying thought that the engine might have cut because it was short of fuel. Thus many a pupil would push the fuel lever forward again hopefully after about five seconds and accentuate the trouble. This indecision usually resulted in the necessity for a forced landing with the pupil ill-prepared to select a suitable field since he had been concentrating on trying to get the engine going again.

'A common sequence of events after that was for the pupil to select a field hurriedly when he was only about 400 feet up and try to position himself for landing in it into wind. He had very likely forgotten which way the wind was blowing. Before his final approach to the field he probably closed the fuel lever again to prevent the engine coming on suddenly and spoiling his landing.

'If he had judged his approach correctly and was well-placed for a landing in a suitable field, the engine would have been slowly "unchoking" itself and, at the moment of touchdown, would have come on with a full-throttle roar, carrying the Avro a long way up the field. The pupil would then decide that all was well after all and the engine was all right, forgetting that he had closed the fuel lever. As the Avro approached the far hedge the engine then cut

again and the ensuing embarrassment usually cost the Air Ministry quite a lot in Avro repairs.'

Pupils were thus well-imbued with the principles of engine management before they were sent off on their first solo, for the lightweight, high-drag Avro gave very little time in which to pick-up gliding speed after an engine failure, particularly on take-off. Failure to set up a glide in the heat of the moment would result in a stall within a few seconds, and perhaps a spin.

As in all rotary-engined aeroplanes, the gyroscopic force of the rotating engine mass affected the Avro's handling. With power on, the nose tended to rise in left turns and drop in right turns, requiring compensating rudder inputs. Nevertheless, the gyroscopic effect was less marked in the Avro than in some contemporary machines, notably fighters such as the Sopwith Camel and Snipe. Again like its contemporaries, the Avro suffered aileron drag from its unsophisticated control surfaces, resulting in pronounced adverse yaw when rolling into a bank.

'The Avro's rudder is very sensitive,' advised the Pilot's Notes, 'therefore it must be held very firmly, very slight movement of the foot moves the machine a great deal. The ailerons are not very sensitive, therefore to turn there is a greater movement of the stick than of the rudder. The elevator is fairly sensitive, all fore-and-aft movement of the stick should be made gently. Owing to the sensitive movement of rudder the machine is inclined to side-slip or skid about in turning. On a turn, if a breeze is felt on the inside, there is too much bank for amount of rudder, correct by lessening bank and slightly increasing rudder. If the breeze is felt on the outside there is too much rudder for the bank used, correct by increasing bank and decreasing rudder. In a correct turn no draught should be felt.'

Landing an Avro presented two interlinked problems for inexperienced pilots. The springiness of the bungee-cord rubber suspension on the undercarriage would return and accentuate every bounce of a misjudged landing resulting in a kangaroo trip across the airfield, and the lack of precise engine control virtually prevented power being used to soften the bounces. If the petrol lever was advanced or the blip switch released, the engine would give a full burst of power which was hardly the way to smooth out an already rough approach. The Pilot's Notes for the Avro 504K recommended the following technique for landing:

'To descend, shut petrol off. When engine is off, machine swings to the right owing to right rudder used to counteract prop torque. Correct by putting rudder neutral. Although pressure is kept up by mechanical pump while engine is running, as soon as engine is shut off pressure must be kept up by hand. Glide down at 55 mph, noting carefully direction of the wind. This machine, being light, is very sensitive to drift and must be landed dead into wind. When about 50-100 feet above the ground put petrol lever to one inch and hold thumb switch down but do not "buzz" engine. Flatten out gently or machine will stall owing to slow glide. Hold machine about one foot off ground by gently pulling back on stick until all speed has been lost, when machine will settle gently, wheels and tail together, not running more than a few yards.'

'If the wheels touched first one was all right.' says Air Commodore Wheeler, 'so long as one did not try to pull the tail down too soon. When firmly on the ground one pushed the fuel lever forward and the engine, still spinning because of its great rotary inertia, would come to life again with a bit of a roar. It could then be controlled by the magneto blip switch on top of the control column until one had adjusted the fuel lever to a very weak mixture, after

Right: early examples of the Avro 504 were powered by 80 hp Gnome rotary engines. Ordered by both the Royal Flying Corps as a training and reconnaissance type, the 504 was also pressed into service as both a Zeppelin interceptor and a bomber. Its most famous exploit in the latter role was the raid on the airship sheds at Friedrichshafen in November 1914, in which three aircraft each carried four 20 lb Hales bombs. An Avro 504 trainer is pictured

which it would attain its rather erratic idling speed with the cylinders firing in short bursts. Some of the very experienced instructors would practically never use the blip switch from start to stop, since they knew the exact position for the fuel lever for slow-running and taxying, but this sort of familiarity . . . was not achieved by pupils.'

Once a trainee had mastered the basics of departure and arrival he would be introduced to the art of aerobatics. With its light wing loading the Avro would loop around a very small radius. The technique was to dive until the airspeed reached 145-160 km/h (90-100 mph), pulling up with a touch of rudder to keep straight, over the top at 72 km/h (45 mph), then pull back on the fuel lever to shut off the engine to prevent overspeeding in the subsequent dive and recovery. 'One must remember that in looping the Avro one had to shut the fine adjustment as one came down in the vertical dive,' says Allen Wheeler, '. . . but if one was a bit slow in pushing the lever forward again when flying level, the engine would slow down and stop and one was faced with the rather embarrassing sight of a stationary propeller. The immediate action was to dive steeply to reach a speed of about 110 mph, when the engine would start turning again and start up.'

The Avro stalled at about 40 km/h (25 mph), and spun quite readily. Recovery was easy, but the aeroplane would spin without warning if stalled carelessly. The Avro's spin was slow, with modest loss of height per turn, so that falling leaf manoeuvres, which are in essence a series of checked spins in alternate directions, could be performed most attractively. Manoeuvres requiring precise lateral control were not its forte, however. The Avro's ailerons were weak, and made rolling all but impossible. The aeroplane could perform half rolls using the effective rudder, and barrel rolls were possible, but few even attempted slow rolls or rolls off the top of a loop.

Despite its role as a wartime trainer, and its subsequent career with the Royal Air Force, the Avro 504 became best-known as the mount of the postwar barnstormers, who purchased surplus aircraft for as little as £20, less the engine. With a variety of power plants up to 180 hp, the weary Avros were given a new lease of life joy-riding eager passengers two, even three at a time, on 'five-bob flips' in the heady, profitable days of 1919 when a hard-working barnstormer could earn £60 on a good summer's day.

Air Commodore Allen Wheeler recalled of the type, 'The Avro 504K as an aeroplane was very easy to fly and very forgiving of pupils' mistakes, even to the extent of (usually) not killing them when they spun it into the ground . . . To start off with, and for some reason I never could understand, the Avro seldom seemed to catch fire after a crash even though its rotary engine seemed to be vomiting flames out of its open exhaust ports and spraying fuel in all directions. Its fuel tank was situated immediately behind the engine.

'The lateral control was soggy by modern standards; the rudder and elevator were more positive but varied in "feel" considerably according to whether the engine was on power or off as one would expect, and the force required to operate the controls varied much according to speed. The available speed range varied between a stalling speed of about 30 mph and a maximum attainable speed of about 140 mph in an almost vertical dive when the controls became almost as solid as those of our early supersonic fighters when they were diving at transonic speeds.

'So far as my experience went in the Avro, I only once, later in my training, got into this unhappy state by trying to fly upside down. As we only had seat belts we had to cling on to the bracing wires under the seat with one hand to keep ourselves in; this left no hand on the fuel lever. In the ensuing confusion which started in an inverted dive and developed into an attempt to pull out as though finishing a loop–but with the engine full on–I think I achieved the Avro's terminal velocity, but by dint of hard pulling on the control column the Avro ultimately regained level flight.'

With its central landing skid, wingtip hoops, two-bay wings and numerous bracing wires, the Avro 504 was undoubtedly an 'ugly duckling' of the air. Despite appearances, however, the type proved both docile and reliable in service with both the Royal Air Force and many postwar civil operators. The 504's twenty years of production attest to its continuing suitability for the training purpose

de Havilland Moth

Although designed in the inter-war 'Golden Age' of private flying, the Tiger Moth was destined to carve its reputation 'in uniform'. Freed from its war-paint, a Tiger is pictured on a cross-country flight flown, as was the custom, from the rear cockpit. The Tiger Moth was descended from the straight-winged DH60 Gipsy Moth which had first flown in 1925 and had added impetus to Sir Sefton Brancker's programme to supply flying clubs with modern equipment

'I had been thinking of an ideal private owner's aeroplane for some long time,' Geoffrey de Havilland said of the original Moth 'partly, or perhaps largely, because I wanted one for my own use. The available engines nearly always dictate the design of an aeroplane, but there was no engine of the right power for the practical lightplane I was keen to build. So we had to create one. I suggested to Frank Halford that we should cut one of the eight-cylinder vee Renaults in half and make a four-cylinder inline engine. He did this with his usual drive and energy, and it resulted in a robust and simple engine known as the Cirrus. This event was to be far more important than we realised at the time. Here we had an engine which, although not ideal, enabled me to design a light aeroplane of the kind that had dominated my thoughts for so long, and to which I could give the intense enthusiasm that is necessary for all good work.

'I had visualised the finished aeroplane long before the design was started, and working drawings soon appeared. Although I did the main layouts and general arrangement drawings, the members of the drawing office soon shared my enthusiasm, so that the project became a co-operative one, with many useful ideas contributed by all of us. As the actual construction advanced day by day, I watched it with growing interest, looking forward to the time when I could step into the cockpit and do the first test flight.

'The new light aircraft was intended, above all, for the amateur, the weekend flier and for instruction. Simplicity and safety were of paramount importance. I did not feel it was suitable of good sales policy to give it only a numeral. A name had to be found, and many ideas were put forward before my enthusiasm for natural history–which remained as strong as ever–led me to seek the solution in

entymology. It suddenly struck me that the name "Moth" was just right. It had the right sound, was appropriate, easy to remember, and might well lead to a series of Moths, all named after British insects . . .'

Geoffrey de Havilland's dream was of 'aeroplanes for all'–cheap runabouts which ordinary people would own and operate just like family cars. In his DH Moth he came nearer to fulfilling that dream than most and, even though the Moth never became the people's aeroplane he envisaged, it and its many successors caught public imagination to the extent that the name Moth is still synonymous with 'light aeroplane'.

'The de Havilland two-seater light aeroplane is being produced for the school, the flying club and the private owner', ran publicity material published in January 1925, just before the first Moth flew. 'Simplicity, robustness and ease of handling and maintenance are features which have been most carefully considered in its design. The de Havilland Moth will not be a delicate and frail craft requiring highly-skilled attention. It will be as sturdy and lasting as the modern light car. First cost of the DH60 will be low and its upkeep correspondingly cheap and simple.'

When the prototype Moth flew a month later, on 22 February 1925, it matched that promise. It was of sturdy, simple construction featuring a plywood box fuselage and fabric-covered wood flying surfaces with two tandem open cockpits. A new Moth cost £885. It was, remarked The Times, 'an aeroplane for youth, the most promising contribution yet made to the difficult problem of getting the youth of the nation into the air.'

Sir Sefton Brancker, the Director of Civil Aviation of the time, evidently agreed, for he ordered 90 Moths for his government-sponsored flying clubs which effectively started the private flying movement in Britain. The Moth appeared in successive guises with Cirrus II and III engines and, when the supply of surplus Airdiscos–from which the Cirrus was made–ran out, the classic Gipsy engine designed by Frank Halford was utilised.

'Anyone can learn to fly a Moth in a few hours', de Havillands claimed. 'Its controls are easy to master and simple to operate . . . the Mark II Cirrus engine is as straightforward as a motorcycle engine; it is robust, reliable and does not require skilled attention . . . any open field is a potential aerodrome for the Moth. It leaves the ground with pilot, passenger and luggage after a run of only a hundred yards.'

Entry into a Moth's front cockpit was never easy, for it was situated beneath the centre-section in a maze of cabane struts, and this lack of easy access was the reason why the DH60 Moth was never accepted by the Royal Air Force for training–getting into, and especially out of, the front cockpit in a hurry, with full flying kit and parachute was almost impossible. Once aboard, the cockpit was cramped, but the proximity of the long exhaust pipe which ran beside the fuselage made it snug and warm, although one had to beware of casually draping ones arm over the side.

The view forward on the ground was hampered in the early Moths by the Cirrus' upright bank of cylinders, and exposed rockers and valve gear. The low compression engines started easily by hand-swinging, and with a minimum of checks a pilot could begin the precarious business of taxying a brake-less aeroplane which did not have a steerable tailskid. Turns called for generous rudder and a blast of throttle. Flying controls were conventional, with the now-familiar de Havilland 'cheese-cutter' trim lever on the port side of the cockpit which altered the tension of springs attached to the control column, adjusting the longitudinal trim of the aircraft without the complexities of trim tabs or adjustable tailplanes. Some pilots felt that the cheese-cutter marred the fore and aft feel of the Moth–and its successor, the Tiger Moth–because one was always pulling or pushing against the spring's tension.

Ready for take-off, into wind, and with the power on, a Moth would take off by itself, as the great adventurer and navigator Francis Chichester discovered when he first flew with a professional pilot in his Gipsy Moth Elijah: '"Let's go", said Joe, pushing the throttle wide, one autumn morning at Croydon. I assumed that he wanted to take off himself, so I let go of the controls. We were a long time leaving the ground and just cleared the trees by a foot or two. "What on earth are you doing?" shouted Joe. "Nothing", I shouted indignantly, "I never touched the controls." "Nor did I", said he.'

Student pilots felt confident in such an aeroplane, as David Garnett recounted 'When we were over the hangars I turned to the Orwell estuary, turned again and flew back. My first glide was just right, but I spoilt it by checking too high up. Clayton put on the engine and took her round, banking sharply about 30 feet off the ground and turning in a small circle. This suddenly gave me complete confidence. The stoical deliberation, the slow, precise carefulness in the face of danger, which had been my recent mood, this was all blown out of me by that lovely low racing turn with one wing stretched down to within 15 feet of the turf, and once more I was swept away by the strength and power of the machine–marvellously strong, it would not dawdle about, but fly like a roaring comet, supple and powerful in my hands.'

In calm weather a Moth was a delight, but they were particularly sensitive to rough air. Stability has often been described as outstanding, perhaps a little too good laterally, for the Moth and the Tiger Moth both suffered from soggy, ineffective roll control. This was due to de Havilland engineer Arthur Hagg's differential gearing which slowed the movement of the down-going aileron to prevent adverse yaw, and roll the aeroplane level if it stalled in a turn. The result was sloppy roll control further aggravated by the absence of ailerons on the top wing.

However, the Moth's stall was docile, a virtue further enhanced by the automatic Handley Page slats on the upper wing's leading edge. These start to move out below 97 km/h (60 mph), creeping forwards as the angle of attack increases. A pilot could monitor his airspeed at such times while looking out of the cockpit, for Moths had calibrated airspeed plates mounted on a starboard interplane strut. A spring-loaded pointer was pushed across the scale by air pressure; simple but effective.

For aerobatics the Moth was limited by its lateral stability, but it looped nicely, and was a

Left: the Tiger Moth had the distinction of being the last biplane trainer to bear the colours of the Royal Air Force. Unlike its predecessor, the Gipsy Moth, the Tiger had swept-back wings, a feature which permitted easy exit from the front cockpit in emergency. Over 1,000 Tiger Moths had been delivered by the outbreak of war in 1939; total production in Britain and abroad eventually exceeded 8,800 airframes. Insets: the rear (left) and front cockpits of the Tiger Moth exhibit similarly sparse instrumentation. The compass binnacle and inter-cockpit Gosport tubes are prominent

popular mount for air display 'stunt' flying. C. Turner-Hughes, who flew with Alan Cobham's flying circus, kept a record of his aerobatics on Moths and Tiger Moths; these totalled 2,328 loops, 2,190 rolls, 567 bunts, 522 upward rolls, 40 inverted falling leaves and five inverted 'outside' loops.

To demonstrate the ease of landing a Moth, Geoffrey de Havilland would approach with power off and the stick pulled right back, sinking at 25 km/h (40 mph) until he made contact with the aerodrome; this impressed customers until his Moth's much-abused lower longerons gave way one day. A Moth instruction manual described the correct landing technique thus: 'The instructor will tell you how you must glide gently down for the landing, the aeroplane facing exactly into wind, and how, as the ground is approached, you must gradually flatten out by easing the control stick farther and farther back until, at the moment the aeroplane touches the ground, the stick is fully back and the aeroplane drops the last few inches to the ground, touching with undercarriage wheels and tailskid together. This is, in fact, the theoretically-perfect "three-point" landing. Many circuits and landings will be made until the pupil has got thoroughly used to the manoeuvre, and then, one fine day when there is a gentle, steady wind blowing, the instructor will say through the earphones: "You're all right now for solo".'

Tens of thousands of would-be pilots heard those

Many Tiger Moths followed their period of service with the Royal Air Force by passing into the hands of civilian owners. The qualities which had made the type the RAF's standard elementary trainer for over 15 years commended it to flying club operators, while its aerobatic performance was exploited by organisations such as the Tiger Club, which performed at airshows with single-seat converted Tigers. Many Tiger Moths still flew in the late 1970s, nearly half a century after the type's debut

words through a Moth or Tiger's Gosport tube. Geoffrey de Havilland's aeroplane for all remained — in one form or other — the standard *ab initio* training machine into the 1950s and beyond. Something of the magic of flying a Moth is captured here in the words of one of its pilots: 'A fiercely bright thread of light tells me that the Thames is eight miles southwest; all around is a hazy patchwork of fields and woods, houses and hills receding into a misty grey, and just above my head the familiar boiler fuel gauge becomes silhouetted as a large bright break appears in the cloud cover. From the gloomy greyness brushing the top mainplane we pass into a bath of brilliance with a ceiling of cerulean blue, crowning those miraculous soft dazzling white piles of cumulus.

'Climbing in a bright spiral away from earthly twilight, we begin a journey up and into another world. The cold here is very apparent, feet are chilling, a pain starts in the forehead, all the little draughts become obvious. Those nagging hardships are suddenly dissolved as the eye alights on the splendour of light and form slowly enlarging as the Moth climbs its way up and over the foothills of a fairy tale, not a green and grey-blue England like the one so quickly abandoned, but a new brilliant white country with an immaculate blue sky. Practical thoughts were left down there. We have arrived in a pilot's Utopia, where all earthly hazards are denied, and all you have to do is fly!'

'The man who could coax a Ford into flying hands-off for even a few minutes was temporarily in luck'

Ford Tri-Motor

'Here is a wonderful old aeroplane,' wrote movie flier and stunt pilot Frank Tallman, 'beloved by nearly all who fly, and known far and wide by the rather pale and wishy-washy name of "Tin Goose". It is most inaptly named, for it should be labelled with an honest-to-gosh, muscle-in-the-shoulders kind of name like "Tin Ox" or "Tin Elephant", for it is most assuredly as slow as an ox, but just as strong and long-lasting as an elephant.'

The elephantine aeroplane was the Ford Tri-Motor, known even more appropriately as the 'Flying Washboard' on account of its distinctive, corrugated Alclad skinning which contributed to its extraordinary longevity and strength. The first three-engined Ford was the model 3-AT, designed by Bill Stout, whose abilities as an aircraft engineer were matched–and probably exceeded–by his talent as a promoter. Stout wrote to leading industrialists in the United States asking them to back him to the tune of 1,000 dollars apiece, promising only that they would never see their money again. Among those who contributed was Henry Ford, who also provided factory space for Stout's aeroplanes. A three-engined version of the successful Ford 2-AT Air Pullman, the 3-AT was a disaster. It was ugly, impractical, and such a poor performer

The pilots' controls of a Ford Tri-Motor viewed from the passenger cabin. The compass is mounted centrally immediately below the windscreen and beneath it, on the instrument panel, is the turn and bank indicator. This is flanked by the airspeed indicator to the left and the altimeter to the right. Between the control wheels are the engine controls. The instruments for the centre engine are mounted on the panel, whereas those for the outer engines are fitted to the sides of their nacelles

that the test pilot who flew it summed up the aeroplane in just two words: 'Forget it'. The 3-AT was conveniently destroyed in a factory fire, along with all design notes and paperwork relating to the project. From that fire, phoenix-like, arose the Ford 4-AT, designed by a Ford-appointed committee and flown on 11 June 1926.

The Ford 4-AT carried 12 passengers, who sat on wicker chairs in a sparsely-furnished cabin. Even so, by the standards of the time it was a luxurious aircraft: 'The public took to the flying washboard like migrant sharecroppers to a deluxe penthouse', wrote Tallman. 'The relative comfort of the Ford's 12 seats and 16-foot cabin with six-foot headroom came as both a surprise and a pleasure. Cabin attendants on some Ford-equipped airlines served such exciting and enticing menus as cold sandwiches and water from a thermos.'

Ernest K. Gann was less enthusiastic: 'Life aboard the trimotored Fords was far from ideal', he wrote. 'For American passengers there was little comparison between the cold box lunches tossed into their laps by the co-pilot, and the soup-to-nuts-on-a-white-tablecloth cuisine offered by equivalent British and European aircraft. Ford passenger cabins were always too hot or too cold and the decibel level assured them a top place among the world's noisiest aircraft.

'Immediately on boarding, passengers were offered chewing gum which would allegedly ease the pressure changes on their eardrums during

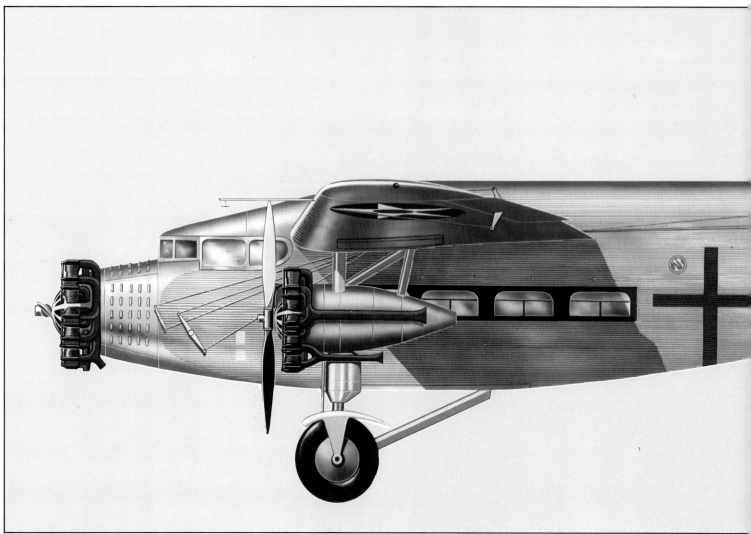

climb and descent, but it was just as much to encourage a cud-chewing state of nerves. They were also offered cotton, which wise passengers stuffed in their ears so they would be able to hear ordinary conversation once they were again on the ground. Wise pilots employed cotton for the same purpose, and many who scoffed at such precaution had trouble meeting the hearing requirements on their physicals for years after their service in Fords was done.'

With three uncowled 300 hp Wright J-6 engines, or 420 hp Pratt & Whitney Wasps in the 15-passenger Ford 5-AT, it was not surprising that the Tri-Motor was noisy. The din was further amplified by the aircraft's metal skin and the slap of the exposed elevator and rudder control cables against the fuselage sides. It was, however, just those factors – the safety of three engines and the strength of all-metal construction – which gave the Ford its public appeal; a lightly-loaded Tri-Motor could stay aloft on just one engine.

The cockpit accommodated a pilot and co-pilot, with a minimum of instrumentation. 'Even on the Fords used by the airlines by 1930 there were only

Left: a Tri-Motor pictured during its engine starting sequence. On most models of the aircraft each engine had to be started by hand-cranking an inertia starter.
Below: the Ford C-9 was flown as an ambulance by the 60th Service Squadron of the USAAC

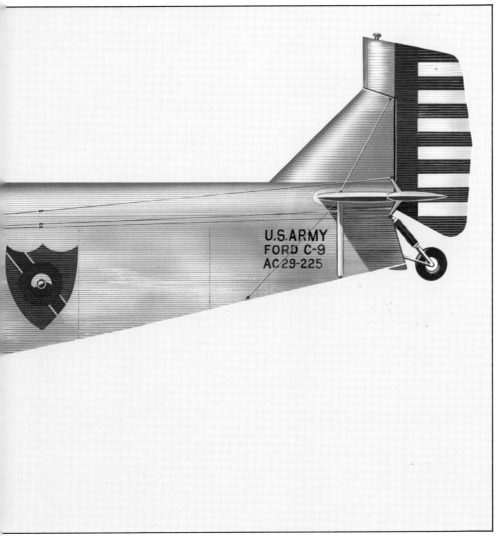

U.S. ARMY
FORD C-9
AC 29-225

thirteen instruments', wrote Frank Tallman, and those for the wing-mounted engines were out there on the nacelles, so that a pilot needed good eyesight to monitor his engines, particularly at night. 'The early Sperry artificial horizon used on the Fords and other aircraft of the day had the rear horizon face tinted a delicate sky colour', Tallman recalled, 'and the pivot point was not an illuminated marker but a real aeroplane, gear, tail surfaces, wings and all . . . Another lovely feature was the wooden control wheels, taken from deluxe Model T Fords. They were as necessary as a Charles Atlas muscle-building course because of the heavy control forces on the Ford in certain flight attitudes.'

Ernest Gann agreed with this assessment: 'Even in smooth air, flying a Ford became a chore if only because it was so difficult to keep in trim. The man who could coax a Ford into flying hands-off for even a few minutes was temporarily in luck and probably did not have any passengers. Even a normal bank in a Ford was an experiment in muscular co-ordination mixed with a practised eye for anticipation, since whatever physical input was directed at the controls, a relatively long time passed before anything happened. To stop or reverse as desired any manoeuvre required a keen sense of anticipatory delay. In rough air these delays and wilfulness were compounded, and just keeping the Ford straight and level became a workout.'

Besides the minimal instrumentation and those massive Model T steering wheels, which seemed to need winding round forever to deflect the ailerons, the Ford pilot had a central console with mixture controls and three throttle levers topped with golf-ball-sized knobs, and a long lever between the seats which operated the aircraft's brakes. This 'Johnson Bar' was pulled up to apply brake, while use of the rudder would select braking action on that side only. During landing roll-out a Ford pilot ideally needed three hands – one for the control wheel, one for the throttles and a third for the Johnson Bar, which also had an irritating habit of hooking and tearing the uniform pockets of anyone entering or leaving the cockpit.

The Ford's engines were equipped with inertia starters activated by external hand-cranks. Ernest Gann describes the start-up procedure like this: 'On signal, a mechanic or the co-pilot inserted a crank in each engine separately and commenced his labours. He wound slowly at first and then faster as his efforts spun a heavy flywheel which was geared to the crankshaft. Once the flywheel was whining at what sounded like full speed, the cranker pulled the cable which engaged a spring-loaded clutch, thereby transmitting the energy of the spinning wheel to turn the engine. The squealing sound was almost identical to that displeasure emitted by a resentful pig kicked in anger. If the oil was not too cold the propeller would turn at least three or four revolutions. Usually this was enough to start the engine, but if the pilot was not alert and missed the moment of truth with mixture and throttle, the cranker was obliged to start his labours all over again. Winding the cranks was very hard work and at times when engines proved unaccountably balky there were impolite exchanges of opinion between cockpit and cranker.'

However recalcitrant in starting, the Ford was

Built in 1929, this Ford 5-AT-B was flown by American Airways in the early 1930s. In 1962 the airline re-acquired the Tri-Motor and it embarked on a nationwide flying tour of the United States before being grounded for display at the Smithsonian Institution's National Air and Space Museum, Washington

no slouch when it came to getting airborne. With a payload of one to two tons, depending on the model, a Ford would be off the ground in little more than four times its own length. Aside from the prohibitive noise level, the exhaust fumes from the forward engine crept into the cockpit, making for a less than comfortable working environment.

Long hours were spent in the cockpit, too, for the Tri-Motor was an inveterate sluggard which cruised between 145 and 160 km/h (90–100 mph), although the optimistic speed promised by Ford's advertising was 193 km/h (120 mph). Long transcontinental trips 'which no sane passenger would endure', in the words of one observer, 'were best endured by confirmed masochists'. An eastbound transcontinental flight in one of National Air Transport's Fords took 28 hours; the return, against prevailing winds, took 31 hours, during which passengers endured many discomforts.

Despite eager acceptance by both passengers and crews, the early Ford was not without its faults. Transcontinental Air Transport's aircraft, which were among the first to enter service, were initially restricted to daylight operations because the vertical glass windscreens of the Fords created confusing reflections at night which made landing precarious. As Ernest Gann points out, the Ford's spritely take-off performance was not matched on landing either: 'Legend has it that Fords could be landed in any small cow pasture, which was not so, particularly if loaded. The ability lies somewhere in between, depending on many factors, including the hunger status of the pilot or airline.

'Take-off performance was actually more remarkable than landing speeds, which were much higher than most historians seem inclined to acknowledge . . . Behind the more spectacular short-field stops made by Fords, which actually touched down between 65 and 70 miles per hour, there was a grunting co-pilot pulling for all he was worth on the long bar which extended from the floor upward between the two cockpit seats . . .

'Like any star of stage or screen the trimotored Fords bred gossip. One particularly uncomplimentary canard concerned the inability of two engines to do more than stretch the Ford's glide if one should fail. This was nonsense. At least a few pilots made a practice of shutting down the centre engine to conserve fuel if headwinds were strong, and a landing for refuelling was inconvenient or meant even greater delay in ground time.'

Frank Tallman's landing experiences in Fords included the following: 'I landed the Ford on many different types of terrain, from hard-surface military runways to grass strips, and its good landing characteristics are legendary. I doubt very much whether, with the size of control wheel and the necessity to get it back in one's lap on a three-point landing, there were ever many fat Ford Captains.

'On final approach one of the very unusual characteristics is that one approaches a landing with power on the centre engine and with both outboards cut back and idling. Also, on a final approach if you get a wing down making a steep turn into landing, you'll find that you need the muscles of a Hercules–you may have to use both arms–to straighten the Ford out.

'You can come in at any airspeed from 80 to 55 mph, power on or power off, but because of the thick wing section and the drag on the aeroplane, it slows down a great deal faster than any other aircraft, so your float is much less than it is in an aeroplane such as the DC-3. You can make perfectly safe wheel landings and then bring your tail down, but you never make a stalled landing where the tailwheel touches first.'

A South American pilot ferrying a load of oil drilling equipment made that mistake, breaking his Tri-Motor in half; the crew repaired it on site with hand tools and flew it away. Freight ferrying became the Ford's most common application when airlines finally gave way to the demand for speed in the mid-1930s with the coming of the Douglas DC-2 and Boeing 247. Formidable loads were carried, notably in the less hospitable parts of South America, where the Fords' corrugated cabins were filled with everything from diesel oil to coal and flown 15,000 feet over the Andes.

In 1963 Trans World Airlines, successor to first Ford operators Transcontinental Air Transport, leased a surviving 5-AT for a marathon, 54-hour transcontinental flight to celebrate the 25th anniversary of the 1938 US Civil Aeronautics Act. One newspaper reporter who went along wrote: 'Last gasp of the Tin Goose; in a ramshackle museum piece a dozen volunteers make a desperate journey down memory's airlane.'

He was wrong for, years after the event, Island Airways were operating Fords on scheduled services from Put-in-Bay Island, Ohio on a 17-mile route, carrying passengers and cargo on a round-trip service which took just 45 minutes, including stops.

*'This fantastic amalgam of corrugated skinning...
demonstrated a total disregard for the most elementary
aerodynamic considerations'*

Junkers Ju 52

While the corrugated-metal skinning of the Ford Tri-Motor was something of an innovation in America, it had long been accepted in Germany, where Professor Hugo Junkers had flown an all-metal aeroplane as early as 1915. Like Ford, Junkers also produced a tri-motor transport which attracted unflattering nicknames–'Tante Ju', (Auntie Ju), 'Iron Annie', 'Corrugated Coffin'–and which played a major part in developing civil air transport in the 1930s.

The Junkers Ju 52/3m first flew in 1932, intended as a passenger and freight transport but with its potential as a bomber and troop-carrier scarcely disguised. In airline configuration the Ju 52 carried 14 to 17 passengers, and was powered variously by three 600, 725, or 830hp BMW radial engines,

925hp Bristol/PZL Pegasus, 710hp Wright Cyclones, or Jumo 5 heavy oil (diesel) engines. The Junkers employed a 'double wing' concept, using full-span ailerons and slotted flaps trailing behind and below the wing's trailing edge. These gave good aerodynamic efficiency and excellent lateral control, but were prone to icing. A few minutes' flying in icy conditions was sufficient to pack the gap between wing and aileron, locking the controls. Deutsche Lufthansa pilots used to waggle the wing at regular

Below: after establishing itself as a civil airliner in the 1930s, the Ju 52/3m found a new lease of life with the Luftwaffe in World War II.
Left: the flight engineer sits behind the engine controls, with the radio operator on the right

intervals to prevent complete loss of control, but, even so, the rapid accumulation of ice often produced a negative lift effect and a control response reversal, which invariably proved fatal.

Iron Annie could never be called an attractive aeroplane, with her nissen-hut skinning, gawky, waddling undercarriage and peculiar, outward-canted engines. However, like her sister the Ford Tri-Motor, she more than made up for lack of aesthetic charm with consistently good performance. In military overload conditions the Junkers could lift nearly its own weight from short, un-improved forward airstrips. It was reliable—Luft-hansa's forced-landing record went down from seven per million kilometres flown to just one-and-a-half when the airline equipped with Ju 52s—and durable almost to the point of indestructibility.

The crew sat beneath a great greenhouse of cockpit glazing with no fewer than 17 panels, through which the view was 'reminiscent of that from the driver's cab on an old London double-decker bus', one British pilot reported. 'The cockpit layout was a mess,' he said, 'with switches and knobs everywhere. How could such a basic aircraft have such a complicated cockpit?' Scott Johnson, an American pilot who flies a restored Ju 52, agrees: 'The panel', he says, 'is a maze of German instrumentation set in chartreuse green; two large wooden-plated control wheels and two more straight-back chairs sporting one dilapidated cushion apiece make up the cockpit.'

Captain Eric Brown, who test-flew many captured Luftwaffe aircraft at the Royal Aircraft Establishment Farnborough during and after the war, recalls that 'the drill for starting up the 725 hp BMW 132A-3 nine-cylinder radials was rather like playing a Wurlitzer organ.' First, the battery master switch had to be turned on, then the ignition retarded, the master ignition knob pulled out, three individual ignition switches set, fuel switches set to prime and mixtures to fully rich, three oil cooler controls closed and, at last, the primer pump to the centre engine actuated. 'After this dazzling prelude,' says Captain Brown, 'the handle for the requisite inertia starter was depressed for ten to twenty seconds and then pulled up. As soon as the engine fired, the ignition had to be set to the *früh* [advanced] position and the engine allowed to tick over at 700-800 revs until oil pressure registered.' Once the oil pressure was up the two outboard engines could be started, causing great clouds of oily smoke which usually attended a Ju 52 start and sometimes obscured the entire forward part of the aircraft from view.

Scott Johnson described his first ever take-off in the Ju 52 like this: 'Annie shuddered as the surging engines nudged her forward. Cursing the tailwheel lock, Bud walked [operated] the brakes in an effort to free it. That's when I noticed that Annie's brakes—the only hydraulics aboard—were worthless! Following much persuasion, the tail-wheel came free, and Annie rocked to and fro over the uneven terrain. Forward visibility was not sensational, necessitating constant 'S'-turning to ensure all was clear ahead. Temperatures and pressures were already in the green, Annie hobbled on to the hard surface.

Bud ordered 25 degrees flaps for take-off.

Reaching for the selector handle behind the big flap/trim wheel beside the bottom of Bud's seat, I jerked it and began cranking while watching the gauge, set into the left side of the cockpit wall abeam the control column beneath the window. The flap/trim wheel, at least one-and-a-half to two feet in diameter, was attached to a shaft extending back into a mechanism driving what closely resembled a bicycle chain which travelled up from and disappeared back into the floor.

'The wheel tension was terrific, at some points requiring two hands. Finally the flap indicator reached 25 degrees and the trim indicator co-located on the same shaft rested on −1·3 degrees; I later learned that this configuration, depending on weight, gave you the best short-field performance available . . . Sounding like three chain saws at a woodcutter's ball, Annie snorted down the runway, 1,900 rpm and 30–32 inches of manifold pressure on the gauges was all she could muster. I should say 'gauge', as Annie's only manifold pressure gauge was connected to the number one engine, the other two displaying 'ATA' information—whatever that meant. Eighty miles per hour was the magic figure, using all of 600 feet of runway! She bolted skywards like a scalded hen, the rate of climb pegged and the airspeed bled back to 60 mph.

'Totally alarmed at this turn of events, I sat upright from my flap retraction duties, diplomatically pushing forward on the yoke. Annie responded to my endeavours, levelling off at 500 feet. Bud showed little irritation toward my breach of command, for which I was thankful. Apparently, he well realised my total unfamiliarity with Annie's flight characteristics, and I caught him in the middle of a very wide grin shortly thereafter.'

The Junkers' flap/trim combination was necessary to compensate for the large trim changes brought about by deployment or retraction of the massive flaps, which were raised in two stages during climb-out, after which the flap/trim combination was disengaged. The aircraft's performance was not outstanding, with a cruise speed around 201–217 km/h (125–135 mph) and an ambling climb rate which put 3,000 m (10,000 ft) fully eighteen minutes away from brake release. 'However,' wrote Captain Brown, 'if the Junkers climbed like the venerable old lady that she was, she also possessed all the docility associated with the venerable, being beautifully stable and virtually capable of being flown hands-off in anything but really turbulent air . . . but if there was a fair amount of turbulence one had to work fairly hard on the controls, although the rudder could be set on autopilot to take the strain out of the footwork.' The 'autopilot', which could also be used in the event of an engine failure to cope with asymmetric loads, consisted of a pair of spring-loaded T-handles projecting from beside the rudder pedals. These handles could be pulled upwards along a ratchet to offset the rudder to whatever degree necessary to retrim the aircraft directionally.

'The landing procedure', says Captain Brown, 'was basically a matter of pulling back the throttles, with the slight complication of engaging the flap/trim combination and winding on full flap (40 degrees) at 93 mph . . . Touchdown was a clattering, jangling affair no matter how delicate one strove to make it, but the landing run in zero wind was a mere

Above: final approach to land in the Junkers Ju 52/3m was accompanied by the deployment of the type's large flaps, which permitted remarkably short landings to be made.

Above right: the distinctive dihedral angle of the mainplanes and the ungainly fixed undercarriage, both characteristic of the Ju 52, became familiar sights in all theatres of war from the Spanish conflict onwards.

Right: a pilot's view of the Ju 52/3m's instrument display. The majority of the type's dials relate to the operation of the engines and appear in triplicate behind the lever array.

Below: despite its early appearance as a bomber, the Ju 52/3m reverted to its designated role as a transport to become the Luftwaffe's standard troop carrier. Italian-based aircraft are pictured

1,050 feet.' Braking was fun, because the Ju 52 had an unusual, possibly unique, system whereby the brakes were applied by pulling back the throttle on the appropriate side, or, if you wanted to brake both mainwheels, pulling back the throttle of the engine in the fuselage nose. Taxying required care and a light-handed touch to avoid a skater's waltz around the tarmac.

Scott Johnson, who was used to flying jet airliners, found the Junkers' short-landing capabilities in no way exaggerated by the passage of time: 'I've always heard that Iron Annie was great for getting into or out of small, unimproved fields. I was about to prove it to myself. The last approach never got past the half-flap mark – this time we would use the full 40 degrees. Turning final for runway 18 Bud wheeled down 40 degrees that all but stopped Annie in mid-air. The airspeed was already back around 65 mph by accident, but she felt all right so I left it there. The fence grew nearer, with airspeed back to 60. We crossed the fence at 60 with touch-

down around 55 mph indicated. Considering head-wind, our groundspeed couldn't have been much over 35–40 mph – unbelievable! Touching tail-low, almost in a three-pointer, Annie rolled perhaps 300 to 400 feet at most – no brakes!'

Tante Ju was slow, noisy, fearsomely draughty and cold, but she was reliable, rugged and simple to fly and maintain. Thirty years after the end of World War II, at the outset of which the Junkers was already outmoded and inadequate for the many tasks thrust upon it, a handful were still in active service with the Spanish air force, and rumours abound of others still earning their livings in South America and New Guinea. As one writer so aptly put it, 'you cannot build a better aeroplane than the Junkers Ju 52. Everything about it is necessary, and unless a man dives it straight into the ground, walking away from a forced landing is almost a certainty.' She was indeed a kindly old lady.

Captain Eric 'Winkle' Brown described the Ju 52 thus: 'Angularly ugly and incredibly cumbersome! How well I recall my reaction on first seeing an example of Dipl Ing Ernst Zindel's Junkers Ju 52/3m transport sporting Deutsche Luft Hansa markings and sitting on the apron at Tempelhof airfield, Berlin over 40 years ago, in the summer of 1936. To my then-youthful eyes, this fantastic amalgam of corrugated skinning, trailing flappery and heavily-braced undercarriage, not to mention a trio of air-cooled radial engines . . . demonstrated a total disregard for the most elementary aero-dynamic considerations! Yet this aesthetically-unappealing contraption possessed, so I was told at the time, very considerable commercial respect-ability; I was of course quite unaware that, probably at that very point in time, this respectability was being somewhat tarnished in Spanish skies by a less pacific and even more hideous version, with an immense "dustbin", accommodating a bomb-aimer-cum-gunner, appended between the rearmost legs of its undercarriage tripods . . .

'To us it seemed that when employed as a troop transport this lumbering monstrosity must surely frighten its inmates silly. It appeared to be so extraordinarily vulnerable; one could imagine it falling victim to a farmer's shotgun. But were we maligning this ugly duckling? Was it in truth an extraordinarily well-camouflaged swan? I began to doubt the validity of my first reactions when, as the fighting in Europe finally petered out, I discovered the very real affection for the "Tante Ju" possessed by the Wehrmacht as a whole, and began to appreciate the fact that this transport had probably played a greater role in shaping the course of World War II than any other combat aeroplane.'

Developed from the single-engined Ju 52 of 1930, the Ju 52/3m was a logical progression in Junkers' successful line of all-metal transport aircraft which had been developed through the 1920s. The prototype, a converted Ju 52, utilised three Pratt & Whitney Hornet radial engines of American origin; flight trials were so successful that all aircraft then on the Dessau assembly line were completed to the new three-engined standard. The majority of production aircraft were powered by the nine-cylinder BMW 132 engine in place of the Pratt & Whitney power plant

Douglas DC-3

'In the hands of a skilled pilot DC-3s can be successfully landed in just about any cabbage patch...'

Above left: the DC-3's distinctive tail-down attitude on the ground placed the crew in an elevated position above and between the type's powerful Twin Wasp engines. Developed from the similarly-configured DC-2, the DC-3 had a limited airline life before the outbreak of World War II, but many military aircraft were subsequently recruited on the resumption of peacetime services by civil operators over the world. A small number of DC-3s soldier on in the late 1970s, almost all used exclusively for freight work

'The DC-3 groaned,' says a former co-pilot, 'it protested, it rattled, it leaked oil, it ran hot, it ran cold, it ran rough, it staggered along on hot days and scared you half to death, its wings flexed and twisted in a horrifying manner, it sank back to earth with a great sigh of relief – but it flew and flew and flew. It took us and ten thousand crews around the globe to where we had to go and brought us home again, honest, faithful and magnificent machine that it was.'

The DC-3 evolved when American Airlines asked Douglas if they could produce a night-sleeper version of the DC-2. Thus the DST – Douglas Sleeper Transport – which was in effect the first DC-3 was born. DSTs, DC-3s, C-47s, Dakotas, 'Gooney Birds', call them what you will, were powered by two 1,200 hp Pratt & Whitney Wasp twin row radials or two Wright Cyclone nine-cylinder radial engines of 1,535 hp. The DST, which carried 14 passengers, entered service in the summer of 1936, inaugurating a nonstop service between New York and Chicago on 25 June; scheduled flight time was four hours, forty-five minutes, compared to eighteen hours by train. Three months later the Douglas transports took over the transcontinental coast-to-coast service between Newark Airport, New York and Grand Central Terminal, Glendale, Los Angeles, via Memphis, Dallas and Tucson. The flight time was 15 hours 50 minutes eastbound, and 17 hours 41 minutes westbound.

'The operation is now routine,' wrote Ernest K. Gann, 'which means that the much-publicised "Mercury" flight to Los Angeles is supposed to depart Newark at 5.10 and touch down on Glendale Airport at 8.50 tomorrow morning – God and the elements willing. The average has been reasonably good, but the prevailing westerly winds across the North American continent often make the public relations people wish the schedule was printed on elastic.

'Once in the air, all souls aboard with the exception of the crew will be served cocktails on the house followed by a fine steak dinner, then Captain Dodson will send back his written flying report to be passed among his guests. It will be signed by his co-pilot, who will be pleased to answer any questions during one of his tours through the cabin.'

Soon other US airlines had DC-3s, most opting

Douglas DC-3 cockpit
1: *Clocks* **2:** *Artificial horizon* **3:** *Altimeters* **4:** *De-icer pressure gauges* **5:** *Rate of climb indicator* **6:** *Airspeed indicators* **7:** *Turn and bank indicator* **8:** *Radio compass indicator* **9:** *Engine speed indicators* **10:** *Automatic pilot controls* **11:** *Automatic pilot instrument panel* **12:** *Azimuth indicator* **13:** *Magnetic compass* **14:** *Fuel pressure gauges* **15:** *Oil pressure gauges* **16:** *Oil temperature gauges* **17:** *Cylinder head temperature gauges* **18:** *Carburettor air temperature* **19:** *Fuel contents* **20:** *Fuel contents gauge tank selector* **21:** *Manifold pressure* **22:** *Propeller speed* **23:** *Throttles* **24:** *Mixture* **25:** *Carburettor heat and filter* **26:** *Fuel selector cocks* **27:** *Throttle friction adjustment* **28:** *Tailwheel lock* **29:** *Elevator trim* **30:** *Rudder trim* **31:** *Aileron trim* **32:** *Parking brake* **33:** *Flap position* **34:** *Rudder pedals* **35:** *Control wheels*

for the smooth-running Pratt & Whitneys, rather than the Wrights which vibrated. Trans-Continental and Western Air flew from Kansas City, and the following contemporary description of a flight to New York via St Louis, Indianapolis, Columbus, Dayton and Pittsburgh captured that era of airline flying perfectly.

'It's ten minutes before scheduled take-off time at 2pm . . . Captain Smith and First Officer Jones walk up to the cockpit. You can stand up now and watch Jones go through his regular before take-off routine. He picks up a check-list titled "Before Starting Engines" and calls out "Battery cart on, gasoline checked, radio checked . . ." He and Captain Smith check each item. He picks up his mike. "Flight 14 to Kansas City, radio check." TWA's radio operator returns: "Kansas City to 14. Transmission normal, time 57, five seven, altimeter 29·80, two niner eight zero."

'Passengers and baggage are already on the ship, and Captain Smith gets the "all clear to start engines" signal from the ground. He starts the right engine, then the left. Jones shifts the electrical load from battery cart to aeroplane battery . . . Captain Smith gets a salute from the passenger agent which means "all clear to taxi". Jones changes radio frequency to the control tower frequency and presses his mike button: "TWA Flight 14 to Kansas City tower. Ready to taxi out." The tower operator returns: "Okay to taxi out TWA 14. Wind northwest three, NW3, traffic taking off north. Your clearance: Flight 14 is cleared from Kansas City to St Louis tower to cruise 7,000 across Weldon Springs 2,500, no essential traffic reported."

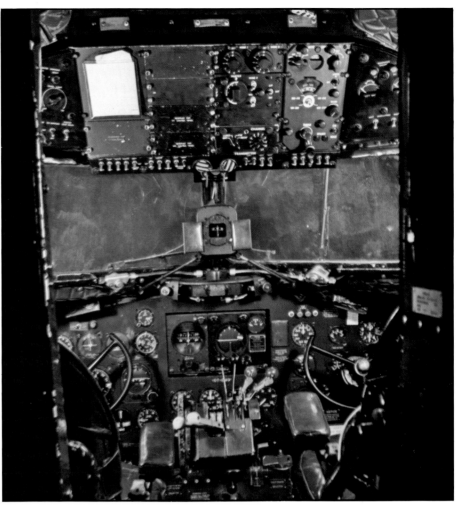

'Jones repeats the clearance as the plane stops at the south end of the north-south runway for the routine engine run-up. Out comes the check-list with items to be checked before take-off: "Flaps up, trim tabs set for take-off, seat belt sign on, carburettor air cold . . ." Captain Smith sets the parking brake, runs each engine up to 30 inches of mercury, tests the magnetos. Jones presses the mike: "TWA Flight 14 ready to take-off", receives the tower's okay and we begin to roll. The throttles go to the full forward position and as we leave the ground Captain Smith says "Up gear". Jones unlocks the safety latch on the floor of the cockpit, pulls the landing gear lever to the up position and in the same motion picks up his mike: "TWA 14 off at zero three, changing over". The control tower repeats and Jones shifts to TWA company frequency and repeats our time off ground. The company radio operator at Kansas City contacts St Louis and gives our time off and also estimated total time to St Louis.

'Now we're at 1,000 feet in the air heading on a course due east, and Captain Smith pulls back the throttles to 30 inches of mercury and synchronises the props at 1,900 rpm. We are climbing at 120 mph. When we reach our cruising altitude at 7,000 feet you see Jones pull out his Wright power calculator. He figures for a moment, glances at the outside air temperature indicator and says "Twenty eight point three for 1,200 horsepower" Captain Smith moves the props to 1,850 and the throttles until the two manifold pressure gauges read 28·3. Now he moves the gas tank selector from the positive tank

Above: the flightdeck of a C-47, showing the instruments carried above the windscreen on the cabin roof. These include radio controls, oxygen instruments, electrical panels, ignition switches and prop feathering buttons. Above left: the passenger cabin of one of KLM's DC-3 airliners on the Amsterdam to Java route in 1937. The Dutch airline was one of the first European operators of this aeroplane. Left: a DC-3 of Bahamas Airways, one of numerous airlines to fly the type postwar, is pictured on take-off

DOUGLAS DC-3

(left main) to the left auxiliary tank and glancing at the gasoline gauge we see that there are 85 gallons in this tank. The mains hold 210 gallons and each auxiliary holds a maximum of 201.

'Captain Smith and Jones seem to be busy every minute, checking oil pressure, moving a lever to increase oil temperature to 150 degrees, or checking the air temperature in the passenger cabin. "Jones", says Captain Smith, "You'd better let down a quart of water. I see the steam pressure in our boiler is dropping." Jones leaves his seat, lets down the required amount of water and notes a steady rise in steam pressure up to 25 pounds. When you ask about the heating system Captain Smith explains that the passenger cabin is heated by a water jacket surrounding the engine exhausts and that steam generated by a quart to three pints of water is generally sufficient for an hour and a half flight. A gauge over the co-pilot's seat shows the exact air temperature in the passenger compartment at all times. Air entering the nose valve of the ship is heated to 70 degrees and passes into the passenger cabin.

'"Flight 14 over New Florence at 44, four-four, 7,000 contact, estimate Weldon Springs at 10, one zero, St Louis at 21, two one, temperature 33, gain 22 . . . Jones." Our speed is slightly more than Jones had estimated since we've picked up a tail-wind of 22 mph. You settle back thinking that's all the work necessary before our arrival at St Louis. But not Jones. He reaches behind his seat and pulls out the aeroplane log–Form 76. This log gives a complete record as to functioning of engines and aeroplane for each leg of a journey. Over his shoulder as he writes we see: engines-ignition-radio-oil pressure and temperature normal. Altitude–7,000, airspeed–175 mph, horsepower–1,200, fuel per hour–90 gallons.

'Jones replaces the log. When we reach St Louis he will enter our total time between Kansas City and St Louis, and the ground crew will enter the number of gallons of gasoline and oil with which they service the ship. Jones makes his report over Weldon Springs, then when we're five minutes from St Louis, picks up his mike and says: "Flight 14 to St Louis. Over the River, go ahead." "St Louis Tower to Flight 14. Okay, over the River, the wind west nine, runway number one, local traffic. You are cleared to the field."

'Smith and Jones keep a sharp watch on two little yellow Cubs circling the field. Jones gets out his "Before Landing" check list . . . "Gas on left main, full rich, props 1,850, tailwheel locked." Captain Smith checks each item and then slows the ship to 150 mph. "Down gear." Jones pushes down the lever which lowers the landing gear and, when the landing gear strut pressure reaches 750 pounds, locks the safety latch and repeats "Gear down and locked, pressure 750 pounds, green light on". We swing to the east of the airport, descend to 1,200 feet, line up with the east-west runway and slow to 110 mph. "Down flaps three quarters", says the captain. Jones lowers the flaps, returns the flap lever to neutral. "Flaps are down three quarters." We touch the ground. Captain Smith pulls back the control column, says "Flaps up"–then pushes the propeller controls ahead to full low pitch, returns the elevator trim tab to neutral, unlocks the tail

wheel and we taxi slowly to gate No 3 where a mechanic in white coveralls stands with his hands over his head. Jones presses his mike button, changes to TWA radio frequency: "Flight 14 on the ground at St Louis at 24, two four." The figure in white below us extends his arms horizontally–we come to a stop. Jones pushes the carburettor controls to the full lean position, Captain Smith reaches overhead, cuts the ignition switches and sets the parking brake."'

'The DC-3s are easy aircraft to fly,' says Gann, 'almost totally forgiving to the most ham-handed pilots. Their inherent stability makes them an

Above: over 1,900 examples of the Douglas C-47 were supplied to the Royal Air Force under Lend-Lease arrangements. Known as Dakota–a name since incorrectly applied to all DC-3 and C-47 aircraft–the type played a major role in many notable operations, including the D-day landings in Normandy.
Inset: the interior of a Dakota equipped as a personal transport for General Sir Bernard Montgomery, commander of the 21st Army Group

excellent instrument aircraft and their low stall speed combined with practically full control response at slow approach speeds allows the use of very short fields. They can be slipped with full flaps or held nose high and allowed to descend in a near power stall. In the hands of a skilled pilot DC-3s can be successfully landed in just about any cabbage patch some optimist dared to call an airfield.'

The approach speed certainly was slow. One pilot claimed that landing 'took as long as an old lady preparing for bed'. The Pilot's Manual recommended a light-load, full flap approach speed of just 75 knots with power on. 'Three-pointing is difficult,' recalls one DC-3 pilot, 'the preferred technique being a cross between a wheel landing and three-points, with just a light forward pressure to hold her down as the big low pressure wheels brush the ground, whipping up the flaps at the same time. Aileron must be used to hold the upwind wheel firmly on the ground, both during the landing and take-off run . . . Once the landing is completed there is still the problem of taxying. As there are no internal control locks, most operators engage the autopilot again, with the gyros caged this time. The control surfaces are large enough to overcome the efforts of two pilots to hold them, but with the hydraulic autopilot servos locked in too, life becomes less of a battle while taxying in strong winds. Plenty of differential wheel brake and throttle are called for, with the added assistance of the tail-wheel lock for straight running.'

The DC-3/C-47's most amazing accomplishments came in World War II (during which it was almost certainly the only major aircraft type used by opposing combatants, for both the Allies and Japanese used them). Quite formidable loads were carried and the rule was to 'shove everything as far forward as it will go.' One pilot recalls winding on full *nose down trim* before take-off to raise the tail as a routine operation on transatlantic ferry flights with the RAF Transport Command. A DC-3 of China National Airlines flying out to Burma once carried 75 passengers–the´ standard load was twenty-one.

Two tributes sum up the Douglas DC-3's continuing contribution to aviation: 'By modern standards the degree of noise and vibration on the flight deck is out of all proportion with the results obtained, but once one becomes used to her, the old "Gooney Bird" flies beautifully, and really flies, sitting up on that fabulous wing, which contributes far more lift than any modern "flying blow-lamp" enjoys . . . For all her years, the Dakota is a gentleman's aeroplane.'

And from Ernest Gann, who began a long and distinguished flying career on DC-2s and DC-3s: 'The DC-3 was and is unique, for no other flying machine has been part of the international scene for so many years, cruised every sky known to mankind, been so ubiquitous, admired, cherished, glamorised, known the touch of so many different pilot nationals, and sparked so many maudlin tributes. It was without question the most all-up successful aircraft ever built, and even in this jet age it seems likely the surviving Douglas DC-3s may fly about their business forever . . . Regardless of the label the Douglas masterpiece was profoundly admired by all who flew it. And still is. Wherever you go in the world there is a very good chance you will see a DC-3 at work, and in some of the less sophisticated regions there is a very strong possibility you will be in one.'

The C-47, as the main military version of the DC-3 was designated, formed the backbone of many air forces' transport squadrons after World War II. The type's ruggedness and reliability, together with its ability to operate from short, improvised airstrips, ensured it a longevity matched by few other military aeroplanes. A former RAF Dakota is pictured in service with the Greek air force in 1970

Bristol Bulldog

Michael Turner's painting shows the aerobatic team of No 19 Squadron RAF going through their paces for the crowds at Hendon during the annual Royal Air Force Display. An impressive formation loop, often with each Bulldog trailing smoke from a canister attached to the fuselage underside, was usually a feature of such displays. However, the fighter's poor elevator response in a dive limited its aerobatic repertoire

Landing the Bristol Bulldog has been likened to trying to lift a loaded wheelbarrow at arm's length. Criticism of an aeroplane long after it has been replaced by more modern designs is perhaps rather unfair for, one assumes, it represents the fruits of the manufacturers' best efforts. The Bristol Bulldog remained in service for eight years with the Royal Air Force, and even saw action abroad (in Finnish service) during World War II.

Although superficially the Bulldog appeared to have advanced little from the designs that appeared at the end of World War I, with its twin-gun armament and bulky air-cooled radial engine, it did in fact represent some progress in basic aircraft design owing to its fabric-covered metal structure. However, despite all the efforts of its 490 hp Bristol Jupiter VII, its top speed remained disappointingly low, at only 280 km/h (174 mph).

At the time of the Bulldog's original design, most fighter biplanes had their share of flutter problems, either with ailerons or elevators, and in early service the Bulldog was prey to these troubles. Later on, the problems were alleviated with the introduction of mass-balanced ailerons.

On the ground the Bulldog displayed its first virtue, an excellent field of view for the pilot, who was seated below an enormous cut-out in the upper wing, fairly high in the cockpit so that forward view of the ground was only restricted by a 10-degree arc blanked by the engine. Take-off was entirely straightforward, the tail coming up after about thirty yards at full throttle; fairly coarse use of rudder was necessary to counter swing. With a fixed-pitch, two-blade wooden propeller, the climb away was simply a matter of setting the throttle to give an indicated speed of 170 km/h (105 mph).

Top: a formation of No 17 Squadron's Bulldogs photographed shortly after the unit received the type in 1929. This squadron flew the Bulldog in both the day and night fighter roles, the excellent visibility from its cockpit being a particular advantage at night.
Above: a pilot climbs aboard a Bulldog Mark IIa of No 23 Squadron

For normal flight manoeuvres the aircraft was light and sensitive on the controls but steep turns below 210 km/h (130 mph) required almost full top rudder to keep the nose on the horizon. Quite what was lacking in directional control never seems to have been fully understood in the Bulldog, despite some early re-design of the rudder and a small increase in fin area. That there may have been some airflow breakaway at the rear of the bulky fuselage, resulting in loss of fine rudder control at low speed, is possible, as more than one famous pilot found to his cost. Stalling and spinning were gentlemanly, there being virtually no natural tendency to drop a wing, the stall occurring at just under 88 km/h (55 mph) indicated and the nose falling sharply.

However, the Bulldog was noted for its many spectacular displays of aerobatics, particularly those at the famous Hendon shows during the 1930s. Yet, although these involved precision manoeuvres, often in formation with coloured smoke, they demanded little that was remarkable in the aeroplane. Given plenty of sky with only high cloud, the pilots of the day gave beautiful exhibitions of great sweeping loops, often reaching 1,200 m (4,000 ft) at the top. The secret was to give oneself plenty of space and speed, using about 320 km/h (200 mph) in the dive before pulling up. Once again the superb field of vision, not often achieved in the old biplanes, was widely acclaimed by 'aerobatting' Bulldog pilots.

Recovery from almost all manoeuvres emphasised the Bulldog's most tricky vice: its relative laziness to respond to elevator in the dive, and its exaggerated 'sink'; on No 23 Squadron, for instance, it was strictly forbidden to perform any high-loading manoeuvre in which the aeroplane was 'likely to pass below 300 m (1,000 ft) above the ground'. Of course pilots could and did fly aerobatics very low, but there was nothing of the ballerina in the Bulldog; climbing turns near the ground were invariably made with plenty of speed and power, but it was regarded as foolhardy below 150 m (500 ft) to attempt rolls as the end of the 'barrel' could easily lie below the trees.

As a fighter the Bulldog never had a real chance to show its paces, although one or two examples with the Finnish air force did put up a good fight against the Russians in the Winter War of 1939–40. It is, perhaps, fortunate that the RAF never had to fire the Bulldog's twin Vickers in anger owing to those wretched guns' perennial tendency to jam after a few rounds; as the British had no other suitable gun at the time, the Vickers' gun bodies were always located just in front of the pilot's face for ease of 'in-flight clearance'. Instead, many a pilot of the 1930s performed what were probably very useful air-to-air cine-gun exercises with a bulky gun-camera attached to the lower wing root.

Back in the landing circuit there were none of today's complicated landing checks; no propeller pitch control, no flaps, no fuel cock juggling and no cooling gills to worry about, just 'straps tight'. Turning from crosswind just outside the boundary, speed about 145 km/h (90 mph) indicated with plenty of throttle at something like 46 m (150 ft), the pilot straightened up, eased off the throttle, let the speed drop to around 93–97 km/h (58–60 mph) before allowing the aircraft to settle into the flare-out. Indeed it was important to judge the final heights very nicely as the nose, as already mentioned, dropped quite sharply on the stall. Hence a modification found necessary early in the Bulldog's Service life was a tougher undercarriage, provoking those remarks about 'loaded wheelbarrows'.

Right: the last airworthy Bulldog started life as the Bristol Company's demonstrator in 1930. In 1961 it was restored in the markings of No 56 Squadron RAF, but its subsequent flying life was short, as it crashed at Farnborough in 1964.
Below: the Bulldog Mark II's lengthened fuselage improved the type's spin recovery characteristics

'I shall always remember the noise of the engine, the smell, the crackle of the exhausts, the vibration of the flying wires.'
Duncan Simpson

Hawker Hart

The Hawker Harts and Furies of the Royal Air Force in the 1930s had always made a deep impression on me, as they no doubt did on thousands of other schoolboys who wanted to join the RAF and fly. Perhaps they were the most elegant biplanes ever built and they flew every bit as well as they looked. Little did I think as I collected pictures of the RAF Hawker-equipped squadrons in 1938 that fourteen years later I should join Hawkers as a test pilot and be given the opportunity of flying a Hart.

Built in 1930 as the thirteenth aircraft on the production line, G-ABMR was Hawker's demonstrator. It had been flown all over Europe on sales and support tours in the 1930s, used for development work at Brooklands in Surrey and served during the war as a communications 'hack' between the Hawker airfields and the squadrons. My only disappointment was to see it finished in a dreadful blue and gold colour scheme and not in the beautiful silver with squadron insignia and polished cowlings as I had remembered the aircraft in its heyday.

I flew G-ABMR towards the end of 1954 and will never forget the experience of starting the magnificent Rolls-Royce Kestrel 12-cylinder engine with the aid of two strong men, the smoke and noise when the engine fired and the lively take-off even at +6 psi

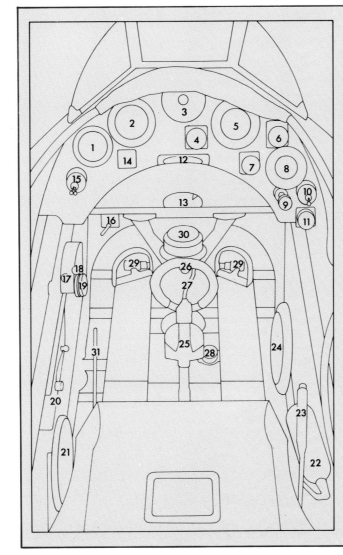

Hawker Hart cockpit

1: *Altimeter* **2**: *Airspeed indicator* **3**: *Turn and bank indicator* **4**: *Oil pressure gauge* **5**: *Engine speed indicator* **6**: *Radiator temperature gauge* **7**: *Oil temperature gauge* **8**: *Fuel contents gauge* **9**: *Engine primer pump* **10**: *Starting magneto switch* **11**: *Boost gauge* **12**: *Inclinometer* **13**: *Radiator position indicator* **14**: *Compass correction card* **15**: *Twin magneto switches* **16**: *Fuel cock* **17**: *Fuel mixture control* **18**: *Throttle control* **19**: *Engine control friction adjustment* **20**: *0·303in Vickers machine gun* **21**: *Tailplane incidence adjustment wheel* **22**: *Fire extinguisher* **23**: *Seat adjustment lever* **24**: *Radiator retraction wheel* **25**: *Control column* **26**: *Machine gun firing button* **27**: *Wheel brake lever* **28**: *Brake pressure gauge* **29**: *Rudder pedals* **30**: *Compass* **31**: *Radiator flap lever*

boost. In the air its exhilarating performance, ability to turn on a sixpence and its climb reflected the aircraft's real performance in the vintage years when, as a day bomber, it outstripped the fighter opposition. No wonder that Sydney Camm regarded this aircraft as one of his masterpieces and considered it his favourite.

Imagine my feelings then, in September 1956, when I found myself only 180m (600ft) above Wiltshire, in poor weather, with a complete engine failure on my hands. There was a sudden thump, the engine seized and, on looking behind, a thin trail of smoke was visible. I had no alternative but to glide and select a clover field almost straight ahead; it was a steep incline and I missed some telegraph wires by feet. A short landing run uphill and I came to a silent halt. Nothing broken and nothing superficially to indicate the supercharger seizure due to bearing failure in the Rolls-Royce Kestrel engine.

The Hart was recovered and it took three long years to find the necessary pieces to put the Kestrel together again. During this time I began to work on the airframe restoration. Time and time again I came up against difficulties such as researching squadron colour schemes. Sir Sydney took a keen interest. He did not quite know what he did want but he was adamant that he could not stand the markings of the pre-war squadrons. In the end I found a happy solution of which he approved.

In 1932, Hawkers borrowed J9941, the ninth production Hart, from No 57 (Bomber) Squadron, and George Bulman flew it to Paris for the Paris Air Show. This was the ninth production aircraft which had completed 707 hours in service without overhaul. My task now was to restore G-ABMR to exactly the condition of J9941 as it flew with 'B' Flight, No 57 Squadron. I ended up with a file some two inches thick! The breakthrough came when I found Group Captain H. N. Hampton RAF (Retd), then living in Norwich. He was a most meticulous officer and had commanded 'B' Flight in 1930–32. In his logbook was a comprehensive record of his Flight's aircraft with details of colours and serial numbers. We finished G-ABMR in these colours down to the last detail and I had also found two guns to mount on the aircraft which provided the final touch. In July 1962 I had the greatest thrill in flying the aircraft up to RAF Marham for the ceremony of Standard Presentation by Her Royal Highness Princess Marina to No 57 Squadron.

I continued flying J9941 up until 1972 when sadly it was grounded and transferred to the RAF Museum at Hendon, where it remains to this day. I was lucky to have flown it for 18 years and I know that it gave so much pleasure to the thousands who saw it flying. I shall always remember the noise of the engine, the smell, the crackle of the exhausts, the vibration of the flying wires, the carburettor icing, the delicate care required when landing the aircraft and the visits from Sir Sydney to see his masterpiece–the Hawker Hart.

Left: Frank Wootton's painting depicts a formation of Harts of No 57 Squadron RAF, which flew the type from Netheravon and Upper Heyford between the wars. The leading aircraft, J9941, was chosen as the model for the restoration of Hawker's Hart demonstrator

John Nesbitt-Dufort DSO recalls: 'In 1930 I first saw a Hart; it was one belonging to No 12 Squadron from Bicester and had just replaced their Fairey Foxes. An old pupil of No 3 FTS Grantham had flown up this gleaming beauty to show it off to an admiring ring of, as yet, wingless acting pilot officers on probation, of which I was one. I can still remember gazing in envy at the junior pilot as he climbed proudly out of, what was to us, the most magnificent machine we had ever seen. Its staggered and slightly swept-back wings, brilliantly polished aluminium cowlings with the big golden "12", and the Squadron crest of a fox's mask painted on it impressed us tremendously.

'Referring back to my log book I find I first flew the Hart in April 1932. We had one in No 25 (F) Squadron which was supposed to be used for converting new pilots to the [Hawker] Fury but so far as I can remember it was never put to this use as most pilots in the squadron went straight from Siskins on to Furies without further dual. However, the Hart provided us with an ideal aeroplane for giving joy rides to our very friendly rugger rivals, the 3rd Battalion of the Royal Tank Corps stationed at Lydd; we used to enter these flights in our logbooks as 'air experience for army officers', and in return it was not uncommon to see an RAF officer at the controls of a medium tank as it charged about the shingle at Dungeness.

'The Hart was much better as far as performance and feel were concerned compared with any other two-seater aircraft of the period, and it was, of course, fully aerobatic. Regarding the latter it was a good deal heavier on the controls than the Fury and the radiator had to be laboriously wound in prior to any aerobatics involving negative 'g'. Failure to do this resulted in a frighteningly loud 'clonk' as the radiator fell inboard, during a slow roll for example. You could hang your Hart up in a really spectacular stall turn, which in my opinion, if properly done, was one of the most exciting manoeuvres.'

Top: the thirteenth production Hart which was flown by the author, Duncan Simpson, on numerous occasions between 1954 and 1972, when it was grounded and presented to the RAF Museum at Hendon.
Above: power plant of the Hart was the Rolls-Royce Kestrel inline engine, the radiator of which is visible between the undercarriage legs

> *'...an ideal aircraft for aerobatic flying, due to its excellent manoeuvrability, high rate of climb and low stalling speed.'*
> *Wg Cdr R.R. Stanford Tuck*

Gloster Gladiator

With flaps on upper and lower wings extended, a Gladiator comes in to land. Although it possessed such relatively advanced features as flaps, enclosed cockpit and wing-mounted machine guns, the Gladiator did not differ in essentials from the fighters of World War I. The last in a long line of RAF biplane fighters, it was well liked by its pilots, as Robert Stanford Tuck attests

I first flew Gloster Gladiator serial number K7938 on 28 May 1937, when I collected it from the Gloster Aircraft Co at Brockworth. Prior to this, from September 1936, I had been flying the Gladiator's forerunner, the Gauntlet and, while they were very similar in handling qualities, the Gladiator was a considerable improvement over the Gauntlet. Naturally, my squadron–No 65 at Hornchurch–was delighted to be re-equipped with this faster, sturdier, and better-armed aircraft, having four Vickers machine guns instead of the two of the Gauntlet.

The Gladiator was a stubby, sturdy, good-looking biplane with a sliding cockpit canopy, a strong fixed cantilever Dowty undercarriage and ailerons in both upper and lower mainplane. It was powered by a Bristol engine of great reliability and, for those days, power, with a large fixed-pitch wooden airscrew. It was an absolute delight to fly as

it had a high rate of climb for those days, would go fast downhill and had a most docile stall. The cockpit was roomy and comfortable but, I thought, had one significant drawback in that there was a complete lack of heating. This became most unpleasant for the pilot at very high altitude, as we frequently got these aircraft up to 8,500m (28,000ft), where they handled very well, providing no excessive 'g' was imposed. However, the cockpit was absolutely frigid and we always experienced great difficulty with frosting up of the canopy and windscreen; woe betide any pilot who was lax in the maintenance of his flying equipment, as one small hole in the fingers of his gloves could result in frostbite. Somehow, these defects just did not seem to matter; they were our machines, our aeroplanes and we were very proud of them.

It may come as a slight surprise to some to learn

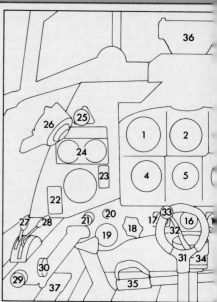

Gloster Gladiator cockpit

1: *Airspeed indicator* 2: *Artificial horizon* 3:
4: *Altimeter* 5: *Direction indicator* 6: *Turn a*

7: *Engine speed indicator*
8: *Oil pressure* 9:
Emergency oil cooler cock
10: *Boost gauge* 11: *Engine
primer pump* 12: *Priming
cock* 13: *Starter switch* 14:
Starting magneto switch 15:
Oil temperature gauge 16:
Brake pressure 17: *Fuel
pressure* 18: *Fuel tank
selector* 19: *Fuel contents*
20: *Carburettor cut-out* 21:
Cockpit light dimmer switch
22: *Magneto switches* 23:
Pitot head heat switch 24:
Oxygen panel 25: *Gunsight
master switch* 26: *Radio
control* 27: *Mixture control*
28: *Throttle* 29: *Air intake
shutter control* 30: *Friction
adjustment* 31: *Control
column* 32: *Brake* 33: *Gun
firing button* 34: *Compass
35: Rudder bar* 36: *Gunsight
37: 0·303 in Browning*

*of climb indicator
k indicator*

that in the evenings in the mess over a pint of beer in 1937–38, we often talked about how our Gladiators would stand up against the much-discussed Bf 109, which would be our main adversary if we went to war with Germany. Although we had also heard quite a lot about R. J. Mitchell's Spitfire and Sydney Camm's Hurricane, to us at the time these were really only rumours of what we might have in the future as a mount with which to engage and destroy the enemy.

One of my greatest thrills in a Gladiator was on a dark night on 27 July 1937. At 2135 hours in K7931 I took off from the grass at Hornchurch along the long line of goose-neck flares stretching into the distance. The Bristol engine gave of its full power and after rumbling along, gathering speed fast, at about 113 km/h (70 mph) tail down, we rose smoothly into the air, climbing easily and steadily into the night sky. I trimmed the aircraft for a steady climb, and then with head down in the cockpit which, with one's eyes adjusted to the pitch outside, was well-illuminated in a dull red glow, quickly scanned around the instruments–all was well–levelled off at 1,070 m (3,500 ft), eased back on the throttle and looked around–R/T call to base could wait for a moment or two.

Ahead I beheld the enormous area of that great city, London, a sight which always thrilled me enormously. I set course dead across this blaze of lights from north-east to south-west, where I wished to see one of my favourite pubs, the King's Head at Shepperton. My Gladiator flew along smoothly and steadily and I was able to occupy myself with the fascinating object of picking out the route I would have taken had I been driving by car. It always amazed me flying over London in these days with the lights full on how easy it was to navigate a route from the air. In due course I found the King's Head and after flying around it for a bit, imagining my many friends there quaffing their ale, I flew back in easy stages to Hornchurch. On receiving a green Aldis signal from the flarepath, I throttled back, reduced speed, came gliding in and touched down nicely just past the first two or three goose-neck flares and rumbled to a halt on the grass. I taxied onto the lighted tarmac and switched off.

When we had become thoroughly experienced on our Gladiators, it was decided to form No 65 Squadron Flight Aerobatic Team, and I was delighted to be selected as one of the four pilots for this team. As I am sure everyone realises, the precision formation flying of a team such as this is of a very high order and requires great flying ability on the part of the leader, who was Flight Lieutenant Leslie Bicknell, and the three other members of the team. Thus in beautiful summer weather with clear blue skies, our time was very happily and fully occupied in constant training for the various manoeuvres we performed. We always flew three in a vic, with one tucked into the box, and found the Gladiator an ideal aircraft for this specialised form of demonstration flying, due to its excellent manoeuvrability, high rate of climb and notably low stalling speed.

However, all my flights in Gladiators were not so pleasant as those I have mentioned. On 17 January 1938, I had what can only be construed as a disastrous forty-minute flight in Gladiator K7940. On

The Gladiator's ease of handling was due to its light and well-harmonised controls, a quality essential to the traditional dogfighting concept of air combat. The Gladiator was a good gun platform, being stable in all three axes, and possessed excellent manoeuvrability. Its armament consisted of four 0·303 in Browning machine guns

GLOSTER GLADIATOR

The Sea Gladiator was a navalised Gladiator, developed in 1939 by fitting an A-frame arrestor hook, catapult points and a dinghy in a fairing between the undercarriage legs. Armament was modified to Navy requirements and provision made for two more machine guns below the upper wing. A three-blade metal Fairey Reed propeller became standard. The Sea Gladiator remained in service afloat until late 1940

this day three of us – myself, Flying Officer Adrian Hope-Boyd and a new sergeant pilot named Geoffrey Gaskell were practicing formation flying at 900 m (3,000 ft) over Sussex. Although at the time I considered flying in tight 'text-book' formations thoroughly bad policy from a military point of view, as I was a member of a formation aerobatic team, I naturally enjoyed it. The weather that day was not really ideal for this type of training as there was a very strong wind and from time to time we flew through rather turbulent air which rocked us about a bit. To add to this Geoffrey Gaskell was fairly new in the squadron and this exercise was to gain him experience in formation flying. So, we kept the formation fairly loose.

Somewhere over Uckfield, I put the formation into line-astern – with Hope-Boyd leading, Gaskell next, and myself last, in order that I could see how he was doing and advise him as necessary over the R/T. Each of the two Gladiators formating on Hope-Boyd were slightly higher than, and a shade to the right of, the one in front – just enough to stay out of the slipstream. At this close range, the invisible wake left by a Gladiator's propellor could buffet as violently as waves churned up by a steamship's screws. Suddenly we hit a patch of rough air and Gaskell's machine, just below and in front of me, bucked violently. He must have over-corrected and, in dropping back and losing a little height, he was directly in Hope-Boyd's violent slipstream, which caught him and threw him over in a steep bank.

All this occurred in the space of one or two seconds and, being just behind and above Gaskell, I was on the point of yanking the stick over and getting out of the way if his aircraft did not settle back into

position very quickly. I was easing off my throttle and starting to fall back when Gaskell, who could have broken away to the left in an empty sky with complete safety, suddenly, unaccountably, hauled his plane up on its tail and broke to the right. I saw him rear up dead in front of me. There was no hope of pulling sideways or upwards to avoid a collision. For one horrifying instant, over the top of my engine cowling, I looked down into Gaskell's cockpit – saw his gloved hands clamped on stick and throttle, the top of his leather helmet pressed against the headrest and the folded map protruding from the big patch pocket on the left leg of his flying suit.

The two machines were almost at right angles. I slapped the stick forward hoping I might be able to dive under Gaskell's tail, but in that second we struck. My engine and propeller crashed into the fuselage of the other machine just behind the cockpit. In front of my windscreen now was nothing but fabric and buckling metal airframe. The wings crumbled upwards and wrapped themselves around my hood with an awful grinding crash. At this stage I fully expected fire to burst out, but fortunately there were no flames, and then I realised that my engine had disappeared outwards as now the only noise was a hideous grinding and flapping from the tangled wings sealing me in my cockpit.

After a lot of struggling I managed to disconnect my R/T lead, oxygen tube and my seat harness, but on trying to open the canopy I found I could not

Right and above right: the Shuttleworth Collection's Gladiator Mark I, preserved in the markings of No 72 Squadron, was originally restored to flying condition by V. L. Bellamy, an ex-Fleet Air Arm pilot, and registered G-AMRK. It was returned to its makers for a token sum on condition that it would be maintained in flying condition. It was donated to the Shuttleworth Collection in 1960, since when it has continued to fly regularly

budge it – the crumpled wings above were holding it tight. From the peculiar 'g' sensation I was experiencing, I realised the wreckage was spinning down faster and faster with me inside it. After trying everything I could think of to budge the canopy, I put both my feet on the instrument panel and pushed the canopy with my head and shoulders. With the machine spinning faster and faster, there was a sudden crashing and grinding and daylight flooded the cockpit again; I realised that the wrecked wings holding me in had parted and floated away somewhere, offering a chance of escape.

A second later the canopy disappeared; I went out and without waiting the specified two or three seconds, pulled my rip-cord. With a crack the canopy opened and I was floating down quietly and peacefully. As I hung in my straps, blood was dripping down my white flying suit and I realised that I had been badly cut somewhere around the head. I remembered leaving the cockpit through a mass of flailing rigging wires and, on putting my hand to my face to try to feel the wound, my fingers went right through my right cheek into my mouth; virtually the whole of the right side of my face had been opened up. A moment later I felt some bits in my mouth and on spitting these into my hand realised they were two teeth from top and bottom of my right gums. I tossed them away angrily a second before I hit the ground with a frightful thump.

I was sitting on the ground trying to staunch the flow of blood from my face when a farm worker came running up to me; several others then arrived and gave me temporary first aid. A car drove me to Uckfield Cottage Hospital, where they proceeded to clean me up and in no time at all I was on the operating table being stitched up. I got one of the hospital staff to phone the Adjutant at Hornchurch

and explain briefly what had happened and that sadly young Geoffrey Gaskell had been killed instantaneously. So ended the brief career of K7940. Having had 28 stitches on the outside of my face, four inside and minus two teeth, I was again flying Gladiator K8002 on 26 January, very little the worse for wear, but a lot wiser. I continued flying the beautiful little Gladiator up until 30 December 1938, when I flew my first Spitfire, with which my squadron was re-equipped.

'The sparkle of a Bugatti coupled with the docility of an Hispano-Suiza.'

Hawker Fury

A Fury Mark I of No 43 Squadron, the first Fury squadron, based at Tangmere in 1931, flown by Sqn Ldr L. H. Slatter. First flown on 25 March 1931, the Fury offered more speed and a faster rate of climb than previous RAF fighters, although with less endurance. Its controls were light and positive, and combined with the instant throttle response and wide, flexible speed range of the 525 hp Kestrel engine to make the Fury a superb aircraft for aerobatic manoeuvres

'When I joined the Royal Air Force in 1935, the aim of nearly all pilots was to go on to fighters', recalls Squadron Leader G. H. Plinston. The fighter which every pilot–and many a would-be pilot–hankered after was the Hawker Fury. The Fury was a small, fast, light biplane whose polished aluminium panels and noisy, open-exhausted engine made it the aerial equivalent of a Blower Bentley.

The Fury epitomised the fighting aeroplanes of the 1930s. It was, arguably, the most beautiful aircraft of its time, thanks largely to the sleek, shark-nosed cowling which tightly enclosed its Rolls-Royce Kestrel IIS supercharged, water-cooled V-12 engine which produced 525 hp at 4,300 m (14,000 ft) and gave the Fury a maximum speed of 333 km/h (207 mph).

'I joined the first course at No 11 Flying Training School at Wittering,' says Squadron Leader Plinston, 'and about half way through the

first term our Furies arrived. They would only be flown by second term pilots, so we could only look at them with envy. Then, a few of us were selected to go on to fighters. What a day! The Furies were lovely little aeroplanes, not very fast, nor very powerful, but what a lovely noise they made!' Another Fury man, John Nesbitt-Dufort DSO, likened its charm to 'the sparkle of a Bugatti coupled with the docility of an Hispano-Suiza'. He reported the handling characteristics to be 'as near perfect as they could be [with] aileron and rudder light and positive; fore and aft control was equally positive but not quite so light, a good point, as nobody wants to be blacked out by a hiccough. Taxying was rather blind with a couple of yards of engine rearing up in front of one, but swinging the nose from side to side was simplified by the very efficient toe-operated brakes.'

Take-off required judicious use of right rudder to counter the torque of the Kestrel and its massive,

KI93

Right: a Fury of the Royal Yugoslav Air Force, one of a batch of ten purchased in 1936. Powered by 745hp Kestrel engines and fitted with cantilever undercarriages, low-drag radiators and four-gun armament, the aircraft followed six Furies, similar to the RAF's Mark I, which were bought in 1931. The Fury had ailerons on the upper wing only but had an excellent rate of roll

fixed-pitch Watts airscrew, which left a ground clearance of just four inches when the tail was raised. 'The unstick came surprisingly quickly,' says Wing Commander Nesbitt-Dufort, 'and after a comparatively short run; the climb at 140mph was outstanding for the period at a fraction below 2,000ft per minute.

The Fury set new standards for fighter performance when it was introduced. It was the first interceptor in service with the RAF to exceed the magic figure of 200mph in level flight, and its rate of climb, which was even better than Wing Commander Nesbitt-Dufort recalls, took it to 3,050m (10,000ft) in four minutes and 25 seconds. The lightness of control and positive response made Furies a pilot's dream; 'Very easy to aerobat,' says Squadron Leader Plinston, 'and easy to land, but of course they had to be flown all the time.' Its great range of speed and the instant throttle response of the Kestrel engine made the Fury a fine formation flying aircraft, and RAF squadrons, only six of which were ever equipped with the Fury, took advantage accordingly. Sixteen-plane tied-together formations were a favourite sight at pre-war air displays at Hendon, where entire squadrons of Furies were able to change formation within the airfield boundary, such was the aeroplane's agility.

Three pilots from 'C' Flight of No 25 Squadron based at Hawkinge, Kent, performed the first ever formation roll in Furies. Indeed such was the machine's aerobatic potential that it was difficult not to succumb to the desire to loop or roll it.

The Fury's armament consisted of a pair of 0.303in Vickers machine guns mounted in the nose top decking and firing through the propeller disc by means of the reliable old Constantinesco interrupter gear first put into service during World War I. The guns were fired by two thumb-triggers on the control column grip, though no RAF Fury ever fired a single one of its 600 rounds of ammunition in anger. 'I did one armament course and managed to get reasonable scores on the drogue, but with only two Vickers guns one had to get fairly close and shoot in short bursts to hit anything,' says Squadron Leader Plinston, whose only 'incident' while serving on Furies occurred when he collided with a puffin on a low-level flight off Flamborough Head, Yorkshire, and the bird carried away his pitot head, depriving him of an airspeed reading. 'Since we always flew by the seat of our trousers in those days it didn't really matter,' he adds.

The Fury's guns provided the means by which newcomers to No 25 Squadron were given a chilling initiation, as Wing Commander Nesbitt-Dufort explains: 'Invariably a day or so after his arrival in the squadron, a newly posted pilot officer would stagger white-faced into the Mess, order a large brandy and, having downed it and probably another, say shakily, "I know none of you chaps will ever believe me, but I have just landed from a flight during which an empty Fury flew in close formation with me." Whereupon a senior flying officer would

slowly lower his newspaper, glare at the young pilot, who in any case shouldn't have opened his mouth until he was spoken to, and remark, severely, "For your information, as it is flown by the spirit of a dead pilot, we never discuss the Phantom in the Mess; do try to remember that in future."

'The newcomer would mumble a confused apology and maintain an awed silence until much later in the day when eventually another junior officer would take pity on him and, having quietly led him into a corner, let him into the secret.

'Like all good illusions it was really very simple. Immediately above the breeches of the guns were two little flaps which had to be raised when it was necessary to change the locks. One of the squadron pilots, while clearing a stoppage in his port gun, discovered that by dropping the adjustable seat down to the bottom of its travel and sticking his head well below the level of the front edge of the cockpit cowling, he could peer out through the open flap and see just enough to formate on another aircraft and remain invisible himself.

Having stalked his victim in this position he would move up into tight formation and draw attention to himself by snapping back the throttle, which produced the characteristic popping from the engine. The new boy would hear this and on looking round find to his horror an apparently empty Fury in close formation with him. The resulting panicky peel-off . . . was invariably spectacular.'

Above: four Furies were bought by the Spanish in 1935 and widely used by the Republicans in the Civil War.
Left: the Intermediate Fury of 1932 was used to test the supercharged 640 hp Kestrel IVS engine, wheel spats, Vee interplane struts, tapered wings and Messier undercarriage legs

*'It was its manoeuvrability, loop, roll, climb and dive capability
which impressed us most.'*
Lt Gen Ira C. Eaker

Boeing P-26

The Boeing P-26 single-seat fighter first came into the US Army Air Corps inventory early in 1934. It was the successor to the P-12, also produced by the Boeing Aircraft Company of Seattle, Washington and the United States' standard fighter for several years previously.

The P-26 and its successor the P-26A were designed to meet a specification which stipulated a gross weight of 1,340 kg (2,955 lb), a maximum speed of 377 km/h (234 mph) at 2,130 m (7,000 ft), a service ceiling of 8,350 m (27,400 ft) and a range of 580 km (360 miles). The P-26A was powered by a 500 hp Pratt & Whitney R-1340-27 engine. Pilots of my organisation, the 17th Pursuit Group, and I flew our 78 P-26s from the factory to our

station, March Field, California, 640 km (400 miles) to the south. We were immediately impressed and delighted with its many advanced characteristics in performance and maintenance. Its low wing permitted excellent forward visibility, while its toe pedal brakes shortened the landing roll greatly. However, it was its manoeuvrability, loop, roll, climb and dive capability which impressed us most. It was also a better gun platform, with improved target visibility for its two 0·3 in machine guns, firing through the propeller disc.

Our base at March Field was frequently covered by low clouds, especially in winter and spring. This interrupted our frequent schedule for ground and tow target practice as our firing range was over the

Right: with its operational service confined to the inter-war years, the P-26 was commonly finished in the olive drab and chrome yellow colour scheme prevalent in the early 1930s. The aircraft illustrated is a P-26A of the 34th Pursuit Squadron, one of the units comprising Major Ira Eaker's 17th Pursuit Group. The author was greatly impressed on first acquaintance with the 'Peashooter' in early 1934

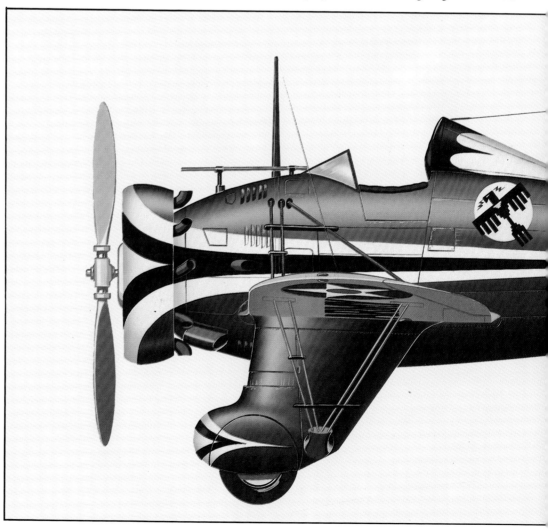

Right: an unusual view of the Boeing P-26A's cockpit from the aircraft's rear fuselage. While considerably more complex than that of a World War I scout, the instrument display still grouped engine and flight gauges together in the upper panel. Armament, fuel and light controls had been relegated to the smaller panel between the rudder pedals. The pilot sat high in the open cockpit, protected from injury in the event of a crash by a steel tripod, retrospectively fitted behind the seat in case of turn-over

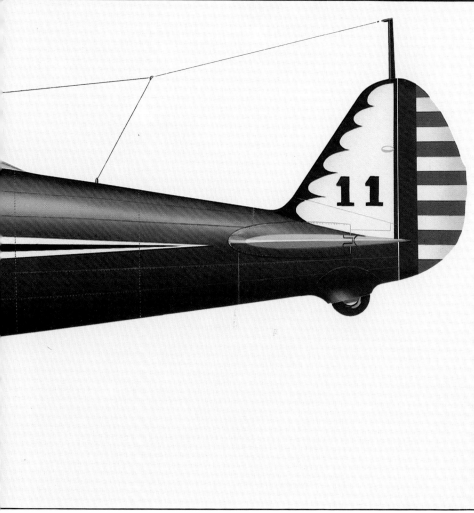

mountains in the Mojave Desert some 160 km (100 miles) distant. This problem was soon solved when we developed a 'baby-buggy' type of cockpit canopy. After a few hours of blind flying practice I could lead a flight of six aeroplanes through several thousand feet of cloud cover, into blue sky and clear the coast range *en route* to desert gunnery ranges.

It was necessary for the formation leader to close the cockpit canopy shortly after take-off and before entering the cloud cover, since clouds blowing over a wing gave the impression that the plane was turning in that direction, resulting in over-controlling and an eventual spin. Under the canopy, relying entirely on the turn and bank indicator, compass and airspeed indicator, flight at any desired rate of climb could be maintained without difficulty. The remaining pilots of the flight needed no canopy, flying formation with the leader and keeping their wings level with his.

The P-26A, although the best the state of the art could produce at the time, was not suitable for combat even in the early stages of World War II. It was, however, an essential intermediate fighter type and was invaluable in the training of the fighter pilots of that period, many of whom became the aces and squadron and group commanders of World War II. It was with the P-26A, with its low wing, that we developed the 'stepped down' rather than the 'stepped up' formations. The two-plane flights, stepped down and back, were also developed, which became standard in the war years.

There was, at first, a slight increase in fatalities in fighter groups equipped with the P-26A. When the aeroplane turned over in landing crashes, pilots were sometimes crushed, since their necks and heads

BOEING P-26

protruded above the cockpit. This was partially alleviated by a steel tripod behind the pilot's seat, designed to bear the aircraft's weight in case of turn-over. All wartime low-wing single-seaters incorporated this feature as a result of the P-26A pilots' experiences.

The armament in the P-26A was, of course, completely inadequate for combat, although one 0·5 in gun eventually replaced one of the 0·3s in later models. It was only when more powerful engines became available that 6 and 8 guns could be carried by fighters and most of these could be housed in the wing, where they fired outside the propeller disc. These more powerful engines also made it possible to include some protective armour in wartime fighters.

All of us who learned our fighter tactics – how to fly and shoot – in the little P-26A weighing only 2,900 lb and powered by a 500 hp engine with no supercharger, always had a real nostalgia for this little toy with which we grew to the maturity and experience required for air battles against the Luftwaffe's Focke Wulf Fw 190 and the Japanese Zero.

Right: a P-26 'Peashooter' awaits flight at Langley Air Force Base, Virginia.
Below: a formation of P-26s of the 95th Pursuit Squadron, 17th Pursuit Group

'…its remarkable steadiness and solidness when eight machine guns crashed into life made it an absolute delight to fly.'
Wg Cdr R.R. Stanford Tuck

Hawker Hurricane

The Hurricane's pilot was seated high in the fuselage; his view over the nose during taxying, take-off and landing was good, despite the size of the engine. The strong, wide-track undercarriage made the Hurricane stable during take-off and landing and able to operate from rough grass airfields, an ability first demonstrated by the RAF Hurricane units operating in France in 1939–40. This factor contributed greatly to the operational flexibility of the Hurricane and its continued use on other roles after it was outclassed as a day fighter

On 11 September 1940, I flew up to Martlesham Heath from Biggin Hill to take over command of No 257 Squadron, which was flying Hurricanes, and was greeted on the tarmac by my old friend Flt Lt Pete Brothers, who was one of the flight commanders. I bade farewell to my lovely Spitfires which I had flown for some 1,000 hours and walked over to my new Hurricane with Pete, who was going to fill me in on the cockpit drill and flying characteristics. Strangely enough, I had never been very close to a Hurricane before, let alone sat in the cockpit. Hurricane P4190 sat there on its wide, sturdy undercarriage, with its slightly down-sloping nose and humpbacked fuselage giving it a slightly hunched, crouching appearance. I was not very impressed, as it looked like a great sturdy carthorse compared with my Spit, which was like a racing thoroughbred.

After walking around it for five minutes, with Pete pointing out various aspects and characteristics, I said 'OK, let's get in the office' and jumped into the cockpit, with Pete leaning in to tell me the layout. I was impressed, as it was roomy and the instruments and various switches, taps and controls came to hand easily. After half an hour or so, I

rehearsed the take-off and landing procedures and was then ready to go. As I roared across the grass of the Martlesham runway, I liked very much the better forward vision over the sloping nose, and particularly the sturdiness of the rugged wide undercarriage. I climbed away over Harwich and at about 3,300 m (10,000 ft) started to fling it about to get the feel of it.

In spite of my first-sight impressions of it, as I dived, climbed, looped, rolled, stalled, spun and did everything I knew with it, I became aware of its virtues. The Hurricane, I decided, was solid and it was obvious she'd take a lot of punishment. She was as steady as a rock, even going fast downhill, and was a very impressive gun platform, having good forward visibility. The two banks of four guns were mounted closely together, each just firing clear of the propeller arc. She hardly shuddered when the eight Brownings blasted off, but it was a different story later when four 20 mm Hispanos were mounted in it, and later still, two 40 mm cannon which were used for tank-busting in North Africa.

After four days of intensive flying with my new

Above: R. R. Stanford Tuck, officer commanding No 257 Squadron, flies low over a Dornier Do 17 bomber which fell to his guns. Although outperformed by the German Messerschmitt Bf 109E fighter in the Battle of Britain, the Hurricane was used successfully against German bomber formations. The Hurricane's original armament of eight 0·303 in Browning machine guns proved ineffective against armour and a twelve gun wing was introduced.

Opposite top right: the Hurricane's cockpit was comparatively roomy and uncluttered. The flap and undercarriage lever was located in an H-gate on the right of the seat. The throttle lever was worked in a slot in the side decking shelf to the pilot's left. Mixture control was fully automatic and there was no pilot control lever

pilots, I took the whole squadron off from Martlesham on our first operational 'Scramble' on 15 September at 1445 hours. At 6,700 m (22,000 ft) over south-east London, and on instruction from the ground controller, we were climbing hard at almost full throttle, when I saw the large enemy formation we had been vectored onto some 900 m (3,000 ft) above me and with the sun in their favour. It consisted of a large number of Heinkel He 111, Junkers Ju 88 and Dornier Do 17 bombers; above them flew a milling mass of Messerschmitt escort fighters.

While I was summing up the situation, with my Hurricanes getting a little strung out as I was forced to climb so hard, I felt a quick flash of anger that we had not been scrambled a few minutes earlier. Had this been the case, we would not be in the unenviable position of climbing to the attack of a heavily-escorted bomber formation with the critical factors of the sun in our eyes and a low closing speed on our targets. However, the one redeeming feature of the situation was that the large enemy bomber formation, probably 60 or 70 aircraft, was restricted in its speed to the slowest of the three types, the He 111, which was leading the formation. This necessitated both the closely-escorting Bf 110 fighters and the higher Bf 109 fighters weaving about to contain themselves to the speed of the great gaggle of the bomber formation.

As I closed in to the rear of the bombers from below, I had reached the same altitude as them and called those of my pilots who had managed to keep up with me into as near line abreast as they could manage, but with a quick glance both sides, I saw that only seven or eight had been able to stay and

pull up into position. Among them I recognised my number two Carl Capon, Pete Brothers, David Coke, Farmer, Lazoryk and Franik Surma; I could not have wished for more sterling characters alongside me, but would have liked far more–it looked a pitifully thin line. We kept out throttles as far open as possible, as every second we gained in delivering our attack would make our interception a few hundred yards farther from the packed city.

The German fighters, above and on either side of their bombers, had seen us coming up very nearly all the way; as we were closing in behind their charges, the Bf 109s picked their moment, peeled off and came screaming down astern of the Junkers and Heinkels. The eight of us were now hauling up fast behind our targets, but if there was to be any hope of hitting the bombers we had to keep going straight at them and as long as possible until it was critical to take evasive action from the Bf 109s dropping down on us.

I had just lined up on a Junkers Ju 88 in the middle of the rear formation, but was still out of range when a Bf 109 above and behind me opened up and tracer stabbed past my aircraft. There was a bang in the cockpit–a bullet had shattered the side panel of the windscreen. There was nothing to do but slam the stick hard over and turn in towards him in a steep turn, as he flashed past going very fast. My number two, Carl Capon, weaved behind me and kept station perfectly. With Carl weaving furiously behind me, I saw below me and to my left the great phalanx of German bombers ploughing ahead. Fortunately, the rest of the formation of my Hurricanes was now joining battle, together with the Spitfires, slicing in like a school of sharks.

Already there were streams of black smoke coming back from one or two of the bombers, and the whole of the rear of their formation was starting to weave about, which indicated their first break-up; above all this, the higher Bf 109s escorting them were diving down towards them. As my eyes scanned again, I saw that Farmer had joined us, and then straight ahead I saw about 20 Bf 110s turning steeply in from the flank, going to the aid of the bomber formation. Fortunately, we had height advantage and turned rapidly down onto them; this time three of us had the sun behind us. I picked out a Bf 110 closing rapidly, quickly glanced down to the turn and bank needle, 250 yards, pushed the fire button and lumps flew off the Bf 110, which tumbled from its formation and burst into flames.

Capon and Farmer were also busy. From the worst possible situation at the commencement of this attack, we had achieved what is in fighter pilots' jargon 'the perfect bounce'—out of the sun and surprise. At once, the rest of the formation began to weave restlessly, some skidding wildly sideways and almost colliding with their neighbours, some pulling up in an attempt to gain altitude and others diving blindly; a few more continued on resolutely to protect their main formation. Within seconds the whole pattern of the great marching phalanx was disintegrating. I felt happy, if one could call it that

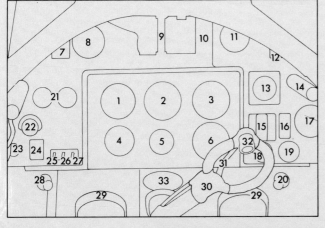

Hawker Hurricane cockpit

1: *Airspeed indicator* **2**: *Artificial horizon* **3**: *Rate of climb indicator* **4**: *Altimeter* **5**: *Direction indicator* **6**: *Turn and bank indicator* **7**: *Undercarriage indicator switches* **8**: *Undercarriage indicator position* **9**: *Reflector gunsight position* **10**: *Spare lamps for reflector sight* **11**: *Engine speed indicator* **12**: *Gunsight master switch* **13**: *Boost gauge* **14**: *Cockpit light* **15**: *Oil pressure gauge* **16**: *Fuel pressure gauge* **17**: *Fuel contents gauge* **18**: *Oil temperature gauge* **19**: *Radiator temperature gauge* **20**: *Priming pump* **21**: *Oxygen regulator control* **22**: *Boost control cut-out* **23**: *Engine starter* **24**: *Magneto switches* **25**: *Pitot head heat switch* **26**: *Navigation lights switch* **27**: *Gun camera switch* **28**: *Supercharger control* **29**: *Rudder pedals* **30**: *Control column* **31**: *Brake lever* **32**: *Machine gun firing button* **33**: *Compass*

HAWKER HURRICANE

A Hurricane Mark II, preserved in flying order by the RAF Battle of Britain Flight is painted to represent a Mark I flown by Douglas Bader when commanding officer of No 242 Squadron. During October and September 1940 the Squadron flew as part of the Duxford Wing, comprising between three and five squadrons, a formation largely instigated by Bader and led by him. Although the wing concentrated 60 aircraft for a mass interception, the formation took time to assemble and was unwieldy to control

in those sort of circumstances, but the affair was going surprisingly well.

This all took place in a matter of seconds, and our piece of sky at 22,000 feet over south-east London was full of Hurricanes, Spitfires, Heinkels, Dorniers and Junkers diving, turning and twisting. Capon and Farmer were still with me, so we cast around rapidly for the next. I swung around again after an He 111, with the others following, overhauled him quickly in a shallow dive, and was just lining up and checking sight, when a Bf 109 came slicing down almost vertically like an arrow out of the sun. I saw him coming just as either Carl or Farmer yelled 'watch out – up-sun coming down fast'. He was firing furiously with what he thought a sure kill, but I executed a tight skidding turn towards him and he went plummeting down past us.

'After him, Carl' I yelled, as Carl was already peeling over in pursuit. Farmer and I turned the opposite way, climbing for height up-sun. I'd crossed off the Heinkel which was my original target, and was looking hard for the number two of the Bf 109 which Carl was after. A split second later we saw it streaming down towards Carl and his target. I swung into a rapid diving turn towards it. All of us were going down fast; from my shattered windscreen side panel a solid jet of ice-cold air was blasting at me and the noise was terrific, but apart from this all seemed well. My target suddenly realised the trap it was in and pulled sharply out of his dive, and in doing so came into my sights as obligingly as a homing pigeon to its loft. Check, turn and bank – a little deflection, and my guns crashed out in a long burst. The Bf 109 rolled smoothly onto its back and then went down vertically, streaming smoke.

I reckoned I had a few seconds more ammunition, pulled up steeply from my dive and went into a medium turn; I looked around for another enemy aircraft, but the battle was over. With astonishing suddenness the sky was empty of all other aircraft. British and German machines had scattered, vanishing in what seemed an instant. After the whirling, twisting confusion, there was a tremendous stillness. All that was left were the tangled filigreed vapour trails, a few smears of oil smoke and a single parachute away to the south, floating tranquilly down into the motionless haze of the great Thames valley.

At this stage I did not know what our casualties were, but I felt sure that No 257 Squadron (the 'Burma Boys') had acquitted themselves well. I put my nose down and headed for base in a long steady dive through the haze, but every few moments doing a gentle turn to look behind and above. Back at base, I learned from Geoff Miles, my Intelligence Officer, that No 257 Squadron had been credited with the destruction of five machines without loss. My ground crew stencilled two more swastikas on my aircraft. That was one of the most important days of my life. It was the day that No 257 Squadron, flying Hurricanes, really became a squadron.

After this first day's combat with my new Squadron in the Hurricane serialled V6555, code-letters DT-A, my first impressions of this magnificent aircraft were completely wiped out, as I realised the sterling qualities of its handling. It had not a vice in its whole make-up. Its wonderful visibility forward over the nose, considering the

great Rolls-Royce Merlin engine in front, and its remarkable steadiness and solidness when the eight machine guns crashed into life made it an absolute delight to fly, but I would have liked more speed. I felt sure that if under heavy attack, it was capable of taking tremendous punishment and this later proved to be the case.

In April 1941 No 257 Squadron was re-equipped with the Hurricane Mark IIC, armed with four 20 mm cannon, and in which I nearly shot myself down. I was carrying out some air-to-ground firing trials, and for this purpose the aircraft was fitted with a container of powdered aluminium which, when dropped on a calm sea, burst and left a bright shiny patch on the surface. Off the Norfolk coast, I duly dropped my aluminium marker on a bright calm morning, banked, and climbed away, and from about 900 m (3,000 ft) saw my shiny patch sitting on the water nice and clear. I had done this several times before, which probably accounts for my casualness on this occasion and the resultant mistake a few seconds later.

Being a very sunny day, I switched my reflector gunsight to 'bright', turned and dived steeply down on to the aluminium marker. Steadying up and checking skid, when the bead was on target I pressed the firing button and the four 20 mm cannon crashed into life. I was spot on target and great showers of spray shot up. I had been over-casual in the angle of my dive, but was fascinated at the fire-power of the four cannon and continued to dive too low. Pulling out at the last minute, far too low for safety, as I climbed away I was astonished to see what I took to be red tracer shooting up in front of my nose very close. It was the cannon shells ricocheting off the surface of the water! As I levelled off and turned back to the coast, breathing a little deeply, I suddenly saw the humour in the incident.

On 21 June 1941, I was flying on a routine patrol and had gone as far as Southend without seeing anything. It was a beautiful clear day, so I flew a wide arc out to sea off the east coast. All I could see were great white clouds and the calm sea stretching to the horizon in all directions. It was very peaceful, calm and restful with the strong sunlight pouring into the cockpit. I must have day-dreamed a little, because suddenly there was an appalling crashing sound in the cockpit as a heavy blast struck me from astern. I pulled up quickly and was immediately hit again from the left. My left hand was suddenly numbed and my arms jarred as the whole throttle quadrant was blown out of my hand. The reflector sight plate exploded and a chip lodged in my forehead between my helmet and goggles. The side door and hood blew off with a great roar, the engine was misfiring badly and I had no throttle.

A few seconds later the engine was spluttering and cutting out, and temperatures were climbing fast. The radio was dead and speed falling off rapidly. Oil and glycol drenched my legs, but somehow the aircraft stumbled on. It was astonishing that the machine stayed in the air at all after the punishment it had taken. It seemed that the airframe could stand almost anything.

After a few more moments, desperately staggering back to the coast, the starboard aileron broke

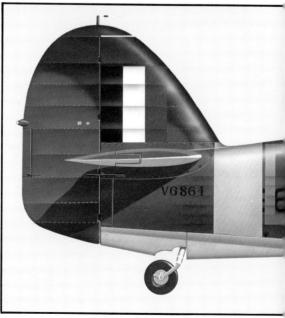

Above: a Hurricane formates with a Supermarine Spitfire Mk I. When possible during the Battle of Britain a Hurricane squadron attacked the German bomber formations, while a Spitfire squadron protected them by tackling the bombers' escort fighters. Right: Hurricane Mk I flown by Sqn Ldr R. R. Stanford Tuck. Tuck was at first unimpressed by the Hurricane, but he rapidly came to appreciate its manoeuvrability, steadiness as a gun platform and ability to absorb heavy battle damage.

Above right: several Hurricanes on the civil register have been used for air racing and displays since World War II, often painted in RAF colours

off and disappeared astern, white smoke and flames started to appear at the bottom of the cockpit under the dashboard. I baled out, shed my boots and 'chute and got my punctured dinghy inflated. I was in the dinghy for two hours before being picked up by a coal barge from Gravesend, and was kept fully occupied getting the chips of glass out of my forehead, staunching the blood and baling out the dinghy. I trailed my left hand in the water, as when I baled out the parachute lines had somehow slipped through the palm of my hand, causing painful blisters. I had been attacked by three Bf 109s, but had had the satisfaction of sending two of them crashing into the sea.

I have related the above incident not merely to describe an aerial combat, but to indicate the tremendous sturdiness of this great aircraft, the Hurricane. Many years later, I was to have the sad honour of writing an obituary to the designer of this magnificent aircraft, Hawker Aircraft's brilliant Sir Sydney Camm.

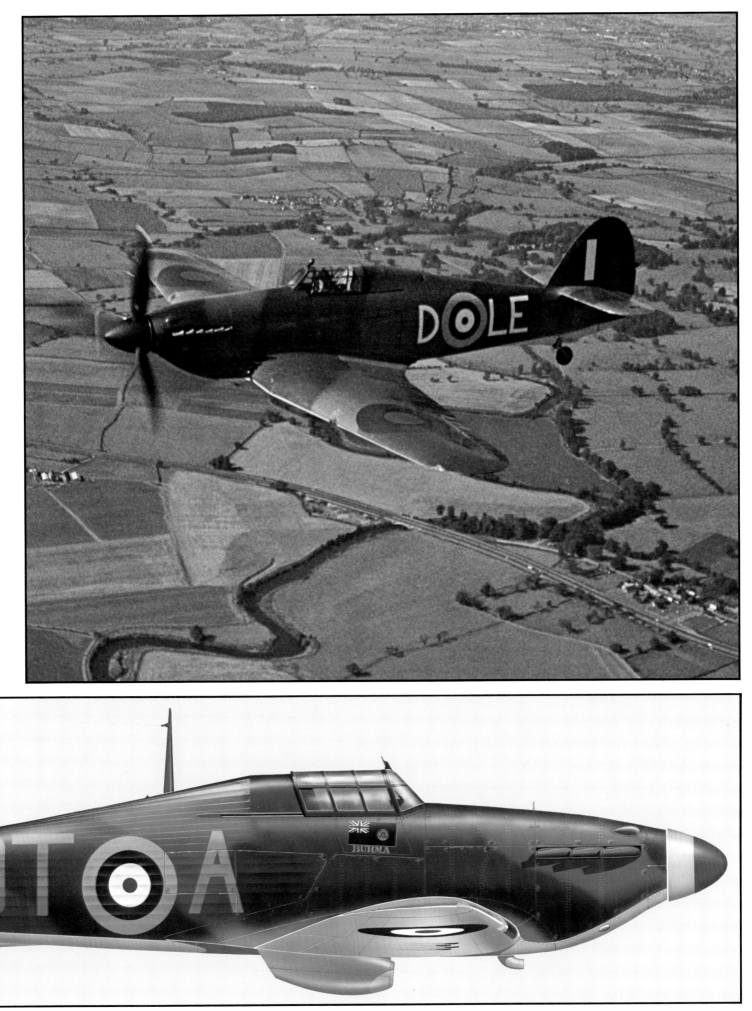

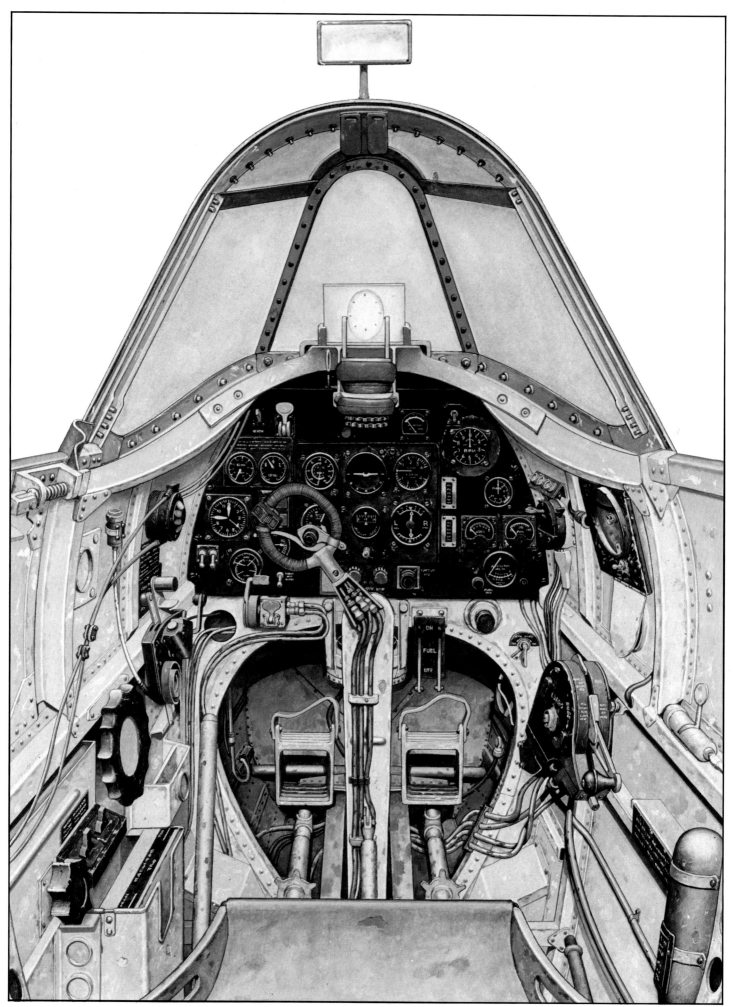

'The Spitfire's superior rate of turn would get you out of trouble – if you saw your attacker in time.'
AVM J.E. Johnson

Supermarine Spitfire

When, in August 1940, I flew the Supermarine Spitfire for the first time I had a total of 180 flying hours in Tiger Moths and Miles Master trainers. My instructor walked me round the lean fighter 'plane, drab in its grey-green camouflage, and explained the flight-control system. Then I climbed into the cockpit while he stood on the wing-root and spoke about the various instruments, and the emergency procedure for getting the undercarriage down. I was oppressed by the narrow cockpit and said that it seemed far more confined than the Master, especially when the hood was closed. 'You'll soon get used to it,' he replied. 'You'll find there is plenty of room to keep turning your head when the 109s are about, and get a stiff neck from looking behind. Otherwise you won't last long!' With this boost to my morale we pressed on.

He told me to start her up. I carried out the correct drill and the Merlin surged into life with its booming song of power–a sound no Spitfire pilot will easily forget. The instructor bellowed into my ear: 'You're trimmed for take-off. Don't forget your fine pitch, or you'll never get off the ground! Good luck.' He sauntered away with a nonchalant air, but I knew he would watch my landing and take-off with critical eyes.

I trundled awkwardly over the grass, swinging the Spitfire from side to side with brakes and bursts of throttle. This was very necessary, for the long nose made forward vision impossible, and more than one pupil had recently collided with other aeroplanes or vehicles. I reached the boundary of Hawarden airfield and made the final cockpit check. I swung her nose gently into the wind. With the throttle firmly open to about four pounds of boost, she accelerates very quickly, much faster than the Master. I push the stick forward to lift the tail, and get a good airflow over the elevators, and correct a tendency to swing with coarse rudder. We become airborne, already climbing into the sky, wheels up. Pitch control back and throttle set to give a climbing speed of 320 km/h (200 mph). After

---

Supermarine Spitfire cockpit

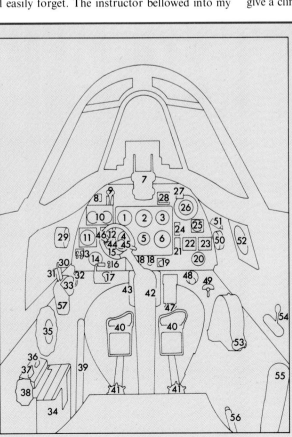

1: *Airspeed indicator* 2: *Artificial horizon* 3: *Rate of climb indicator* 4: *Altimeter* 5: *Direction indicator* 6: *Turn and bank indicator* 7: *Reflector gunsight* 8: *Navigation lights switch* 9: *Flap control* 10: *Oxygen regulator panel* 11: *Clock* 12: *Undercarriage position indicator* 13: *Main magneto switches* 14: *Brake pressure gauge* 15: *Elevator trim tab indicator* 16: *Landing lights switch* 17: *Landing light lowering control* 18: *Cockpit light dimmer switches* 19: *Engine starter button* 20: *Fuel contents gauge* 21: *Oil pressure gauge* 22: *Oil temperature gauge* 23: *Radiator temperature gauge* 24: *Fuel pressure gauge* 25: *Boost gauge* 26: *Engine speed indicator* 27: *Generator switch* 28: *Voltmeter* 29: *Wireless remote controller* 30: *Thrtottle control lever* 31: *Mixture control lever* 32: *Airscrew control lever* 33: *Undercarriage horn cutout* 34: *Map storage box* 35: *Elevator trim tab control* 36: *Gun camera master switch* 37: *Pitot head heat switch* 38: *Rudder trim control* 39: *Radiator flap lever* 40: *Rudder pedals* 41: *Rudder control adjustment wheels* 42: *Control column* 43: *Compass* 44: *Brake lever* 45: *Gun camera button* 46: *Machine gun firing button* 47: *Fuel tank cock controls* 48: *Primer pump* 49: *Fuel tank pressurisation control* 50: *Signalling switchbox* 51: *Spare lamps for reflector sight* 52: *wireless remote contactor* 53: *Undercarriage control lever* 54: *Pilot's release harness* 55: *Fire extinguisher* 56: *Seat adjustment lever* 57: *Engine controls friction adjuster*

SUPERMARINE SPITFIRE

a struggle, during which the nose rose and fell, like the flight of a jay, I closed the perspex canopy and the cockpit seemed more restricted than before. I thought about flying with the hood open, but one could not fly or fight in this fashion.

I made an easy turn and tried to pick up my bearings. Not more than four or five minutes since take-off, we were already more than twenty miles from the airfield. A few barrel rolls; a slow roll to port, and another to starboard; a loop, a roll off the top. A Master looms ahead; I overtake him, oozing confidence, attempt an upward roll. However, I forgot to allow for the heavy nose of the Spitfire with sufficient forward movement of the stick and slop out of the attempted manoeuvre, losing an undignified amount of height.

Over Hawarden again. Throttle back, and join the circuit at 300 m (1,000 ft). Hood open. All clear ahead. Wheels down, and curve her across wind. Flaps, and a final turn into the wind, 177 km/h (110 mph) on the approach, and we are too high. Throttle back, and she drops like a stone. More power to clear the boundary at 160 km/h (100 mph); too fast. Stick back, and head over the side to judge the landing. Too high. Eventually we drop out of the sky and hit the unyielding ground with a hefty smack. The instructor, nonchalance gone, was waiting: 'I saw the Spit get you into the air, and given a fair chance she would have made a better landing than yours! If you make a mess of your approach, open up and go round again. You've been told that since you began flying. Get into the front seat of that Master and I'll show you a Spitfire circuit!'

A few days later, with less than twenty Spitfire hours I joined No 616 (South Yorkshire) Squadron of the Auxiliary Air Force at Coltishall, Norfolk; they had been in the front line, at Kenley, but had lost more than half their pilots in a few days, and were at Coltishall to train replacement pilots like me. This was a lucky break, because I could hardly fly the Spitfire properly and had I joined the squadron at Kenley I would not have lasted long against Messrs Galland, Mölders, Wick and Co.

Our Spitfire Mark Is (1,030 hp Rolls-Royce Merlin) with their eight 0·303 in Browning machine guns, had a ceiling of about 9,750 m (32,000 ft).

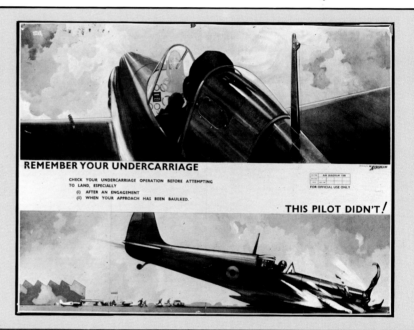

Left: two pages from the Pilot's Notes for the Spitfire Marks IX, XI and XVI. Right: a Spitfire Mk II (left) and a Hawker Hurricane Mk II preserved by the RAF Battle of Britain Flight. Below left: an information poster often seen in wartime crew rooms. A wheels-up landing invariably resulted in a 'written-off' Spitfire. Red indicator tabs protruded through the wing upper surfaces above each wheel well, when the undercarriage was lowered and locked. Below: the Spitfire Mk IX flown by 'Johnnie' Johnson when he commanded the Canadians in the Kenley Wing. Previous pages: Frank Wootton's painting depicts Douglas Bader's Spitfire Mark VA in combat with a brace of Messerschmitt Bf 109s. As commander of the Tangmere Wing, Bader was quick to notice Johnson's potential in his early operations

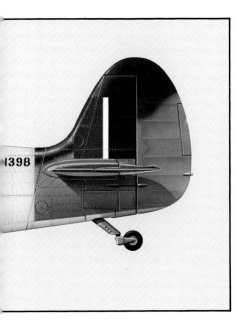

The Messerschmitt Bf 109E, our principal opponent, had a higher ceiling and better guns than either the Spitfire or the Hurricane, and the Bf 109F, which was soon to make its debut over England, had one cannon firing through the hub of the airscrew so that the pilot had a great advantage of aiming and firing along his line of flight. Our Spitfires were more manoeuvrable, but manoeuvring does not win air battles, and tight turns are more of a defensive than an offensive tactic. The Spitfire's superior rate of turn would get you out of trouble–if you saw your attacker in time. On balance the Bf 109F was a slightly better fighting aeroplane than the Spitfire Mark I.

One year later I was still with the South Yorkshire Squadron. We had switched from the defensive fighting of the Battle of Britain to offensive fighter sweeps and bomber escorts over France and the Low Countries. Air fighting was tougher in 1941 because we were always flying over hostile territory and apart from the Bf 109s, had to contend with the light and heavy flak, and a two-way Channel, or North Sea, crossing on each mission.

Our losses testified to the intensity of the fighting. Douglas Bader, our wing leader, had been shot down in August 1941 and was a prisoner of war. Bob Tuck, of Biggin Hill fame, was also 'in the bag'. We, in No 616, had lost no fewer than 17 pilots during the season's fighting. Some were prisoners of war, a few evaded capture and made dangerous journeys back home, aided by courageous men and women of the Resistance, but the majority had been killed in the cauldron of the Pas de Calais. On the credit side we had accounted for a fair number of 109s and, thanks largely to Bader, the squadron was a far better fighting unit than in 1940. It now had a panache, style and toughness, and rated with the best in Fighter Command.

I had some 380 Spitfire hours, had flown 66 operational missions over Europe, had been pro-

SUPERMARINE SPITFIRE

*Below: Spitfire Mark Is of No 610
Squadron patrol in 'vics' of three
aircraft during the Battle of Britain.
The vic formation was soon replaced by
the more flexible 'finger four'.
Inset right: the 360 degree 'bubble'
cockpit canopy greatly improved
rearward vision from the Spitfire.
Inset below: the cockpit of a Seafire
FR Mark XVII naval recce fighter.
Inset below right: Spitfire trainers
appeared late in the fighter's career*

moted to flight lieutenant and commanded 'B'
Flight. Whaley Heppell – a 20-year-old from New-
castle who had an ice-cold combat temperament –
and I had just been awarded the Distinguished
Flying Cross. We began the 1941 season with
Spitfire Mark IIs, and their constant-speed airscrews increased both speed and ceiling. Our
armament, however, still consisted of eight 0.303 in
machine guns – a calibre of weapon probably pretty
good in World War I, but useless for our contest.

However, some Fighter Command squadrons
were re-equipping with the Spitfire Marks VA and
VB. The engine of the Mark V was only slightly
bigger than that of our IIs, and consequently there
was little difference in performance. The VA still
had the dear old 0.303s, but the VB had, at last, two

20mm cannon and four machine guns. Another
important difference between the Spitfire Mark II
and the Mark V was that the former had fabric
ailerons whilst the latter had an improved metal
type. In the air the difference was quite remarkable,
for the previous heavy stick-pressures were greatly
reduced and the rate of roll, at high speeds, was more
than doubled. The new ailerons were exactly the
same size and shape as their fabric counterparts.

We heard from Jeffrey Quill, perhaps the greatest
test pilot of his day, that the new ailerons were
being manufactured at Hamble and after various
clandestine meetings, at which higher authority was
not represented, it was arranged, between the
factory and the South Yorkshire Squadron that our
aeroplanes should be flown, one by one, to Hamble
for this essential modification. Various documents
had to be signed when we collected our Spitfires,
which we did with gay abandon.

Naturally, Bader's Spitfire was the first to have
the new ailerons, and a day or so later we bounced a
gaggle of Bf 109s over St Omer. The Messerschmitts

evaded, as usual, by their half-roll and steep dive. Bader tore after them, leaving the rest of the Squadron trying, unsuccessfully, to keep up. Our squadron commander, Billy Burton, called his superior officer to order: 'Douglas, we can't keep up because we haven't all got bloody metal ailerons!'

The Whitehall bureaucracy caught up towards the end of 1942 when I received an official letter demanding an explanation as to why No 616 Squadron had fitted metal ailerons to its Spitfire Mark IIs. Who had authorised the work at Hamble? And who was going to pay? This letter, somehow, vanished, but after several more I replied that doubtless Wing Commander Douglas Bader could throw more light on the matter, and he could be contacted at Stalag Luft III.

The Spitfire Mark IX was 'the best of them all', writes Air Vice-Marshal 'Johnnie' Johnson, who scored all his 38 air victories while flying Spitfires. The aircraft pictured has been restored in the markings of No 130 Squadron RAF at the time of the D-day landings

In the summer of 1942 I was given command of No 610 (County of Chester) Squadron, Auxiliary Air Force, flying Spitfire Mark Vs. We were based at Ludham, hard by Hickling Broad, and our job was convoy patrols of the east coast, enemy shipping reconnaissances off the Dutch coast, a few fighter sweeps and plenty of those deadly Rhubarbs. Rhubarbs were low-level strafing missions over France and the Low Countries. The idea was to take full advantage of low cloud, slip sections of Spitfires across the enemy coast, and then let-down below the cloud to search for opportunity targets– rolling stock, aeroplanes on the ground, enemy transport and troops and the like. They were usually arranged on a voluntary basis, and a very small minority of fighter pilots seemed to prefer this type of individual ground-strafing to the teamwork of air fighting. Most of us thought that the dividends yielded by the numerous Rhubarb operations fell far short of the cost in valuable aeroplanes and trained pilots.

When on such a mission, it always seemed to me that the German light gunners were ready and waiting. Airfields were always well-defended, and it was a dangerous business to try and make more than one low, fast attack. The Germans prepared unpleasant surprises against these operations. Here and there decoy targets were established, such as a stationary locomotive emitting steam that could be seen for miles. The engine and wagons were heavily armoured and ringed by many camouflaged light flak guns, arranged to provide a deadly concentration of fire against our Spitfires.

We took some bad knocks on Rhubarbs, largely because our engines were cooled by a liquid called glycol, held in a small tank just below the spinner. This tank and radiator were always exposed to groundfire, and one hit meant that the engine seized up or caught fire within a matter of minutes. I loathed these missions, and regretted the hundreds of fighter pilots lost on either small or mass Rhubarbs; when I had more authority my strong views were given a sympathetic hearing and they were discontinued, except for very special occasions.

With our two cannon there was little to choose between the Spitfire Mark VB and the Messerschmitt Bf 109F, but when the redoubtable Focke Wulf Fw 190 entered the arena we were completely outclassed, to the extent that we had to curtail our offensive missions; even so, our casualties increased. This splendid fighter aeroplane was faster, had a higher ceiling and, with its four 20mm cannon and two machine guns, completely outclassed our Spitfire Mk Vs. When, soon after the war ended, I flew one of these superb machines I was greatly impressed with its ease of control and its incredible aileron turns at high speeds.

In August 1942, we took part in the ill-fated Dieppe raid, and we flew top cover to a fighter wing consisting of No 485 (New Zealand) Squadron and No 411 (Canadian) Squadron. Our job together with other Spitfire wings, was to maintain an air umbrella over Dieppe–but umbrellas sometimes leak. Briefly, the aim of this combined operation was to get Canadian troops ashore at Dieppe for a few hours to destroy enemy defences, radars, power stations, dock and rail facilities and take prisoners.

On our first patrol, just after dawn, we climbed to our allotted height of 3,000m (10,000ft), and about ten miles from Dieppe I could see a heavy pall of dark smoke over the town. On the radio some Spitfire leader was ordering his pilots to fight their way out, and another reported more enemy fighters approaching from inland.

Ahead of us a mass of aeroplanes milled about the sky. I could see 190s above and my flight commander, Denis Crowley-Milling called the break. We swung round together to find the 190s at our own level, in pairs and fours. A 190 zoomed from below and appeared ahead of my section of four Spitfires. I gave him a long burst, cannon and machine guns, from the maximum range. Surprisingly, it began to smoke; the wheels dropped and it fell into the sea.

The Messerschmitts and Focke Wulfs came down on us from astern and the flanks. They were full of fight, and for the moment I thought only of evasion and staying alive. During a steep turn I caught a glimpse of more German reinforcements flying towards Dieppe from inland, and I called the wing leader, 'Jamie, strong enemy gaggle coming in. About fifty-plus. Over.' Wing Commander 'Jamie' Jameson, a great New Zealander and veteran fighter was also hard at it, but he found time to call No 11 Group and ask for assistance. My own section had been reduced to three Spitfires, and during a lull in the attacks we fastened on to a solitary Bf 109 and sent it spinning down.

Then they came at us again, and we later estimated that we saw well over one hundred enemy fighters. Three of my squadron had already been

With the substitution of a Griffon engine for the Merlin in later marks of Spitfire, the fighter's performance and handling characteristics changed considerably. This was mainly due to the heavier and more powerful power plant and to the airscrew rotating in the opposite direction to that on Merlin-powered Spitfires. A Spitfire PR Mark XIX is illustrated

briefed not to fly below 1,200 m (4,000 ft) over Royal Navy ships otherwise they would open fire. I hoped they would, and ramming the throttle into its emergency position I raced, at sea-level, straight at the destroyer. The sailors, bless them, were true to form. Their flak and tracer came at me, and slower tracer, from the 190 still behind passed over my cockpit. At the last moment I pulled over the destroyer, slammed the nose down, broke hard to the left, and searched for this determined enemy pilot. He was no longer with me. Either the gunners had put him off, or nailed him.

Such was the all-round superiority of the Focke Wulf 190 over our Spitfire Mark Vs. On this day the Luftwaffe bested us in the air fighting, and shot down two of our aeroplanes for every one lost to them. On the broader canvas the Dieppe operation was a complete failure, and the record of the (Canadian) Essex Scottish, who brought back 52 soldiers from a force of 553, gives some indication of the desperate situation on the ground. 'The Dieppe raid', wrote Chester Wilmot, 'yielded bloody warning of the strength of the Atlantic wall.'

In the spring of 1943 the squadron, once more, was based at Tangmere but our fighter penetrations over France were considerably less then when, two years previously, Bader had led the same wing. On one occasion when we were badly bounced by Bf 109s I lost four pilots, and a few days later Reg Grant, a splendid aggressive New Zealander, lost three of his pilots, one of whom was his younger brother. Sometimes I led the Tangmere Wing, and I tried to avoid combat, unless sun and height were in our favour.

We heard that all would be well when we got the new Spitfire Mark IX which, it was said, could hold its own against the Fw 190. I was soon to find out, for in March 1943, with about 1,000 hours on Spitfires and more than 100 offensive sweeps over occupied Europe, I was promoted to wing commander and posted to Kenley to lead Nos 403 and 416 (Canadian) Squadrons with their new Spitfire Mark IXs.

The new 1,600 hp Merlin 61 engine was designed for bombers but it was soon found that it could be housed in an extended Mark V airframe. Individual ejector exhausts were fitted and a four-blade Rotol airscrew absorbed the extra engine power at high altitudes. The supercharger cut in automatically at about 6,000 m (19,000 ft) which gave a top speed of some 660 km/h (410 mph). In short, the Spitfire Mark IX was the best fighting aeroplane of its day. Its great tactical advantage was that, apart from its longer nose and more numerous exhaust stacks, it looked exactly like the inferior Spitfire Mark V, and in the air the Germans would not know the difference – until we hit them.

Because of the poor winter weather the Canadians had not had many combats in their new fighters, but they were an extremely aggressive outfit and, with the advent of spring, were anxious to get at the Fw 190s. Our turn came when, one fine Saturday afternoon, freelancing over the Pas de Calais, John Hunter, a splendid controller, quietly told me that there were twenty plus 'bandits' a few miles away, well below, and he would try and bring us out of the sun. He did just that, and I was able to take the wing in a long slanting dive against two gaggles of Fw

shot down when I saw my own wingman, 'South' Creagh from Australia, planing down towards the sea streaming white glycol from his engine. It was impossible to protect him, for once we took our eyes off the enemy fighters we would get the same treatment. I still had another Spitfire alongside, but I lost him when we broke in opposite directions to face an astern attack.

Once alone, especially in a hostile sky, the golden rule was to get out, because no solitary pilot could search all the sky. I was getting out when I spotted a lone fighter over Dieppe. It was an Fw 190 and since, for once, I was not harried I turned towards him. At the same time he saw me and snaked towards me – head on. He passed a few feet below my Spitfire. We both turned hard to the left, and whirled round on opposite sides of a tight circle.

At this time I was not aware of the 190's turning ability, and drawing on past experience thought that in a couple of turns I would be on his tail for a quick burst and home. But although I held my Spitfire in the tightest of shuddering turns I could not see him ahead. Little wonder for the 190 was gaining on me, and in a couple of turns would have me in his sights!

Not relishing this prospect, I plunged into a near vertical dive, pulled out over the rooftops, turned as tightly as I could and saw the 190 hanging on like a leech. For some seconds we dodged round Dieppe, and I caught a glimpse of stationary tanks on a deserted beach and, offshore, a destroyer surrounded by a clutter of smaller ships.

The Royal Navy, of course, invariably fired first and identified later! Not unnaturally, and especially on this day, they were trigger-happy. We had been

The Spitfire's aileron response was crisp and powerful, especially on the later fighters fitted with metal ailerons. The rate of roll of the clipped-wing variants intended for low-level operation was further improved. The pilot's notes for the Spitfire Mark XIV (illustrated) recommended that rolls be initiated at an indicated airspeed of between 354 km/h (220 mph) and 402 km/h (250 mph). Flick rolls were forbidden

large bunches of enemy fighters and we often saw 50 or more. With more Spitfires than my wing of 24 I reckoned we could destroy more Germans, and I put my case to Air Vice-Marshal 'Ding Bat' Saunders, AOC No 11 Group, who immediately gave permission for me to lead a 'Balbo' comprising the Kenley Wing (two squadrons) and the Hornchurch Wing (three squadrons), a total of 60 Spitfires.

Our large Balbos were not successful. When the controller told me to make fairly large changes of direction to intercept the enemy formations the two wings were difficult to hold together as a balanced striking force. Also, our mass of Spitfires could be seen from afar, and the German leaders simply half-rolled and dived away when they wanted to avoid the issue.

Sometimes I succeeded in bouncing enemy formations, but I found it difficult to control and re-form the Balbo. It was no use taking part in one brief skirmish over France and returning a few minutes later as a disorganised rabble. The Balbo must be kept together as a fighting unit, which seemed impossible to achieve in our fast-moving combats. Both Al Deere of the Biggin Hill Wing and Bill Compton of the Hornchurch Wing led these huge Spitfire formations, but we were soon agreed that they were far too cumbersome for this type of offensive fighting.

The Americans were developing their own force of long-range fighters, and soon the twin-engined Lightnings and sturdy Thunderbolts escorted their bombers far beyond the range of our Spitfires. Sometimes the bombers made long penetrations, beyond the range of their own fighters: it was on some of these operations that the Luftwaffe reacted with great skill and, during one black week, almost 150 bombers were lost together with their crews.

Despite these setbacks, the Americans never lost sight of their goal—the massed daylight bombing of Germany—and eventually attained it through their characteristic energy and perseverance. Bomber formations were increased. Fighters were fitted with long-range tanks, and eventually the Mustang made its debut and could fly as far as the bombers.

So began the Battle of Germany, for us a sort of Battle of Britain in reverse, but of longer duration and greater intensity. Sometimes more than 1,300 bombers supported by 800 Mustangs and Lightnings ranged far and wide over Germany against a German defensive system including 900 fighters, some carrying rockets. Often the Luftwaffe pressed home determined attacks but eventually they were out-numbered and out-fought. The Eighth Air Force won a great victory, for they wrested command of the skies from the Luftwaffe and exposed all Germany to daylight bombing.

Our Spitfires, through lack of offensive thinking in Whitehall, did not have anything like the range of Mustangs. So our contribution to this tremendous contest was to escort the bombers to the Dutch-German border, or during their long withdrawal.

For fighter pilots this, in my view, was the toughest air fighting of World War II. In our small fighters, which could be brought down by a bullet from a machine gun, we had twice to cross the North Sea. Sometimes we had to fly over heavily-defended areas, and when we crossed the Ruhr we faced the

190s. It was a perfect bounce and we hammered six of them in less seconds.

Thus began a long bout of air fighting which, for me, was to last until the autumn of 1943. These six months were the peak of my fighting career, because I far preferred this clean type of fighting to Rhubarbs and beating-up ground targets. Also, I soon discovered, my Canadian fighter pilots were splendid, aggressive, highly-disciplined, well-trained young men. The squadron and flight commanders were veterans and the newcomers averaged at least 50 hours on Spitfires. In our trusty Spitfire IXs we outclassed the opposition.

On most days I led the wing on freelance fighter sweeps, or we escorted RAF bombers over France and the Low Countries. Sometimes we escorted the Boeing B-17 Fortresses of the US Eighth Air Force which, against much advice from our top brass, set out to bomb Germany by day—which task our bombers had found impossible. We liked to support these ever-increasing formations of Fortresses and Liberators, for the enemy saw the writing on the wall and reacted with large, mixed formations of Bf 109s and Fw 190s. We had many combats on these missions and invariably got the better of our opponents.

Sometimes the radar controllers put me on to

greatest concentration of flak in the world. More-over, German civilians began to maltreat and some-times kill Allied airmen who crashed or baled-out.

September 1943 came, and it was more than three years since I joined No 616 Squadron. During the previous six months I had led the Canadian Wing on 120 fighter sweeps and bomber escorts. We had destroyed a satisfactory number of German aeroplanes and my own score was 24—all enemy fighters. I was posted to No 11 Group head-quarters for a rest from operational flying.

During this 'rest' period at No 11 Group head-quarters I flew regularly with various fighter wings, and at Tangmere flew a Spitfire Mark XII which had a 2,000hp Rolls-Royce Griffon engine and clipped wings. At low and medium altitudes the Mark XII was faster than the Mark IX, and its best fighting height was about 3,700m (12,000ft). The wing leader, Ray Harries, explained that he flew between 3,000 and 3,600m (10,000 and 12,000ft) and usually the German formations were above his wing. Then his tactics were to let the enemy leader begin his attack, and at the right moment Ray's men would break into the 190s and out-fight them.

Over France the controller gave Ray various courses to steer, and eventually we were flying below a swarm of Focke Wulf Fw 190s. For a few minutes we flew some 1,500m (5,000ft) below the enemy fighters. Ray followed every move of the Germans and held us below them, and I felt like a lamb being led to the slaughter. However, eventually the Fw 190s made off, and Ray did not have the opportunity to demonstrate his remarkable yet successful tactics.

In the spring of 1944 I was appointed to lead another Canadian Wing equipped with Spitfire Mark IXs, which was classified as a fighter-bomber unit, because in addition to our primary role of air fighting, our Spitfires would be required for strafing and dive-bombing missions during the forthcoming invasion. In June we were the first fighter wing to move into Normandy, which meant that we could range deeper over France in search of the Luftwaffe.

The enemy now began to appear in large for-mations. On one of these occasions we bounced a large gaggle over the River Seine, and I soon got a brace of Fw 190s, the second at low-level. I was alone and since there were a lot of German fighters milling about, I cautiously began to regain height, keeping a very sharp look-out and clearing my tail every few seconds. At 4,300m (14,000ft) I thought I saw six of my Spitfires, slightly above. I called whom I thought to be the leader, and told him that I was just ahead of him and form-up to me.

I learned of my stupid error when the leader of the six Messerschmitts opened fire, and during the subsequent fight—one of the hardest—my Spitfire took a cannon shell in the wing root. Eventually, I managed to throw them off, and on returning found we had destroyed twelve for the loss of three Canadians.

This was the first time I had been hit. The vicious fight had shaken me so, as was the custom, I took to the air in another Spitfire, and when we flew over a strongly-held German position the heavy flak surrounded us. My Spitfire pitched violently when it took a chunk of shrapnel in the

'Johnnie' Johnson is pictured leading the Spitfire Mark IXs of his Canadian Wing in a strafing attack against a Luftwaffe airfield in this painting by Michael Turner. The Spitfire was ill-suited to such missions, as the glycol coolant tank under the nose was especially vulnerable to ground-fire. If this tank was holed, it was only a matter of minutes before the engine seized

SUPERMARINE SPITFIRE

tail unit. She felt sluggish and heavy on the controls, so I staggered back to our airfield and managed to get her down in one piece.

Our trusty Spitfire IXs were suddenly replaced by Spitfire Mark XVIs. The Mark XVI was a close relative of the IX, but it had a Packard-built Merlin engine, and its armament had been improved by replacing the old 0·303s with two Browning 0·5 in machine guns. Soon after this, I began to lose pilots in mysterious circumstances. For example, a pilot flying over Germany would say his engine was on fire and he was bailing out. Sometimes Spitfires exploded in the air without giving the pilot a chance to bail out.

When these losses first occurred I thought the Spitfires had been hit by heavy or light flak, but our casualties increased and sometimes pilots bailed out or crash-landed when we knew they had not encountered either enemy flak or fighters. Eventually it was admitted that this particular batch of Rolls-Royce Merlin engines, built by Packard, was faulty and would be replaced, but with the war drawing to and end it was hard to lose so many of my Canadian pilots in this fashion.

In March 1945, I was promoted to group captain and given the command of No 125 Wing, equipped with three squadrons of the new Spitfire Mark XIVs. 'A nice, fast flying machine but its not a Spitfire any more', was my comment after my first flight in a Spitfire XIV, for the additional power of the 2,050 hp Griffon engine, and the fact that the airscrew rotated in the opposite direction to the Merlin engines made it feel quite different to the earlier models.

Since the Griffon-engined fighter was so different I think it should have had another name. The Spitfire Mark XIV was designed as a high-altitude fighter, but its powerful engine produced a lot of torque, which meant that the aeroplane required constant trimming, especially when manoeuvring. I flew the Mark XIV several times in combat, but I preferred the Mark IX – the best of them all.

The greater power and weight of the Griffon-engined Spitfire Mark XIV enabled it to dive faster than Merlin-engined marks. It retained the tendency to become increasingly tail-heavy as speed was gained and had to be 'trimmed into' a dive. Maximum diving speeds were imposed, above which control became difficult and recovery violent

Fairey Swordfish

Popularly known as the Stringbag, a number of factors contributed to the Swordfish's survival into the monoplane age. Its ability to carry a great weight and variety of ordnance enabled it to be adapted to several roles. It had a very short take-off run which suited it to operations from small escort carriers. It was rugged and dependable and could absorb tremendous battle damage, but, despite being very large and heavy for a biplane, it was highly manoeuvrable, particularly at low speeds, an advantage used to evade fighters

'You don't mean to say you actually fly those things? They look more like four-poster bedsteads than front-line aeroplanes!' said an American naval officer attached to HMS *Illustrious* in 1940 when first he saw her Fairey Swordfish torpedo bombers ranged on her deck. Small wonder, for the US Navy's standard torpedo bomber of the day was the Douglas TBD Devastator, an all-metal monoplane itself already due for replacement by the Grumman TBF Avenger. The British, however, were taking on the German fleet in open-cockpit, fabric-and-wire biplanes.

Compared to most biplanes the Swordfish was a mammoth, standing almost as tall as a double-decker bus on giant undercarriage legs. The airframe was all-metal; the welded steel-tube fuselage was metal clad and armour-plated forward of the cockpit area, with wing and tail surfaces of duralumin and steel, the whole structure being fabric-covered and wire-braced. Mark II versions had a

strengthened lower wing with metal underskinning with hard-points for rocket launchers. It was the Swordfish's remarkable load-carrying capability–torpedoes, bombs or rockets–which earned it the now famous nickname of 'Stringbag' when someone remarked: 'No housewife on a shopping spree could cram a wider variety of articles into her string-bag.'

The engine was a 750 hp Bristol Pegasus nine-cylinder radial driving a fixed-pitch, three-bladed Fairey-Reed propeller of nearly 3.7 m (12 ft) diameter. The Pegasus had an inertia starter whose heavy flywheel had to be spun up to very high speed by a plug-in handcrank. Cheeks puffed, faces scarlet, the deck crews would crank ever faster, energising the flywheel which started the engine by means of reduction gears and clutch. It would take about two minutes to get the Pegasus running and on an icy cold deck out in the Atlantic it was, at least, a good way of keeping warm. The wings had

Above: cockpit fitting and layout varied between Swordfish marks and between aircraft used in different roles. The aircraft illustrated has a radio altimeter and altitude limit setting dial for torpedo attack below the dash board, absent from the cockpit in the artwork (left). The button on the control column hand grip fired the machine gun (if fitted), and released the torpedo, bombs, depth charges, flares or rockets, the options being controlled by a main selector operated by the observer, from his position behind the pilot

The Fairey Swordfish cockpit

1: *Airspeed indicator* 2: *Artificial horizon* 3: *Direction indicator* 4: *Altimeter* 5: *Compass correction card holder* 6: *Compass lamp dimmer switch* 7: *Compass lamp plug* 8: *Compass* 9: *Fire extinguisher button* 10: *Main starting switch* 11: *Engine speed indicator* 12: *Fuel pressure warning indicator* 13: *Engine priming pump* 14: *Oil temperature gauge* 15: *Turn and bank indicator* 16: *Oil pressure gauge* 17: *Cylinder head temperature gauge* 18: *Suction gauge* 19: *Power failure warning light* 20: *Landing light control* 21: *Brake pressure gauge position* 22: *Engine priming pump* 23: *Boost gauge*

24: *Starter lights* 25: *Starter switches* 26: *Engine cut-out* 27: *Oil by-pass valve control* 28: *Carburettor air intake shutter control* 29: *Lighting control box* 30: *Landing light on/off switch* 31: *Fuel mixture control* 32: *Throttle control (with press to transmit radio button)* 33: *VHF radio* 34: *Elevator trim wheel* 35: *Seat height adjustment lever* 36: *Rudder bias trim* 37: *Carburettor de-icing controls* 38: *Arrestor hook release control* 39: *Signalling switch* 40: *Fuel tank selector* 41: *Rudder pedals* 42: *Control column* 43: *Wheel brake lever* 44: *Weapons release button* 45: *Very pistol cartridges*

to be folded back manually, and were locked in flying position by a pair of simple latches at the inboard root position. These could be flipped into place with a couple of fingers, hardly inspiring confidence in those making their first trips.

'You could pull a Swordfish off the deck and put her in a climbing turn at 55 knots', wrote Terence Horsley. Indeed, with a steady wind over the deck a Swordfish would be airborne almost as soon as the throttle was opened, and those flying off short-decked MAC-ships (merchant aircraft carriers) could even be rocket-assisted for near helicopter-like ascents. 'The Stringbag could be very roughly handled in incredible attitudes', says Commander Charles Lamb DSO DSC, 'provided the pilot knew what he was doing. To stall a Swordfish by mistake was almost an impossibility . . . given a stalling speed of 55 knots, and no pilot,

Right: the defensive armament of the Swordfish was a relic of World War I. It consisted of a 0·303 in Lewis machine gun on a Fairey high-speed flexible mounting for the rear gunner, and a fixed forward-firing 0·303 in Vickers machine gun on the right of the pilot's cockpit. Although obsolete as a weapon, the Lewis had an excellent field of fire upwards and rearwards, but the Vickers had limited usefulness and was removed from many Swordfish. However, the Swordfish's manoeuvrability constituted its best means of defence

however ham-handed, could allow his speed to drop to that extent without noticing. To induce it into a spin was quite hard work: the aircraft could be stood on its tail in mid-flight so that it became almost stationary before it would drop into a stalled turn, and then recovery could be instantaneous. Quick application of throttle and opposite rudder, and a speedy lowering of the nose, would provide almost immediate stability . . .'

The Swordfish's astonishing manoeuvrability at low speed was fully exploited in service, where the lumbering biplane was much less of a sitting duck to enemy fighters than it seemed. During the Norwegian Campaign, pilots of the Fleet Air Arm would fly low right up against cliff sides, luring Luftwaffe Messerschmitts into narrow fjords from which the faster, less nimble fighters were unable to escape. A number of enemy aircraft were destroyed in this way.

Defensive armament was not a strongpoint, however. 'Its armament was a pathetic hangover from the First World War', says Commander Lamb, 'The Vickers gun in the front cockpit was fired by the pilot through the propeller, and was all of one stage more advanced than a bow and arrow. The Lewis gun in the rear cockpit, fired either by air gunner or observer, had been very successfully used in the First World War, but was quite valueless in the second. The sensible Swordfish pilot ignored these weapons and put his faith in his ability to out-manoeuvre the other man. Given enough height and

space in which to throw the aircraft about, the Stringbag could outfly almost every other aircraft, with the possible exception of the Gloster Gladiator.'

The rear cockpit was occupied by an observer and telegraphist-air gunner, who endured misery in the bitterly cold, draughty dug-out behind the pilot's seat. Flying far out over grey Atlantic waters, from small merchant ships whose living quarters were as cramped as their aircraft's cockpits, these men were tormented by stomach disorders from bad food and assailed by bitter slipstream blasts. Further north in the Arctic Circle where winds were raw, crews were cruelly savaged by the climate because an administrative oversight sent their fleece-lined flying suits to Blackburn Skua-equipped squadrons, whose pilots were quite snug in their enclosed, heated cockpits.

Exhausted by endless hours of duty, stiff and numb from the merciless cold, the pilots would fall asleep at their controls to be woken by hearty thumps from observers, whose tiny cubicles were scarcely conducive to slumber. These were frequently cluttered with parachute, charts, chart-board, protractors, dividers, course-and-speed calculator, Wilkinson Computer, pencils and rubbers. With frozen fingers the observers struggled to make drift sightings through the perspex window in the floor beneath their folding camp-stool seats, or fought the slipstream to take compass bearings, dead-reckoning across tens of thousands of square miles of featureless ocean, often in darkness, to find their way back to the insignificant specks of floating steel which were their homes.

'I always felt the deepest respect for the observer and air gunner, exposed in the rear cockpit, sitting with their heads lowered away from the slipstream, concentrating on their exacting but less exciting task of navigating or tuning the radio,' writes Charles Lamb. 'They were entirely in the hands of the man in the front seat and had to rely on him to get them safely there and back. He had the excitement of delivering the weapon and avoiding the flak, while they sat helplessly in the rear cockpit, praying that he would not make a mistake. They were brave men indeed, and I would not have changed places with them for all the inducements on earth.'

The Swordfish was a heavy, underpowered monument to high drag whose published maximum speed of 125 knots (120 knots with torpedo) was in practice more likely to be 90 to 100 knots, and even that could be reduced to almost nothing by strong winds. 'There was a well-known jest among Swordfish pilots', recalls Commander Lamb, 'that the enemy had no speed settings on their gunsights as low as the Stringbag's cruising speed of 90 knots, and therefore a Swordfish could only be hit by shells aimed at a flight astern. This was an exaggeration, of course, yet there was an element of uneasy truth in the statement.'

Worst affected by the Swordfish's sluggardly performance were crews flying from merchant ships, for a sudden change in wind speed or direction while they were patrolling astern could mean a struggling return trip into a 60-knot headwind, reducing groundspeed to 30 knots or even less, with perhaps 100 miles between them and a fast-moving convoy which dared not stop for fear of being attacked by a U-boat. On occasions the Swordfish had to ditch, fuel exhausted in the futile chase, and with little hope of rescue and death from exposure a near-certainty. Patrols astern of convoys were not popular with Swordfish crews.

The type's ponderous performance could, however, be turned to advantage. When approaching a rolling, sea-swamped carrier whose deck was pitching high as a house, instant controllability at airspeeds of 55 knots or below was a worthwhile asset. The relative movement between a Swordfish and the deck of a ship steaming into wind could often be reduced to but a few knots, in contrast to the bone-crunching, oleo-jarring arrivals of faster machines which had to be flown onto the deck.

Ian Cameron described a typical heavy-weather landing-on of a Swordfish thus: 'A good many of the Swordfish were damaged. All the aircrew were exhausted–some of them having made three exceptionally difficult operational sorties within twenty-four hours–and several were wounded. The light was fading. Wind and sea had risen to a frenetic malevolence and the *Ark Royal* was pitching and rolling like a cork in a mill-race. The landing-on of fifteen Swordfish, which would normally have taken about ten minutes, took that evening just over half an hour.

'It seemed impossible that any aircraft could land on so wildly plunging a deck. For the carrier's round-down was now rising and falling by a full sixty feet, and one moment the approaching plane would be far too high, poised near stalling some fifty feet above the deck, the next moment too low, about to shatter itself against the up-flung plates of the carrier's stern. Under these conditions the task of the deck landing officer was, to say the least, difficult in the extreme.

'Patrick Stringer had been batting aircraft on to the *Ark* for a good many months and the pilots had come to trust his judgement; It was as well that they had, for that evening his skill and patience saved their lives. No matter how wildly a carrier is pitching there is always, sooner or later, a period of a few brief seconds when its deck is level and relatively steady. This period can't be judged from the cockpit of an approaching plane, but it can be judged from the batting platform. Provided therefore that the pilot and batsman have confidence in each other and are possessed of sufficient patience, they can almost always engineer between them a landing of sorts.

'It was this confidence and this patience which, that evening, saved the lives of the Swordfish aircrew. Again and again a plane would make a perfect approach, only to find itself waved off as, at the crucial moment, the deck either fell away from it or rose too sharply. Round and round went the aircraft: again and again and again, with the light fading and their fuel running low. One plane was waved off seven consecutive times, but at the eighth attempt it got down. Another landed so heavily that it snapped off its undercarriage and squelched to the deck like an over-ripe plum, breaking its back, but the crew clambered out unhurt. Another flew straight into the barrier. Another ended up in the catwalk. But from every landing the crew walked away. And therein lay the value, and the reward, of Stringer's batting.'

Loaded with its 18 in, 1,610 lb torpedo, 1,500 lb mine or equivalent bomb-load on underwing racks, the Swordfish had an 870 km (540 mile) range, which could be nearly doubled in the reconnaissance role by the addition of an overload tank in the observer's position. One pilot operating in the Western Desert once loaded his Swordfish with 1,135 kg (2,500 lb) of bombs. His take-off run across the sands lasted for 18 km (11 miles), but the Stringbag got off eventually!

'Of all its many weapons,' says Commander Lamb, 'the most devastating was the Swordfish's aerial torpedo. To deliver this weapon in the face of intense opposition in daylight, pilots were taught to attack from a steep dive, at speeds of 180 knots and more. They have been known to reach 200 knots in that dive–*in extremis*–but there was a real danger of the wings folding back or tearing off.' Even in a near-vertical dive from 3,000 m (10,000 ft) the airspeed indicator would never go much over 200 knots anyway, thanks to the Stringbag's drag-ridden airframe. One could safely hold one's dive to within 60 m (200 ft) of the water, drooping all four ailerons to act as dive brakes if necessary, although this facility–operated by a knurled wheel let into the upper wing's centre section–was seldom used in service.

The Swordfish's torpedo sight was foolproof. 'Whoever designed it was a genius', says Charles Lamb. 'Two rods, one on either side of the front cockpit, fixed to the trailing edge of the top main-

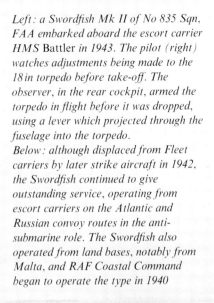

Left: a Swordfish Mk II of No 835 Sqn, FAA embarked aboard the escort carrier HMS Battler in 1943. The pilot (right) watches adjustments being made to the 18 in torpedo before take-off. The observer, in the rear cockpit, armed the torpedo in flight before it was dropped, using a lever which projected through the fuselage into the torpedo.

Below: although displaced from Fleet carriers by later strike aircraft in 1942, the Swordfish continued to give outstanding service, operating from escort carriers on the Atlantic and Russian convoy routes in the anti-submarine role. The Swordfish also operated from land bases, notably from Malta, and RAF Coastal Command began to operate the type in 1940

FAIREY SWORDFISH

Ian Cameron, who flew Swordfish on Atlantic and Russian convoys, wrote of the Swordfish hunting the *Bismarck*: 'Aboard the carrier, conditions were so bad that many of her ship's company thought flying was impossible. Her flight deck, sometimes awash and constantly swept by spray, was slippery as a skating rink. Her wind-over-the-deck recorder was wavering between forty-five and fifty-five knots and her round-down was rising and falling by fifty-six feet – the height of a four-storey house! The *Ark* had flown her Swordfish in bad weather before, but never in weather like this. Yet fly she must, if the *Bismarck* was to be halted . . .

'Ranging the Swordfish [on deck] that morning called for the strength of Hercules and the patience of Job. Time and again, as the flight deck tilted at fantastic angles, a plane would slide bodily towards the catwalks, dragging with it the forty to fifty ratings who were struggling to manhandle it aft. But somehow, by 8.30am ten planes were ranged and ready to fly off on a broad-fronted search to locate *Bismarck*. At 8.35am the carrier reduced speed and swung into wind. Traill, choosing his moment carefully, dropped his flag, and aboard both *Ark Royal* and *Renown* ship's companies held their breath as the leading plane gathered way. Would she make it?

'As the flight deck tilted down, the take-off degenerated into a frantic, slithering glissade. It looked, for one terrible moment, as though the aircraft were plunging straight into the maw of an approaching wave. But Traill had timed his signal well. At the last second the deck swung up and the plane was flung off through the spume of a sixty-foot wave as it cascaded over the carrier's bow. And the almost unbelievable thing was this. The miracle was repeated not once, but nine times, until the whole of the searching force was airborne and fanning out on their respective courses.'

plane, displayed a neat row of electric light bulbs, spaced equally far apart. The distance between each bulb and the next represented five knots of enemy speed. By arriving over the sea at right angles to the enemy ship at a range of about two thousand yards, the pilot would steer towards the ship with the correct light bulb in line with the ship's bow . . .

'In a daylight attack, because the aircraft was most vulnerable during this breathtaking run-in, the time spent low on the water had to be reduced to seconds if the pilot was going to be able to deliver his weapon and survive; the assessment of enemy speed had to be made before the pilot started his dive. Last-minute yawing – by use of rudder – to keep the bulb in line only served to throw the torpedo out of true when it was released, and then it might run in circles. Torpedoes were temperamental weapons which required accurate flying if they were to run properly. They had to be dropped from a height of sixty feet, no more, no less. At the

Below: the only remaining airworthy Swordfish, a Mark II, is maintained at RNAS Yeovilton. It was handed back to Fairey after the war by the FAA and allocated the civil registration G-AJVH on 28 May 1947. Painted blue and silver it flew until 1954 when it was dismantled. Restored to flying condition in 1956, it was returned to the Royal Navy and repainted as LS 326 in 1959

beginning of the war we had no sensitive altimeter or "blind flying" instrument panel, and could only read our height above sea level to the nearest one hundred feet, so this dropping height required accurate judgement by the pilot.'

Narvik, Bomba Bay, Cape Matapan, Taranto, North Atlantic, Mediterranean, Western Desert and the sinking of the *Bismark* – the Swordfish's battle honours are legendary. Its role as a torpedo bomber ended in 1942 with the catastrophic attempt to prevent the break-out of the battleship *Scharnhorst*, *Gneisenau* and *Prinz Eugen* from Brest harbour. In this action six Swordfish, led by Lieutenant Commander Eugene Esmonde – posthumously awarded the Fleet Air Arm's first Victoria Cross for his part in the action – had been pulverised by the German guns and all but three of their crew members killed. Thereafter, largely unsung, the Swordfish performed its greatest work as reconnaissance spotter, coastal patrol bomber, minelayer and submarine hunter-killer.

'Long, lean monarchs of the sky, that pilots would be proud to fly', enthused an idealistic wartime poet. The Swordfish inspired in those who flew it a fierce, undying loyalty. What was its special charisma? Not looks, nor speed, nor comfort, but its sweet handling, vicelessness and old-fashioned, rugged dependability. It was an aeroplane to which

pilots entrusted their lives confidently, secure in the knowledge that whatever happened, their aeroplane would never let them down, would take all the punishment that they could and, often more dead than alive, bring them home again. 'A friend', wrote Terence Horsley, 'when you are fighting your way through darkness towards a lurching flight deck, or are 100 miles out over empty waste, is something worth having.' The Swordfish was a friend indeed.

A Swordfish in the final stage of a carrier landing approach, its hook about to engage an arrestor wire. Although the pilot's view over the nose was not good, the Swordfish was comparatively easy to land. It could be landed onto a carrier at 111km/h (69mph). Flaps were rarely needed or used as they tended to make the aircraft float across the deck and miss the arrestor wires

Short Sunderland

A Sunderland Mk III taking off from sheltered waters. Sunderland pilots had to combine airmanship with seamanship, as it was necessary to keep the aircraft in a planing condition until take-off speed had been reached. To build up speed only the outer engines were opened up to full throttle; the inner engines were opened up when they were clear of spray and sufficient speed had been gained. To keep the aircraft straight in a rough sea it was often necessary to keep one wing slightly down into the wind. If the nose fell, the aircraft could plough under a wave; if it rose, a wave might throw the aircraft prematurely into the air

'She was a wonderful boat,' recalls former Sunderland pilot Charles Potter, 'and a dream to fly. I never heard a bad word said against her.' Typical affection for the aeroplane known to the Luftwaffe as Fliegende Stachelschwein–the Flying Porcupine –because of its portly appearance and bristling defensive armament.

The Short Sunderland served with the Royal Air Force for 21 years and was the last flying boat operated by that service. Developed from the Imperial Airways Empire boats it did sterling service in World War II seeking and destroying U-boats and gained an unlikely reputation as an aeroplane not to be dismissed lightly in aerial combat. On occasions this lumbering flying boat proved to be anything but a sitting duck target and successfully fought off a half-dozen or more enemy long-range fighter aircraft.

The atmosphere aboard Sunderlands was more akin to a ship than an aircraft. 'The captain had almost complete autonomy,' says Charles Potter, 'very much like the captain of a ship. He was responsible for all decisions, and since we operated far away from higher command and were to some extent self-sufficient, a quite unusual spirit of comradeship grew among the crew, who stayed together as a unit and made the boat a "home from home", with little personal touches–curtains, pictures and so forth.'

A typical Coastal Command Sunderland crew numbered 11 men, whose long patrols always began with a pinnace ride out to the flying boat at its mooring buoy. 'The stench of diesel fuel from these boats is another vivid impression that has remained with me ever since–one I'm sure I share with quite a few Sunderland crews', remembers one Sunderland crew member. Checking the equipment aboard a Sunderland when first taking over the aircraft must have been a lengthy job. Here, for example, is part of the equipment checklist: 'Miscellaneous Items: blinds, sun (4); ranges, cooking (1); kettles, tea, tinned; pot, tea, enamelled;

stew pans; pans, frying; spoons, tea, small (11); cloths, tea, wiping . . .' These were vital items indeed on far-ranging flights lasting up to 20 hours. The Sunderland had a well-equipped galley in the lower hull forward of the bomb compartment where the air gunner, who doubled as chief cook, prepared meals on Primus stoves and a Clyde Cooker oven.

Another Sunderland crewman remembered how every take-off in the big flying boat was for him a thrilling experience. 'Standing between the two pilots one saw the control column pulled back and the bows come up as the throttles were eased forward in pairs. The spray being pounded from the hull, the floats skimming the water and finally the boat lifting majestically to the roar of its engines. It

it back into planing attitude. Nose-up and you were in a good position to be thrown into the air again, while nose-down meant straight into the next green one and possible damage.'

The Sunderland was a delight to fly. Very stable with light control forces on ailerons and elevators, a little heavier on the rudder. She cruised at an unhurried 120–125 knots and it was said – unkindly – that she had 'built-in headwinds' thanks to the unusual installation of the engine nacelles, which were canted outwards and did not align with the direction of flight. In fact it was not the engines which were out of line, but the entire wing. When the first Sunderland was built, a C-Class flying boat wing was employed, but the aircraft's centre of gravity was too far aft. Rather than relocate the

Right: depth charges on the port wing weapons rack of a Sunderland, seen through the fuselage hatch below the wing. The racks were carried inside the fuselage and were winched out under the wing before the weapons were dropped. A long-range general reconnaissance and anti-submarine patrol flying boat, the Sunderland could carry an ordnance load of up to 907 kg (2,000 lb), including depth charges, bombs and mines. From the Mark III onwards, the Sunderland was fitted with air-surface vessel (ASV) search radar, which improved it as a reconnaissance, aircraft, convoy escort and anti-submarine aircraft

never failed to excite me. A night take-off, with full petrol and bomb-load, was a much more protracted affair which often seemed interminable before coming unstuck.'

The RAF Pilot's Manual for the Pratt & Whitney Twin Wasp-powered Sunderland Mark V called for $2\frac{1}{2}$ divisions of rudder trim and neutral elevator trim at take-off, one third flap and cooling gills fully open. 'Hold the control column hard back and open up the outer engines gradually to full throttle', it advises. 'When the nose rises and spray is clear of the inner propellers, open the inner engines to full throttle. Any tendency to swing may be checked by throttling back slightly on one outboard engine until rudder control is gained. At 50,000 lb take-off speed is approximately 75 knots; at 60,000 lb take-off speed is approximately 80 knots.'

'In rough conditions it was necessary to keep the floats clear of the waves, a little wing-down into wind to help keep the aircraft straight; wing-up into wind could give you an uncontrollable water loop and possible loss of a float,' said one skipper '. . . in rough seas, especially in swell conditions, the problem was to keep the boat on the water and in a planing attitude until sufficient flying speed could be attained. One could be thrown into the air quite a few times in these conditions, returning each time with a resounding thump. The main thing was to ease the aircraft back onto the water again and get

entire mainplane, Shorts' designers simply swept it back slightly from the root position, hence the 'splayed' engines. Although there may have been minor drag penalties in this configuration, the outward-pointing engines helped maintain directional control in the event of an engine failure, reducing asymmetric loads, particularly on the Bristol Pegasus-powered Marks I, II and III, which did not have fully-feathering airscrews.

Sunderland patrols were usually flown at low level, around 300 m (1,000 ft) or lower. 'The choice of patrol, weather conditions *en route*, time of day over operational area explained to us at briefing could be a nail-biting experience', said one pilot. 'It could happen that we would be making for the Spanish coast, cruising at about 110 knots in brilliant sunshine and a cloudless sky – with a resultant twitch in one's system at the prospect of meeting German fighters in deadly unfavourable circumstances.'

One such encounter is described by Ivan Southall in his book *They Shall Not Pass Unseen*: 'Shells and bullets crashed into the Sunderland. Tail had a go at the rapidly nearing fighter on the port but midships didn't. Fuller's guns lay fully depressed with his turret turned starboard. He rested over his guns, eyes slitted. Little Fuller, no more than a boy – he even looked a boy – sat on his guns, barrels down, and watched the 88 on the starboard side hurtle at him, watched the bullet holes spatter all round him, yet didn't waver. He watched until that thundering 88 filled up the sky, head on, and was fifty yards off the wing-tip.

'Fuller flashed his guns up, sighted and shot. Hundreds of round slaughtered the 88 as it broke away. Fuller poured them into it and suddenly it was a cloud of flame and black smoke and bits and pieces. It screamed vertically into the sea.

'"Straighten up", said Simpson, not unmoved. "Straight and level. Get some height. They're coming again, two more of them in line astern on the port quarter. Twelve hundred yards. Prepare to turn and dive to port. One thousand yards and they're firing cannon. Eight hundred, Hold your fire. Turn and dive to port. Go."

'Shells and armour-piercing bullets crashed into the hull, shot away the elevators and rudder-trimming wires, severed the tail hydraulics, and slammed the turret violently against the stops.

'Still the enemy came in. Still the Sunderland held its fire. All it did was scream round its turn and didn't fire a shot. The first 88 broke away. The second came on and in to two hundred yards.

"Fire", yelled Simpson.

'They fired, Nose and Midships together, Fuller and Watson as one man. Tracers spun their lazy arcs towards the Junkers. It pulled up sharply. It was almost a positive movement and broke away. Fuller and Watson followed him without pause or mercy. A thin stream of smoke came from the fighter's starboard engine; then a sudden burst of dark flame . . .

'It dropped towards the water and struck the surface in a smother of foam. It bounced vertically, hung for a split second, then plunged into the sea. A column of oily smoke shot up like a rocket.

'"Superb", said Simpson. 'Two destroyed. There's another coming in now on the starboard. Prepare to turn and dive to starboard . . .'

'Walker turned and yelled at Amiss, "Get another message away, Two shot down".

'"And now they're coming up from below. Watch them, Galley. One on each quarter. Fire as soon as you like. Tail, he's yours, too. Get into him. Good shooting Galley, you've scared him off. 88 on the starboard is still coming in. Don't hold your fire, Tail, get into him! Tail . . . Captain, Tail's bought it."

Right: the Sunderland cockpit layout conformed to the pattern of other four-engined RAF aircraft. The standard blind-flying panel, containing the basic six flight instruments, was mounted in front of the pilot, seated on the left. The co-pilot had four basic flight instruments. The main engine instruments were mounted centrally and the engine controls were mounted between pilot and co-pilot, throttle levers at the top, mixture levers centre and airscrew speed levers at the bottom

A Sunderland Mark V is preserved at the Royal Air Force Museum, Hendon. The Sunderland was not amphibious and wheels (illustrated here) were fitted to the fuselage sides when it was necessary to beach the aircraft. Sunderlands were usually moored to a buoy between missions and minor repairs and maintenance could be done while they were afloat. However, major work had to be done on land

Westland Lysander

With its enormous spatted undercarriage and long, high-aspect-ratio, dragonfly-like wings, the Lysander was designed for army co-operation work – picking up messages and artillery spotting. However, during World War II it performed such diverse roles as ground-attack aircraft, target tug, supply-dropper, air-sea rescue craft and secret agent transport.

To facilitate the Lysander's prime role as an army co-operation aircraft, Westland designer W. E. Petter employed a 15 m (50 ft) long wing on the Lysander, with the entire leading-edge equipped with Handley Page slots, the inner portions of which were directly connected to the split trailing-edge flaps. These enabled the aeroplane to operate over a wide speed range, from a maximum of 381 km/h (237 mph) down to a loitering speed below 89 km/h (55 mph). Lysanders were powered by 890 hp Bristol Mercury XII, 905 hp Perseus XII sleeve-valve, or 870 hp Mercury XX radial engines. Armament, when carried, consisted of a pair of 0·303 in Browning machine guns mounted in the wheel spats and firing outside the propeller arc, and a manually-fired 0·303 in Vickers or Lewis gun at the rear cockpit position.

'The comfortable pilot's cockpit', a Lysander pilot recalls, 'was well laid out, warm and roomy and, as is nearly always the case in a high-wing monoplane, the forward all-round view superb. Both sides and the top of the perspex covering could be slid down and back respectively to give a fully open-cockpit effect – most welcome in hot climates – and the rear cockpit covering, a single perspex canopy, slid back to reveal a roomy space for the gunner or two passengers at least.'

The Lysander was the first true short take-off

Below: the Westland Lysander's remarkable short-field landing characteristics were specified for the aircraft's original role of army co-operation and five squadrons equipped with Lysanders accompanied the British Expeditionary Force to France on the outbreak of war in September 1939. A Lysander in the pre-war markings of No 4 (Army Co-operation) Squadron is illustrated

(STOL) aircraft in the Royal Air Force's inventory. John Nesbitt-Dufort reported that 'in a moderate breeze using the automatic boost control cut-out I have actually taken off in 36 yards.' Once in the air, the Lysander could be 'turned on a postage stamp at low speeds'.

Although the Lysander's versatility saw it in many unusual roles, perhaps the most useful and certainly the most exciting was a clandestine transport for British agents of the Special Operations Executive. In this guise the aeroplanes were stripped of guns and armour plate, equipped with an underbelly, long-range fuel tank and a tubular metal boarding ladder and painted matt black overall. Between 1941 and 1944 these Lysanders ferried 293 agents to France and brought back more than 500,

Below: the Lysander's cockpit panel had blind flying instruments mounted in the centre and engine instruments to the right. Bomb selector and fusing switches occupy the left of the instrument panel on army co-operation versions of the Lysander, but they are not fitted to this aircraft. A three-way gun selector and control button is attached to the control column handgrip and operates the fixed machine guns, cannon (when fitted in lieu of bombs) and recce camera

greatly contributing to the Allied intelligence effort.

Landing any aeroplane in a strange, short field at night needed plenty of practice, but the Lysander's extraordinary tractability at low airspeeds made the task easier once the pilot became accustomed to its idiosyncrasies, as Wing Commander Nesbitt-Dufort recalls: 'The aeroplane was completely different from any other that I had flown . . . and my first approach was rather similar to someone descending a shallow flight of stairs, until I got the hang of it . . . The whole leading edge of each wing was divided into two sets of automatic slots and the inboard set was connected directly to trailing-edge split flaps [whose deployment was thus controlled by airspeed, rather than by the pilot].

'On reducing speed on the approach to below 80 mph the outboard slots open and further reduction in speed immediately results in the opening of the inboard slots and automatic lowering of the flaps, producing a further reduction in speed and a steeper angle of descent. Naturally, unless the nose-down tendency is corrected or trimmed out at once, up goes the speed and up come the flaps again, giving a tail-heavy effect, and so on *ad nauseam*. Thus the answer was to reduce speed to well below the slot-operational 80 mph and, when the flaps came down, slow up even more and control the rate of descent with the throttle, so that a normal approach can be made at 65 to 70 mph . . . and at 60 mph a very steep angle of approach presented no difficulty.'

The Lysander's undercarriage could take great

punishment for it consisted of a massive, one-piece Elektron box casting in the shape of a horseshoe, originally made in Switzerland. When supplies were cut off during the war a built-up horseshoe shape was tried, held together with countersunk screws, but they soon loosened in jarring, rough-field landings. Such was the strength of the original one-piece unit that the undercarriage would often be the only whole piece of the machine left after the not-infrequent crashes, standing admonishingly unmarked amid the wreckage.

Wing Commander H. S. Verity DSO DFC drew up *Notes for Pilots* for the Special Duties Lysander crews operating full-moon agent-dropping flights. The following are excerpts from this publication. 'Emergency kit: if you get stuck in the mud, it is useful to have in the aeroplane some civilian clothes. Do not put these in the passengers' compartment or they may be slung out. A good place is in the starting handle locker. You should also carry a standard escape kit, some purses of French money, a gun or two, and a thermos flask of hot coffee or what you will. A small flask of brandy or whisky is useful if you have to swim for it, but NOT in the air. Empty your pockets of anything of interest to the Hun, but carry with you some small photographs of yourself in civilian clothes. These may be attached to false identity papers . . .

'Before take-off: you must make sure that the escorting officer for the agent knows the form. If he does not, you must attend to your agent yourself. Make sure that he knows how much luggage he is carrying and where it is stowed. He must know how to put on and operate parachutes, if carried, and helmets and microphones. He must try the working of emergency warning lights. He must understand the procedure for turning about on the field. This is, briefly, for Lysanders, that one agent should stay in the aeroplane to hand out his own luggage and receive the luggage of the homecoming agent, before he himself hops out. In the rare case where the agent has night flying experience over the area in question, it may be of use to give him a map of the route. One operation failed when the pilot was very far off track and the agent, a highly experienced Air Force officer, knew perfectly well where he was but could not tell the pilot as the intercom was switched off.

'Crossing the enemy coast: it is generally safer to cross the enemy coast as high as possible up to 8,000 feet. This gives you a general view of the lie of the coast and avoids the danger of light flak and machine gun fire which you might meet lower down. On the other hand, your pinpoint at the coast is of vital importance, for by it you gauge your wind and set your course for the interior along a safe route, so it may be necessary to fly along a much lower route than 8,000 feet to see where you are in bad weather. Don't think that you will be safe off a flak area within four miles. I have been shot at fairly accurately by low angle heavy flak three miles off Dieppe at 2,000 feet, so, until you know where you are, it is not wise to make too close an investigation of the coastline. In this case you may identify the coast by flying parallel with it some miles out to sea. Notice the course which it follows and any general direction which it takes. By applying these to your map you will generally find that you must at least be on a certain length of coastline and, at best, at a

definite point. When you know your position you may gaily climb above any low cloud there may be and strike into the interior on dead reckoning.

'Target area procedure: on approaching the target area, fish out your target map, refresh your memory of the letters and do your cockpit drill. This involves switching on the fuselage tank, putting the signalling lamp to 'Morse', pushing down your arm rests, putting the mixture control back and generally waking yourself up. Don't be lured away from your navigation by the siren call of stray lights. You should aim to find the field without depending on lights, or to find some positive landmark within two miles of the field from which you will see the light.

'If you don't see the light on ETA [Estimated Time of Arrival], circle and look for it. One operation was ruined because the pilot ran straight over the field twice but did now see the light because the signal was given directly beneath him and he failed to see it because he did not circle. Once you have seen the light, identify the letter positively. If the letter is not correct, or there is any irregularity in the flare path, or if the field is not the one you expected, you are in NO circumstances to land. There have been cases when the Germans have tried to make a Lysander land, but where the pilot has got away with it by following this very strict rule.

'In one case where this rule was disobeyed, the pilot came home with thirty bullet holes in his aircraft and one in his neck, and only escaped with his life because he landed far from the flare path and took off again at once. Experience has shown that a German ambush on the field will not open fire until the aeroplane attempts to take off, having landed. Their objective is to get you alive to get the gen, so don't be tricked into a sense of security if you are not shot at from the field before landing. I repeat, the entire lighting procedure must be correct before you even think of landing. On take-off it is generally worthwhile to pull out your boost override and climb away as speedily as you safely can.'

By overriding the automatic boost control – normally only done at altitude – the pilot was able to extract maximum power from the specially-tuned Bristol Mercury XXX engines installed in the Lysanders. Despite orders expressly forbidding it, some adventurous pilots also sought to extract maximum performance from the Lysander by performing aerobatics. 'I used to think that a slow roll was easier than a loop,' wrote one such pilot, 'but either was fun.'

Looping a Lysander was considered a most

Inset far left: a Lysander of No 208 Squadron based in Egypt practices message pick-up drill. A detachable hook was fitted beneath the Lysander and this engaged a cord with the message attached, which was strung between posts on the ground. The trailing-edge flaps and leading-edge slats, which can be clearly seen, were operated automatically according to airspeed.
Inset left: it was imperative to open the Lysander's cowling gills fully before taxying to prevent the Bristol Mercury engine from overheating.
Left: this preserved Lysander is painted in the markings of No 414 Squadron RCAF and it flies from Booker airfield in Buckinghamshire

creditable achievement—except by the authorities—and among those who performed the manoeuvre was the former Chancellor of the Exchequer, Anthony Barber, and Wing Commander Ken Wallis, designer of the successful Wallis gyrocopter series, who recalls: 'The Lysander looped very well, but rolling aerobatics were liable to result in loss of the leading-edge slots and could well be disastrous . . . During one of my loops I was failing to get the aeroplane around quickly enough. I looked down to see the pitch trim wheel rapidly winding itself to give full nose-down pitch on the large stabiliser! This would more than take over control of a Lysander, as pilots quickly found when opening up to go round again, on landing trim setting. To avoid an uncontrolled pitch-up one had

to feed on power gently, while re-trimming hard, for many turns of the wheel.

'After eventually extricating myself from my elongated loop, I found that any stick-induced pitch change, other than the most gentle, would be countered by the stabiliser changing trim in the opposite sense . . . In fact, many handling characteristics [of the Lysander] were similar to autogiros, but you needed to be much earlier opening up the Bristol engine to save an almost vertical, fully-slotted and flapped disaster if the speed got too low. Any panic throttle opening merely produced woofling noises, and any stick movement only compounded the problem, [but] once you got the hang of its very special features you realised what a wonderful piece of aerodynamic design it was.'

Right: Michael Turner's painting shows a Lysander of No 161 (Special Duties) Squadron during a pick-up operation in Occupied France. The aircraft landed at night with the aid of a dim flarepath of torches laid out by a reception committee of the local Resistance. Time on the ground was kept to a minimum. Below: a Lysander Mark IIIA specially modified for Special Duties operations. The ladder attached to the rear fuselage helped agents to embark and disembark quickly and the auxiliary fuel tank under the fuselage allowed sorties deep into enemy-occupied territory

North American B-25 Mitchell

Named after 'Billy' Mitchell, the campaigning US Army officer who was court-martialled for his fearless belief in the value of air power, the North American B-25 was produced in greater numbers than any other American twin-engined aircraft and is widely held as the best medium bomber of any nationality in World War II. It was powered by two 1,700 hp Wright Double Cyclone 14-cylinder twin-row radial engines.

The Mitchell became world-famous when Lieutenant-Colonel Jimmy Doolittle led a flight of 16 B-25Bs on a daring and morale-boosting attack on Tokyo on 18 April 1942, after taking off from the deck of the aircraft carrier USS *Hornet* (CV-8). Captain Ted Lawson, who took part in the raid, recalls his early training on the B-25: 'Our first B-25s came to us virtually untried. That made our test flights so much more interesting. We flew them across the country to Langley Field, Virginia, and never spared their feelings. We tested their speed, firepower, gas consumption, ability to take rough handling and bomb capacity. I dropped a 2,000 pounder near Langley one day that had the citizens

pretty indignant, even though it had been advertised in newspapers three days in advance.

'The main trouble with the first B-25s was that the ship was so fast that the slipstream kept the rear gunner from giving us much real protection. His single 50-calibre machine gun wasn't operated from a power-driven turret. The barrel just stuck out. The next model put the gunner in cramped quarters at the extreme end of the fuselage, still with one 50-calibre gun. But the third model we got – the type we used on the Japanese raid – placed the rear gunner under a power-driven plastic turret about three-quarters of the way to the end of the fuselage and gave him two 50-calibre stingers.

'A group of Russian aviators barged into McChord one night, [and] they loved the B-25s as much as we did. A Russian General, an interpreter and I got into the plane. The General asked us – or told us – that he was going to take the controls just after we got off the ground. He wasn't kidding. He took us for a ride I'll never forget. When we were just a few feet off the ground he banked the ship and laid it over at a 90-degree angle. I was a passenger,

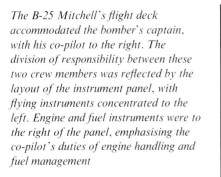

The B-25 Mitchell's flight deck accommodated the bomber's captain, with his co-pilot to the right. The division of responsibility between these two crew members was reflected by the layout of the instrument panel, with flying instruments concentrated to the left. Engine and fuel instruments were to the right of the panel, emphasising the co-pilot's duties of engine handling and fuel management

standing up, but with the side window just in front of my face. The General insisted on staying right over the city of Washington, and not very high, while he gave that B-25 a test that would frighten a test pilot. He was a wild man, that General, but one hell of a flier.

'Back at Jackson, Bob Gray was nearly killed and nearly took me with him. The B-25 he was using that day had a bad left wheel-brake. I landed just ahead of him, rolled to the end of the runway and turned off to the right. I braked my ship and stopped, for there wasn't any more room for me to roll, and Bob was coming in. I was cornered. As soon as Bob put the brakes on, his plane swerved towards my parked job, because only his right wheel was slowing down. So he revved his right engine and that straightened him out on the runway again. Then he braked again, and once more he headed for me. Then he revved the right engine again. It was a good idea, but those B-25s like to roll on forever. He was rolling much too fast to turn to the left, for that would have rolled off his tyres and tipped him over. Finally his right tyre blew out from the uneven pressure put on it. The B-25 swung around, just short of my hemmed-in plane, and simply fell to pieces. You should have seen those fellows pouring out of it!'

The Mitchell's brakes were mightily effective when working properly, as postwar cinema pilot Frank Tallman discovered on his first flight in a B-25. The brakes, he said, were 'set so delicately that a mayfly landing upon the pedals can send a pilot through the windshield like catapult ejection. My taxi to take-off position was a sight to behold: it looked like Bojangles Robinson doing a shuffle off to Buffalo.'

Getting aboard a B-25 was never easy if the under-belly hatch did not have a ladder. One had to

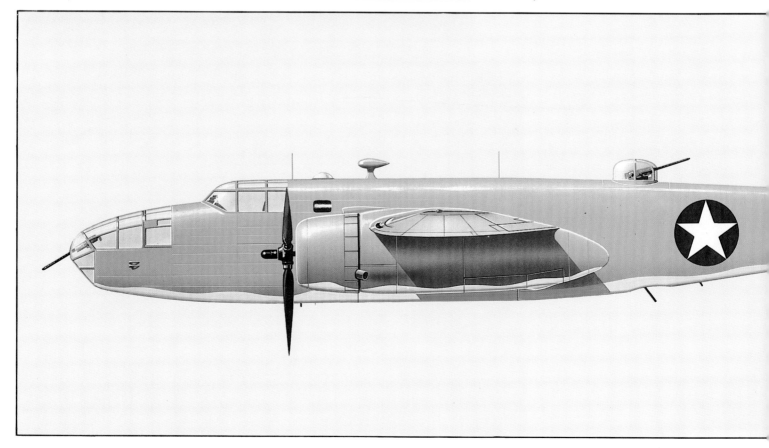

grip the sides of the hatchway opening and swing oneself bodily upwards like a trapeze artist. 'The most dangerous part of the flight', recalls one former B-25 ferry pilot, 'was getting through that hatchway. The risk of slipping and cracking your elbows or pelvis on the ground was very real.' Another pilot noted: 'When you climb up, you find yourself in a small room, about six feet square, going from the top to the bottom of the fuselage. It has a couple of jump seats and a plexiglass bubble in the top for navigation work. The forward side of this area is only about three feet high, opening into the back of the cockpit. Getting up into the pilot's seat is a major operation. The cabin roof is fairly low and the seats are close together, which means you have to walk on the row of knobs and levers that cover the space between the seats.'

'Take-off' wrote this pilot, 'is really, really exciting–possibly even more so than in a Mustang, because you know the tricycle gear will take care of the take-off roll and you have time to bask in the glory of flying a bomber . . . After making sure that everything on the quadrant was full forward and the boost pumps were on, I'd call for one quarter flaps and start the throttles forward. As soon as the aeroplane is moving, the rudders are effective and you only have to touch the brakes just once before the rudders come in. The power must come up slowly to keep the prop governors from surging and you have to monitor manifold pressure to keep it under 44 inches. Considering the amount of aeroplane around you, the acceleration is fantastic and the noise even more so.' A Mitchell lifted off around 90–100 knots, depending on load, and density altitude. The take-off from the deck of the *Hornet* was accomplished with 2,000 pounds of bombs and a total fuel capacity of 1,141 gallons– sufficient for a round trip of 2,400 miles–and the take-off roll could be no more than 700 feet. 'If you men have any idea that this isn't the most dangerous thing you've ever been on, don't even start this training period', Doolittle told his crews.

Ted Lawson described his own take-off thus: 'I was on the line now, my eyes glued on the man with the flag. He gave me the signal to put my flaps down. I reached down and drew the lever back and down. I checked the electrical instrument that indicates whether the flaps are working. They were. I could feel the plane quaking with the strain of having the flat surface of the flaps thrust against the gale and the blast from the props. I got a sudden fear that they might blow off and cripple us, so I pulled the flaps up again, and I guess the Navy man under- stood. He let it go and began giving me the signal to rev my engines.

'I liked the way they sounded long before he did. There had been a moment, earlier, when I had an agonising fear that something was wrong with the left engine. It wouldn't start at first. But I had got it going good. Now, after 15 seconds of watching the man with the flag spinning his arm faster and faster, I began to worry again. He must know his stuff, I tried to tell myself, but when, for God's sake, would he let me go?

'I thought of all the things that could go wrong at this last minute. Our instructions along these lines were simple and to the point. If a motor quit or caught fire, if a tyre went flat, if the right wing

badly scraped the island, if the left wheel went over the edge, we were to get out as quickly as we could and help the Navy to shove our plane overboard. It must not, under any circumstances, be permitted to block traffic. There would be no other way to clear the forward deck for the other planes to take off.

'After 30 blood-sweating seconds the Navy man was satisfied with the sound of my engines. Our wheel blocks were jerked out and when I released the brakes we quivered forward, the wind grabbing at our wings. We rambled dangerously close to the edge, but I braked in time, got the left wheel back on the white line and picked up speed. The *Hornet*'s deck bucked wildly. A sheet of spray rushed back at us. I never felt the take-off. One moment the end of the *Hornet*'s flight-deck was rushing at us alarmingly fast; the next split second I glanced down hurriedly at what had been a white line and it was water. There was no drop nor any surge into the air. I just went off at deck level and pulled out in front of the great ship that had done its best to plant us in Japan's front yard. I banked now, gaining a little altitude, and instinctively reached down to pull up the flaps. With a start I realised they were not down. I had taken off without using them . . .'

In the air the B-25 was heavy to fly, with positive ailerons, rudders which 'were about equal to moving the anchor of the Queen Mary with one foot' and elevators which required strong biceps to counter an out-of-trim condition, as one pilot recalls: 'A slight out-of-trim condition caused the nose to drop. I automatically pulled the nose up–or at least, I tried. I was flying with my left hand, my right resting lightly on the throttles. I could hardly pull the wheel back with one hand! I released the throttles and brought the other hand over to help, barely getting the nose up level. I finally had enough sense to wheel in some trim. The controls couldn't be that heavy! I made a turn to the left, or at least my hands did, but the control wheel resisted my attempts to move it. Grasping it firmly, determined to do it with one hand, I forced one end down and the wings responded smartly enough by rolling obediently into a left bank–then the nose started to fall. With the 30-degree bank I was holding, I had to force the wheel to the rear to keep the nose from falling. I had started losing altitude the second I started to roll. I wasn't prepared for the heavy control pressures.'

Experienced B-25 pilots soon grew accustomed to its heavy controls, and some even performed aerobatics in the 35,000-pound bomber. Ted Lawson recalled: 'Lieutenant Butler wasn't as lucky on those manoeuvres. He was killed near the end of the tests. His B-25 went into a slow roll while taking off the short Augusta, Georgia field. Its 100-octane [fuel] went all over the place and ignited. There wasn't much left of anybody or anything by the time the ambulance and fire apparatus reached it. The same apparatus came out after me at Augusta twice. There was a broad ditch at the end of the runway. I used to run the length of the runway on take-off, duck the nose of my B-25 down in the ditch for extra speed, then go up. The boys thought I was crashing and I got a bawling out for it.'

'Single-engine drills in the B-25 are really fun,' wrote one new Mitchell pilot with more than a touch

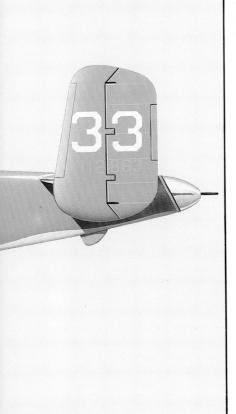

Above left: B-25B variants of the Mitchell took part in James Doolitte's raid on Tokyo in April 1942, taking off from the aircraft carrier USS Hornet.
Left: the final production variant of the Mitchell was the B-25J, which served primarily as a low-level bomber in the Pacific theatre of operations.
Below: a B-25C Mitchell of the US Ninth Air Force painted in desert camouflage

Much modified for aerial film work, this Mitchell was operated by Frank Tallman. Tallman's lasting impression of the filming of Catch 22 was 'the indescribable excitement of a gang take-off with 17 other B-25s only 100 feet apart'

of sarcasm. 'One thing is certain, when an engine shuts down, there is no doubt which is the "idle foot". My good foot was working so hard that after each hop it took several hours for my knees to stop shaking . . . There are only two things to remember when feathering a B-25: remember what your Vmc [single-engine minimum control speed] is for your weight, and move forward in the seat because you have to be seven feet tall for your legs to push the rudder all the way down. I found myself wedging my shoulder against the seat and practically standing on the rudder, lying sideways in the seat, right hand frantically cranking in rudder trim. Once the trim is in, the aeroplane is a pussycat, but if you don't start cranking trim right off the bat, the pussycat will eat one leg, and maybe your entire lunch . . . During single-engine stalls, I got very good at leaping on the power and bringing it back quickly. You forget to reduce power only once in a power-on, stalled, engine-out situation, then the B-25 does all the talking and you do all the listening.'

What of other B-25 crew members? The gunner operating the remote, faired-in twin-gun turret installed in the lower rear fuselage of early Mitchells had to adopt a position once described as 'akin to milking a cow', while aiming through an optical sight facing down and backwards. As a result the gunner's effectiveness was severely reduced by the peculiar optical effects, and he was a near-certain candidate for airsickness. That turret was abandoned on later B-25s, because, wrote one former occupant, 'it was about as useful as a pickpocket in handcuffs.' The B-25G packed a 75mm M-4 cannon in its solid nose. The navigator doubled as gunner on this weapon, and had to hand-feed the shells, while keeping clear of the gun's 21-inch recoil. The Mitchell proved a steady platform for the 75mm gun, which needed careful aiming, but the aeroplane would be almost stopped in mid-air at each firing, and eventually the M-4 gave way to a quartet of 0·5in guns though not before one had sunk a Japanese destroyer with a single shell.

'For my first landing', says a B-25 pilot, 'we flew a wide downwind [leg of the circuit] at 120 knots and I ran through the landing check as fast as I could because the airport was disappearing rapidly. I called for the gear and at the same time pushed the props up to 2,200 rpm, where they would stay until we were on the ground. Mixture went to auto-rich, and boost pumps went first to low, then to high. By this time I was way past the airport, so I brought the power back a little and started to turn on to base [leg]. The second I started to turn I knew what Junior had been talking about when he mentioned heavy aircraft and the way they need power and don't need steep banks. When the wing went down, the aeroplane started sinking immediately, and I had to advance power to catch it . . . On base, I found myself using a lot of power just to maintain the status quo, cranking in trim every few seconds. I stuck up two fingers, indicating I wanted half flaps, adding more power and trim. As I turned [on] final [approach to land], I stuck up four fingers for full flaps and started gently reducing power and struggling with the nose to get 110 over the fence. Then I had 110 knots and Burchinal was yelling to bring the power back. I thought he was crazy, that we'd never make the runway, but I killed the power anyway, keeping my nose pointed at the numbers, 110 knots on the gauge.

'I started bringing the nose up and Burchinal started yelling "Pull, pull". He grabbed the wheel and helped me. It turned out I was flaring in the right place, but I would have touched down on all three, or just a little nose-high, but I would have been too hot. Burchinal kept me pulling and we touched down with the nose at an impossibly steep nose-high attitude, completely hiding the runway. Roll-out was arrow straight, and Junior cautioned me to be very, very gentle on the brakes, because they are sensitive. My toes crept up on the top of the rudder pedals and pushed as gently as they could . . . the nose strut compressed as I nearly locked the brakes. They have double discs and just need a whisper of pressure to stop the wheel. Trying to taxi smoothly was a near impossibility.'

DH Mosquito

The Press dubbed it the 'Wooden Wonder' and, in a generation of outstanding wartime aeroplanes, the Mosquito was a magnificent example of British ability to equate experience with operational demands. Added to this are the facts that its development was undertaken when Britain's fortunes were at their lowest ebb, and that its concept embraced the maximum possible use of non-strategic materials and radical tactical employment. The Mosquito thus emerges not only as an outstanding aeroplane but as a landmark in aviation history. Although few would argue that the Mosquito was essentially a 'pilot's aeroplane' – owing to the diverse demands of its original specification, not to mention its necessarily accelerated wartime development – it was exceptionally adaptable and, provided its flying and operating limitations were respected and accepted, exhilarating to fly.

Aerodynamically the 'Mozzie' was a beautiful shape, the sharply-tapered wing located on the smoothly-contoured fuselage at mid position. The engines were closely cowled in low-profile nacelles, their radiators being incorporated within the wing leading-edges adjacent to the fuselage. Spruce-sandwich construction was employed throughout the aeroplane, an expedient adopted by the design team which had produced the famous Comet racer half a dozen years before the war. Pilot and navigator sat side-by-side in the nose, while the four 20 mm Hispano cannon, carried by the fighter and fighter-bomber versions, were located under the cockpit floor.

Entry to the cockpit was by means of a telescopic ladder leading to a hatch in the lower starboard side of the nose, the pilot entering first to occupy the port seat and the navigator following. Bearing in mind that this hatch was also the emergency exit through which the crew bailed out, it always seemed to the uninitiated that the starboard propeller was uncomfortably close to the hatch. However, although it was recommended that, if there was time, the propeller should be feathered before stepping over the side, a perfectly safe bail-out was possible without doing so.

After switching on the electrics and checking that the 24-volt battery was fully charged and the

The instrument panel of a B Mark 35 illustrates the basic layout of Mosquito bombers. On the right is the hatch to the nose compartment, found on both bomber and reconnaissance variants, for bomb-aiming and observation respectively. Mosquito bomber and reconnaissance variants had no gun armament and relied on their speed to escape interception. Panel layout was similar in fighter-bomber variants but the hatch was blanked-off

pneumatic system showed a pressure of 200 psi, the outer fuel tanks were selected for use first. This was because, in the event of an engine failure, it was not possible to cross-feed fuel from the outer tanks of one wing to the engine on the other side.

To start up, port engine first, the throttle was set slightly open, constant-speed propeller controls fully forward, supercharger set at 'moderate' and fuel pressure venting cock switched on. The ignition switches – two per engine – were switched on and the starter and booster-coil buttons pressed. As the ground-crew feverishly operated the priming pump, the engine would fire to an accompaniment of loud irregular bangs from the exhaust manifolds scarcely six feet from the canopy windows. This was always an impressive moment when starting engines at night for, even when fitted with exhaust shrouds, the excess fuel in the cylinders exploded to cause pyrotechnic flashes that lit the night vividly.

As soon as both engines settled down to an even firing, the throttles were eased forward to give about 1,200 rpm and the radiator flaps opened. As with many Merlin-powered aircraft – particularly the Mosquito with its slim wing radiators – overheating on the ground, either when stationary or taxying slowly, was a feature of engine handling that had to be watched carefully. If the coolant temperature rose much above 70 degrees centigrade it was essential to turn the aircraft into wind and run the engines up to about 2,000 rpm for a short period.

Before taxying, normal checks were carried out to ensure propeller constant-speeding, flaps operating and that, with take-off boost, the engine revs reached 3,000 rpm. Testing the operation of the magnetos was by ensuring the engine speed did not drop by more than 150 rpm when each magneto was switched off in turn.

Taxying the Mosquito was straightforward as the view over the nose of the bomber and fighter-bomber version was excellent, although the later AI Mark X-equipped night fighters with bulky nose radome demanded fish-tailing to see the taxi-track ahead. The powerful wheel brakes were operated from a lever on the control column, differential effect being achieved by use of the rudder bar.

Arriving at the take-off area it was customary to swing into wind and, with the control column held hard back, run the engines up to 3,000rpm to clear the spark plugs. Take-off checks were brief: check trimmers–elevators slightly nose heavy on most versions, rudder slightly right and ailerons neutral– propeller pitch controls fully forward, fuel cocks set to outer tanks and tank contents checked, flaps selected up or about 15 degrees down as required, supercharger at 'moderate' setting and radiator flaps open.

After being given take-off clearance the throttles were pushed slowly forward, leading slightly with the port control to counteract a fairly marked tendency to swing to the left. Acceleration after releasing the brakes was most impressive, and the moment at which the pilot would raise the tail varied

(170mph) indicated. It was customary for pilot and navigator to use oxygen from take-off onwards during night flights, and in daytime to switch over to oxygen at 2,400–3,000m (8,000–10,000ft).

Fighter-versus-fighter air combat in the Mosquito by day presented some difficulty owing to the field of vision from the pilot's seat being severely restricted by the large engine nacelles, located so close to the cockpit, and by the side-by-side seating. In combat against bomber aircraft and such targets as the flying bombs, two criteria were essential– heavy armament and high speed, both possessed in abundance by the Mosquito. That is not to suggest that the aeroplane lacked manoeuvrability, and aerobatics were a delight to perform, the sensitivity of the controls for what was, after all, a fairly big aeroplane, being particularly memorable.

Top left: the starboard side of the cockpit of a Mosquito TT Mk 39, a high-speed target tug converted from the B Mark XVI for the Fleet Air Arm. The aircraft served postwar with the Navy's Fleet Requirements Units.

Left: the port side of the cockpit of a Mosquito NF Mk 38, showing the pilot's seat, the control column and the engine control quadrant. The instrument panel of Mosquito night fighter variants differed from that of other variants, because of the space occupied by the AI radar equipment on the right of the two-man cockpit.

Below: a Mosquito NF Mk 36 of No 85 Squadron based at West Malling in 1951. The Squadron began operating Mosquito night fighters in August 1942, and only relinquished them for the Gloster Meteor NF Mk 11 in October 1951. Postwar, Mosquito NF Marks 36 and 38 were the backbone of home defence units until the arrival of jet night fighters.

Right: two pages from the Pilot's Notes for the FB Marks VI, XVIII and 26

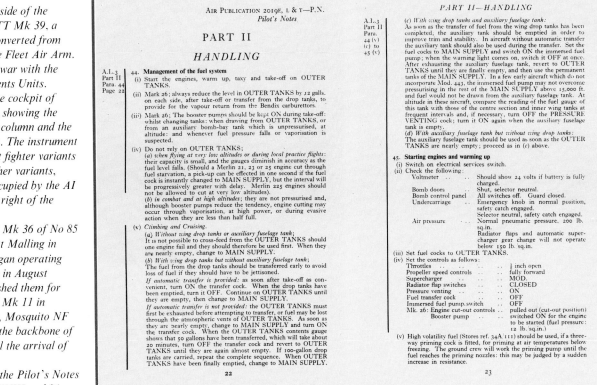

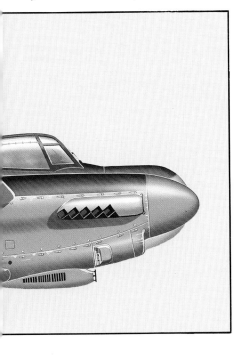

from version to version. The night fighters, which had more equipment in the nose, tended to assume a tail-up attitude fairly quickly and it was necessary to check this with slight backward pressure on the stick. Unstick occurred at around 200–210km/h (125–130mph) indicated; it was then essential to hold the aircraft level, raising the wheels as soon as possible to allow speed to build up quickly to the fairly high critical speed of 320km/h (200mph)–the minimum speed necessary to maintain control of the aeroplane should an engine cut out on take-off. The relatively small, high-placed rudder, combined with the low-slung engine nacelles, imposed this lack of directional control at low airspeeds, and it was an unfortunate feature of early Mosquito operations that accidents due to engine failure after take-off were fairly frequent. Later Mosquito versions, with more power available on take-off, reached their critical speed appreciably quicker.

Once the safety speed was reached the aircraft could be trimmed into the climb, flaps raised (if used) and engines throttled back to climb at 274km/h

A slow roll was relatively difficult to execute as the speed dropped off quickly and the nose dropped fairly sharply during the second half of the roll, so that a fair amount of height was lost; it was necessary to barrel the nose round the horizon to maintain height. If the roll was too slow there was a risk of one or both engines cutting while inverted. It was, however, quite possible to barrel-roll the Mozzie fighter-bombers with one engine's propeller feathered, provided the entry speed was at least 480km/h (300mph) indicated. Before executing aerobatics involving entry speeds of over 515km/h (320mph), a good deal of nose-down trim was needed to counter tail-heaviness, which increased as the speed built up.

The best way to do a climbing roll was to open the throttles in a shallow dive to about 600m (2,000ft) and ease back on the stick as the speed built up to around 595km/h (370mph) indicated, and start the roll as the nose rose about 40 degrees above the horizon; the speed would drop off quickly, and to avoid stalling it was necessary to ease off the stick as soon as the roll was completed. For a straightforward loop the same entry speed was needed, although it was usually recommended that the minimum height should be greater. The backward pressure on the stick had to be maintained so as to 'fly the aircraft round' fairly tightly, easing off some throttle when inverted otherwise excessive height would be lost in recovery.

An entry speed of not less than 610 km/h (380 mph) was needed for a roll off the top, and the rolling out had to be started as soon as the nose touched the horizon. In an aircraft with plenty of fuel left the roll-out was a bit uncomfortable as the speed would have dropped off quite close to the stall. Despite the use of constant-speed propellers there was a tendency for them to overspeed during high-speed diving in later versions of the Mosquito, especially during recovery from the loop. The best way to minimise this was to avoid using the throttles during the aerobatics themselves, other than throttling back during recovery.

Stalling was again straightforward, the stall in the 'clean' condition being induced by holding the stick firmly back and closing the throttles. The stall was heralded by slight pitching, followed by the nose dropping fairly steeply and possibly one wing. Spinning was generally frowned upon owing to the lack of rudder effect at low speed. With wheels and flaps down the stall was somewhat more energetic, being accompanied by a good deal of pitching and vibration. If the stick was held right back in this condition, one wing would drop quite sharply. Recovery from the stall required little effort from the controls, apart from easing the backward pressure on the stick, as the speed built up very quickly in the glide.

Aerobatics, other than gentle rolls, were not as a rule encouraged in the Mosquito night fighters as excessive 'g' was not considered conducive to efficient operation, either of the radar or its operator. In any case the greater nose-heaviness rendered the aircraft very sluggish in climbing and looping manoeuvres.

Gun firing in the Mosquito was always a stimulating experience, particularly in those versions armed with the full four cannon and four

Below: a Mosquito T Mk 3 maintained in flying condition. The T Mark 3 was developed as an unarmed two-seat dual control trainer from the NF Mark II, to which it was generally similar. Entering service in 1943, it served in Flying Training Command and the Operational Conversion Unit of Bomber Command until some years after the war

Right: a Mosquito attacks German vessels in a Norwegian fjord. The Mosquito FB Mk VI began to enter RAF Coastal Command service in early 1944 in the anti-shipping role. It usually carried eight 60lb rocket projectiles – devastating against unarmoured shipping – in addition to cannon and guns

machine gun battery. The aircraft was an extremely steady gun platform, there being little change of trim while firing in a curve of pursuit, and none in level flight. The crash of gunfire from the cannon less than a foot beneath the cockpit floor was possibly amplified by the lightweight wooden structure of the airframe. When dropping bombs from the fuselage bomb-bay there was little change of trim, although opening the bomb doors resulted in a slight nose-up change.

In later life, particularly in the postwar RAF, Mosquitoes suffered quite a high rate of engine failures as their service lives were stretched well beyond that originally envisaged. There were also instances when, following recall from duties in tropical and humid theatres overseas, their spruce airframes deteriorated without the flaws being detected. Of course, careful monitoring of engine temperatures would enable incipient engine trouble to be avoided, even if this simply meant closing down an overheating engine to avoid the possibility of more serious problems.

Battle damage to a radiator would almost invariably result in engine overheating and, unless stopped quickly, eventually fire or failure. Shutting down an engine was effected by throttling back and switching off the relevant magnetos, and then pressing the propeller feathering button. A windmilling propeller caused considerable drag on that side, so much so that too little rudder control would remain for a safe landing. If an engine fire had occurred, the relevant fire extinguisher button would be depressed. As always, once the extinguisher had been operated, it was never wise to attempt to re-start the engine owing to the possibility of a recurrence of the fire without further means of extinguishing it. The fire extinguishers operated automatically in the event of a crash.

Control of one engine gave no trouble, as there was adequate trim available from the rudder tab to hold the aircraft straight at a reasonable speed. However, care had to be taken in turns not to allow the aircraft to tighten up when turning towards a dead engine.

In the event of dire emergency, unless speed and altitude dictated otherwise, it was not recommended to ditch the Mosquito in the sea. There was a tendency for the weight of the engines to 'bury the nose' and the lightweight wooden structure could break up very quickly. Both crew members carried K-type dinghies in their parachute packs, and most Mosquitoes were equipped with L-type two-man dinghies which popped out by operation of an automatic immersion switch. Exit from the cockpit either after ditching or a wheels-up landing was through the roof emergency panel which should have been jettisoned before touch-down.

Although bailing out was recommended in preference to ditching, it could be a rather confusing process unless thoroughly practised by crews on the ground, owing to the confined nature of the cockpit. As already mentioned, it was best if the starboard engine was stopped and the propeller feathered. The hatch by the navigator's right leg was jettisoned by pulling the large red handle and kicking out the panel. The navigator would leave first, followed by the pilot – who had to negotiate the control column, being careful not to snag his harness on any of the numerous controls, knobs and switches, particularly in the radar-equipped night fighters.

Rejoining the landing circuit was a procedure that varied according to the duty performed by the Mosquito. The bombers tended to make long, flat, powered approaches, whereas the fighters and fighter-bombers usually completed a tightish circuit of the airfield on to the approach quite close to the boundary. Unless on a 'straight-in' instrument approach, the night fighters generally compromised with a larger circuit, aiming to straighten up for the final approach about one or one-and-a-half miles downwind of the runway threshold.

During the downwind leg, checks for landing were carried out while reducing speed to about 290 km/h (180 mph) indicated. Brake pressure was checked to ensure a minimum of 200 psi, superchargers set at 'moderate', radiator flaps open and undercarriage lowered (if returning on one engine, the wheels took a good 30 seconds to extend and

Left: Mosquitoes of the RAF Coastal Command Strike Wing, based at Banff, Banffshire take off at dawn on 4 December 1944 to attack shipping off the Norwegian coast.

Right: the FB Mk VI, most widely-used fighter variant of Mosquito, pictured in 1943, shortly after its service debut. A very stable gun platform, it was armed with four cannon and four machine guns, and could carry four 500 lb bombs, two below the wings and two in the bomb bay. Entry to the Mosquito was by a hatch in the starboard nose.

Below: de Havilland Mosquito B Mk IVs of No 105 Squadron depicted during a low-level raid. Too fast to be intercepted by fighters, Mosquito bombers were used extensively for low-level and pinpoint bombing attacks, and achieved the lowest loss rate of any aircraft in RAF Bomber Command during the course of World War II

lock down). Propeller pitch controls set fully forward and the fullest fuel tanks selected. Flaps were then selected fully down – requiring a lot of nose-down trim, and by the time the aircraft turned cross-wind and started to descend the speed would have dropped to about 257 km/h (160 mph).

Using throttle to adjust the rate of descent, the aircraft was turned on to the final approach at about 225 km/h (140 mph), and to check its fairly high rate of descent a good deal of power was needed, aiming to cross the threshold at a height of 4·6 m (15 ft) up at about 193 km/h (120 mph), when the throttles could be closed and the stick eased back. The aircraft at average landing weights stalled at about 169 km/h (105 mph), and the night fighters slightly higher.

Landing on one engine presented no real difficulty provided a longish approach was made, enabling the speed to be kept above about 160 mph, and the rate of descent controlled by use of the good engine. The descent rate was a good deal faster and a rather steeper approach than normal was advisable. The author recalls an instance when, returning at night on one engine, the other engine failed at the moment of touchdown. The aircraft swung quite violently towards the windmilling propeller and careered across the unlit airfield, between the air traffic control tower and a hangar, before it sat down on its belly, having knocked off both main undercarriage members on an obstruction. The fuselage fuel tanks ruptured, but fortunately there was no fire.

In the event of a baulked landing and the need to 'go round again', it was again essential to accelerate as quickly as possible to gain that vital critical speed, so the throttles were pushed open fairly smartly and the aircraft held down, and the wheels retracted immediately. The flaps were left down until a height of about 150 m (500 ft) was reached, as raising them caused the aircraft to sink quite appreciably.

Once finally down on the runway the deceleration caused a slight tendency to swing to the right but this could be checked quite easily by use of the left rudder and possibly a bit of brake. However, the radar-equipped night fighters were difficult to land in a fully tail-down attitude and with the weight in the nose it was inadvisable to use the powerful wheelbrakes until the tail had finally dropped firmly on to the runway. Turning off at the end of the landing run, the flaps were raised, and back at dispersal the engines were stopped by pulling the slow-running cut-outs.

The foregoing recollections may serve to give some idea of routine flying in the Mosquito. Yet the demands of war upon this outstanding aeroplane were so diverse that it would be impossible to convey more than a superficial impression of the many exploits undertaken which emphasised its extraordinary adaptability to combat operations.

There were, for example, the photo-reconnaissance Mosquitoes which were the first versions to enter operational service and the first to fly sorties over enemy territory in September 1941. Without bomb gear or guns, and flying at 7,000 m (23,000 ft) over Bordeaux and Paris, they easily outpaced the Messerschmitt Bf 109s sent up to intercept them. Later the Mosquito Mk IX became the RAF's standard twin-engined photo-reconnaissance aircraft, capable of a range of 5,600 km (3,500 miles) and a speed of 684 km/h (425 mph) at over 9,000 m (30,000 ft). Sorties far out over Europe and the Middle East of eight hours' duration were commonplace but imposed great strains upon the crews in their cramped cockpits. These operations demanded quite outstanding qualities from the photo-reconnaissance pilots and navigators who endured all the physical discomfort of cold and psychological pressure of loneliness while flying deep inside enemy airspace. Pinpoint accuracy in navigation – not simple to achieve at high altitude in an aircraft whose pilot's field of vision was somewhat restricted – with only speed for defence, singled out the photo-reconnaissance Mosquito crews as among the finest in the wartime RAF.

It was for their countless bombing attacks that

the Mosquitoes were best remembered, and it seemed astonishing that an aircraft which had started life essentially as a light bomber was eventually developed to carry a 4,000lb Blockbuster bomb all the way to Berlin. Loaded with this weapon and a full fuel load, the Mosquito Mk XVI with 1,680hp Merlin 72s could still take off in about 1,100m (1,200 yards), and normally operated from standard 1,800m (2,000 yard) runways. Deprived of the Blockbuster's weight over the target, the Mozzie shot up as much as 240m (800ft). The critical speed of this version at take-off weight was 350km/h (220mph), and more than ever it was the pilot's instinctive habit to brace his left hand hard against the throttle levers as the aircraft left the ground.

Flying the Mosquito in the low-level fighter-bomber and intruder role was particularly exhilarating, and the impression of great speed at low level was heightened by the excellent view over the short nose that was absent on single-engined fighters. Again those big Merlins, growling away 'just outside the window', gave a feeling of power that no jet engine could convey. With such excellent forward vision it was no wonder that the Mosquito achieved such pinpoint low-level bombing accuracy as in those memorable attacks on Amiens Gaol by Group Captain Percy Pickard's Mosquito Wing on

18 February 1944, by No 613 Squadron's destruction of the Gestapo records in the Kleizkamp building at The Hague on 11 April 1944 and No 464 Squadron's attack on the Gestapo headquarters in Copenhagen on 21 March 1945.

As a night fighter the Mosquito reigned supreme during the last three years of the war, remaining the backbone of Britain's night defence for six years afterwards. As most pilots will testify, the power and noise of the engines appeared to be accentuated when flying at night, and this was never more apparent than in the Mosquito. Yet there was also something akin to added comfort in the very proximity of those Merlins even if the visible effect of speed was concealed. Needless to say almost all the highest-scoring RAF night fighter pilots flew the Mosquito, not only on home defence operations but also on widespread intruder sorties.

Despite its wooden structure, there was nothing flimsy about the Mosquito in the air and in battle and it was capable of withstanding considerable combat and flak damage. As an all-round weapon the Mozzie was a masterpiece, possibly even the greatest example of a successful marriage of aerodynamic perfection with the demands of warfare. Certainly this was a classic instance of 'once flown, never forgotten'.

Above: the B Mark 35 appeared too late to see action in World War II, but was the last Mosquito bomber to serve in Bomber Command. The Mosquito remained the fastest bomber in the Command until the introduction of the English Electric Canberra which superseded it in 1952–53. The B Mark 35 was an improved B Mark XVI, which had been developed for No 8 Group's Light Night Striking Force, which specialised in lightning 'nuisance' raids on German industrial centres

Left: the Mosquito Mk XVIII, designed for ground attack and anti-shipping duties, was armed with a 57mm Molins gun in place of the 20mm cannon battery, although it retained the four machine guns. The Molins was equivalent to a six-pounder field gun. About 27 Mk XVIIIs were built, serving with Nos 248 and 254 Squadrons of Coastal Command. The variant went into action in November 1943 and was particularly effective against shipping, submarines and shore installations

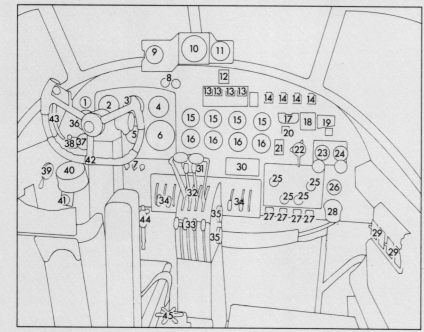

Avro Lancaster cockpit

1: *Stopwatch* 2: *Airspeed indicator* 3: *Artificial horizon* 4: *Rate of climb indicator* 5: *Direction indicator* 6: *Turn and bank indicator* 7: *Identification light switches* 8: *Landing light switches* 9: *Direction finder (DF) indicator* 10: *Dead reckoning (DR) compass repeater* 11: *Clock* 12: *DR compass deviation card holder* 13: *Engine ignition switches* 14: *Engine starter switches* 15: *Boost gauges* 16: *Engine speed indicators* 17: *Identification friend or foe (IFF) detonator switches* 18: *Bomb containers jettison button* 19: *Bomb jettison button* 20: *IFF switch* 21: *Vacuum pumps suction gauge* 22: *Vacuum pump change-over cock* 23: *Oxygen regulator control* 24: *Oxygen regulator gauge* 25: *Feathering buttons* 26: *Triple pressure gauge* 27: *Engine fire-extinguisher buttons* 28: *Signalling switchbox (identification lamps* 29: *Radiator shutter controls* 30: *Supercharger gear change control panel* 31: *Flap position indicator (below throttle lever)* 32: *Throttle control levers* 33: *Propeller speed control levers* 34: *Master engine fuel cocks* 35: *Control levers friction adjusters* 36: *Beam approach indicator* 37: *Undercarriage position indicator* 38: *Auto controls clutch* 39: *Auto controls cock* 40: *Magnetic compass* 41: *Auto controls pressure gauge* 42: *Control wheel* 43: *Brake lever* 44: *Harness release lever* 45: *Rudder trim tab controls*

Avro Lancaster

The pilot of the Lancaster was the captain of the aircraft regardless of his rank. There was no relief pilot, which put great strain on pilots who often flew night missions of eight hours' duration. However, the flight engineer would assist the pilot during take-off and landing with the engine controls and, as required, in co-ordinating controls in flight and for manoeuvres. Although normally light and sensitive, the elevators tended to become heavy in turns and the ailerons and twin rudders became heavy at high speeds and great force often had to be exerted on the controls. The pilot generally flew without reference to the ground, using the blind flying panel in front of the control column

Everything about the Lancaster was big. True, it was no bigger than the Short Stirling and Handley Page Halifax which preceded it into service, yet the scale of effort to introduce it into widespread use, and to produce the tens of thousands of aircrew to fly and crew this truly classic aircraft was unprecedented anywhere in the world. Yet only fourteen months elapsed between the prototype's first flight in January 1941 and the Lancaster's first operational mission in March 1942.

The secret of the Lancaster's success lay largely in its superb power plants, the reliable and well-tried Rolls-Royce Merlins, which were introduced into the airframe after failure of the Vulture in the similar but smaller Manchester bomber. Indeed it was the expedient of substituting four Merlins in place of two Vultures that not only bestowed the increased safety and survival factors, but permitted the carriage of hitherto unheard-of bomb-loads. Of all bombs delivered by RAF Bomber Command during World War II, Lancasters dropped 63·8 per cent (over 600,000 tons). No wonder Sir Arthur Harris spoke of it as 'the greatest single factor in winning the war'.

The customary bomb-load of the Lancaster was around 12,000lb, usually including a single 4,000lb 'Blockbuster' and combinations of 1,000lb, 500lb or 250lb bombs, or 250lb Small Bomb Containers (carrying incendiary bombs). Other combinations included 14 1,000lb bombs (GP short-tail type), six 1,500lb mines, six 2,000lb High Capacity bombs, or a single 8,000lb and six 250lb bombs. Lancasters with bulged bomb doors were able to accommodate the 12,000lb 'Tallboy' deep-penetration bomb, and – the ultimate in conventional bomber arsenals of the war – the 22,000lb 'Grand Slam' was lifted by specially-modified Lancasters.

In its normal configuration the Lancaster was crewed by seven men (compared with ten in the American B-17 Flying Fortress and B-24 Liberator), comprising the pilot (captain), navigator, flight engineer, radio operator, bomb-aimer/front gunner, mid-upper gunner and rear gunner. There were early variations to this crew, principally as a left-over from the days when wireless operators doubled as gunners, and also when the Lancaster was occasionally equipped with a ventral gun turret, or special jamming equipment. Unlike the crews of German bombers, who tended to be grouped together in a compartment in the nose, the British heavy bombers of World War II, including the Lancaster, featured

dispersed crew stations, some crew members being physically isolated from their colleagues, except for the intercom, for eight or ten hours of cold, discomfort and danger. Being in an unpressurised aircraft, each man breathed oxygen throughout the flight, and failure of the supply of oxygen might well prove fatal unless a periodic crew check on the intercom brought no response, when the mid-upper gunner would be sent aft to discover the trouble.

Apart from the loneliness endured by the rear and mid-upper gunners, most of the crew had to contend with extreme cold, for the Lancaster was quite widely regarded as a draughty aircraft, the icy slipstream managing to penetrate numerous small cracks and apertures in the fuselage, particularly the front turret, cockpit canopy and bomb-bay; once again the unfortunate rear gunner suffered most. Irvin jackets, fleece-lined boots and electrically-heated suits alleviated the discomforts, but occasional malfunctions in the heating circuits either caused burns and blisters through overheating, or frostbite through total failure. While the rear gunner might be shivering, the radio operator, on the other hand, would probably be sweating, for his crew position was located abaft the two hot-air louvres from the wing centre section. The rear fuselage obtained none of this hot air as a bulkhead was designed to retain the heat, or at least most of it, in the forward half of the fuselage.

Before attempting to describe a typical Lancaster mission, it is necessary to set out the principal duties of the crew members to demonstrate that it was entirely the result of a tightknit team that such missions were possible. This teamwork and comradeship existed from the moment the crews assembled during their training until they were eventually disbanded or shot down. It permeated their whole lives on the ground and in the air. Prior to the introduction of the RAF's four-engined heavy bombers, there had been no necessity for such mutual trust and dependence among so many men assembled in a single aircraft.

Unlike the American B-17 and B-24, the Lancaster came to feature only a single pilot, assisted on certain occasions by the flight engineer. Although the pilot was frequently an NCO with officer crew members, he was invariably the aircraft captain, responsible in the final resort for decisions regarding mission aborts, crew safety and overall defence against the enemy. (This was occasionally not the case in different Canadian units.) His position, high in the nose of the aircraft, was the only one in the aircraft with armoured protection–a single sheet of armour behind his back. Apart from the obvious job of flying the aircraft, the pilot actively commanded his crew, calling crew checks on the intercom, and being responsible for the crew's proficiency in emergency and dinghy drills. In the event of the crew being ordered to bale out, the pilot was the last to go–often holding the aircraft steady until the last moment.

The flight engineer, as his title indicates, was responsible to the pilot for the general functioning of the engines and systems, assisting the pilot during take-off, managing the distribution of fuel throughout the flight, carrying out running repairs– where possible–to components in the hydraulic, electrical and oxygen systems. His crew station, surrounded by fuel gauges and cocks, ammeters, system switches and warning lights, was immediately behind and to the right of the pilot, though a fold-down seat on the right-hand side of the fuselage enabled him to operate the throttles and pitch controls during take-off.

The navigator, occupying a compartment behind the pilot, was fully engaged throughout the flight with frequent course checks, taking fixes, maintaining the flight log, passing checks and changes of course to the pilot and, being the only crew member whose station was illuminated, was curtained-off. So engrossed in his work was many a navigator that he was–and undoubtedly preferred to be–oblivious to the noises and hazards of battle that raged about the aircraft.

With radio silence almost invariably imposed on bombing operations, it might be thought that the radio operator, in his crew station opposite the wing leading edge, would normally have little to do. Yet throughout the flight he had not only to keep a listening watch on his Group frequency in case of recall, but also detect enemy radio traffic between intercepting fighters and their controllers on the ground, and operate such jamming equipment that was carried in his aircraft. Later on in the war the radio operator also managed and employed the H2S radar equipment for navigation purposes, and the Monica tail warning radar which gave indications of enemy fighters astern.

In the nose the bomb aimer had three principal duties–apart from notifying the pilot of approaching landmarks during the flight, for his field of vision was the best in the aircraft. (Although he was not supposed to take up his position in the nose until after take-off, it was extremely difficult to negotiate a way past the flight engineer in full parachute harness, and most bomb aimers did in fact install themselves in their crew station before take-off.) On the outward flight he would most likely man his turret and keep a look-out for enemy fighters. It was however his job to release the numerous bundles of Window at pre-briefed intervals (often as frequently as two or three times every minute) during the approach to the target, an unpopular chore owing to the large piles of these bundles that cluttered his already restricted compartment. On the actual bombing run he was of course responsible for fusing and selecting his bombs, guiding the pilot up to the point at which he assumed limited control through the automatic

control system. After release of the bombs a photo-flash would be discharged to synchronise with a photo taken by a camera under the cockpit, operated by the pilot, to show ground details of the point of impact of the aircraft's bombs.

The duties of the two gunners were of course vital for the survival of the aircraft and its crew. Just prior to crossing into enemy airspace they would fire a short burst to test their guns, but thereafter they would be scanning the sky to watch for other aircraft–friendly aircraft that might inadvertently stray dangerously close, and enemy aircraft. Theirs was the responsibility to maintain a commentary of enemy tactics so that the pilot could take effective evasive action. The majority of Lancasters in RAF service were not armed with the ventral turret, indeed could not be so armed when equipped with H2S radar whose large radome occupied the position otherwise taken by the turret. This almost universal absence of ventral defence rendered the Lancaster terribly vulnerable, a fact the Luftwaffe eventually exploited with its introduction of the upward-firing cannons in their night fighters.

The mid-upper gunner was provided with twin rifle-calibre Browning machine guns in a Frazer-Nash turret usually firing only 'ball' ammunition without tracer. His hydraulically-operated turret possessed a 360-degree traverse with taboo track to prevent him firing at parts of his own aircraft in the heat of action. The rear gunner was located within an enclosed cylindrical turret with hinged doors at his back (to bail out he simply turned his turret sideways and pushed himself backwards through these doors). Almost throughout the war the tail Frazer-Nash turret was armed with four 0·303in Browning, although later on some aircraft were fitted with enlarged Rose turrets mounting two 0·5in Browning guns. The ammunition boxes for the rear turret were located approximately abaft the mainplane trailing edge with long chutes passing down each side of the rear fuselage to a point under the centre of the turret mounting ring.

So much then for the duties of a Lancaster crew. Mere words can give no more than an impression of these duties in the reality of a dark night in a hostile sky. No amount of training could fully condition these young men to the sudden onset of unseen dangers, death and destruction and constant fear.

It was not uncommon for news of a raid to be received twelve hours before take-off, a period of daylight in which the aircrew could do little but try to rest and relax. Elsewhere however the bomber base would be seething with activity. Daylight hours were spent in the countless preparations for the

Inset above: entry to the nose was via the hatch on the right of the cockpit.
Inset above right: the navigator's position. The crew breathed oxygen during missions; the intercom was in the mask.
Right: Lancaster serialled PA474 is maintained by the Battle of Britain Flight. Built as a PR Mark I, it served with No 82 Squadron which used the Mark to make an extensive aerial survey of Africa in 1946–52. Subsequently PA474 became a flying test-bed. In 1965 it was refurbished to represent the B Mark I of No 44 Squadron in which Sqn Ldr J. D. Nettleton won the VC

Above: a Lancaster B Mk I of No 101 Sqn based at Ludford Magna, Lincolnshire and flown by Flt Lt George H. G. Harris DFC. The aircraft was equipped with Airborne Cigar (ABC), revealed by the two dorsal masts. ABC, one of the earliest airborne electronic countermeasures devices, searched out and then jammed enemy radio transmission frequencies by producing a constantly-varying audible note which ran up and down the enemy channel. It was used to disrupt communications between enemy night fighter pilots and controllers. A specially-trained German-speaking operator was carried. The ABC-equipped Lancasters carried a normal bomb-load less the weight of the equipment and operator. No 101 Squadron first took ABC into action on the night of 7/8 October 1943 on a raid on Stuttgart, and between then and April 1945 flew 2,477 sorties in support of the main bomber force with ABC

raid, during which the base was sealed off from the outside world for security purposes. While a small army of engine and airframe fitters exhaustively checked and re-checked every part of the aircraft itself, armourers examined and tested turrets and guns. At the bomb dump the loads to be carried were assembled with the various pyrotechnics and the bombs fused and loaded onto the trolleys for delivery to each aircraft at its distant dispersal bay. At the various sections of the base specialist officers worked out signalling procedures, examining weather forecasts and target information. Others assembled all the latest information on enemy defences and tactics, on diversion airfields and on other Bomber Command activity, such as spoof raids designed to distract German fighters. Elsewhere equipment stores were checking parachutes and other emergency kits.

It was fairly common for an RAF Bomber Command base to accommodate two Lancaster squadrons, each of which might be required to dispatch twenty aircraft on a night raid. Thus an evening's effort would involve some 280 aircrew members. The preparation of their aircraft demanded a carefully co-ordinated timetable of preparation in case an air test was required after an aircraft's inspection.

Pre-raid briefing of all aircrew was undertaken by a number of specialists, introduced by the station commander, namely the armament officer, navigation officer, intelligence officer, signals officer and meteorological officer. The following raid was one of many launched during the war against Berlin – 'the Big City' – the bombers' track lying out across the North Sea before turning south-east across northern Germany towards the target. Window was to be dropped before crossing the enemy coast and for much of the remainder of the outward journey. Most of the bombers carried a single 'Blockbuster' and incendiary bombs for a typical 'area bombing' attack. The high explosive bomb was intended to smash the city's water and electricity services and block streets with rubble, thereby preventing the civil defence forces from

reaching the countless fires started by the tens of thousands of incendiaries. Diversionary raids were to be carried out by small forces of bombers against southern Norway and France in attempts to disperse the German fighter opposition.

The main briefing over, the various crew members dispersed to their own briefings and then to their messes for an evening meal. After donning their flying clothing in the locker rooms and collecting their personal safety equipment and flight snacks, they made their way to their dispersed aircraft – often well over a mile from the station buildings – to await the moment to embark. With the knowledge of a long, hazardous flight ahead, this waiting time strained the nerves to the utmost. Some crews played football with the ground personnel, others played cards, smoked a cigarette or even tried to snatch a few moments' sleep.

About half an hour before take-off each crew assembled at the rear of the Lancaster to enter the aircraft through the door on the starboard side. A quick final check of their personal equipment and each man climbed the short ladder and made his way to his crew station. Those in the nose probably barked a shin on the great wing spar that constricted the midships passageway. As each man carried out his pre-flight checks, the pilot and flight engineer prepared to start the engines.

It was customary to start the two inboard engines first, followed by the outer. The ground starter battery was plugged in and the ground/flight switch set to 'ground', throttle set about half-an-inch open, propeller pitch set fine, slow-running switches off, supercharger in M-gear, air-intake control on cold, radiator shutters in automatic and the fuel tank selector cock on No 2 tank. As the groundcrew operated the priming pump, the ignition and booster coil was switched on and the starter button pressed. As the engine gave a few preliminary bangs, the groundcrew continued to pump away until the Merlin picked up on the carburettor and fired regularly. This process was repeated on the other engines.

As darkness gathered over the station, the air

Below: Lancasters depicted on a night mission. Although used in 1942 on daylight bombing raids, the Lancaster was vulnerable during the day, and Bomber Command subsequently used the type almost exclusively as a night bomber until the Allied air forces had achieved air superiority over Europe in early 1945. On night raids, the heavy bombers flew in streams, generally in three waves, to provide the maximum protection from night fighters

A 12,000 lb Tallboy deep-penetration bomb being loaded into a Lancaster's bomb-bay. The Lancaster could carry a maximum bomb-load of 8,165 kg (18,000 lb), including one 4,000 lb bomb and, from mid-1943, an 8,000 lb bomb, basically two 4,000 lb bombs joined together. These bombs were essentially huge cans of high explosive, designed to produce surface blast waves. They were highly successful in built-up areas. Later Lancasters could carry a 12,000 lb bomb. However, the 12,000 lb Tallboy and the 22,000 lb Grand Slam were 'earthquake' bombs, designed to provide deep penetration before exploding, and were known to penetrate 10·7 m (35 ft) of concrete before exploding

was full of noise as eighty 1,200 hp Merlins started and each pilot ran up against the chocks to 1,500 rpm to check the eight magnetos and then to 3,000 rpm to check boost. Further checks followed, prior to taxying. Flaps were selected down and up, bomb doors checked closed, booster pumps off, radiator shutters open, brake pressure at least 250 lb/sq in, altimeter set to airfield height, vacuum pumps for instrument panel showing minus 4½ lb/sq in and navigation lights on.

Waving away the chocks, the pilot gunned the throttles to move his 25-ton aircraft out of dispersal to join the queue of other Lancasters taxying slowly towards the end of the runway. No weaving was necessary as his view over the front turret was sufficient to see the aircraft ahead. A check call was made on the intercom to ensure all crew members were ready for take-off and that their equipment, including oxygen supply, was functioning satisfactorily. As each Lancaster turned onto the runway, it was cleared for take-off by a green Aldis light from the control tower (no radio could yet be used). Take-off checks included auto-pilot clutch in, cock out, DR compass set, pitot head heater on, trim set (elevator slightly forward, rudder and aileron neutral), propeller pitch fine. Fuel was checked (contents OK, master cocks on, selector cocks on

No 2 tanks, crossfeeds off, booster pumps in Nos 1 and 2 tanks on). Superchargers were set in M-gear, air intakes at cold, radiator shutters on automatic, and flaps selected at about 15 degrees down.

On receiving take-off clearance, the pilot released the brakes and advanced the throttles slowly, the flight engineer assisting and leading with the port levers to check a slight tendency to swing to port. With throttles wide open and held there by the flight engineer and the engines at plus-9 boost and 3,000 rpm, the pilot eased forward on the control column, at the same time applying fairly coarse right rudder to hold the swing. At around 100 mph indicated airspeed, he began a firm but gradual backward pressure on the column and the Lancaster became airborne. Applying the brakes momentarily to stop the wheels spinning, the undercarriage was retracted and, after gaining at least 500 feet, the flaps were raised. Safety speed was about 125 mph indicated and once this speed was reached, the throttles were pulled back to give plus-6 boost at 2,850 rpm for the initial climb to operating height.

The Norfolk coast was crossed and the H2S radar gave a clear indication of Yarmouth, enabling the navigator to make a rough check on the briefed wind speed and direction. At this time it was not realised in Bomber Command that the operation of

gunfire would be heard over the background hum in the crew's earphones.

The turn towards the enemy coast was followed almost immediately by the first discharge of Window bundles. The bomb aimer started to push the brown paper packages down the chute, to be caught and burst open by the Lancaster's slipstream. Notwithstanding this effective means of confusing the enemy's radar, the pilot now warned his gunners to be particularly alert for enemy fighters.

Conscious of the fact that theirs was only one of several hundred similar bombers, all flying an identical course in a great invisible corridor in the sky, the pilot and gunners strained to catch a glimpse of other aircraft. Suddenly out of the corner of his eye the pilot sighted a line of white specks some distance to port; at once the mid-upper gunner reported a bomber being attacked by a night fighter. Not waiting to watch the result of the attack, the pilot started to fly an erratic course, corkscrewing gently so as to provide a more fleeting target for any other fighter that may be stalking his Lancaster from astern. There was no further call from the gunner and the crew took comfort in the belief that perhaps the bomber managed to evade the German fighter.

Five minutes later the radio operator passed a further wind broadcast from home to the navigator, who told the pilot that the Lancaster was crossing the German coast, a fact confirmed on the H2S. Crossing in near Hamburg, the coastline easily recognised at this point, Berlin was still an hour's flying time away. The German fighter assembly beacon nearby was passed, but another assembly point was not far distant to port of the bomber stream. At this stage there was little flak and no searchlights penetrated the cloud below.

Suddenly a great burst of light exploded ahead and above the Lancaster, casting a weird, flickering glow on the surrounding cloud tops and momen-

the H2S equipment would be detected by the Germans at very long range, thereby giving ample warning of the assembly and approach of a large raid. Later on in the war, orders were given that the H2S should only be switched on as the enemy coast was crossed.

Soon the first wind information at the head of the bomber stream was passed back to Britain by the 'windfinders'. This was collated and broadcast to the bombers following. The radio operator received the information and passed it to the navigator, who made the necessary adjustment to his course and informed the pilot.

Arriving at 22,000 feet the pilot throttled back slightly to maintain a speed of just over 200mph indicated. After about three hours' flying the navigator warned that the change or course towards the German coast must be made shortly and gave the anticipatory instructions to the pilot. One by one the gunners asked permission to fire a short burst from their guns to clear any icing and the clatter of

Left: the bomb aimer had an optically flat plexiglass panel in the nose cupola through which to sight. He lay in a prone position looking through the bombsight – a Mark XIV – throughout the bomb run, during which he selected and fused the bombs through a main control box in the nose, and guided the pilot onto the correct course via the intercom. Below: a Lancaster of No 15 Squadron. The markings on the tail fins indicate the aircraft is carrying GH airborne radar, although it also has the H2S radar ventral radome. GH airborne radar allowed RAF squadrons to undertake daylight blind bombing, for instance through total cloud cover. A limited number of Lancaster squadrons of Nos 3 and 6 Groups Bomber Command were fitted with GH equipment

THE DAMS RAID

Wg Cdr Guy Gibson recalled his attack on the Möhne Dam in his book *Enemy Coast Ahead*. 'The Lancaster was really moving and I began looking through the special sight on my windscreen. Spam had his eyes glued to the bombsight in front, his hand on his button; a special mechanism on board had already begun to work so that the mine would drop (we hoped) in the right spot. Terry was still checking the height. Joe and Trev began to raise their guns. The flak could see us quite clearly now. It was not exactly inferno. I have been through far worse flak fire than that; but we were very low. There was something sinister and slightly unnerving about the whole operation. My aircraft was so small and the dam was so large; it was thick and solid, and now it was angry. My aircraft was very small.

We skimmed along the surface of the lake, and as we went my gunner was firing into the defences, and the defences were firing back with vigour, their shells whistling past us. For some reason, we were not being hit.

'Spam said, "Left–little more left–steady–steady–steady–coming up." Of the next few seconds I remember only a series of kaleidoscopic incidents. The chatter from Joe's front guns pushing out tracers which bounced off the left-hand flak tower. Pulford crouching beside me. The smell of burnt cordite. The cold sweat underneath my oxygen mask. The tracers flashing past the windows–they all seemed the same colour now–and the inaccuracy of the gun positions near the power-station; they were firing in the wrong direction. The closeness of the dam wall. Spam's exultant, "Mine gone".'

Right: two pages from the Pilot's Notes for the Lancaster Mks I and II. Left: a photograph taken from a cine-film made by the RAF Film Production Unit during the Thousand Bomber Raid on Essen on 11 March 1945, showing bombers releasing Window on the flight to the target. Window consisted of slivers of aluminium foil, released by the bomb-aimer in loosely-tied bundles which scattered in the slipstream. Radar reflections from the foil combined with reflections from the bombers to produce a confused picture on enemy radar displays, often obscuring them entirely and concealing the size and direction of a raid. During the Essen raid 1,079 RAF bombers dropped 4,661 tons of bombs through total cloud cover, made possible by GH blind-bombing radar

tarily lighting the cockpit. Someone in the crew reported a 'scarecrow', a pyrotechnic thought to be fired from the ground to simulate an exploding bomber. It transpired that no such devices were ever fired by the Germans during the war and it was likely that these explosions were either bombers exploding, or large flares dropped above the bomber stream by German reconnaissance fighters.

The gunners now started calling in to report tracer being fired at aircraft on both sides of the Lancaster, which was still weaving gently from side to side. The mid-upper broke off suddenly in mid-sentence and then called urgently to warn of a single-engine fighter sweeping in from the rear quarter. As the pilot banked sharply towards the attack, he was immediately aware of minute shafts of light passing close ahead. There was an angry clatter of gunfire from the mid-upper. Five seconds later the gunner

reported that the fighter had disappeared. Pilot and flight engineer anxiously scanned their instruments to spot any tell-tale loss of power or pressure and there was a quick check of crew members on the intercom. Fortunately the fighter had overshot the Lancaster and disappeared.

Events now occurred in swift succession as the navigator warned the pilot that the target was only ten minutes away. The bomb aimer reported that he had completed his Window dropping and was taking up his position at his bombsight. At this moment the rear gunner reported another aircraft closing from astern, but the pilot, sensing rather than seeing cloud towering ahead, warned the gunners to hold their fire in the hope of evading the enemy fighter. There was a brief clattering sound from somewhere aft and then the Lancaster was swallowed up in the grey shroud. The pilot banked the aircraft sharply one way and then the other. Moments later the Lancaster emerged from the towering cumulus and the bomb aimer reported that he could see the ground ahead. The crew was conscious of a vibration that passed right through the Lancaster, and the mid-upper called back to report sparks streaming back from the starboard outer engine. The flight engineer reported a loss of power on the engine and that its coolant temperature was climbing fast. A fire warning light flickered on. The vibration was getting worse and the pilot ordered the engine to be stopped. The flight engineer immediately switched off the Merlin's master fuel cock, operated the fire extinguisher on that engine, feathered the propeller and switched off.

As the pilot re-trimmed the aircraft to counteract the drag from the stopped engine, he was aware that there had been no further word from the rear gunner and, receiving no reply to a check on the intercom, ordered the mid-upper gunner aft to find

own fine control corrections on the auto control, the bomb aimer was oblivious to the noise and chaos about him as the Lancaster rocked from the explosions of nearby shell bursts. Suddenly the great bomber seemed to be lifted by some invisible hand. 'Bombs gone', came the call from the bomb aimer. Still the pilot had to maintain a steady course for some moments until the photo-flash recorded the impact point of the bombs.

The all-important photograph taken, the navigator passed a new course to clear the target area. The mid-upper gunner reported to the pilot that the rear gunner had been slightly wounded in the arm, that the oxygen supply to the rear turret was no longer functioning and that the turret was partly jammed. He assisted the gunner forward into the fuselage and gave him a portable oxygen set. The pilot ordered the mid-upper to remain in his turret and told the radio operator to help the wounded gunner further forward and attend to his wound.

AIR PUBLICATION 2062A, C & F—P.N.
Pilot's and Flight Engineer's Notes

PART IV

EMERGENCIES

51. Engine failure during take-off

(i) If for any reason the booster pumps in the tanks being used are not ON, the master fuel cock of the failed engine must be turned off before feathering.

(ii) If one outer engine fails, the aircraft can be kept straight provided 130 (125) m.p.h. I.A.S. has been reached.

(iii) Climbing speed on three engines should be 135 (130) m.p.h. I.A.S. at moderate loads, or 140(135) m.p.h. I.A.S. if heavily loaded.

(iv) As soon as the undercarriage is up, raise the flaps a little at a time, retrimming as necessary.

52. Engine failure in flight

(i) If an engine is stopped, air may be drawn into the fuel system through the carburettor of the failed engine. To prevent this, the master fuel cock must be turned off before feathering, unless the booster pump for the tank in use is on. If an engine seizes up, its master fuel cock should be turned off immediately to ensure that the fuel supply to the other engine on the same side is not affected.

(ii) If the failed engine cannot be made to pick up again, feather its propeller and switch off. On Lancaster III and X, set mixture control to IDLE CUT-OFF.

(iii) *Handling on three engines.*—The aircraft will maintain height at full load on any three engines at 10,000 feet, and can be trimmed to fly without foot load. Maintain at least 145 (140) m.p.h. I.A.S. The automatic pilot has sufficient power to maintain a straight course with either outboard engine out of action, but only if assisted by the rudder trimming tab.

34

PART IV—EMERGENCIES

(iv) *Landing on three engines.*—Lowering of flaps to 20° and of undercarriage may be carried out as normally on the circuit, but further lowering of the flaps should be left until final straight approach. The final approach should be made at 120–125 m.p.h. I.A.S. using as little power as possible, and rudder trim should not be wound off until definitely committed to landing. Use all good engines to regulate approach. (*See* A.P. 2095, Part IV, Note D.)

(v) *Handling on two engines.*—It should be possible to maintain height below 10,000 feet at 140 (135) m.p.h. I.A.S. on any two engines after release of bombs and with half fuel used; but with two engines dead on one side, the foot load will be very heavy. The automatic pilot will not cope with flight with two engines dead on one side.

(vi) *Landing on two engines.*—The circuit should be made with the good engines on the inside of the turn, and undercarriage and flaps left as late as practicable. Keep extra height in hand, if possible, and lower the undercarriage later than usual, but have it locked down just before the final approach. The approach should be made at 130–135 m.p.h. I.A.S. in a glide. When certain of getting into the airfield, lower flaps for landing. Do not wind off trim until final approach can be made in a glide, as some power may be necessary in the early stages. (*See* A.P. 2095, Part IV, Notes C and D.)

(vii) Do not attempt to maintain height above 10,000 feet, either on three or two engines.

(viii) *Fuel system.*—The cross-feed cock should only be turned on when it is desired to feed fuel from port (or starboard) tanks to starboard (or port) engines. In this case all live engines should be fed from one tank and the fuel booster pump for this tank should be on. The fuel selector for the tanks on the other side of the aircraft should be off. At all other times, the cross-feed cock should be off.

53. Feathering

(i) (*a*) *Practice feathering.*—Check that booster pump in the tank feeding the engine to be stopped is on. *See* para. 52 (i). Set propeller control to low r.p.m. and throttle to give a moderate cruising boost.

35

---

out what had happened. The Lancaster was approaching the target area, and with the flak intensifying there seemed less chance of being attacked by enemy fighters. The climax of the flight approached, as the bomb-aimer reported that he could see the first target indicators. All around the ground was a sea of flashing explosions, among the countless pinpoints of white twinkling incendiaries huge shimmering bowls of fire erupted as the huge blast bombs shattered the streets far below.

As he had to keep the Lancaster steady on a straight course, the pilot completed his final trimming as the great bomb doors were opened, causing a slight nose-up tendency. These were the most hated moments of the whole flight as the crew sensed that every German gunner on the ground was aiming at their own aircraft as it flew up to the point at which it released its deadly load of bombs. Making his

Although the Lancaster was perfectly capable of maintaining altitude on three engines, the crew was painfully aware that it still had a long flight home. With the airspeed reduced to about 160 mph indicated and a strong headwind, it would be covering enemy territory at only about 120 mph. Experience on previous raids suggested that the German night fighters had concentrated their efforts upon the bomber's approach to the target, and that only occasional attacks were made on the returning stream. Nevertheless, aware that his defences had been severely reduced, the Lancaster's captain warned the mid-upper to keep a sharp lookout for other aircraft. The bomb-aimer volunteered to go aft to the rear turret with a portable oxygen set to keep a watch astern. The navigator passed a new course for base.

Time passed slowly. Soon the Lancaster was

again flying over unbroken cloud. After eight hours in the air there was a perceptible lightening in the east as dawn approached over eastern Germany. The pilot ordered the bomb aimer forward to his position in the nose as the navigator reported that the H2S showed the aircraft to be crossing the Belgian coast. The radio operator called up to say that the wounded gunner had lost a lot of blood and, though conscious, was in some pain despite a morphia injection. Calling for a course to steer for Manston, the pilot decided to make for the nearest diversion airfield to get medical help for the gunner as quickly as possible.

Another ten minutes passed and the bomb aimer reported that the cloud was breaking up below. Easing back the throttles, the pilot started descending towards the Kent coastline. Still he dared not break radio silence in case there were enemy intruders over south-east England awaiting the bombers' return.

At 4.30 it was already beginning to get light. At 5,000 feet the bomb aimer called up with a sighting of the coast. The pilot now called Manston for permission to land, stating that he had a wounded crew member aboard. The airfield replied, giving landing instructions; the huge runway was quite adequate even for a Lancaster without brakes.

With the runway lights in sight, the pilot started a wide circuit to the left, thereby keeping the two good port engines on the inside of his turns. Lowering of the undercarriage caused a slight nose-

down trim change, but this was corrected with selection of 20 degrees of flap. Keeping the speed at about 140mph, the pilot turned onto the approach about two miles from the runway with plenty of power. Now he eased off throttle to reduce speed to about 125mph, gradually winding off the coarse rudder trim and maintaining his heading by use of rudder. Once over the runway threshold at about 50 feet, he selected a bit more flap and firmly eased back on the control column. As the Lancaster touched down at about 90mph the flight engineer closed the throttles and the pilot started applying the brakes. The great bomber slowed rapidly and the engineer shut down the remaining outer engine for taxying on the inner Merlins.

Above: Lancasters bombing a V1 flying bomb launching site. The V1 offensive began on 12 June 1944, and on 16/17 June Bomber Command began attacks on the launching sites in France in an intensive effort which lasted until 6 September, shortly after V1 launching from France ceased. Below: a Lancaster B Mk III of No 207 Squadron. The B Mark III was similar to the B Mark I but had Packard-built Merlins in place of the Rolls-Royce-built engines. No 207 Squadron, in common with other Lancaster Squadrons, flew B Marks I and III concurrently

Mitsubishi A6M Zero

Below: the A6M2 Model 11 was the first production version of the Zero. The highly manoeuvrable, heavily-armed Zero achieved a myth of invincibility over China and in the first months of war with the USA, but once its vulnerabilities – light structure and lack of armour – had been discovered, it was soon outclassed by opposing fighter aircraft.

Bottom: the A6M5 Model 52 was developed from the A6M3 in 1943 to meet urgent demands for a fighter able to restore Japanese air superiority in the Pacific. It had a stronger wing to allow it to dive faster, a critical factor because US fighters exploited their superior diving speeds in combat with Japanese fighters. The A6M5b introduced an armoured windscreen and fuel tank fire extinguishers to decrease the Zero's vulnerability

If ever a single aeroplane type truly symbolised a nation's air power it was surely the Mitsubishi A6M Reisen–Japan's Zero fighter. From that infamous December day at Pearl Harbour, the Zero heralded a new era in naval aviation and created a myth of Japanese invincibility.

The Zero was designed as a replacement for the Mitsubishi A5M Navy Type 96 Claude carrier fighter, to a demanding Imperial Japanese Navy specification calling for a top speed in excess of 500km/h (310mph), a 3,000m (10,000ft) climb in three-and-a-half minutes, and range and especially manoeuvrability in excess of any existing type. So impossible did the requirements seem that Nakajima, Mitsubishi's rivals for the contract, pulled out within three months of starting design work, believing the project to be unrealistic. By careful use of a light, tough alloy called Extra-Super Duralumin in the airframe, and the selection of a lightweight engine, Mitsubishi designer Jiro Horikoshi was able to keep the A6M prototype's weight and frontal area to the minimum, so that

by the time the third prototype had flown late in December 1939, all the navy's requirements had been achieved or exceeded.

Even in its early form the Reisen came as a shock to American pilots and a delight to the Japanese airmen who flew them. 'The Zero excited me as nothing else had ever done before', wrote Japanese ace Saburo Sakai. 'Even on the ground it had the cleanest lines I had ever seen in an aeroplane. We now had enclosed cockpits, a powerful engine and retractable landing gear. Instead of only two light machine guns, we were armed with two machine guns and two heavy 20mm cannon as well. The Zero had almost twice the speed and range of the Claude, and it was a dream to fly. The aeroplane was the most sensitive I had ever flown, and even slight finger pressure brought instant response. We could hardly wait to meet enemy planes in this remarkable new aircraft.'

From the Sino-Japanese conflict, during which they made short work of a motley collection of Russian Polikarpov I-16s, and American Curtiss P-40s, to Pearl Harbour and the attack on Dutch Harbour in the Aleutians in June 1942, Zeros won and held Japanese air superiority and fostered this myth of invincibility among Japanese and Allied pilots. Recounting one air battle over the Yangtze Valley, Sakai wrote: 'I pulled out at low altitude, coming up behind one I-16 fighter as it rolled down the field. It was a perfect target, and a short cannon burst exploded the fighter in flames. I flashed across the field and spiralled sharply to the right, climbing steeply to come around for another run. Tracers and flak were to left and right of me, but the Zero's unexpected speed threw the enemy gunners off. Other Zero fighters dived and made strafing passes over the runways. Several of the Russian fighters were burning or had crashed. I pulled out of a dive to catch another plane in my sights. A second short cannon burst and there was a mushrooming ball of fire. There was nothing left to strafe. Our attack had cleared the field of enemy planes and not a single Russian aircraft was able to fly. . .'

The Zero was faster in both climb and maximum speed than any Allied aircraft and US Navy pilots flying Grumman F4F Wildcats quickly discovered that the only way to down a Zero was to dive through the Japanese formations from above, firing all the while, before dashing away out of

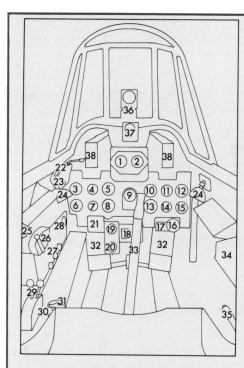

gauge 4: *Clock* 5: *Airspeed indicator*
6: *Radio direction indicator*
7: *Magneto switch* 8: *Altimeter*
9: *Magnetic compass* 10: *Rate of
climb indicator* 11: *Fuel and oil
temperature gauge* 12: *Engine speed
indicator* 13: *Manifold pressure gauge*
14: *Oil temperature gauge*
15: *Cylinder head temperature gauge*
16: *Oil cooler control* 17: *Ignition
booster switch* 18: *Cannon master
switch* 19: *Pilot's oxygen supply gauge*
20: *Hydraulic systems pressure gauge*
21: *Engine primer pump* 22: *Fuel
mixture lever* 23: *Boost switch*
24: *Cockpit lights* 25: *Throttle
quadrant* 26: *Fuel mixture control
lever* 27: *Lighting control box*
28: *Lighting voltmeter gauge*
29: *Bomb release levers* 30: *Drop
tank release* 31: *Fuel tank selection
control* 32: *Rudder pedals* 33: *Control
column* 34: *Radio equipment stowage*
35: *Seat height adjustment lever*
36: *Reflector gunsight* 37: *Gunsight
control* 38: *7.7mm machine gun
breeches*

Mitsubishi A6M Zero cockpit
1: *Artificial horizon* 2: *Turn and bank
indicator* 3: *Exhaust temperature*

range. To hang around for a dogfight with the nimble Reisen was to ask for trouble. Sakai recalled of his first encounter with an F4F that he 'realised that the Grumman's fighting performance far exceeded that of any other American, Dutch or Chinese fighter planes. . . [but] I had full confidence in my ability to destroy the Grumman, and decided to finish off the enemy fighter with only my 7.7mm machine guns. For some strange reason, even after I had poured about five or six hundred rounds of ammunition directly into the Grumman, the aeroplane did not fall but kept on flying. I thought this very odd–it had never happened before–and closed the distance between the two aeroplanes until I could almost reach out and touch the Grumman. To my surprise, his rudder and tail were ripped to shreds, looking like an old torn piece of rag.'

In Sakai's surprise at the Wildcat's ability to fly with so much combat damage lies the key to the Zero's biggest failing. When two almost undamaged Zeros fell into American hands in 1942 the aircraft quickly revealed itself as far from invincible; indeed it was distinctly vulnerable. By paring away excess weight, Mitsubishi had achieved outstanding performance, but at the cost of structural strength and a near-total inability to absorb any serious combat damage and remain airworthy. Although nimbler than many Allied aircraft, the Zero had no armour protection for pilot or fuel tanks. After examining the captured specimens, the Intelligence Service of the United States Army Air Force offered this advice to American combat pilots: 'Never attempt to dogfight a Zero; never manoeuvre with a Zero below 300mph unless you are directly behind it, and never attempt to climb behind a Zero at low speed. Aeroplanes to be used against the Zero should be

嵐-131

as light as possible. All equipment not absolutely necessary for combat should be removed.'

The Zero, especially the clipped-wing A6M3 version, was also deficient in range for the Japanese attempts to hold a front extending from Malaya to the Aleutian Islands. When the Americans took Guadalcanal in August 1942, the Japanese found themselves trying to drive back their advance from Rabaul, 900km (560 miles) away, and many Zeros were ditched on the long round-trip.

Saburo Sakai and his colleagues developed a technique for extending the range: 'The Zero was designed to remain in the air on a single flight for a maximum of six or seven hours. We stretched this figure to from ten to twelve hours, and did so on mass formation flights. I personally established the record low consumption of less than seventeen gallons an hour; on average our pilots reduced their consumption from thirty-five gallons per hour to only eighteen. . . To conserve fuel we cruised at only 115 knots at 12,000 feet altitude. Under normal full-power conditions the Zero was capable of 275 knots and, when overboosted for short emergencies, could reach its maximum speed of about 300 knots. On our long-range flights we lowered propeller revolutions to only 1,700 to 1,850rpm and throttled the air control valve to its leanest mixture. This furnished us with the absolute minimum power and speed, and we hung on to the fringe of losing engine power at any time and stalling.'

Until the turning point at the Battle of Midway, the Zero had reigned supreme in the Pacific War, not just because of its superior performance, but because the Allies had seriously underestimated Japanese air power. Australian pilot Gregory Board, who flew Brewster Buffaloes against the

Japanese in Malaya, Singapore and Burma in 1942, summed it up thus: 'Intelligence briefings almost daily by the most learned of men, who came in from the other side of the Japanese bamboo curtain, told us that the best of the Japanese fighters were old fabric-covered biplanes which wouldn't stand a chance against the Buffaloes. With this ringing promise of slaughtering the Japanese in the air should they get too big for their britches, we concentrated on flying and learning different methods of drinking gin and tonic.' When Board's squadron encountered Zeros 'the entire squadron was wiped out to a man. Suddenly we realised what we had in the Buffalo – a barrel which the Zero could outfly, outclimb, outgun, outmanoeuvre and outdo in almost anything else that was in the book for fighting aircraft.'

Gregory 'Pappy' Boyington, who flew Curtiss P-40s with the American Volunteer Group in China and later US Marine Corps' F4U Corsairs in the Pacific, had been similarly misled about the Japanese. His recruiter in the AVG told him:'The Japs will be flying antiquated junk over China. Many of your kills will be unarmed transports. I suppose you know that the Japanese are renowned for their inability to fly. And they all wear corrective glasses.'

Once the surprise element had been overcome, and the Americans had learned the Zero's weaknesses, its nemesis was not long in coming. The Grumman F6F Hellcat and Chance Vought F4U Corsair effectively put an end to the Zero's superiority, both aeroplanes surpassing it in every respect except low-speed manoeuvrability. 'The F6F', wrote Japanese staff officer Masatake Okiyuma, 'has a higher maximum speed than the Zero, can outclimb and outdive and outgun it,

An A6M5c Zero of No 221 Naval Air Corps, Imperial Japanese Naval Air Force, a land-based fighter unit, depicted in January 1944 when the unit was formed on Shikoku Island. Serving in Japan, Formosa and the Philippines, it was in action until the Japanese surrender. The A6M5c was the last major production variant of the Zero. It was intended to meet an urgent Navy requirement issued as a result of the 'Marianas Turkey Shoot' of 19 June 1944 when its A6M5a and b fighters had been decimated by the US Navy's Grumman F6F fighters. The A6M5c introduced armour for the pilot, more fuel tankage for increased range and heavier calibre guns. Although these changes resulted in greater weight, engine power was not increased and performance was poor

and retains the benefits of high-structural strength, armour-plating and self-sealing fuel tanks. In fact, with the exception of turning radius and range, the Hellcat completely outperforms the Zero. . .'

Saburo Sakai found the Hellcat no easy kill for his Zero: 'I snapped back in a tight turn. The manoeuvre startled the enemy pilots as I climbed at them from below, swinging into a spiral. I was surprised; they didn't scatter. The lead fighter responded with an equal spiral, matching my manoeuvre perfectly. Again I spiralled, drawing it closer this time. The opposing fighters refused to yield a foot. This was something new. An Airacobra or a P-40 would have been lost trying to match me in this fashion, and not even the Wildcat could hold a spiral too long against a Zero. But these new Hellcats–they were the most manoeuvrable enemy planes I had ever encountered. . . I ran. I gunned the engine to give every last ounce of power and pulled away sufficiently to get out of their gun range for a moment. . . I slammed my right foot against the rudder bar, skidding the Zero to the left. Then the stick, hard over to the left, rolling sharply. Sparkling lights flashed beneath my right wing, followed by a plummeting Hellcat. . . I cannot remember how many times the fighters attacked nor how many times I rolled away. The perspiration rolled down my body, soaking my underclothes. My forehead was all beads of sweat, and it began to drip down onto my face. I cursed when the salty liquid trickled into my left eye. . . I couldn't take time to rub it with my hand. All I could do was to blink, try to keep the salt away, try to see. I was tiring much too quickly. I didn't know how I could get away. But it was very clear that these pilots weren't as good as their planes. An inner voice seemed to whisper to me. It repeated over and over the same words. . . speed . . . keep up your speed. . . forget the engine. . . burn it out, keep up your speed. . . keep rolling. . . never stop rolling. . .'

Sakai recalled an air battle over Guadalcanal on 8 August 1942: 'Finally I saw them, about 1,500 feet below me – a single Wildcat pursued three Zero fighters, firing in short bursts at the frantic Japanese planes. All four planes were in a wild dogfight, flying tight left spirals. The Zeros should have been able to take the lone Grumman without any trouble, but every time a Zero caught the Wildcat before its guns the enemy plane flipped away wildly and came out again on the tail of the Zero. I had never seen such flying before. . . The Wildcat was clinging grimly to the tail of a Zero, its tracers chewing up the wings and tail. In desperation I snapped out a burst. At once the Grumman snapped away in a roll to the right, clawed around in a tight turn, and ended up in a climb straight at my own plane. Never had I seen an enemy plane move so quickly or so gracefully before; and every second his guns were moving closer to the belly of my fighter. I snap-rolled in an effort to throw him off. He would not be shaken. He was using my own favourite tactics, coming up from under. . .

'Neither of us could gain an advantage. We held to the spiral, tremendous 'g' pushing us down in our seats with every passing second. My heart pounded wildly, my head felt as if it weighed a ton. A grey film seemed to be clouding over my eyes. I gritted my teeth; if the enemy pilot could take the punishment, so could I. The man who failed first and turned in any other direction to ease the pressure would be finished.

'On the fifth spiral the Wildcat skidded slightly. I had him, I thought. But the Grumman dropped its nose, gained speed, and the pilot again had his plane in full control. There was a terrific man behind that stick. He made his error, however, in the next moment. Instead of swinging back to go into a sixth spiral, he fed power to his engine, broke away at an angle, and looped. That was the decisive split second. I went right after him, cutting inside the Grumman's arc, and came out on his tail. I had him. He kept flying loops, trying to narrow the distance of each arc. Every time he went up and around I cut inside his arc and lessened the distance between our two planes. . .

'When I was only fifty yards away, the Wildcat broke out of his loop and astonished me by flying straight and level. At this distance I would not need the cannon; I pumped 200 rounds into the Grumman's cockpit, watching the bullets chewing up the thin metal skin and shattering the glass. I could not believe what I saw; the Wildcat continued flying almost as if nothing had happened. A Zero which had taken that many bullets would have been a ball of fire by now. . .'

A Zero suicide aircraft is hit by anti-aircraft fire from its intended victim, the cruiser USS Vicksburg. By October 1944 the Japanese Navy had lost its aircraft carriers and few of its experienced fighter pilots survived. However, although kamikazes accounted for half of the American warships damaged or sunk during their ten months of use, suicide attacks were finally defeated by anti-aircraft fire and fighter patrols

> *'With the usual pitching and yawing of the carrier on the open sea, that narrow flight deck posed special hazards. The Hellcat's stability and trim capabilities really made the difference...'*

Grumman F6F Hellcat

This pair of Grumman F6F-3 Hellcats illustrates the type's characteristic tail-down 'sit'. The F6F-3 entered US Navy service at the beginning of 1943 and by the end of the year it had replaced the Grumman F4F Wildcat aboard the principal American carriers

From the outset of America's involvement in World War II, the US Navy was continually challenged to produce a carrier-based fighter aircraft to defeat the excellent Mitsubishi A6M Zero-Sen series used by Japanese fighter squadrons. Lacking both the speed and manoeuvrability of the Zero-Sen, the Grumman F4F Wildcat achieved success through superior tactics and pilot proficiency. However, it was the Grumman F6F Hellcat series which gave US Navy fighter pilots the speed and diving ability to master the Zero-Sen and other Japanese fighters. To the Hellcat's credit, it established a 19-to-1 kill ratio during the war in the Pacific.

The Grumman F4F was in production and the Chance Vought F4U Corsair series was well along in development when the 7 December 1941 Japanese attack on Pearl Harbour brought the United States into World War II. However, the Corsair was experiencing problems – particularly in its ability to operate from aircraft carriers – and it was apparent that the Wildcat alone could not fill the fighter gap in the Pacific. The other front-line fighter – the Brewster F2A Buffalo – was clearly no match for Japanese fighters. Hence, work was accelerated on the 'improved F4F' which Grumman had contracted on 30 June 1941 to build for the Navy.

The design team headed by company founder Leroy Grumman and William T. Schwendler did more than simply 'improve' the Wildcat. Although they were advised to stay close to the basic F4F design, to enhance the speed of development of the new fighter, they came up with an aircraft which was bigger, heavier and considerably faster. In adhering to Navy specifications for more ammunition and fuel – both of which added more weight – the design team had to use the largest wing area of any American single-engined production fighter of World War II.

F6F-3 Hellcats of fighter squadron VF-8 fly in formation before embarking on USS Hornet (CV-8). In combat with Japanese fighters, Hellcat pilots avoided tight manoeuvring dogfights and exploited their superior speed in diving attacks on the enemy. When caught at a disadvantage, the Hellcat had sufficient power to evade an attacking Japanese fighter and it was sturdy enough to absorb a considerable amount of battle damage

The Hellcat wing was mounted at the minimum angle of incidence to obtain the least drag in level flight. However, since a relatively great angle of attack was desirable for taking off from a carrier flight deck, a negative thrust line was adopted for the engine. In turn, that produced an angle on the propeller shaft that gave the Hellcat a tail-down 'sit' while in level flight.

The Grumman design team knew that the Mitsubishi Zero-Sen series was so successful because of its clean, lightweight design which made the pilot particularly vulnerable to heavy enemy firepower. The risk was unacceptable to the American designers, to whom the sobriquet 'Grumman Iron Works' was a tribute to the ruggedness of their aircraft. Hence, the obvious answer was to equip the Hellcat with the most powerful engine available to give it the speed to pursue the Zero-Sen.

Initially, the 1,700hp Wright R-2600-10 Cyclone 14 engine was considered for the Hellcat. Development problems with that power plant encouraged Grumman and the Navy to consider the 2,000hp Pratt & Whitney R-2800 Double Wasp. Following development of the series through the XF6F-1 and XF6F-2 prototypes led to the XF6F-3, which eventually became the first production Hellcat. The experimental variant first flew on 26 June 1942 and the first production variant made its maiden flight on 30 July 1942.

Fighter Squadron VF-9 was the first unit to be equipped with F6F-3 aircraft and was deployed aboard USS *Essex* (CV-9). VF-5 aboard USS *Yorktown* (CV-10) was the first unit to fly the Hellcat in combat, sending F6F-3s into the 31 August 1943 attack on Marcus Island.

Carrier suitability problems with the Vought F4U Corsair made it imperative that large num-

bers of new F6F-3s be produced to fill the flight decks of the new American aircraft fleet, which was growing at a fast pace. In addition to the large new *Essex*-class carriers (CVs), a number of cruiser hulls were being converted to light carriers (CVLs) and merchant ship hulls were being used to build small escort carriers (CVEs). All three types of carriers eventually operated Hellcats, which became so sought after that Grumman had to build a new plant specifically to produce them.

Pilots were also needed to man the growing number of Hellcat squadrons. In the case of Lieutenant (junior grade) James R. Ean, that meant forsaking slower dive bombing aircraft for the fast and manoeuvrable environment of the fighter. Now an executive with the US office of Lufthansa, Ean recalls: 'After I had completed my naval flight training, I had been assigned to a Douglas SBD Dauntless dive bomber squadron. The SBD was a great dive bomber, which performed very well, although it was slow during bombing runs. To fill the obvious need for a faster means to deliver weapons, the Navy ordered a number of dive bomber pilots be retrained as fighter-bomber pilots.

'I was an obvious choice for retraining, as I had logged time in the FM-2, the General Motors licence-built variant of the Grumman F4F Wildcat. The FM-2 was a good, true aircraft and, after having flown it, I looked forward to flying the F6F. The Hellcat was, of course, a much bigger aeroplane than the Wildcat. The F6F was armed with six 0.5in Colt-Browning machine guns and carried bombs under each wing, as well as a 500lb bomb slung under the fuselage.

'The Hellcat was a big, solid-looking aircraft. It dwarfed any other naval fighter aircraft I had encountered. The cockpit was comfortable and

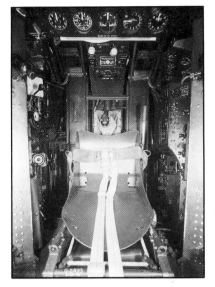

Above and above right: the cockpit interior of an F6F-3 Hellcat shows the neat and logical arrangement of the instruments and controls. Flying instruments are concentrated on the main panel, together with engine instruments. Fuel and oil gauges are below and to the right of this panel, together with electrical switches. On the left are the undercarriage retraction control and the throttle, supercharger and fuel mixture levers

roomy. The instruments, gunsight and aircraft controls were all readily available and laid out in a very orderly manner so there was little chance for confusion during the stressful moments of aerial cambat. One aspect of the Hellcat that I particularly liked was its stability, even during formation flying. It remained stable during cross-overs and cross-unders and was not difficult to control when you encountered slipstream; you could bring it right back into position.

'Another feature of the Hellcat which endeared it to the average pilot was that during Field Carrier Landing Practices (FCLPs), you could literally "hang" the aircraft on its propeller – with gear and flaps extended into the slipstream – and still feel as though you were exercising sufficient control over the aircraft. FCLPs were the final step before qualifying for take-offs and landings aboard a carrier and we made those flights "on" and "off" a portion of the runway at the US Naval Air Station at Glenview, Illinois that was marked off to resemble an actual flight deck. We flew FCLPs in both the SBD and the F6F, but then we hit a period of inclement weather that kept us at Glenview so long that we had to requalify our FCLPs using the North American SNJ Texan trainer. It was not until the weather lifted a bit that we could head out to Lake Michigan, where our "carrier" waited for us.'

There were, of course, no surplus aircraft carriers available to provide US Navy pilots with experience in shipboard flight operations. More-over, the danger of enemy submarines severely restricted the use of American territorial waters for such training. The US Navy showed considerable ingenuity in solving both problems. Two old paddle-wheel steamers were converted into the training carriers USS *Wolverine* (IX-64) and USS *Sable* (IX-81). To young Lieutenant James Ean, the procedure for making the initial carrier qualification flights was quite simple. He remembers: 'About an hour before I was to begin my carrier qualifications, I bounced a few FCLPs with my F6F. When the Landing Signal Officer (LSO) was satisfied, he gave me a piece of paper on which was written the direction and distance to the *Wolverine*. Then off I went, in fog, to find the training carrier. All of my training paid off, however, and when I did find the ship, I made a very easy, slightly nose-up landing that was quite smooth.

'The Hellcat always responded in great style and as one became more accustomed to its response, one's feeling of confidence in the air-craft increased. That was coupled with excellent visibility for approaching the carrier. There was no trouble in spotting and keeping the LSO in view during all phases of the approach to the carrier.'

When aircraft are being recovered aboard US Navy aircraft carriers, the 'Charlie' maritime signal flag is hoisted to notify all naval elements in the area that this phase of flight operations is being conducted. Hence, preparation for landing aboard a carrier is called 'Prep Charlie'.

James Ean relates: 'When the carrier was ready to recover aircraft, we had to be ready and have the first aircraft in our flight in position to land. The ship had to turn into the wind and maintain a fairly straight course to keep a steady wind down the centreline of the flight deck. In a training situation that was no problem; but in combat, the longer the carrier had to stay on one heading, the greater the danger it would be attacked by enemy submarines or surface craft.

'While other aircraft in the flight got into what

we called the "Charlie pattern", a long counter-clockwise orbit leading to the final approach, the rest of us circled until it was our turn to get into the pattern. When we did receive the signal to land, we were expected to do so quickly, so the ship could complete the recovery operation and change course.

'Being in the "Charlie pattern" required great speed control, which was a virtue that the F6F certainly had. It was not unusual to start from perhaps 10,000 feet and literally dive the aircraft, while still controlling the speed to the extent that you would not come down too far from the carrier or go so fast that you would be unable to maintain landing pattern altitude and speed. You had to have just the right combination of speed and sink rate to make a swift, safe landing aboard ship. And with the Hellcat you could perform that manoeuvre with great confidence, because you knew the bird could do it.'

After Lieutenant Ean completed his carrier qualifications in the F6F-3, he was assigned to VF-22 aboard the light carrier USS *Cowpens* (CVL-25), which set out on its second Pacific combat cruise on 16 January 1944. Taking off and landing aboard the 190m (622ft) long flight deck of this smaller type aircraft carrier brought out the Hellcat's best characteristics, as James Ean notes. 'The same sterling qualities that enabled the Hellcat to execute FCLPs so successfully proved just as reliable during actual carrier landings. With the possible exception of the

Grumman TBF Avenger, the F6F was the best aircraft designed for carrier operations. A good pilot, with the help of the LSO and the aircraft's inherent stability, could literally "spot land" the Hellcat – put it right down on a given spot.

'That capability was especially valuable in operating aboard a CVL, which did not have either the almost 875 feet in length or 150 feet in width that the larger *Essex*-class carriers enjoyed. The length of the carrier flight deck was not as important as the width, which on the *Cowpens* was about the same as that of a shore-based taxi strip. With the usual pitching and yawing of the carrier on the open sea, that narrow flight deck posed special hazards. The Hellcat's stability and trim capabilities really made the difference in landing right square on the centreline–or drifting off to the side and going into the catwalk if you were lucky or right into the drink if you were unlucky.'

USS *Cowpens* had one hydraulically-powered aircraft catapult on the port side of the forward portion of the flight deck. While the catapult required less wind over the deck to launch aircraft, it was also a slower means of deploying the ship's aircraft. Hence, in combat situations, aircraft were generally positioned well aft on the flight deck, with their engines warming up until the signal was given for them to 'deck launch' – simply to take off into the wind under their own power. As James Ean notes, the F6F Hellcat was a particularly good aircraft for deck launching. 'The

The Hellcat's appearance in the Pacific Theatre wrested control of the air from the Mitsubishi A6M Zero, which had mastered Grumman's Wildcat. The type accounted for three-quarters of the kills registered by the US Navy's carrier-based pilots. The aircraft depicted was flown from USS Intrepid in 1944 by Lt Alexander Vraciu of VF-6

Pratt & Whitney Double Wasp engine gave the Hellcat enough power to make a deck launch easily – even from the relatively short flight deck of a CVL. You made a smooth run down the deck, made a slight dip just as you left the end of the deck, over the bow of the ship, but then you pulled up and away.'

The Grumman F6F-3 Hellcat had a maximum range of 1,745km (1,085 miles), which was derived from its normal fuel load of 946 litres (250 US gallons) stored in a fuselage tank and two tanks in the wing centre-section. That range could be extended to 2,606km (1,620 miles) with the addition of a 568 litre (150 US gallon) long-range auxiliary fuel tank, which would be jettisoned. Even with the belly fuel tank, or a napalm bomb for jungle operations, 'the Hellcat was still aerodynamically sound', James Ean remembers. 'It required very little trim change when flying with the auxiliary fuel tank or a napalm bomb – and little change was needed after either was dropped. You could also carry fuel tanks under the wings and if you jettisoned only one of them, you would have some difficulty and you would have to use trim tab to make up the difference.'

Lieutenant James Ean took part in numerous combat sweeps deployed from USS *Cowpens* and was involved in a number of aerial combats. US Navy records show that he shot down at least four enemy aircraft and contributed to the destruction of another four or five. In operations such as the so-called 'Marianas Turkey Shoot' of 19 June

1944, there were so many US Navy fighters in the sky that it was often difficult to determine which Hellcat shot down which Japanese fighter.

In all cases, however, Ean and his comrades were well-versed in using the Hellcat's strengths to exploit the Zero-Sen's weaknesses. Recognising that the Japanese fighter aircraft was better-suited than the Hellcat for close, tight manoeuvring that produced more high-G stress, the US Navy fighter pilots used their superior speed and diving ability to draw the Zero-Sen into a combat environment favourable to the F6F. For example, the F6F could hang onto a tightly-turning Zero-Sen long enough to fire several blasts of its six 0.5in machine guns, which was often enough to bring down the lightly-armoured Japanese fighter. Conversely, the F6F possessed enough 'Grumman Iron Works' durability to absorb considerable fire from the Mitsubishi A6M's two fuselage-mounted 7.7mm machine guns and even the four wing-mounted 20mm cannon. When pursued by the Zero-Sen, the Hellcat could exercise its tremendous horsepower to escape.

'During overhead gunnery runs,' Ean recalls, 'which were essentially a split-'S' in which you exercise great 'g' forces, the F6F did not skid or slip while you were concentrating on your target. The Hellcat also held steady when you fired the five-inch rockets that could also be carried under the wings. To get the rocket to hit at the proper angle of impact, you had to be in a dive of almost 60 degrees. When you start to pick up that ad-

Hellcats await deck-launching from an Essex-class aircraft carrier during World War II. A device inherited from the Wildcat and visible here was the Hellcat's so-called Sto-Wing feature, in which the wing pivoted at the root to fold back flush with the fuselage. The resultant space saving was considerable

ditional speed in a lot of other aircraft, they have a tendency to "skid" away from you. But with the Hellcat, you always had great control and that enhanced your accuracy in firing rockets or machine guns. It is, of course, essential for a fighter to be stable if it is to be an effective gun platform–and the Hellcat consistently provided the stability necessary to ensure that accuracy.'

The great reliance that the Hellcat inspired can be seen in a mission flown by VF-22 after the successful recapture of the Philippine Islands. James Ean recalls: 'On one occasion we went out on a routine strike, which was almost a milk run because we controlled so much of the area. About a third of the way to our target, the 12 Hellcats from USS *Cowpens* received a message from the Task Force Fighter Directional Officer. He requested that four of us leave the formation and head off in another direction to provide fighter cover for a downed naval pilot, who was being besieged by Japanese torpedo boats and peppered by shore-based batteries.

'Three other pilots and myself were vectored to the location and 20 minutes later we came upon the scene. We had not operated in that area before, but we didn't think about that, as we set to work to discourage the Japanese from devoting so much attention to the pilot in the water. We spent the better part of an hour driving back the torpedo boats and shooting up the shore batteries while one of our surface units came in to rescue the pilot.

'During this encounter we were using some rather abrupt types of aerobatics – split-'S' and other manoeuvres – in order to get in our best shots and quickly return to the scene of the action. While this fight was going on, however, my gyroscopic compass had precessed [rotated from its given heading]. I hadn't "caged" it to give me an accurate direction for the return flight.

'By the time we got through with driving back the Japanese, I found that mine was the last aircraft at the scene. Now I was all alone and, since my gyros had precessed, I had no idea how I could hold a proper heading to get back to the carrier. To make matters worse, I was running low on fuel. The best I could do was to head in the direction I thought I should be going and set my gyros at 000 so I would follow that course and not stray to either side. I was heading east by northeast, where I assumed the fleet would be by that time.

'My low fuel state and the fact that I had to obey strict radio silence made for a tense situation. But I had such confidence in the Hellcat that I knew that, even if I had to make a water landing, the durability of the aircraft would get me through it. As it turned out, I spotted the *Cowpens* just as my fuel gauge showed I was nearly out of gasoline and I managed to come aboard on the first pass.'

James Ean also points out that he found the F6F Hellcat to be dependable in other ways: 'The aircraft wore well, which proved to be a delight to our squadron engineering officer, as well as to the maintenance officer. It was seldom necessary to "scratch" an operation because of a "sick bird" and whenever you were slated to be a stand-by pilot for a mission, there was little chance of being pressed into service in another flight due to mal-

GRUMMAN F6F HELLCAT

Below left: this F6F-5 Hellcat is preserved in the overall midnight blue finish adopted for carrier aircraft early in 1944. The F6F-5 differed from the F6F-3 primarily in having an improved, flat-fronted windscreen and a new engine cowling. Inset far left: ratings manhandle a Fleet Air Arm Hellcat on the deck of HMS Indomitable in January 1945. Ten squadrons of the FAA flew Hellcats, most of them operating in the Pacific. Inset left: one of VF-9's Hellcats flies from USS Yorktown (CV-10) late in 1943. The fuselage marking denotes the air group commander

function of other aircraft.

'F6F pilots were generally scheduled to participate in Combat Air Patrol (CAP) flights, in which they took off from the ship, rendezvoused and then circled above the fleet to protect it from attacks by enemy aircraft. On other occasions we flew strike missions. CAPs were most often assigned to the CVL-based squadrons and they consisted of long, fatiguing and boring hours of flight. In this instance, one of the real beauties of the F6F is that it trimmed very true; you could maintain a constant throttle and rpm setting on long formation flights, which greatly aided in conserving the energy of both aircraft and pilot.'

Other pilots of other air arms found the F6F series to be a good, reliable mount in combat. The US Marine Corps, a branch of the Navy, began receiving Hellcats in 1945 and, prior to that, F6Fs had been provided to Britain under the Lend-Lease programme. No 800 Squadron was the first Fleet Air Arm unit to become operational with the Hellcat and was deployed aboard HMS *Emperor*. In March 1944, four of No 800 Squadron's Hellcats were jumped by German fighters off the coast of Norway. The Fleet Air Arm lost one Hellcat, but the other three each claimed an enemy aircraft. Eventually, 252 F6F-3 and 930 F6F-5 types – operated as Hellcat I and Hellcat II, respectively – were provided for the Royal Navy. To meet the need for a ship-based radar-equipped night fighter, an 'N' version was developed and subsequently became the F6F-3N and F6F-5N.

Towards the end of World War II, the F6F Hellcat series was gradually replaced by the Vought F4U-4 Corsair as the front-line carrier-based fighter. In the postwar era it was soon succeeded by the F8F-1 Bearcat before the 'Grumman Iron Works' began the development of jet-powered aircraft, notably the F9F Panther series.

Ex-US Navy Hellcats went on to see service in the air arms of Argentina and Uruguay, as well as with the French Armée de l'Air and Aéronavale. Indeed, the latter Hellcats were used in combat into the 1950s to support the ill-starred French attempt to retain colonial interests in Indo-China. The ruggedness and dependability of the Hellcat was highly praised by French pilots whose counter-insurgency missions took them to ever lower altitudes. The Hellcat allowed them to zero in on Vietminh targets while absorbing heavy return fire from the ground. The Hellcat continued to give good service long after the demise of the Mitsubishi Zero-Sen fighter it was intended to defeat.

Vought
F4U Corsair

In common with the majority of US Navy fighters, the Vought F4U Corsair was equipped with wing-folding apparatus for ease of shipboard stowage. It was not until 1944, however, over three years from its first flight, that it was deemed ready for service aboard carriers. Handling problems having been overcome, however, the aircraft performed well

It was late one afternoon in early 1943 over the waters around the Solomon Islands of the South Pacific when I first saw the Vought F4U Corsair. After a dive, the US Marine Corps pilot had pulled the Corsair up steeply in a spectacular performance truly worthy of an aeroplane of tomorrow. Guadalcanal, the first major offensive action for the US Navy and Marine Corps had just been successfully concluded after some of the bloodiest land and sea battles of World War II. The Japanese air force had been driven from the skies over the Solomons back to Rabaul by courageous Navy and Marine pilots flying the Grumman F4F Wildcat. This short stubby mid-wing aeroplane was tough but aerodynamically inferior to the swift, manoeuvrable Japanese Zero. Something else was needed, and fast.

Then the finest carrier-based fighter of World War II, the Corsair, came on the scene. Ordered in 1938 and first flown in 1940, over 10,000 Corsairs of more than a dozen models were delivered before production ended in 1952.

It was in World War II that the Chance Vought Corsair achieved its greatest fame. Against Japanese pilots, the Corsair pilots scored an incredible eleven-to-one victory ratio. The clean aerodynamic design, powered by a 2,000hp Pratt & Whitney R-2800 Double Wasp engine and armed with six 0.5in machine guns made a for-

midable aerial weapon.

Although as commanding officer of Fighter Squadron VF-44, I flew the F4U-4 during the final phase of America's involvement in the Korean conflict, my first flight in a Corsair was in 1947 when I was regularly flying the small, speedy, manoeuvrable Grumman F8F Bearcat. The pilot of the petite Bearcat 'wore' the aeroplane, being seated right over the wing, just aft of the engine. In the Corsair, the pilot rode well aft, behind the engine and fuselage fuel tank. The seat was mounted on the floor and the rudder pedals were only slightly lower than the level of the seat. Thus, a pilot's legs were almost horizontal. Sitting well aft in the aeroplane, I occasionally felt like a chariot rider, steering a team of horses. In fact I was steering and aiming the equivalent of some 2,000 horses at full power.

Operating aboard a carrier day and night is the greatest thrill a pilot can experience. As noted earlier, the Corsair was originally restricted to land-based operations because of the poor visibility in the 'groove' coming in astern of the carrier. At low speeds of 85 to 88 knots, the 4.6m (15ft) nose ahead of the cockpit made it easy to lose sight of the landing signal officer (LSO) on the port quarter of the carrier. This problem was solved in two ways: first, a perfect level, low altitude pass would have the pilot arriving at the

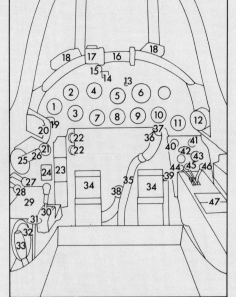

Vought F4U Corsair cockpit
1: *Engine speed indicator* **2:** *Altimeter*
3: *Boost gauge* **4:** *Direction finder*
5: *Compass repeater* **6:** *Artificial horizon*
7: *Airspeed indicator* **8:** *Turn and bank*
indicator **9:** *Rate of climb indicator*
10: *Cylinder head temperature gauge*
11: *Oil pressure gauge* **12:** *Gyroscopic*
gunsight dimmer **13:** *Carburettor*
temperature warning light **14:** *Stall*
warning light **15:** *Water injection*
indicator light **16:** *Gunsight position*
17: *Gunsight control* **18:** *Armament*
switches **19:** *Drop tank control* **20:** *Flap*
control **21:** *Ignition switches* **22:** *Gun*
charging controls **23:** *Undercarriage*
indicator **24:** *Hand pump selector*
25: *Throttle* **26:** *Radio button*
27: *Propeller pitch lever* **28:** *Mixture*
control lever **29:** *Circuit breaker reset*
buttons **30:** *Undercarriage and dive brake*
controls **31:** *Fuel tank selector*
32: *Elevator trim wheel* **33:** *Emergency*
hydraulic hand pump **34:** *Rudder pedals*
35: *Control column* **36:** *Gun-firing button*
37: *Stores release button* **38:** *Ventilator*
39: *Brake pedal adjusters* **40:** *Fuel*
contents gauge **41:** *Hydraulic pressure*
gauge **42:** *Voltmeter* **43:** *Fuel pressure*
gauge **44:** *Oil cooler flap control*
45: *Intercooler flap control* **46:** *Cowling*
gills control **47:** *Main switch panel*

carrier ramp just rolling out of the left turn in time to level the wings for a 'cut power' signal from the LSO and subsequent landing and engagement of the arrestor gear with the tail hook. The second method which was employed in the non-perfect carrier approaches (of which all of us made quite a few) was a combination of a bit of top (right) rudder and left wing slightly down so that the LSO could be kept in sight. The Corsair wasn't called the 'hose-nose' for nothing!

The 'hose-nose' was also useful for aiming the aeroplane in a dive. The Mark 8 gunsight was the principal aid, but fifteen feet of nose was a good arrow to point at the target. It was in glide and dive bombing practice in preparation for deployment to Korea for combat operations that we discovered something that had been forgotten since World War II. As the Korean War heated up, the word came back that the Communists had moved in 37mm and 57mm guns. These were in addition to immense quantities of smaller calibre anti-aircraft guns which appeared to be as numerous as wild flowers in a summer field. The larger guns had put premiums on higher altitude for rolling in to the bombing runs, accuracy of delivery on the first pass and higher speed to limit time in the bombing run and over the target.

As we practiced higher and faster entries into our bombing practice runs, we noticed a tendency for the aeroplane to start rolling on its own at the bottom of the dive. After checking and adjusting the rigging of the ailerons and flaps, with little corrective action noted, an old Chance Vought representative from World War II provided the answer: warped ailerons. We had forgotten that the ailerons were made of plywood and were thus subject to warping. At lower than maximum speeds a slight malformation went unnoticed; at very high speeds, the warping turned into unexpected, and thus unwanted, rolling. A frantic call went to the supply system for more unwarped ailerons which, when installed, solved the problem of involuntary rolling at high speeds. In combat in Korea we were grateful for the unwarped ailerons which permitted us to enter high and exit fast after a good steady bombing run.

Like its World War II contemporaries, the Corsair was a tough aeroplane and able to take a great deal of punishment. Not nearly as densely packed as today's modern jets, the Corsair was able to remain airworthy even after having had large holes blown into it. Modern jet fighters achieve survivability by an amazing system of redundancy, doubling (or tripling) up so that the loss of a single system does not result in loss of the aircraft. The Corsair achieved this by sheer toughness.

The Corsair was a fine acrobatic aircraft, easy to turn, roll, loop, dive and climb; the trim tab-assisted ailerons ensured light control stick forces. With excellent visibility from the cockpit, especially in the later models with the 'bubble' canopy instead of the 'birdcage' of the earlier models, formation manoeuvring and aerobatics were easily mastered. The Corsair had a bad reputation for being difficult to recover from spins, however, and thus the rule was to keep the speed up. A flight of four to eight Corsairs in a tail-chase was a sight to behold as the inverted gull wings seemed to be soaring effortlessly.

An unusual event occured over the Naval Air Station, Miami, Florida in 1946, just after World War II. A flight of about six Corsairs manned by one instructor and five students was climbing over the field *en route* to 'altitude' at about 7,600m (25,000ft), for a high-altitude orientation flight. Around 4,600m (15,000ft) in the tail-chase formation, one pilot inexplicably entered an inverted spin. He promptly left the aeroplane and floated

Below left: ordnancemen arm the 0.5in machine guns of an F4U-4 Corsair of Air Group 2. Stationed aboard the carrier USS Boxer, the Group was involved in the early stages of the Korean War in September 1950. The conflict signalled a new lease of life for the Corsair, which was retained in production at Chance Vought's Dallas factory until 1952

Right: a 500lb bomb is mounted on a Corsair aboard USS Philippine Sea off the coast of Korea. The F4U was pressed into service in the ground attack role, in which it frequently employed bombs and rockets to supplement its machine gun or cannon armament.
Below: a Corsair of VF-44 returns to the rain-swept flight deck of USS Lake Champlain in June 1953. An unexpended bomb remains on its rack

The Corsair's operational debut in the colours of the Fleet Air Arm took place on 3 April 1944, when aircraft of No 1834 Squadron from HMS Victorious took part in an operation against the German battleship Tirpitz. Fleet Air Arm aircraft incorporated certain modifications, including longer-stroke landing gear oleos to assist carrier touchdowns and clipped wingtips to reduce the aircraft's height

to the ground with his parachute visible to all at the air station. The Corsair, freed of its human burden, recovered from the spin and dived down north of the field through the puffy cumulus clouds. It had great speed as the engine was in 'supercharger' and the throttle undoubtedly well forward, perhaps fully so. As the elevator was trimmed for climbing flight, the speedy unmanned aeroplane climbed back into the clouds to disappear to the west over the Everglades, likely to be lost forever in the Florida swampland.

Such was not to be the case, however, for this homesick angel turned devil. After climbing through the clouds it came down again, this time over, and in line with, the duty runway at a speed estimated to be well above 300 knots. I was in the parking ramp at the time and saw this monster boresighting the place where several of us were standing. We all started to run and, knowing that I could not get behind the hangar about 200 yards away before the aeroplane crashed, I 'hit the deck' at full speed. Having undergone *kamikaze* attacks aboard a ship in the Pacific about a year earlier, I knew the air would be full of flying debris and

projectiles and thus wanted to present as small a vertical target as possible. The aircraft hit about 150 yards behind me, not more than 100 yards from where it was parked on the ramp before the fateful flight. Damage was extensive, two persons were killed and a number of others suffered injuries. The incident added to the folklore about not getting into a spin with the Corsair.

The versatility of the F4U Corsair was the key to its longevity. A superior air combat fighter aeroplane in World War II, it also had a wing which permitted it to accomplish many other missions. Up to eight wing-mounted bomb and rocket racks were added to later models. Bombs from 100 to 1,000 pounds could be carried and all rockets from the sub-calibre rocket for training to the then-monstrous 11in diameter 'Tiny Tim'. This latter was a very large rocket whose warhead was a 500lb bomb. Long before the space age, Corsair pilots firing the 'Tiny Tim' had a minor version of what space personnel would witness two decades later: a rocket roar resembling the noise of a freight train as a major piece of apparatus took off from the pylon beneath the fuselage under rocket power.

So versatile was the Corsair that several carrier air groups were equipped solely with Corsair aeroplanes after World War II–the fighter and bomber squadrons were all equipped with the 'bent wing beauty'. On the *Midway*-class carriers, then the largest in the US Navy, our Corsairs would be lined up for a deck take-off in two lines instead of one as on *Essex*-class carriers and smaller flat-tops. Aeroplanes in the starboard column would be launched for the corner of the port bow and those in the port column for the starboard bow. The flight deck officer would allow only about six seconds between take-offs, starting an aeroplane down the deck when the one just ahead from the opposite column was about halfway to the bow and the previous aircraft was rotating off the bow at just over minimum flying speed. This was an efficient rapid way to clear the deck but it also added a bit of spice to the flight: just before the aeroplane reached the bow, it would swing about

five to ten degrees out of the launching direction as it was buffeted by the prop-wash of the aircraft just ahead leaving the deck at the other corner.

Returning aboard, the Corsair proved to be a splendid carrier aeroplane. With large flaps and outer wing dihedral, it was a very stable aircraft. As noted earlier, a good carrier approach avoided a 'long-in-the-groove' final. After the 'cut' signal by the LSO, a slight nose dip followed immediately by back stick and a flare resulted in a tailhook engagement and immediate deceleration, characteristic of all successful carrier landings. On the roll-out, while the aircraft was decelerating by courtesy of the arrestor gear, the pilot raised the hook handle. Thus, when the Corsair stopped and rolled back slightly, the wire dropped clear and the pilot taxied forward. The smart carrier pilot also released the manual wing lock and started the wings folding as he was taxying clear of the landing area.

A good Corsair squadron could achieve landing

Above right: US Marine Corps Corsairs bearing 500lb bombs underwing are pictured awaiting take-off at their Pacific airfield. Land-based USMC units were first to fly the type operationally in February 1943.
Right: flown by a US Navy pilot, a Corsair presses home an attack with 5in rockets during the Pacific War. Eight such weapons could be carried underwing by fighter-bomber Corsair variants, which also featured engine water injection

197

intervals of 15 to 18 seconds, a time which contrasts with the 35 seconds and higher required for today's modern jets with their higher speed and longer deck roll-out before stopping. The cross-deck propeller aircraft launch and short-interval landing recovery was one of aviation's smartest peacetime military manoeuvres. Besides being militarily precise, this rapid, disciplined launch and recovery method had – and still has – a valuable purpose. It reduced the time a carrier must spend on a steady course and speed while launching and landing aircraft, during which it is much more vulnerable to submarine and air attack.

My combat experience with the F4U-4 in Fighter Squadron 44 began on 13 June 1953, when the squadrons of Air Group 4, deployed aboard USS *Lake Champlain* (CVA-39), escorted US Air Force Boeing B-50 bombers on a raid over North Korea and bombed enemy positions. From that point until the ceasefire was announced on 27 July, our Corsairs carried out one or two missions per day, generally of three hours' duration, from USS *Lake Champlain* and USS *Boxer*.

Although VF-44 was a fighter squadron and we had practiced all of the fighter tactics that had made the F4U famous, we performed a different combat role in Korea. We did not encounter any hostile aircraft, as we were operating principally on the east coast and along the battle line all the way to Seoul. Communist fighters, most notably

the MiG-15, generally operated in the northwestern corner of the Korean peninsula, near Sinanju. They did not come as far south as we were, nor did our missions take us as far north as they were. The MiG-15s were game for the Air Force's North American F-86 Sabres in 'MiG Alley' along the Yalu River. Our principal role was to assist United Nations ground forces, as well as to interdict enemy coastal watercraft and hit trains, trucks or other vehicular traffic that might be bringing supplies down to Communist front-line troops. We performed road reconnaissance and struck a variety of targets far behind the enemy's lines as another means to keep him constantly off balance.

Throughout all of these missions the F4U-4 proved to be a solidly reliable aircraft. Indeed, it even had an advantage over the jet-powered fighters in our air group that performed similar missions. When *Lake Champlain's* hydraulic catapults malfunctioned, the deck-launched propeller-driven aircraft were the only ones that could carry the war to North Korea, because the jets couldn't get off the deck without the assistance of the catapult. Thus, during one period off the coast of Korea, the Skyraiders and Corsairs carried the full load from *Lake Champlain*.

Soon after arriving in Korean waters my squadron was transferred to USS *Boxer* (CV-21), an unmodified *Essex*-class carrier whose catapults

The Corsair F4U-7 was similar to the AU-1 ground attack aircraft flown by the US Marine Corps in Korea. Sole operator of the F4U-7 was the French Aéronavale, which operated the type from land bases during the Indo-China War. The pictured aircraft was returned to the United States for preservation

Above: Corsairs are stowed aboard a British aircraft carrier in the Pacific Theatre near the war's end. Fleet Air Arm Corsairs underwent their baptism of fire in the Theatre on 19 April 1944, when Nos 1830 and 1839 Squadrons commenced operations.

Left: bombing-up Corsairs on the flight deck of the USS Philippine Sea off the coast of Korea in September 1950.

Below: practice carrier landings were common tasks for the inexperienced Corsair flyer. The aircraft's soubriquet of 'Hose Nose' hinted at the lack of forward visibility afforded the pilot during the approach for a landing

were less powerful than those of *Lake Champlain*. An F9F-5 Panther squadron was exchanged with us. On *Boxer* we found a minor version of the catapult story which we experienced on *Lake Champlain*. The H-4 catapults on *Boxer* were designed to launch propeller aircraft in World War II. The early jets with their relatively underpowered engines therefore needed lots of wind to help them get off the deck with a useful payload of bombs, rockets and gun ammunition. On days when the winds were light, the F9F-2 Panther jets would be launched from *Boxer* with only a load of machine gun ammunition for strafing and perhaps a 'teeny-weeny bomb'. The Skyraiders packed the biggest wallop with the Corsairs next. The catapult dilemma was solved permanently a few years later when the steam catapult developed by the Royal Navy made its appearance on the US Navy aircraft carriers. The steam 'cats' were so powerful that a carrier pilot could lock his brakes during the catapult shot and still be

launched at safe flying speed, but with no tyres and flat wheels as he left the deck.

The graceful World War II Chance Vought fighter started its life as the 'Corsair', the name of the famous pirates of the late eighteenth century. Soon after introduction in World War II, it was dubbed the 'Ensign Eliminator' because of the accidents the young ensigns of World War II experienced in handling the Navy's hottest fighter. It later acquired the sobriquet of 'Bent-Wing Bastard' in a tribute to its inverted gull wing.

Its last nickname was the 'Hog', a deprecating monicker awarded to the oldest operational aeroplane in the US Navy's inventory. While it suffered in this inelegant description, there was some comfort in the fact that all of its early stablemates had long since gone to the aircraft boneyard to be melted down. When the occasional Corsairs remaining in flyable condition appear today in airshows, they are still voted best of the breed among their contemporaries.

Preserved examples of three famous fighters of the Pacific Theatre in World War II fly in formation. The Corsair is in the lead, followed by a North American P-51 Mustang and a Bell P-39 Airacobra (background). Whereas the P-39 helped to hold the ring during the defensive fighting of 1941–42, it was the Corsair's support of the island-hopping campaigns and the Mustang's protection of strategic bombers which helped to bring about Japan's defeat in the air

Boeing B-17 Flying Fortress

The Boeing B-17 Flying Fortress is the most famous American combat aircraft of World War II. This exalted status is due to a combination of a name which appealed to the public and the bomber's part in the go-it-alone daylight raids over Europe, the latter resulting in some of the fiercest air battles of all time. The Fortress epitomised the bravery of the US airmen who, day after day, fought it out with the Luftwaffe fighters or flew through formidable concentrations of anti-aircraft artillery fire to attack their targets. No other bomber was constantly exposed to such fearful opposition and exhibited such a high rate of survival. Many historians point to the high losses sustained by the B-17s in their forays over Hitler's Festung Europa during 1943, but the really remarkable thing is that such large, slow aircraft could sustain so much heavy damage and still return to England with their crews.

As the original vehicle for the USAAF's doctrine of high-altitude daylight precision bombing, the Fortress was subject to a considerable amount of laudatory publicity before it ever got into combat. This was largely due to the USAAF's endeavours to sell the concept of strategic bombardment to sceptical government agencies and in the face of considerable opposition from the US Navy. A great deal of effort was expended on coaxing the media to extol the virtues of this superlative aircraft; the huge investment in producing a large force of strategic bombers had to be justified and, without proof of

Left: the co-pilot's control wheel of a B-17, situated on the cockpit's left; the first pilot sat on the right and had an identical wheel.
Below: the B-17 was generally considered to be viceless to fly and forgiving of mistakes

of what their particular brand of strategic bombing could achieve, the USAAF could not risk unfavourable publicity. Thus the B-17 became known as 'The Glory Wagon' to US airmen associated with other aircraft types. The B-17 crews, however, were delighted with their charge and often referred to her as the 'Queen of the Skies'. The status accorded the Fortress was particularly irritating to the B-24 Liberator crews and the outcome was an enduring rivalry between those who flew or administered the two types of four-engined heavy bomber.

In truth, the original Fortress design was close to being obsolete when the United States finally entered the war. The prototype had first flown in 1935, then the world's first four-motor monoplane bomber. The original configuration was for an aircraft designed to operate at medium altitudes (below oxygen level), primarily on long-range, maritime bomber patrols. With the installation of turbo-superchargers to allow the aircraft to operate at the then extremely high altitudes of 7,620–9,150 m (25,000–30,000 ft), and its adaptation to the role of stratospheric bomber, the original design soon exhibited a number of deficiencies. The tail area was insufficiently large to maintain the aircraft as a stable bombing platform in the thin atmosphere at these heights.

As an offensive weapon, the defensive armament was obviously totally inadequate to meet the advances in fighter interceptor design and armament highlighted in the first two years of the war in Europe. In consequence the Fortress was subject to hurried redesign, featuring a completely new structure of the trailing edge of the wing. The first of these so-called 'Big Tail' Fortresses was the B-17E model and, with power turrets and eleven 0·5 in

heavy machine guns. It was also the first of the famous Boeings to be worthy of the grand title of Flying Fortress. The similar B-17F and G models saw most of the action in World War II and were to become beloved by many thousands of US and Allied airmen.

When the first of the models with the big tail appeared the aircraft was considered something of a giant among USAAF combat aircraft. This is borne out by Lt George Hale's description of his first flight in a Fortress. 'My first trip in a B-17 was at Pyote Field, Texas. This was also the first time I had seen one of these ships on the ground. Previously the largest aircraft I had inspected was a Douglas A-20 so the size of the B-17 really impressed me. After the war I was to fly bombers and transports that dwarfed the B-17 but even so that first introduction was to leave me with the lingering impression that the Fortress was the giant of its times. For a start it was the first aeroplane I had seen with an access door. I clearly remember entering the rear fuselage through this portal and being amazed at so much room for men to move around inside the aircraft. Again this was engendered by my having only flown in aircraft where the crew were restricted to their cockpits.

'That rear fuselage was really rather cramped, for you could stretch out your arms and touch both sides at any point. On this occasion both the waist guns were stowed and the waist hatches were in position to add to the illusion of spaciousness. Later I was to learn that the two gunners could not manipulate their weapons without banging each other in the back. If you were a tall guy, as I was, you found that you had to hunch your shoulders as you made your way forward for fear of striking

Right: B-17s of the 1st Bomb Wing, US Eighth Air Force begin the return flight over the North Sea after a mission. The B-17s normally flew at heights where condensation trails appeared, which were a great help to German fighters. Massed formations were characteristic of US bomber operations in Europe. The B-17 flew in tight boxes for maximum protection from the crossfire of their guns. Losses inevitably broke up the boxes and enemy fighters concentrated on the stragglers.
Below: a B-17G of the 535th BS, 381st BG, 1st Bomb Wing, US Eighth Air Force depicted in 1943. The Group was based at Ridgewell, Essex

your head on the top of the fuselage.

'Through the forward door was the bomb-bay, a narrow catwalk running between the bomb shackle supports. On this occasion the bomb doors were closed and the precarious nature of this walk-way was not immediately apparent. This was only discovered when, at a later date, I had to cross from the cockpit to the radio room clad in heavy flying gear at high altitude. Another bulkhead door had to be negotiated before arriving in the forward cabin. Edging round the upper power turret base you could go down under the flight deck to the bombardier and navigator's positions in the nose, or up forward into the cockpit.

'For my first trip in the B-17, I was invited to take a jump seat behind the pilots. I recall that first impression of size on peeping out of the cockpit side windows with those great broad wings blotting out most of my view of the ground. The instrument panel looked a pilot's nightmare. There were so many clocks, gauges and switches it seemed far too complicated for even two men to handle. This wasn't really the case but that is how it seemed to the novice. The whole procedure of starting engines and wheeling out off the ramp to the runway was done against a check-list, with the pilots working together. I was never a nervous flier but I distinctly recall thinking about the problems of getting such a large and weighty bundle of metal into the air.

'When the moment came the Fortress was liberated from the ground with surprising ease. The pilot was obviously intent on impressing the fledgling aviator behind his seat, for the lightly loaded aeroplane was put through surprising (to me) manoeuvres, with some of the steep turns skidding me off the jump seat. On our approach

to land I distinctly remember the pilot asking me—shouting would be a truer description—if I fancied flying B-17s. Like most guys who had just won their wings I saw myself as a budding fighter pilot but answered with a diplomatic "sure would". "This is a pilot's ship, and if you've gotta go to war in it that's worth a lot" was the gist of his reply. I don't even recall his name now, but he was right. The fact that the Fortress was easy to fly and always predictable gave you a head start when the going got rough.

'Fate and the Air Corps decided that fighters were not for me and I found myself heading for Europe across the North Atlantic in the left-hand seat of a B-17. My subsequent experiences in that location and good fortune in surviving numerous attempts by Hitler's flak and fighters to see I didn't re-cross the Atlantic may have left me with an unfailing loyalty to the Fort. That admitted, I am convinced a deal of the credit for surviving was due to the B-17 being such a fine flying plane. The advice given by the pilot on that first ride in the Boeing was sound indeed. No one could say she was an exciting plane to fly; the Fort handled easily and in a non-combat situation you had to be a real sloppy pilot to get into trouble. That is within the limits of the pilot's notes.

'Local flying with a light load could be almost a bore and that is why most of us liked to indulge in a little buzzing. The Fort was so predictable you could hop over the hedges with ease and cut some really impressive manoeuvres with safety. I often wonder how many former B-17 pilots were killed trying to execute the same sort of buzz jobs in a less forgiving

plane. She took off and landed sweetly. Landing speed was a little over 70 mph which was way below many of the World War II multi-engined contemporaries. You had a problem when landing light in that the Fort tended to float above the runway. You learned to get the tyres onto the surface quickly otherwise you could find yourself in a situation where you were running out of runway.

'Going to war was a different matter. Uncle Sam wanted the best out of his investment and I can't recall a mission where my ship wasn't loaded to capacity with fuel and bombs. We frequently flew with an overload—and a prayer that we wouldn't lose an engine on take-off. The B-17 took a long while to make altitude and sometimes, when the

Top: a B-17G pictured during its bomb run against the Baltic port of Swinemunde. The bombardier in the nose compartment lined up the target with his Norden bombsight and the bombs were automatically released at the point computed by the sight. The bombardier could feed course corrections directly to the controls by adjusting the sight. Above: engine starting on the B-17 was usually accomplished with the aid of a ground starter battery to prevent too heavy a drain on the aircraft's batteries. All production Fortresses utilised four Wright R-1820 Cyclone engines

A.P.2099B,C,D,E,F-P.N.

(ii) During a descent from high altitude the turbo-
superchargers should never be shut off completely.

49.   CHECK LIST BEFORE LANDING

Trailing aerial	- Retract (check visually)
Turrets	- Centralised and locked
Auto pilot	- off
Intercoolers	- COLD
Gills	- Slightly open and LOCKED
Hydraulic pressure	- 600 - 800 lb/sq.in. (See para.66)
Hydraulic valve (Fortress ITA only)	- Set to NORMAL position for emergency brake operation
Superchargers	- Set up to take-off position
Tail wheel	- Locked - warning light OFF
Reduce speed to 150 mph (130 knots) IAS	
U - Undercarriage	- DOWN - green indicator light. Check by horn (if fitted) and visually.
M - Mixture control	- RICH
P - Propeller	- Set for 2,300 r.p.m.
F - Fuel	- Booster pumps ON
F - Flaps	- Fully DOWN, or less in a high wind
Generators	- OFF (Fortress 11 and 11A)

50.   APPROACH SPEEDS

Recommended speeds in mph IAS for the approach are:-

	At 54000 lb.	At 47000 lb
Engine assisted	110 (96 knots)	105 (90 knots)
Glide	120 (104 knots)	115 (100 knots)

51.   MISLANDING

(i) The aircraft will climb away with undercarriage and
flaps down at climbing power provided that the
speed has not fallen below 100 mph IAS; if the
use of full take-off power is found to be necessary,
rpm should be increased to 2500 before boost exceeds
41½ inches.

(ii) Switch on generators (Fortress 11 and 11A) and
raise undercarriage immediately.

(iii) Raise the flaps in stages above 200 feet.

Issued with A.L./2   A.P.2099B,C,D,E,F-P.N.

52.   AFTER LANDING

(i) Shut off turbo-superchargers and, on Fortress 111,
switch off the generators.

(ii) Raise the flaps and open the gills. Unlock
tailwheel before taxying.

(iii) Switch OFF booster pumps

(iv) Stopping engines:-

(a) Idle engines at approximately 800 r.p.m. until
cylinder temperatures drop to 150°C.

(b) Before stopping engines, run at 1200 rpm for
30 seconds.

(c) Stop engines by moving the mixture controls
to ENGINE OFF.

(d) Switch off ignition after engines have stopped.

(e) Switch off all electrical services.

(v) Allow time for the brakes to cook before applying
parking brakes: brakes should never be left locked
when they are hot. Use chocks for parking
whenever possible.

(vi) Oil dilution. The oil dilution period is 4
minutes; while diluting, on Fortress 11A and 11,
operate supercharger regulator controls to get
diluted oil to the turbo-superchargers.

Top: a section of the pilot's notes issued to RAF crews who flew the Fortress. In British service the Fortress flew anti-submarine patrols with Coastal Command and two squadrons took part in Bomber Command's night offensive, undertaking radio-countermeasures duties.
Above: the B-17G spanned 31·62m (103ft 9in) and had a wing area of 131·91 sq m (1,420 sq ft). It was powered by four 1,200 hp Wright R-1820-97 Cyclone radials, giving it a cruising speed of between 265 and 298 km/h (165 and 185 mph) depending on bomb and fuel load

target was on the French coast, we spent longer gaining our operating level than we did actually flying the mission. The makers' performance data may give the Fort a top speed of around 300mph but we flew our combat missions at half that. She was a slow old lady and when things got hot you felt you were only making a snail's progress. A 170 IAS was no pace for tracking through a flak field. The overloads and the climb to altitude put considerable strain on the engines and my biggest problem with the B-17 was fighting the overheat problem. The temperature gauges had to be constantly monitored as we always flew with the temperatures crowding the red lines. The Wright engines were hardy if noisy. [I] can never figure why

they didn't fit the Pratt & Whitneys to later models as these were better engines in my view. The Wrights were always plagued with oil leaks.

'A fault that the Air Force took a while to recognise and put right was concerned with the hydraulic feathering of the propellers. If an engine crankcase was fractured it sometimes happened that the oil was gone so quickly there was not enough left to operate the propeller feathering mechanism when the pilot hit the button. The unfeathered prop would then start to windmill and would eventually wind itself right off the engine. I guess the nearest I came to not coming back from a mission was when a flak fragment went into No 1 engine over Bremen. By the time I saw something was wrong most of the oil had gone and there was no response to attempts to feather. Very soon the prop on No 1 had run away and set up heavy vibration. The knowledge that at any moment that 500lb prop could twist itself off its hub and come slashing across towards the cockpit didn't make for a happy situation. When it did finally separate it took off down without damaging No 2. By that time we were out of formation and alone and lucky to make it back without being picked off by a fighter. Modifications were eventually made to engines to ensure that there was always a supply of oil for feathering.

'The cockpit heating system was good and while we flew in sub-zero conditions at 25,000ft I never had the problems with cold that the men in the nose or the rear of the aircraft endured. We had provision for electrical heated suits but didn't always use them. The most uncomfortable problem was the

BOEING B-17 FLYING FORTRESS

wearing of oxygen masks for long periods and I think most B-17 men will agree on this point.

'A lot has been written about the B-17's ability to absorb battle damage. On the reckoning of one member of my crew we took 16 hits to our aircraft in 31 missions. This is not a large number of hits compared with the battering taken by some Forts, caused substantial damage, two of the three different aeroplanes we flew having to go for major repair as a result. An air-launched rocket did the most damage, taking out a large part of the rear fuselage and fin as well as wounding both waist gunners, although not seriously. Eight of the hits were 20mm cannon shells which knocked large pieces out of the tailplane and stopped an engine but luckily didn't hit a gas tank. The rocket hit took out a number of control cables which could have been fatal on a less stable ship.

'It was because the '17 handled so well that you could compensate for such damage. Three-engine flying was no real problem and many aircraft came back for successful landings on two. I did know a pilot who made our field with only one prop turning, but that is not a situation I would like to have experienced. Photographs showing Forts that càme home with complete tail stabilisers missing and other severe damage prove what a tough old lady she was, worth all the praise she collected.'

The US Army had demanded a dual pilot configuration in all its multi-engined bombers since World War I. Although questioned as being wasteful in manpower, the policy proved itself time and again during World War II where, apart from easing the pilotage load on long duration missions, the presence of a second pilot frequently ensured a safe return of the bomber when the other pilot was wounded or killed in action. The co-pilot of a B-17 shared duties with the captain and was not along just for the ride as an insurance.

In view of the laudatory comments of Fortress pilots on the handling qualities of the aircraft, it is interesting to read the more studied observations of test pilots. The official pilot's notes gives the following summary of flight characteristics. 'The B-17 possesses many outstanding flight characteristics, chief among which are directional stability, strong aileron effect in turns, ability to go around without change in elevator trim, exceptional satisfactory stalling characteristics and extremely effective elevator control in take-off and landing.'

Official observation on other flight characteristics were as follows: 'Turns: because of the inherent directional stability of the B-17, dropping one wing will produce a notable turning effect. Very little rudder and aileron will enable you to roll in and out of turns easily. Avoid uncoordinated use of aileron. In shallow turns the load factors are negligible, but in steeper turns proportionately more back pressure is required, thereby increasing the load factor. If the aeroplane tends to slip out of turns, recover smoothly without attempting to hold bank. Decrease to bank. Use proper coordination of rudder and aileron. Trim: the aeroplane will go around without changes in elevator trim tab settings. However, trim must be changed with adjustment of cowl flaps and power settings for the

Left: a B-17F of the 534th BS, 381st BG, 1st Bomb Wing, US Eighth Air Force exhibits the oil, coolant and exhaust stains with which B-17s rapidly became begrimed in service.
Below: the B-17F incorporated many improvements made to early series B-17s as a result of combat experience in the Pacific. It had engines giving improved high-altitude performance, and introduced a frameless nose transparency and an improved ventral ball-turret. Further modifications, incorporated during production, centred around armour, armament and, most significantly, fuel capacity

Right: a B-17G restored in the group markings and codes of the 457th BG, 1st Bomb Wing, US Eighth Air Force, and maintained in flying condition. The armament has been removed. The B-17 was not only a good-looking aircraft, but it was extremely pleasant to fly out of formation and at moderate altitudes. Although not exciting to fly, it was difficult to make an irretrievable mistake in the B-17. Even in formation at high altitude it was remarkably stable and superior to all its contemporaries. However, formation flying was tiring and demanded considerable vigilance from pilots with the necessity to keep a constant watch on other B-17s' positions. The ease with which a formation could be flown depended very much upon how smoothly the lead B-17 was handled. The B-17's controls became sluggish at about 8,550m (28,000ft) and it was thus harder to keep in tight formation. Inset above right: the nose of the B-17G. The bombardier, who also controlled the nose turret, was accommodated in the nose, and the navigator was positioned behind him. The engineer, who doubled as mid-upper gunner, was accommodated behind the pilot and co-pilot. Inset right: B-17Gs of the 452nd BG, 4th Bomb Wing, US Eighth Air Force pictured in formation in spring 1944

following reasons. Increased power on the inboard engines causes the aeroplane to become slightly tail heavy and closing the cowl flaps on the inboard engines also causes tail-heaviness. With the aeroplane properly trimmed for a power-off, flaps-down landing, you can take off and go around again by applying power and putting the flap switch up with no change in trim. The flaps will retract at a satisfactorily slow rate.

'Stalls: the stall characteristics of the B-17 are highly satisfactory. The tendency to roll–commonly caused by lack of symmetry in the stalling of either wing–is minimised by the large vertical tail. Under all conditions a stall warning at several mph above the stalling speed is indicated by buffeting of the elevators. If airspeed is reduced rapidly near the

stall, the speed at which the stall will occur will be lower than when the stall is approached gradually. The stall will also be more violent because the wings' angle of attack will be considerably above the stalling altitude. The stalling speed of the B-17, like that of any other aeroplane, depends upon the gross weight, the load factor, the wing flap setting, the power, de-icer operation and ice formation.

'The procedure for recovering from a stall is normal. Regain airspeed for normal flight by smooth operation of the elevators. This may require a dive of up to 30 degrees. While regaining airspeed use rudder to maintain laterally level flight. After airspeed is regained use ailerons also for lateral control–but not until airspeed is regained. The important thing is to recover from the dive smoothly.

Penalty for failure to make smooth recovery may be a secondary stall or structural damage to the aeroplane, both because of excessive load factors. Rough or abrupt use of elevators to regain normal flying speed may cause the dive to become excessively steep. The additional airspeed necessary to regain normal flight need not be more than 20 mph. This means that excessive diving to regain airspeed is absolutely unnecessary. Remember these additional facts about stalls: stalls with wheels down will increase stalling speed about 5 mph; stalls with wheels and flaps down will decrease stalling speed about 10 mph; stalls with de-icer boots operating will increase the stalling speed 10 to 15 mph. In recovering from stalls with de-icer boots operating, regains slightly more than the usual 20 mph needed

for recovery. Such stalls are apt to be more abrupt, with a greater tendency to roll.

'Spins: accidental spinning of the B-17 is extremely unlikely. The directional stability and damping are great, and it is possible that even a deliberate spin would be difficult. However, remember that the aeroplane was not designed for spinning and deliberate spins are forbidden. Dives: the maximum permissible diving speed in the B-17 (flaps and wheels up) with modified elevators is 270 mph IAS; without elevator modifications, the maximum diving speed is 220 mph. The structural factors limiting the diving speed of the B-17 are the engine ring cowl strength, the wing leading-edge de-icer boot strength, the cockpit windshield and canopy strength and the critical flutter speed. The

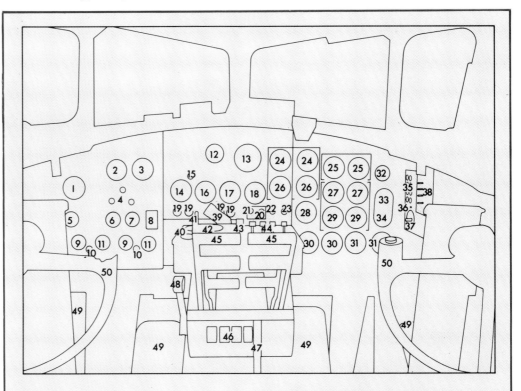

Boeing B-17 cockpit

1: Radio compass 2: Magnetic compass 3: Directional indicator 4: Systems failure warning lights 5: Voltmeter 6: Hydraulic pressure gauge 7: Suction gauge 8: Airspeed alternate source selector 9: Pilot's/co-pilot's oxygen flow indicators 10: Pilot's/co-pilot's oxygen indicator lights 11: Pilot's/co-pilot's oxygen pressure gauges 12: Directional indicator 13: Artificial horizon 14: Altimeter 15: Marker beacon indicator 16: Airspeed indicator 17: Turn and bank indicator 18: Rate of climb indicator 19: Propeller feathering buttons 20: Undercarriage warning light 21: Undercarriage warning light test button 22: Bomber's call light 23: Tailwheel lock warning light 24: Manifold pressure gauges 25: Fuel pressure gauges 26: Engine speed indicators 27: Oil pressure gauges 28: Flap position indicators 29: Oil temperature gauge 30: Cylinder head temperature gauges 31:

Carburettor air temperature gauges 32: Outside-air temperature gauges 33: Fuel contents gauge 34: Fuel contents gauge tank selector 35: Carburettor air-intake filter indicator lights 36: Air-intake filter switch 37: Fluorescent cockpit lighting control 38: Oil dilution switches 39: Cockpit light 40: Magneto switches 41: Master engine ignition switch 42: Turbo-supercharger regulator 43: Turbo-supercharger and mixture controls lock 44: Mixture controls 45: Throttle controls 46: Propeller speed controls 47: Propeller speed controls lock 48: Throttle controls lock 49: Rudder pedals 50: Control wheels

engine ring cowl has been designed to withstand 420 mph. The windshield and cockpit canopy have ample margin at 305 mph. The wing leading-edge de-icer boots begin to raise slightly from the wing at 305 mph, and any additional speed would be likely to lift the upper part of the boot above the wing surface, possibly causing structural failure. Therefore, it is obvious that simply diving the aeroplane to 270 mph involves no danger whatsoever. The only danger that must be considered is in recovery. Recovery must be smooth and gradual.'

For take-off the official pilot's notes for the B-17 give 177–185 km/h (110–115 mph) as the speed when the aircraft will become airborne with moderate back pressure on the control column. The optimum climb speed at all loadings was 225 km/h

(140 mph) IAS, while 200 km/h (125 mph) with half flaps was recommended for touchdown; the B-17 could, however, be landed at even slower speeds.

Another verdict on the Fortress comes from Colonel George Van den Heuval who was involved in the postwar programme where drone B-17s were used as aerial targets for the development of the early guided missiles. Acknowledging the aircraft's predictability, stability and reliability, he points out that it was these very qualities that were the reason for this particular surplus warplane type being chosen for radio control. 'The problems that we had with the control of these drones were many and it was essential that we start off with a fundamentally good flying aircraft. There was none better for our purpose than the Fortress.'

Right: for normal landings flaps were selected fully down. When flaps were fully lowered, the B-17 had to be retrimmed because the flaps caused a nose-down change of trim. When flying low, especially in bad visibility, 20 degrees flaps could be used to lower airspeed to about 240 km/h (150 mph). Recommended landing speed was somewhat lower at 200 km/h (125 mph). Below: a B-17G of the US Fifteenth Air Force, based in south-east Italy in mid 1944, pictured during a 'shuttle' mission, in which US bombers struck targets far in the east of Germany and flew on to bases in Russia. The B-17G had an effective range of 2,735 km (1,700 miles) with its maximum internal bombload of 2,721 kg (6,000 lb), but a typical load was nearer 1,810 kg (4,000 lb)

'The Mustang was well-named, for it could be a wild beast if you did not know its ways.'

North American P-51 Mustang

Although the P-51 is best-known for its operations as an escort fighter during the US Eighth Air Force's daylight bombing offensive against Germany, it was also widely used in other campaigns and roles. In Italy the US Fifteenth Air Force used the type for bomber escort duties, flying across the Alps into Austria, Hungary and Romania, while the US Twelfth Air Force used the type both in Italy and the Balkans for ground support duties. The P-51 also reached the Pacific Theatre towards the end of the war, where its long range was a great asset

Generally held to be the best all-round fighter aircraft of World War II, the North American P-51 Mustang was undoubtedly in a class of its own. It combined high speed in level flight and dives with the ability to maintain a top-rate performance whether at 12,000 m (40,000 ft) or just above the tree-tops. Good manoeuvrability and firepower combined with extraordinary range made the Merlin-powered Mustang one of the most versatile combat aircraft ever built.

The early Allison-engined version had a more restricted performance and gave of its best at altitudes below 4,600 m (15,000 ft). Pilots of the Royal Air Force – the service for which the aircraft was originally built – found the Allison engine dependable and smooth-running at normal speeds. This model was chiefly used for ground attack and tactical reconnaissance, the RAF still having many of the original Mustangs it had received in 1942 on operations at the end of hostilities three years later.

Wing Commander Tom Fazan, having previously flown the slow Westland Lysander spotter aircraft, anticipated that his transition to the Allison-engined Mustang might be difficult, when he took command of one of the first squadrons equipped with the type early in 1942. He later recalled that the Mustang was surprisingly docile and he always felt the aircraft was flying him and not he it. It was very stable and he particularly liked the wide track undercarriage which was a boon on

the small bumpy grass aerodromes from which they generally operated. The Mustang was also a very solid aircraft; one felt the construction was good and that it would stand up to the rough and tumble of operational use very well – and it did.

The Mustang's airframe was considerably heavier than that of most of its European contemporaries and thus it took the Packard Merlin with its two-speed, two-stage supercharger to provide the power match required. Mass-produced at two large plants, the Merlin-engined Mustang became the main USAAF fighter during the final year of World War II. While it is not surprising that such a powerful aircraft should be adapted in postwar years for racing and sport, what does say much for the inherent good design and construction of the aircraft is that, more than three decades after the last example left the production lines, nearly 60 civilian-operated Mustangs are still flying in the United States alone.

The reputation of the Mustang as being 'a hot ship' led to occupancy of its cockpit becoming one of the most sought-after assignments by USAAF pilots. The cockpit was of a comfortable size, much roomier than the glove-like positions in the Spitfire or Messerschmitt Bf 109. The original 'coffin hood' type canopy restricted vision, but no more than in similar-styled contemporaries. The introduction of the so-called bubble canopy on the P-51D giving all-round visibility was a vast improvement, although its predecessors were said to be faster.

The flight controls in a Mustang were the conventional stick and rudder pedals arrangement. All control surfaces had fibre trim tabs adjustable by three knobs on a control pedestal installed on the left side of the cockpit. This control pedestal also sported the operating levers and switches for propeller pitch, fuel mixture, throttle, landing gear and flap control. Switches on the right side of the cockpit were for electrics, radio and oxygen supply. There were normally 14 gauges and dials on the instrument panel, below which were switches to operate weapons release and fuel supply. As the two-speed, two-stage supercharger cut in automatically with changes in altitude, operation of the Mustang was considerably easier for the pilot than either the Republic P-47 Thunderbolt or Lockheed P-38 with their sensitive turbo-superchargers.

The pilot's seat was designed to accommodate either a seat or back type parachute, but the bucket had no fore or aft movement and adjustments had to be made on the rudder pedals to accommodate the very large man more comfortably. The seat could, however, be raised and this was an advantage when taxying. The back of the seat was armoured and the pilot was afforded additional protection by a steel panel aft of the engine and a bullet-proof windshield in front of him.

One young American who was successful in his desire to go to war in the cockpit of a Mustang was Richard Burns. His objective was only achieved after considerable experience in other single-seat fighter types while instructing at bases in the United States. 'The Mustang was well-named for it could be a wild beast if you did not know its ways. A lot of men got killed finding out. I have heard it described as an unforgiving aeroplane. It was no more unforgiving than any other aeroplane where the pilot didn't know its limitations or ignored them. The '51 had a lot of power up front and very clean lines and it would quickly go wild on you if you didn't keep a tight rein. I was lucky in that I first flew the early A model with the Allison engine and this was a tamer beast. I don't think I would have liked to go straight from an AT-6 [Harvard] to a P-51B or D model as some guys did. It was a big step unless you were cautioned what could happen.

'Take-off and landing are always the most dangerous times in a new type and this is where the P-51 could really bring you trouble. On take-off the throttle was opened up until pulling 61 ins of manifold pressure and 3,000 rpm. With all that power, acceleration was rapid. The tendency was to feel you had flying speed before you really had and hoist the tail up by pushing forward on the stick. If you did this too soon there would be insufficient airspeed to give effective rudder control. Unless she got plenty of right rudder the torque of the prop' would have her right off the runway in a matter of seconds. I saw a man get killed through losing directional control during take-off. The other hard one for the novice was stalling out on landing. You had to learn not to let the speed drop below 110 IAS on final approach. Many a Mustang got bent because a greenhorn lost too much speed on approach. As soon as he broke his glide the plane just fell out of the sky.

'The chances were that a newcomer would have trouble getting the hang of the tailwheel control. The lock for this was different to that on most other planes of the day in that it was operated by the control stick. With the stick halfway or pulled back the tail wheel was locked and steerable by the rudder pedals. You had to push the stick right forward to unlock the tail wheel and make it fully swivelling. At the training base you would see some guy gun the engine with the stick forward and suddenly be surprised as hell to find himself swung way off the ramp. Alternatively, you'd see someone doing his best to wrench the tyre off the tailwheel by trying to do a pivot turn while holding the stick back.

'If you knew its limitations the '51 was a sweet-flying ship. She was light on the controls and pretty stable. Only light pressure was needed on the controls which helped a deal on return from long escort missions. She would trim out nicely but the trim tab controls were pretty sensitive and had to be carefully used – so sensitive that a heavy hand on the stick when turning or coming out of a dive could quickly pull so many 'g's that you would momentarily black out. This was particularly so when the rear fuselage tank was full of fuel. The weight shifted the centre of gravity back and reduced the amount of pressure necessary to pull the stick back. You were warned only to fly straight and level with that tank full, and not to engage in any aerobatics or sharp manoeuvres if the tank was more than a third full.

'Normal operating procedure was to take off on the fuselage tank and draw half the fuel, then switch to the drop tanks, switching from one to the other to balance them out. This way if you got into combat and let go the drop tanks your plane was

Above: a P-51D of the 352nd Fighter Squadron, 353rd Fighter Group, US Eighth Air Force, based at Raydon, Suffolk in October 1944. The Group began to fly the P-51 in combat from 2 October 1944, having previously flown the Republic P-47 Thunderbolt. Right: a P-51D fitted with non-standard long-range tanks and carrying a passenger in a 'buddy-seat'. The latter could be installed for non-combat duties and conversion training by removing the rear fuselage tank and the radio installation behind the pilot's seat. A number of aircraft was later converted to two-seat dual control standard by Temco for training by fitting a larger cockpit and canopy

clean and in good flying trim, plus you had two full main tanks to get you home. With full drop tanks and rear fuselage tank the plane couldn't be trimmed for hands-off flight. This was tiring and you were glad when some of that fuel was gone and the centre of gravity moved forward. Only once did I get into combat with a fairly full rear tank and it wasn't nice. The stick forces tended to reverse in a sharp turn. On that occasion we were bounced over the sea, but happily the two enemy fighters didn't want to mix it and made off after their initial pass.

'The Mustang was such a clean design that it would quickly pick up speed in a dive and if you weren't careful you could get into compressibility. The airspeed indicator was red-lined at 500mph but, of course, at high altitude you could be hitting the 500 figure when the dial only showed 300mph. A lot of men got killed because they didn't compensate for altitude, got into a high speed dive at 30,000ft or more and suddenly found the aircraft in compressibility when the pointer was still way below the red line. The Mustang was tough, but if you got into

an uncontrollable dive it only took a heavy hand on the stick to shed wings and tailplane.

'In my outfit there were several cases of P-51s having structural failure in flight. It is a pretty sure thing that most of these break-ups occurred because the pilot was heavy on the controls at high speed. The unwary could easily get into such a situation. We got a lot of this when people started to chase Jerry jets. Sometimes it would look that no more harm than popping a few rivets had been done. As we didn't have the equipment in those days to check for metal fatigue the plane would be put back into service only to break up next time a pilot pulled a sharp turn.

'How a Mustang behaved in a stall depended very much on its loading. Clean and with no fuel in the rear tank the stall was fairly gentle and recovery quite comfortable. Spins in a '51 were to be avoided. Even a power-off spin was nasty, the nose snapping up and down all the time. I never got into a power spin, but understand you were lucky if you came out alive. The guys who got into power spins

Top: three Mustangs and a Curtiss P-40 (left) preserved in the United States. Both the P-40 and P-51 originally had Allison engines, but whereas the Packard-built Merlin radically improved the P-51's performance, the P-40 was not greatly improved by the Merlin. Top right: the cockpit of the P-51D was one of the neatest and most uncluttered of World War II fighters. The basic six flight instruments were grouped centrally on the dashboard, while the main engine instruments were positioned logically on either side. Above: a fin strake was added to P-51Ds to compensate for loss of lateral stability caused by the cut-down rear-fuselage. Nearly 8,000 P-51D aircraft were built. Right: Power was used and flaps were fully powered for normal landings, but only 20 degrees of flaps could be used with drop tanks in place

had usually attempted snap rolls. We were advised not to attempt snap rolls in a Mustang . . . Apart from that, the Mustang had good aerobatic qualities and with those light control pressures she was a joy to stunt around. The P-51D and K models that I flew were pretty reliable and the malfunctions experienced were of a minor nature.

'We did a lot of ground strafing; nobody liked it. The Merlin was a superb engine but its liquid coolant system was highly vulnerable to battle damage. The coolant radiator was under the centre fuselage and there was no armour protection for this or the coolant lines which ran to the engine. A bit of flak or a bullet through one of these lines and that was the end. Your engine would seize in a matter of seconds once the coolant was gone. I have no figures to prove it but believe that nearly all the many pilots we lost ground strafing had to belly-in or bail out after the coolant system was hit. The Mustang was not the best of fighters to belly-in. That large scoop radiator usually crumpled on impact but if there were large rocks or other hard obstructions in its way the fuselage could be torn apart. They said it was possible to ditch a P-51 but I don't know of anyone who did it and lived. Most pilots preferred to bail out. The only time I ever saw a ditching attempted . . . the plane nosed right in as soon as it hit the water; the pilot didn't have a chance.

'When I got into the action in Europe the Luftwaffe was rarely met in the air but I believed that the '51 was superior to anything that we were likely to meet in combat. With the K-14 gyro-gunsight and the six 0·5 in machine guns you could be pretty sure of a kill once you had an enemy aircraft in range. The only superiority that the Bf 109s and Fw 190s appeared to have was in climb performance. Those that I encountered usually broke downwards, which was a bad mistake as we could always overhaul them. Most of the long-range escort we flew brought no aerial opposition and these five or six hour duration trips could be monotonous. We had one pilot in the squadron who was always horsing around on the return trips. His favourite stunt was to fly inverted, particularly if there was a new man leading the flight. He'd say something over the radio to draw the new man's attention and when the guy looked over his shoulder he'd be amazed to see a '51 alongside flying forma-tion upside down. The limitation on inverted flight was 10 seconds, the reckoning being that thereafter the engine lubricant pump would be starved of oil.'

Not all Mustang pilots of the time would have agreed with Richard Burns' assessment, however. One omnipresent problem on long-range operations was the necessity to retain a half-full main tank (situated directly behind the cockpit) to return home in the correct trim. Violent manoeuvres frequently undertaken while bombing or strafing, for example, could lead to trouble with little chance of salvation.

The Mustang's optimal angle of climb was considerably less than the Spitfire's, but the P-51D could outstrip the British fighter in diving, if not level, turns. Compared with the Messerschmitt Bf 109, North American's P-51D could outclimb and outdive its adversary; level flight characteristics were more evenly matched. The German's initial

the premier escort fighter of the war. Its relative comfort was much valued by pilots engaged in accompanying the Eighth Air Force's 'heavies' on their frequent forays to Berlin and other inland targets, with round trips of seven hours or more. Handling qualities above the stall were such that inexperienced pilots could be misled into over-confident and careless flying. The unexpected snap roll which heralded a stall invariably ended such behaviour.

The RAF Pilot's Notes for the Mustang Mk III gave this information about stalling: 'with empty fuselage tank, slight tail buffeting occurs about 3 to 4 mph above the stall, at which the right wing drops gently. With the fuselage tank full or half full, there is no buffeting ... but a series of stick reversals occurs just above stalling speed; at the stall the right wing drops sharply, and unless immediate recovery action is taken, a spin may develop. The control column must be pushed firmly forward for recovery ... The aircraft sinks rapidly as stalling speed is approached. If the control column is held back at the stall, a wing will drop very rapidly. ...'

An interesting test was carried out by the Air Fighting Development Unit (AFDU) at RAF Wittering early in 1944, comparing a Mustang Mark III (the British designation for the P-51B) and similar British and German fighters. The following observations were made: 'Endurance: with a fuel capacity of 152 gallons [this example did not have the rear fuselage tank] and a consumption rate on a par with that of the Spitfire Mk IX, the Mustang had nearly double the range. At similar power settings the Mustang Mk III was approximately 20 mph faster in level flight, thus adding to its range benefit. In comparison with the Griffon-engined Spitfire Mk XIV the Mustang's range was still double that of the Spitfire on internal fuel. This also applied to the Tempest Mk V, the Fw 190A and the Bf 109G, against which it was tested.

'Speeds: for the same engine settings the Mustang Mk III was between 20 to 30 mph faster in level flight at all heights than the Spitfire Mk IX, but its maximum speed was practically identical to that of the Spitfire Mk XIV. The Tempest Mk V was some 15 to 20 mph faster up to 15,000 ft, thereafter losing its advantage and at 30,000 ft the Mustang was over 30 mph faster. The top speeds of the two German fighters were also inferior, particularly that of the Fw 190A which was nearly 50 mph slower at all heights, dropping to 70 mph above 28,000 ft. Against the Bf 109G the Mustang Mk III proved to have its best advantage in speed below 16,000 ft where it was 30 mph faster, and above 25,000 ft where the advantage was also 30 mph increasing to 50 mph and more above 30,000 ft.

'Climbs: being a much heavier aircraft with a higher wing loading, the Mustang climbed far more slowly than both the Spitfire models at all heights. The US fighter did have, however, a better zoom climb in that it could dive 5,000 ft or more and then use the momentum gained to reach its original altitude at a greater speed than the Spitfires. It also needed less increase of power to regain its previous altitude and speed. The Tempest Mk V had a much better climb at lower altitude with up to 20 mph advantage. For the next 10,000 ft there was little to choose between the two, but at 25,000 ft and above

Above: Mustangs have seen diverse service since World War II and the Korean War as executive transports, racing aircraft and chase planes in US Army test programmes, as well as being flown by minor air forces. A Mustang re-built by Cavalier in the 1960s is illustrated.
Top left: two Mustangs are seen taxying out before take-off. Flaps were not normally lowered for take-off, but a 20 degree setting could be used to obtain the shortest possible run.
Centre left: a P-51 is seen shortly after take-off, with the inner under-carriage doors about to retract.
'Cripes A' Mighty 3rd' was flown by Maj George E. Preddy in mid-1944 when he served with the 352nd FG, US Eighth Air Force.
Left: the pictured Mustang is preserved in the colours of the RAF

acceleration advantage, however, was sometimes enough to enable it to make good its escape.

A couple of undesirable characteristics marred the otherwise-impeccable performance of the P-51D's licence-built Merlin engine. The normally-automatic air scoop door control occasionally stuck closed, resulting in a rapid rise in coolant temperature if this occurred during operations requiring high engine revolutions. Lack of corrective action meant a loss of coolant and, subsequently, power, in a very short time.

The other major problem with which the Mustang pilot had to contend was the difficulty encountered when attempting to bail out. The airflow around the cockpit once the canpoy had been discarded contrived to force the would-be escapee back into the aircraft and behind the armour plating. Certain pilots found that rolling the aircraft upside-down was the only sure method of obtaining egress.

In spite of the aforementioned problems, the Mustang was almost universally acknowledged as

the Mustang rapidly pulled ahead, being about 30 mph faster at 30,000 ft. There was little to choose between the Mustang and the Fw 190A, although the Mustang was considerably faster at all heights in a zoom climb. The Bf 109G had a slightly better rate of climb below 20,000 ft, whereas the Mustang had a slight advantage above 25,000 ft. In a zoom climb, however, the Bf 109G was equally as good as the Mustang.

'Dives: the Mustang Mk III could pull away rapidly from both marks of Spitfire in a dive. On the other hand, the Tempest could dive as fast as the Mustang and tended to accelerate away. The Fw 190A could always be out-dived by the Mustang and, while the Bf 109G had an initial advantage, the Mustang could overhaul it in a prolonged dive. Turning circle: the Spitfire Mk IX could easily out-turn the Mustang and the Spitfire Mk XIV was also superior in this respect. The Mustang could out-turn the Tempest and was greatly superior to the Bf 109G, but was only slightly better than the Fw 190. Rate of roll: the Mustang could not roll as quickly as the Spitfire Mk IX at normal speeds, but the two aircraft were comparable in this respect

at very high speeds. This was also the case when pitted against the Spitfire Mk XIV. The Mustang's rate of roll was better than that of the Tempest, similar to that of the Bf 109G, but far inferior to that of the Fw 190A, which was renowned for its speed in this manoeuvre.'

In the same report the AFDU noted that the Mustang had better forward and downward vision than the British fighters and, while the original hood severely restricted rearward vision, the installation of a blown canopy (Malcolm hood) would give a pilot better all-round visibility than from a Spitfire. The armament of four 0·5 in machine guns was considered light in comparison with that of British fighters; the armament was increased to six guns in later models. Firing tests brought a verdict that the fighter was a steady gun platform. Final observations made in the report were that the only serious drawback in performance was the comparatively poor rate of climb and a warning that pilots flying the Mustang should understand the effect of compressibility speeds. Summing up, the report stated, 'The Mustang Mk III is a delightful and easy aircraft to fly.'

Top: a line-up of P-51Ds preserved in airworthy condition in the United States. The Merlin-engined Mustang has often been called the finest all-round fighter of World War II, by reason of its combination of excellent dogfighting qualities, toughness, good performance at all heights and long range.
Above: The view over the P-51's nose during taxying was poor and snaking was necessary. The tail-wheel was locked when taxying and during take-off, while the tail was kept down during the initial part of the take-off run to eliminate a tendency to swing

Yakovlev Yak-1 to Yak-9

Following the success of Yak's wartime fighters, all-metal versions of the Yak-3 and Yak-9 were placed in production at the close of hostilities. The Yak-9P was powered by a 1,700 hp Klimov VK-107A engine and served in the Korean War. The pictured example is preserved in the markings of the Polish air force

I spent two years with the Royal Air Force, the first with No 253 Squadron which specialised in night fighting and a technique called 'Turbinlite' [airborne searchlight] which was particularly instructive from a professional standpoint. Following this, I was posted to the Free French 3rd Groupe de Chasse, which later became known as the 'Normandie-Niemen' regiment. We were subsequently transferred, via Lebanon, to Ivanovo some 200 km (125 miles) north-east of Moscow.

The Soviet authorities gave us a choice of aircraft – British, American or Russian – and we chose the latter. Thus we became acquainted with [the two-seater version of] the Yak-1 which became the basis for the design of a great number of fighters. The simple two-seater, which was principally used for training, was equipped with fixed landing gear capable of taking either wheels or skis, and was perfectly adapted to its task. Its silhouette was reminiscent of the Dewoitine D.520, which arrived in the French squadrons too late in 1940. Was a two-seat D.520 possible? In the USSR it certainly was. The Russians showed us – to our great astonishment – a Hurricane whose characteristic hump had

been replaced by a gaping hole which was supposed to be protected by a ridiculously small plastic windscreen. Even the minute I-16 'Rata' was endowed with a second seat for the good of the Soviet cause!

In a country where the winter sun shows itself so rarely, everything had to be done to make the most of the few hours of daylight there were. Without doubt the climate was responsible for the extreme simplicity of all the machines which were developed to run on airfield surfaces prepared for hours on end by tractors towing long trains of enormous rollers. It was impossible to clear the snow and for this reason the only solution was to pack it down to allow aeroplanes with low-pressure tyres to operate. It was icy cold and on certain days the temperature dropped to below thirty degrees centigrade, making it necessary to change the radiator liquid daily. A glycol mixture would have no effect and would only have complicated the logistics in this immense country with its severe climate and reduced and difficult means of communication. The lubricating oil made the mechanics' task even more difficult and they had to heat the liquid before

Developed from the Yak-7, the Yak-9 entered first-line service in 1943 and was subsequently produced in several different variants. The pictured formation consists of Yak-9Ds flown by the Red Banner Guards Regiment of the Soviet Black Sea Fleet

they could even begin to make even the slightest preparation for the flight.

Luckily this drawback was compensated for by the extreme simplicity of the aircraft's equipment—no gyroscopic instrument except for the turn and bank indicator. Other instruments were restricted to essentials such as the rev-counter, a pressure meter and indispensible thermometers. This would suggest that blind flying was impossible for the fighter. We were to learn quickly that the principal role of Soviet aviation—if not the only one—was ground-support. This explained the basic simplicity of the fighters destined to operate over vast territories, far from the industrial centres transferred east of the Volga following the advance of the German troops. To protect against the failures of compressed air starting, a Hucks starter could be engaged in the exposed end of the propeller shaft.

Our training began, and was initially limited to flights in two-seaters only. The Yak-7, in spite of all its good qualities, left much to be desired for

solo flying. For all that, it did not prevent us from utilising the six available hours of daylight. For those who had left Britain, the inactivity began to weigh heavily. Why wouldn't they agree to taking a tour in a Yak? Because the aircraft had agreeable handling characteristics, we were permitted brief spells to admire a sumptuous countryside of whiteness and light where it was easy to confuse land and sky. However, we hadn't long to enjoy this as the first two single-seat Yak-1s arrived.

The Yak-1's silhouette was a little different from that of its two-seat brother. A simple glance enabled one to distinguish between them, the difference being in the bubble-like cockpit canopy. The Yak-1 was the first single-seat fighter to allow the pilot a complete 360 degree view around him, thanks to a sheet of armoured glass which took the place of the armour plate at the pilot's shoulder height. A plate of the same kind served as frontal protection. There was another cunning device, less visible but just as useful. The gauges of the fuel tank

were placed on the wings, allowing them to be read directly, and the fuel tank itself received the burnt gases – purified through a filter – as they gradually emptied themselves. In the air, the dangers of explosion in combat were thereby reduced. However, we had to wait a very long time before being able to verify just how good this invention was.

The cabin of the single-seat aircraft showed changes only in armament. The aircraft had the same instruments as the Yak-7, including the radio-telephone, an instrument which caused us casualties in battle. Each aeroplane was equipped with an oxygen mask which hooked on the right wall – an item that with time we were to forget about. It was also endowed with a mask for radio-telephone communications, but as we rarely flew at altitudes above 4,000 metres, we abandoned these restricting masks to eternal silence in order to keep our heads and eyes free to move. This ability to move around 360 degrees which this wonderful cockpit canopy allowed, particularly so for the 180 degrees behind,

made life far easier. To help this rotation movement we buckled the seat straps in a way that left us full movement of the shoulders. The opposite was true for western planes which were equipped with shoulder straps, leaving the top half of the body completely free to move, unlike the Yaks with their restriction on movement. Curiously enough, this fault was not even eliminated with the Yak-3 – a plane of exceptional qualities.

Of course another difference other than size distinguished the Yak-1 from the Yak-7 – the armament and the direction of fire. The 20 mm cannon, firing through the hub of the propeller, could be reloaded in flight by the pilot. Unfortunately jamming did occur, and always seemed to happen at crucial moments. This was to be our morning awakening; as the dawn patrols took off, each pilot fired a trial round, as if by pure chance, at the very moment when they flew over our dormitory.

The first Yak-9s arrived after the hard battle of July 1943 on the north flank of the front at Kursk.

A typical Soviet propaganda shot depicts a line-up of Yak-3 lightweight low-level interceptors, with a single Lavochkin nearest the camera. The speedy Yak-3 was considered by many, including General Risso, to be Yakovlev's most advanced fighter of World War II

Pneumatically-controlled firing had made way for electrical control; the ring which surmounted the joystick of the Yak-1 had disappeared. The aircraft's silhouette gave the impression of a great robustness, a solid charger. The cockpit of the Yak-9 revealed the genius of the Russians. A 37mm cannon was installed in place of the 20mm cannon, without the aeronautical qualities of the aeroplane suffering. This installation demanded a few precautionary measures owing to the reduction in visibility during manoeuvres on the ground and the fall in speed after a round of three shots fired at an enemy plane. This drawback could, however, be turned to our advantage; when a landing was too long, three shots from a 37mm put an end to the burst of speed. Moreover, this excess weight resulted in research into finding a means of lightening the load. This was only possible by reducing the quantity of fuel carried on board and thus the range of the fighter, thereby considerably reducing its effectiveness.

The robust Yak-9 was succeeded by the slender and elegant Yak-3 – last of the Yakovlev family. A marvel of aerodynamics, it must have delighted even the most exacting of fighter pilots. It was light –

weighing 2,670 kg (5,900 lb) in full battle array – was powerful, thanks to the 1,350 hp of her 12-cylinder vee engine, and climbed with vivacity, holding tenaciously in turns and reaching hitherto unknown speeds. The Yak-3 was an extraordinary surprise to the Germans who confused it with its ancestor, the Yak-1, with which it had only one point in common to the untrained eye – the silhouette. Of course as with all new aircraft, there were teething troubles. Its undercarriage occasionally refused obstinately to hook back into the retracted position, giving the pilot the illusion of everything having retracted, only to extend again sharply with the slightest possible acceleration.

The machine's great finesse led some pilots to break the speed limit – something hitherto unknown. In spite of these few, quickly-repaired faults, this was an admirable companion with which we returned to France. With it we helped the Allied forces recapture French territory at le Bourget on 20 June 1945. Of the 42 given to France by Russia, a single example perpetuates their memory and that of Normandie-Niemen, being preserved in the Musée de l'Air at le Bourget.

Above: reputedly inspired by both the Supermarine Spitfire and the Messerschmitt Bf 109, the Yak-1 appeared at the beginning of 1940. The all-round vision afforded the pilot by the bubble canopy and the armoured glass to his rear was especially appreciated. Below: the Normandie-Niemen regiment arrives at le Bourget on 20 June 1945 on the liberation of France. With their tricolour propeller spinners and the cross of Lorraine on the fin, the regiment's Yak-3s won an unique place in the annals of air warfare

'She was a joy to fly. Control was very sensitive and the aircraft had excellent manoeuvrability.'
Ladislav Valousek

Lavochkin LA-5FN

With a ground handler at each wingtip, a Lavochkin La-5FN scrambles from Tri Duby airfield, Czechoslovakia. Developed from the earlier La-5, the FN variant featured an all-round vision canopy and a more powerful Shvetsov radial engine. Late production aircraft introduced weight-saving metal wing spars, an innovation which was retained by the type's successor, the La-7

With the consent of the Royal Air Force and according to an agreement between the exiled Czechoslovak government and the Government of the USSR, 20 highly-experienced Czechoslovak fighter pilots and one ground-staff officer were discharged from the RAF and sent to the Soviet Union as the nucleus of the Czechoslovak air force within the framework of the Soviet air force. The transfer of the small group started in February 1944 at Liverpool and ended in April in Ivanovo, about 290 km (180 miles) north-east of Moscow. Two of these pilots – Ladislav Valoušek and František Fajtl DFC recall their impressions of the Lavochkin La-5 single-engined fighter.

Two weeks of intensive lectures covered every aspect of the characteristics of the La-5FN and provided a thorough run-down of Soviet fighter tactics. At the beginning of May we started flying. We performed our first familiarisation flights in a tandem two-seat UTLá-5 and a couple of days later an intensive conversion course began.

The pilot's forward view when taxying was as poor as that from the cockpit of a Spitfire, but the view aft through the bullet-resistant screen pro-tecting the pilot's head was very good. The small mirror attached to the cockpit framing appeared to cover all that the pilot needed to see. The cockpit lacked an entry flap, as in the Spitfire, and clambering in over the high sill was rather awkward. Instrumentation was austere; the lack of artificial horizon and gyro compass was particularly noticeable, while the compass was fairly elementary. Frequency selection for the single-channel radio was by means of a knob under the starboard side of the instrument panel and we guessed that tuning would be somewhat complicated. However, the press-to-speak transmission button on the throttle lever appeared to be an excellent device.

A cock positioned on the starboard side of the cockpit was activated in case of fire to pump inert filtered exhaust gases into the fuel tanks. The PB-1a gunsight was a lens of about two inches diameter instead of the more normal flat, inclined glass plate. There were two deflection rings, but it was obvious that no fine degree of deflection could be obtained. No cockpit heating system was provided for the pilot.

The close-cowled Shvetsov M-82FN engine was

225

LAVOCHKIN LA-5

a 14-cylinder two-row radial with two-speed super-charger and direct fuel injection. Its maximum output of 1,850hp at 2,500rpm for take-off could be used for only two minutes, its nominal maximum continuous power at 2,400rpm being 1,650hp. The power plant drove a three-blade, controllable-pitch propeller of three metres (9·8ft) diameter, the hub incorporating a Hucks-type starter dog in case compressed air bottles were not available. The engine cowling embodied adjustable louvres for controlling the flow of cooling air, while front and rear fans were provided for warm-weather operation.

The fuel was housed between the wing spars in a self-sealing three-tank set. Armament comprised only two 20mm belt-fed gas-operated ShVAK cannon, which were mounted in the forward fuselage immediately ahead of the cockpit and were synchronised to fire through the propeller disc. The hydraulically-operated undercarriage retracted inwards in the fuselage centre-section.

The structure of the 'Lavochka' – the familiar nickname which we had already begun to use – was almost exclusively of birch and so-called delta wood. Automatic leading-edge slats were fitted outboard

and the entire trailing edge was occupied by metal-framed, fabric-skinned ailerons and all-metal split flaps. Our general consensus was favourable overall, apart from some criticism in respect of instrumentation, radio, armament and pilot comforts.

The propeller pitch was set to fully-fine and the right rudder was applied to counter torque during take-off. Only slight elevator movement was called for to take the aircraft off the ground. When airborne, we moved the undercarriage control lever to the 'up' position and watched the green indicator lights blink out. The undercarriage control lever was immediately returned to 'neutral' to avoid damage to the hydraulic system. Boost and revs were reduced for the normal climb regime. We had to watch the cylinder head temperature gauge very carefully as there had been cases with this engine of cylinders literally losing their heads. After levelling off, boost and revs were again reduced for cruise. We had been warned that prolonged cruise at low revs fouled up the spark plugs of the lower cylinders and it was necessary, therefore, to increase revs for a few seconds every 15 minutes to clean the plugs.

Whatever shortcomings the 'Lavochka' posses-

Right: September 1944 saw the arrival of the Czech-flown Lavochkins at Zolná, where some of the heaviest air fighting of the National Slovak Uprising was to take place. Messerschmitt and Focke Wulf fighters were to fall prey to the Lavochkins' cannon. An La-5FN aircraft is pictured shortly after landing with pilot's kit in the foreground. Below: the Lavochkin of Ladislav Valoušek is pictured undergoing maintenance at Rohozná, a relief landing ground near Brezno, Czechoslovakia. As with many of its Soviet contemporaries, the La-5FN was a functional aircraft which required little attention in the field

Above left: pilots Valoušek (left) and Matušek are pictured with Flight Commander Chábera and a camouflaged 'Lavochka' at Tri Duby aerodrome.
Left: a close-up view of the La-5FN highlights the Hucks-type starter dog in the airscrew hub and the cannon port in the cowling to starboard.
Above: developed from the La-5FN, the La-7 appeared at the end of 1943. Czechoslovak units received the type too late in the war to fly it operationally

sed, handling characteristics, once airborne, were not among them. She was a joy to fly. Control was very sensitive and the aircraft had excellent manoeuvrability. She was a superlative low-to-medium altitude air superiority aircraft, excelling in close combat and the master of any Messerschmitt Bf 109 or Focke Wulf Fw 190 in such a dogfight. Spin recovery procedure was quite normal and diving characteristics were good. It displayed some capriciousness when landing; on touching down it tended to bounce. Our Soviet instructors told us to disregard this tendency, but we found this very disconcerting nonetheless. A lot of Spitfire routine must have remained in our subconsciousness for we immediately gave her a little power and eased gently back on the stick – a cardinal mistake insofar as the Lavochkin was concerned. Finally we solved this problem by a compromise; we partly tamed her headstrong temper and partly got used to it.

On 3 June our group became an organised unit, the first Independent Czechoslovak Fighter Air Regiment and it was sent to Slovakia on 17 September 1944 to help the National Slovak Uprising. Our 21 Lavochkin La-5s landed on a hard, large meadow near the village of Zolná north-east of Zvolen and immediately went into action against the encircling German ground and air forces. Due to the wide experience of the pilots and to the sturdiness, outstanding manoeuvrability and high performance of our 'Lavochkas' we very soon stopped the daily intruders' raids completely. We engaged in twenty dogfights and won them all, including those with Bf 190s and Fw 190s, and enjoyed superiority throughout the combat zone until the very end of the organised uprising on 25 October.

Furthermore, we helped the soldiers and partisans by attacking all sorts of targets on the ground with our two-cannon armament.

Ladislav Valoušek recalls, 'Once in combat I touched 447 mph indicated airspeed at around 3,280 ft and although the controls stiffened up considerably, the 'Lavochka' behaved perfectly well. Though we had been informed of the general principles of using the La-5FN for bombing, we had been given no instruction in the technique, and thus had to teach ourselves. The bomb release was placed rather awkwardly very low on the left-hand side of the seat, the pilot having to bend over to reach it at a critical moment at low altitude "in hilly country". [This problem was partially solved by fuses for automatic releasing of the 55 lb and 110 lb bombs.] The cloud was sometimes as low as 500 ft and in such circumstances I endeavoured to drop the bombs from about 165 ft in a climb and turning steeply as the bombs were released.'

After the retreat from Slovakia to Poland, we went on fighting in April 1945 against Schörner's German army near the north-eastern Czechoslovak frontier. František Fajtl remembers that, 'on 16 April in a dogfight I experienced the big advantage of direct fuel injection. I was escorting our [Ilyushin] Il-2 dive-bombers when two Bf 109s appeared. I immediately went into a steep vertical dive . . . There was no short stoppage at the very beginning of the dive in my Lavochka that I had experienced during such a manoeuvre in planes with engines aspirated with a carburettor. We overtook them, opened fire and drove the enemy away.' Undoubtedly the modern Lavochkin La-5 was among the best and most successful Soviet warplanes.

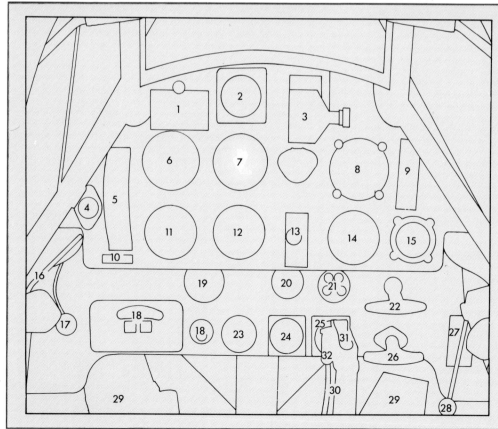

Messerschmitt Bf 109E cockpit

1: *Data card* 2: *Clock* 3: *Gunsight location* 4: *Circuit breaker* 5: *Engine starting control* 6: *Altimeter* 7: *Compass* 8: *Manifold pressure gauge* 9: *Compass deviation card* 10: *Pitot-head heating warning light* 11: *Airspeed indicator* 12: *Turn and bank indicator* 13: *Airscrew pitch control* 14: *Engine speed indicator* 15: *Airscrew pitch indicator* 16: *Hood jettison lever* 17: *Fuel cock* 18: *Gun-arming panel and control* 19: *Gun-sight dimmer control* 20: *Fuel and oil pressure gauge* 21: *Undercarriage position indicator* 22: *Undercarriage control lever* 23: *Fuel contents gauge* 24: *Oil temperature gauge* 25: *Coolant temperature gauge* 26: *Undercarriage emergency control lever* 27: *Mechanical undercarriage position indicator* 28: *Filter pump control* 29: *Rudder pedals* 30: *Control column* 31: *Gun-firing button* 32: *Press-to-transmit radio button*

Messerschmitt Bf 109

A Bf 109E preserved in the UK in Battle of Britain period markings of the Gruppen Adjutant of II Gruppe, Jagdgeschwader 3. The Bf 109E was the primary equipment of the Luftwaffe's fighter arm during the campaigns in Poland, the Low Countries and France, rapidly gaining air superiority over the battle-fields. However, the fighter arm failed to vanquish RAF Fighter Command during the Battle of Britain. Adolf Galland attributes this failure to the Luftwaffe High Command's tactical misuse of the Bf 109E, rather than to any intrinsic inferiority to the RAF fighters

One of the first of a very small number of fighter pilots who were fortunate to fly the Hawker Hurricane, Supermarine Spitfire and a Messerschmitt Bf 109E was that outstanding airman, Bob Stanford Tuck. After the German fighter had force landed in friendly territory, it was repaired and brought to England where Tuck flew it in mock combat against a Spitfire before changing places with the other RAF pilot. He was quick to praise the enemy aircraft for its ingenious design, excellent performance and handling characteristics. He particularly highlighted the enemy's ability to perform negative-g manoeuvres on account of its fuel injection system, an ability which in many situations gave enemy pilots a distinct advantage over the British pilots who relied on conventional carburettors and whose Merlin engines lost power in negative-g conditions.

Forewarned of these handling advantages, Tuck and other British pilots who flew the Bf 109E in 1940 devised tactics to enable Spitfire and Hurricane

pilots to meet the 'Emil' on more equal terms. Indeed all three aeroplanes possessed individual strengths and weaknesses; the Spitfire and Bf 109 were both faster and quicker climbing than the Hurricane, but the latter was capable of the tightest turns. Both the Spitfire and Bf 109 were more tricky to land than the Hurricane with its sturdy, wide-track undercarriage. View from the British fighters' cockpits was much better than from the Bf 109, but the German aircraft could generally out-dive the Hurricane and Spitfire.

The relative weight of armament of British and German fighters was subject of much argument and opinion. Both RAF fighters were armed with eight rifle-calibre machine guns which delivered a high weight of fire, but lacked the punch to penetrate enemy armour, whereas the slower-firing 20mm gun of the Bf 109 demanded more aiming skill to achieve decisive damage to an adversary.

In his book *The First and the Last*, Adolf Galland discussed the relative merits of the Bf 109E and the

Bf 109F. 'It was chiefly a question of armament. The Bf 109F carried only one 20mm cannon and two normal machine guns . . . this armament, too, constituted an incomprehensible regression in the Bf 109F compared with the E series, whose production had stopped in the previous year [1940]. The latter had two 20mm cannon mounted in the wings and two ordinary machine guns. The one cannon of the 109F was, of course, more modern, with a quicker rate of fire, a better trajectory and, what is more, was centrally mounted over the engine and fired through the hub of the airscrew. Nevertheless there were conflicting opinions as to whether the new armament should be regarded as a step forwards or backwards. Mölders shared Udet's opinion that one centrally mounted cannon was better than two in the wings. I regarded one cannon as completely inadequate, particularly as I considered machine guns outdated for aerial combat– merely senseless "fireworks". One could hardly impress an enemy fighter with them any more . . . Not every pilot was as good a sharpshooter as Udet or Mölders.'

By the outbreak of World War II the Bf 109E, widely referred to by the Luftwaffe pilots as the 'Emil', was established as Germany's standard

Inset left and far left: the pilots' instrument displays of two Messerschmitt Bf 109 fighter-bombers. Note particularly the auxiliary bomb selector panel installed below the level of the flight and engine instruments.
Below: Bf 109G aircraft of JG 104 are pictured on a training flight. A contemporary of the Spitfire Mark IX, the 'Gustav' was tiring to handle due to the effects of heavy elevators and lack of a rudder trim tab. Control responses generally lacked the Bf 109E's attractive characteristics

single-seat fighter, cherished by the *jagdverband* as the finest fighter in the world. Lest this view is too hastily brushed aside by exponents of the Spitfire and P-51 Mustang, let it be remembered that it was in the Emil and Gustav (the later Bf 109G) that air victory scores were achieved that eclipsed all those of the Allied air forces by enormous factors. Moreover, although the Focke Wulf Fw 190 later came to be regarded as Germany's finest fighter aircraft of World War II, the highest victory scores were still being amassed in the Bf 109! Indeed it is fairly certain that the Messerschmitt Bf 109 destroyed more enemy aircraft by day than any other aircraft in history.

The Bf 109's narrow stalky undercarriage was the feature that incurred criticism of the aircraft throughout its life. The toe-out of the mainwheels gave rise to some instability while taxying and the fishtailing necessary for the pilot to see forward over and round the nose imposed a heavy strain on the oleo legs. The marked outward cant of these oleos demanded a finely judged kick-off of drift during landing, otherwise the Bf 109 was liable to ground loop and almost certainly an oleo would shear.

The cockpit was entered only from the port wing as the canopy hinged sideways to starboard, and this had to be closed when the engine was started as airframe vibration could strain the canopy hinges. Small transparent hood panels could, however, be slid open. The hood was another source of criticism owing to its extensive strutting which severely restricted the view from the cockpit both upwards and sideways (until introduction of the much-improved 'Galland' hood).

Another of Stanford Tuck's criticisms concerned the narrow confines of the cockpit. The fuselage of the Bf 109 was a beautifully contoured structure, but this in turn bestowed a markedly cramped cockpit, so much so that even a pilot of only average stature had no clearance at shoulder height with the seat set at its lowest limits. The controls and instrument layout were tidy and logically positioned, although some German pilots complained that the undercarriage lever could be accidentally knocked in flight – thereby lowering the wheels, sometimes at an embarrassing moment!

The cockpit, systems and engine controls underwent progressive improvement during the life of the Bf 109, and the Gustav represented the zenith of the design (it was in effect contemporary with the Spitfire Mark IX). Engine starting was by means of an inertia flywheel, which was cranked up by a groundcrewman before being released and clutched into the starter by the pilot pulling out a lever on the left side of the cockpit. While warming up the DB605A engine at 1,900 rpm, fuel system and magnetos could be checked. Taxying, like so many other wartime fighters, necessitated constant fish-tailing – a rather awkward manoeuvre in the Bf 109 owing to that stalky undercarriage – using the powerful toe-operated differential wheelbrakes.

Take-off was brisk and, owing to the tendency to swing to port, it was customary to raise the tail as quickly as possible, not only to gain rudder effect, but so as to see the runway over the long nose. It was also advisable to allow the Bf 109 to fly itself

Top left: the ground handling problems with which every mark of Bf 109 was dogged stemmed from both the narrow-track undercarriage and the inadequate forward visibility from the cockpit.
Left: the Bf 109's power plant was the Daimler-Benz DB 601 engine which, on the pictured E-3 variant, housed a 20 mm MG FF/M cannon between the cylinders.
Above: a chief weakness of the Bf 109E was its limited range, which made bomber escort duties particularly hazardous. The 'Emil' proved superior in many respects to Hawker's Hurricane during the Battle of Britain

Above left: the Spanish Hispano HA1112-M1L fighter was essentially a licence-built Messerschmitt Bf 109G, re-engined with a Rolls-Royce Merlin. The type served with the Spanish air force until its retirement in the 1960s.
Above: a Messerschmitt Bf 109 preserved in the markings of I Gruppe, Jagdgeschwader 51, with which it flew during the Battle of Britain.
Left: a successful pilot of JG 53 is congratulated by his squadronmates, while groundcrewmen prepare his Bf 109E for another sortie

off the ground, as attempting to pull it up too early might result in the wing slats opening unevenly. At about 160 km/h (100 mph) the wheels would be retracted, their retraction being hydraulically operated. The flaps were raised manually, using one of two concentric handwheels on the port side of the cockpit; the other wheel adjusted the tailplane incidence, so that by moving the wheels together the change of trim due to the operation of the flaps could be countered simultaneously.

Although the Gustav climbed fairly steeply and rapidly, it was tedious on the controls both in the climb and in the dive. Not being fitted with any rudder trim tab, it was necessary to apply a firm pressure on the right rudder pedal on the climb and a considerably greater pressure on the right pedal during a dive. Control harmony was extremely poor for, although the rudder was light, the elevators were very heavy. This was probably intentional so as to avoid the possibility of applying too coarse longitudinal movements during combat, which might have caused the wing slats to spring open, thereby inducing aileron snatch and upsetting the aim of the Bf 109G's pilot.

One further criticism levelled at the Gustav was the manner in which its controls became extremely heavy as true airspeed increased beyond about 610 km/h (380 mph). In a dive beyond 644 km/h (400 mph) to low altitude all controls seemed to seize solid so that recovery could only be achieved by throttling back and applying a steady but firm pressure on the stick. The Gustav was, however, intended to operate above 7,600 m (25,000 ft), and at this height it was an extremely

manoeuvrable and pleasant aeroplane to fly. In attacks on enemy aircraft, particularly heavy bombers, the most preferred tactic was a quarter attack, as, when approaching from astern, the opponent's slipstream often activated the Bf 109's wing slats, upsetting gun aiming.

The approach to landing was fairly steep, elevator control remaining entirely positive and sensitive. Thus on round-out there was a substantial change of flying attitude. The stall, in the landing configuration, occurred at fractionally under 160 km/h (100 mph), the slats opening about 32 km/h (20 mph) above this figure. The onset of the stall was heralded by elevator buffeting, followed by gentle nose and port wing dropping.

Unfortunately, on touchdown, the lift did not spill quickly and it was fairly difficult to avoid some ballooning, particularly on uneven ground. However, once the tailwheel was firmly on the ground it was possible to brake quite harshly without fear of nosing over. Once again it was essential to start fishtailing at the end of the landing run in order to see beyond the nose. As previously remarked, the undercarriage was not exactly robust and many aircraft came to grief during landing.

The character of the Gustav was markedly different from that of the Emil in much the same respects that the Spitfire Mark IX differed from the Spitfire Mark I and Mark V. The wing loading had been substantially increased, and the sensitivity of control suffered accordingly. This was the inevitable penalty that had to be paid for the progress of tactical demands: more power, higher speeds and heavier armament.

237

Messerschmitt Me 262

Below: an Me 262A-2a fighter-bomber of Erprobungskommando Schenk, formed in June 1944 from pilots detached from 3 Staffel KG 51 'Edelweiss', depicted in late 1944. Commanded by Major Wolfgang Schenk, the unit went into combat in late July 1944, in support of the German ground forces fighting the Allied invasion forces in north-east France. Other elements of KG 51 subsequently converted to the Me 262A-2a. The Me 262A-2a differed from the Me 262A-1a fighter solely in having provision for two SC 250 bombs or one SC 500 bomb on pylons under the nose. The bombs reduced the Me 262's top speed, bringing it into the speed range of Allied piston-engined fighters

When the radical Messerschmitt Me 262 jet fighter entered operational service in 1944 with the Luftwaffe it represented the pinnacle of technical development achieved in four years of the most difficult conditions imaginable, conditions of privation and political wrangling, of rapidly worsening military situation and changing tactical demands. That the aircraft's role was changed from fighter to bomber and back to fighter, and represented a very serious threat to Allied air superiority was due not only to its sound design but also to the very high calibre of men selected to fly it. With few exceptions, the pilots who introduced the Me 262 into Luftwaffe service and fought in it during the last seven months of the war were the cream of the *jagdverband*, men like Adolf Galland, Gordon Gollob, Günther Lützow, Heinz Bär, Walter Nowotny, Hajo Herrmann, Gerhard Barkhorn and Johannes Steinhoff.

Flying the 'Schwalbe' was considered tricky only

insofar as its engines demanded careful handling and were otherwise unforgiving. This was an aeroplane which, in effect, balanced on the furthermost knife-edge of technical knowledge; that balance had to be maintained in the hustle of mortal combat –a daunting task that demanded the flying skill and experience of the finest men of the German air force.

Perched on its tricycle undercarriage, the Me 262 featured twin axial-flow Junkers Jumo 109-004B turbojets mounted under the swept-back wings, the single-seat cockpit being situated well aft in the fuselage with an excellent field of view both forward and aft of the wing, not to mention that over the long nose which housed the exceptionally heavy armament of four 30mm MK 108 cannon. The pilot's principal concern–as in all the early jets– was to avoid exceeding the jet pipe temperature limits, a fact emphasised by the prominent red

segments on his engine temperature gauges. This was particularly critical in the Jumo turbojets owing to the limitations encountered in German metallurgy in the desperate environment as the war approached its end. In later versions of the 004B engine the Germans employed hollow turbine blades to assist cooling, though this stretched manufacturing technology to its limit. Only marginally excessive temperatures would inevitably result in disintegration of the turbine and probably fatal damage to the airframe caused by fractured blades.

Starting up, the pilot selected the inboard generators, energised the ignition circuit and selected the low pressure fuel system. The starter motor was switched in and as this reached about 500 rpm it was clutched into the main turbine. As the engine

the time-of-flight indicator, the pilot eased open the throttles to 7,000 rpm and released the brakes. As the revs built up to 8,700 (maximum take-off), the aircraft accelerated fairly rapidly with no inherent swing, and at about 130 km/h (80 mph) the nose could be lifted, unstick occurring at about 185 km/h (115 mph) after a ground run of about 914 m (1,000 yards) in a light wind.

As the jet-pipe temperature would be at the danger level throughout the take-off, the pilot would throttle back to 8,300 rpm as soon as speed had built up to about 225 km/h (140 mph) braking the mainwheels and retracting the undercarriage before reaching 257 km/h (160 mph). Speed now built up quickly and the flaps were retracted before reaching 354 km/h (220 mph); the throttles were left

Right: the Junkers Jumo 109-004B turbojet was put into production in June 1944 even though numerous technical problems remained unsolved. The basic problem resulted from acute shortages of high-temperature resistant chromium and nickel for the compressor blades, which thus frequently broke up under the high operating temperatures of the engine. The throttle had to be handled with great care because the fuel flow was very difficult to control, and irregularities would cause the engines to burn out and disintegrate, or flame-out. Re-starting in the air was extremely difficult. Although it could fly, manoeuvre and land on one engine, the Me 262 was then vulnerable to attack from enemy fighters

accelerated to 800 rpm, the ignition switch was pressed, thereby igniting the fuel/air mixture in the six combustion chambers and starting the engine.

Keeping the ignition switch depressed, the pilot waited until the revs increased to 2,000, then de-clutched the starter, selected high-pressure fuel delivery system and eased open the throttle. At 3,000 rpm the ignition switch was released and, provided the jet-pipe temperatures were not climbing too quickly, the fuel tank immersed pumps selected. The other engine was then started.

Flying instruments were then switched on and checked, together with radio and electrical control trimmers. Checking the engines involved running each up to 6,000 rpm to ensure that jet pipe temperatures remained well below the danger marks, a further increase to 8,100 rpm to check fuel pressure at 850 psi and oil pressure not below 15 psi. Those vital temperature needles might now just reach the danger mark, but rise no further.

All movements of the throttle, which controlled engine thrust by movement of a jet-pipe cone, had to be made slowly to avoid flaming out (as on the early Gloster Meteors) or disintegration of the turbine. Taxying was carried out at revs of about 2,000 with the cockpit hood closed, and it was necessary to taxy fairly briskly to avoid nosewheel shimmy, steering on the mainwheel brakes.

At the end of the runway the aircraft was lined up and braked, the elevators trimmed slightly nose-down and flaps set at 20 degrees. After depressing

at 8,300 rpm to give a climb-out speed of about 580 km/h (360 mph). With this setting an altitude of 8,230 m (27,000 ft) could be attained in 12 minutes.

Trimming into level flight at 8,300 rpm at around 9,000 m (30,000 ft) would produce a speed of about 770 km/h (480 mph) indicated, and for short emergency bursts opening the throttles to 8,700 rpm gave a top speed of about 837 km/h (520 mph) indicated (but subject to correction owing to a fairly marked position error). Diving speeds of up to 965 km/h (600 mph) were possible although the controls became very heavy and recovery only possible after engine speed reduced considerably (there were no airbrakes). Constant monitoring of engine temperatures (far from simple during combat) was essential. In the event of failure of one engine, although the aircraft was controllable, it was necessary to handle the Me 262 very gently, not least the remaining engine controls owing to the small margin of power remaining and the reduced flight envelope.

As a gun platform the Me 262 was considered steady although there was a noticeable pitch-up during gun-firing, which of course tended to increase the deflection and tighten a curve of pursuit attack. In the event of the pilot's decision to bail out in an emergency, he would throttle back to about 354 km/h (220 mph), jettison the hood, release his seat harness and microphone leads, roll the aircraft on to its back and drop free of the vertical tail. There was no ejector seat.

On approaching the base airfield to land (whether

preparatory to joining a circuit or on a straight-in approach – as was often necessary in the presence of prowling Allied fighters), for which at least ten per cent of the remaining fuel or sufficient for four minutes' flying at 8,000 rpm was necessary, the engines were throttled back to 6,000 rpm and speed reduced to about 338 km/h (210 mph) indicated. The wheels were lowered and, with so much fuel used forward of the centre of gravity, this resulted in a marked nose-up change which had to be checked if sudden wing-drop was to be avoided. As the speed settled at 298 km/h (185 mph) and the undercarriage lights confirmed the wheels locked down, the flaps were then selected at 20 degrees. To maintain a low rate of descent at about 275 km/h (170 mph) it was now necessary to increase throttle to about 6,500 rpm. Easing back on the stick reduced the speed to 257 km/h (160 mph) and flap could then be increased to the full extent, aiming to cross the boundary at 233 km/h (145 mph) and touching down at about 200 km/h (125 mph).

As the mainwheels touched, the throttles were eased back to the idling position, being careful not to reduce below 3,000 revs otherwise both engines might flame-out. As the nosewheel dropped at about 113 km/h (70 mph) it was necessary to brake fairly heavily on a 2,000-yard runway, and it was this that severely reduced the life of the Me 262s tyres – their life seldom exceeding five or six landings.

This then was Germany's most advanced in-service fighter of World War II. It demanded more than average flying ability owing to a high proportion of the pilot's attention being devoted to his instruments rather than the business of searching the sky for his oponents. A relatively large loss rate was suffered, not necessarily because any Allied aeroplane or pilot was superior, but because of situations which made the Germans vulnerable. Others were victims of their own temperamental – albeit advanced – engines which, despite careful handling and maintenance, failed at a crucial moment during take-off or landing. In the final event it was the nation's chronic shortage of aviation fuel that grounded the last surviving Me 262s.

Above and below: the Me 262 was very smooth to fly and was very quiet in its cockpit. Adolf Galland commented of his first flight in the Me 262, in May 1943, that it was 'just like being pushed by an angel'. He later reported to Reichsmarschal Goering: 'This aircraft opens up entirely new possibilities insofar as tactics are concerned'. Indeed, the Me 262 fighters were able to concentrate upon their primary allotted task of destroying bombers because their great speed advantage over Allied piston-engined fighters enabled them, upon sighting enemy fighters, to accept or refuse combat, the jets usually using their speed to dive or climb away

Grumman Bearcat

Below: the Bearcat's photographic reconnaissance variant was designated F8F-2P. It was distinguishable by a camera port just aft of the trailing edge of the wing. Sixty such aircraft, armed with only two cannon, were built. Bottom: a preserved example of the F8F-2, which was introduced in 1948. Some 293 machines with this designation saw US Navy service with a dozen squadrons. Its taller fin was a distinguishing feature

One of the often-discussed feats of post-World War II aviation is the ease with which a Grumman F8F Bearcat could out-manoeuvre a North American P-51 Mustang in a mock dogfight. A US Navy fighter pilot who emerged triumphant from such an encounter was Lieutenant James Ean, formerly a member of fighter squadron VF-18. He recalls: 'My squadron was one of the elements of Air Group 18 that were ordered to take part in ceremonies to mark the opening of the Squantum Naval Air Station outside Boston, Massachusetts. The ceremony was scheduled for a Saturday to draw a big

crowd of people to the event and hopefully to attract recruits to the Naval Air Reserve unit that was to be based there.

'We flew in about an hour or so before we were to perform a series of aerobatic manoeuvres as part of the day's festivities. Just after we had touched down and were taxying toward the display area, I spotted a P-51 with the words 'Enlist in the US Army Air Force' emblazoned in big letters on both sides of the fuselage. I couldn't help but admire the . . . attitude of the AAF in bringing the aircraft to a Navy show. But I was determined that the Navy should do something to keep from being upstaged by the appearance of the beautiful AAF fighter and its formidable reputation.

'There were no formal plans to pit the Mustang against the Bearcat, which would surely demonstrate the Bearcat's superiority. Therefore, we would have to do something on a less formal basis. Later in the day, after we had performed our stunts and the P-51 was preparing to depart from Squantum, I sat in my F8F at the end of the runway and waited.

'I had the engine at full power and was practically standing on my brakes. I waited for the Mustang to begin its take-off roll. When he was about halfway down the runway, I released my brakes, gave the

bird full throttle and went after him. I came in under him as he was taking off, before he could even get his landing gear up, I did a barrel roll right around him. As the Mustang pilot pulled up and applied maximum power, I did another barrel roll around him and topped my demonstration with a few feints which, in a combat situation, would have spelled the end for him.'

Navy brass at NAS Squantum, who were usually quite sensitive about such unauthorised displays, apparently missed Lieutenant Ean's performance. In any event, he heard nothing further of his apparently successful effort to outshine the P-51.

The Grumman F8F Bearcat, which began life in 1943 under the company designation G-58, was easily the fastest and most manoeuvrable American piston-engined fighter of the World War II era. It was the last propeller-driven fighter produced by the Grumman 'Iron Works' of Bethpage, Long Island and was the purest refinement of the line of small, carrier-based fighters which began with the F4F Wildcat. Indeed, although the Wildcat was succeeded by the F6F Hellcat, the US Navy needed an even faster, more manoeuvrable fighter to maintain its superiority over waning Japanese air power. Moreover, such a small, powerful fighter would have to operate from the escort carriers (CVEs) with the smallest flight decks of any flat-tops. The answer to the Navy's requirements was unmistakably the F8F Bearcat, which arrived too late to see wartime service, but which prepared a generation of carrier pilots for the jet age.

'The Bearcat was a very sleek aeroplane', James Ean remembers. 'It was all engine, with short stubby wings, and could climb like a homesick angel—something on the order of 4,800 feet per minute . . . The Bearcat cockpit was a snug fit: the space was so small that even the pilot's plotting board was smaller than that used in other aircraft to carry navigational and other flight information. In keeping with the "space economy" of the Bearcat, the cockpit was very nicely laid out and the pilot could instantly reach anything he needed.

'Prior to receiving the Bearcat, I had flown the Grumman F6F Hellcat for a little over two years, including a combat tour in the Pacific. The Hellcat was a very fine aeroplane, it was rugged and dependable and it saved my life on several occasions. But I also gained great respect for the Japanese Zero-Sen fighters and I had to admire their great manoeuvrability, which we could never quite match with the Hellcat. But the Bearcat was all we had ever hoped for—and more. It was fast, highly manoeuvrable and beautifully responsive to the controls. If we had the Bearcat in combat, there was not a Japanese fighter that could have come close to us, not even the exotic jet designs they received from the Germans. The secret of the Bearcat's success was that it responded so well to the controls, whereas the early jets and other high-performance aircraft were sloppy in the controls.

'The Bearcat was appreciably smaller than the Hellcat and appeared at first glance to be simply a bulkier version of the Wildcat. But the Bearcat's

Above: designed as a high-performance development of the earlier F6F Hellcat, the Bearcat was substantially smaller than its predecessor, despite sharing the same engine. Performance was generally good but range poor, necessitating the use of the centreline fuel tanks carried by the pictured formation.
Top and above right: power plant of the F8F was the 2,100hp Pratt & Whitney R-2800 radial, making the Bearcat the US Navy's fastest piston-engined fighter of its day. The end of the war reduced official requirements for the type, but it continued in front-line service until 1952.
Right: an F8F-1 is brought to an abrupt halt by the crash barrier aboard USS Kearsage, while cruising in the Caribbean. A total of 24 units, including VF-3A, to which the pictured aircraft belonged, had equipped with the F8F-1 by 1948

bubble-type cockpit canopy offered much greater visibility than any other Navy fighter I had flown.'

James Ean began his career as a Navy fighter pilot in the FM-2 Wildcat, the General Motors licence-built version of the F4F. Following his combat tour as an F6F pilot of VF-22 aboard the light carrier USS *Cowpens* (CVL-25), Ean remained with the Squadron when it was redesignated VF-18 and re-equipped with the F8F.

Powered by a 2,100 hp Pratt & Whitney R-2800-34W engine, the Grumman F8F-1 entered squadron service on 21 May 1945, when the first batch of production aircraft was assigned to VF-19. The second squadron to be equipped with Bearcats was VF-18, of which James Ean was a member. In view of the F8F's intended role as an escort carrier-based fighter, it was perhaps fitting that VF-18 was deployed aboard the smallest of the US Navy's big carriers, USS *Ranger* (CV-4).

James Ean remembers his introduction to the F8F Bearcat: 'A vice president from Grumman came out to brief the Squadron prior to first flights in the new bird. He pointed out the F8F's peculiarities and how it differed from other fighters. He particularly cautioned us about the Bearcat's braking action and how little clearance there was between the propeller and the deck. When the brakes were not judiciously applied during taxying, it was very easy for the Bearcat to nose right over and ruin the propeller. Once ground handling was mastered, however, the Bearcat was a sheer delight to fly.

'The excitement far outweighed the anxiety and slight apprehension as I sat at the end of the runway, preparing for my first flight in the Bearcat. Holding brakes and applying power, the awesome potential of the aircraft became quite evident. After a brief re-check of the control trim, I released the brakes and applied full power. I roared down the runway, very much aware of the Bearcat's tremendous thrust capability. I purposely held the aircraft in a nose-level position to build up speed and after I had used up about two-thirds of the available runway, I brought the stick back into the pit of my belly and experienced for the first time what could best be described as a ride on a rocket.

'I continued to climb to 5,000 feet and levelled off in about a minute. The Bearcat's great ability to climb quickly away from the deck was later used with dramatic effect in the air shows in which I subsequently participated. During that first 40 minutes, the F8F performed every manoeuvre I could think of—and in an admirable fashion.

'After some time of various flight manoeuvres, I practiced slow flight, with wheels and landing flaps extended. Utilising cloud tops as a make-believe carrier deck, I spent ten minutes in familiar-ising myself with response and reaction to sudden throttle and altitude changes at slow speed. I mentally visualised different carrier approaches and the subsequent signals that would be given to me by the Landing Signal Officer (LSO) with his landing paddles: arms extended horizontally when the approach is satisfactory, arms held up to form a "V" when I was too high, arms in an inverted "V" when my approach was too low, and the breast stroke gyrations that indicated my approach speed was too slow.

GRUMMAN F8F BEARCAT

'I would respond to each imagined signal: when too slow, I applied power and maintained altitude by slight forward pressure on the stick; when too low, applying slight power to compensate for loss of speed when the stick is brought back to gain altitude; when too high, slightly reducing the power so as not to gain speed when lowering the nose to attain less altitude.

'The Bearcat accepted my corrections graciously and it passed my personal examination with flying colours. But finally that first flight was over and with great reluctance I proceeded back to a naval air station near San Diego, where I touched down, and taxied back to the hangar. After that one flight I became a staunch supporter of the Bearcat.'

In view of the Grumman F8F-1's high performance capability, particularly in climbing and diving, the US Navy required Bearcat pilots to wear pressurised flight suits. The use of g-suits, as they were informally known, is described by James Ean: 'The first g-suits were form-fitting, heavy green nylons that covered almost the entire body. A long tubular umbilical cord-like device came out of the side of the suit and was inserted into a socket in the F8F's cockpit. When g pressures were encountered in the aircraft, air would be forced into three balloon-type inserts on the thigh and stomach area of the pilot's body. The exterior pressure in these areas prevented the excess flow of blood away from the brain that results in black- or grey-out that occurs when a pilot experiences excessive g-factors.'

With the cessation of hostilities in the Pacific on 14 August 1945, many of the US Navy air squadrons which had been concentrated on the American west coast for deployment to the Orient were assigned to east coast bases. In the case of VF-18, this meant sailing aboard USS *Ranger* from San Diego through the Panama Canal and up to the Gulf of Mexico. The ship's air group then participated in its first air show, a victory event in honour of Navy Day in New Orleans, Louisiana.

The F8F-1's impressive capabilities made it an ideal air show performer. Indeed, when the US Navy formed the flight demonstration team known as The Blue Angels, Grumman Bearcats were the first aircraft assigned to the stunt fliers. As James Ean points out, however, air show flying was not much different from a good portion of standard US Navy air operations: 'Looking at the Bearcat, one would almost think it was specifically designed for air show work, but it really just carried out the basic Navy mission–and performed extremely well. Formation flying and close work together, which is found in air shows, is second nature to Navy pilots. With very few exceptions, we were always flying with someone else. In combat it's a fighter sweep. In an air show it would be the starburst, which was probably our most sensational manoeuvre, flying straight up with three other planes and splitting off at the top of the climb.

'When flying together we simply became accustomed to "tucking in" our wings so they were close to the section leader's fuselage. We always flew in close formation. We got to the point that, when the section leader accelerated, everyone else instinctively followed suit. Whether it was a cross-country flight or a tight air show manoeuvre, the single most important person in the air is the flight

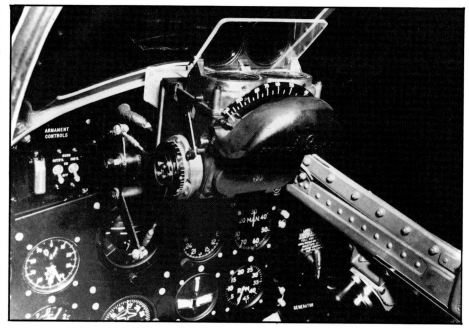

leader. He couldn't "jockey" his throttle back and forth, especially in as sensitive an aeroplane as the Bearcat, or he would just compound the difficulties of maintaining order in the flight. A change in attitude, adjusting the nose or the trim, would be acceptable but, other than that, he had to rely on the good stability of the F8F. He usually tried to maintain a constant throttle setting in the manoeuvres and that made it relatively easy for the men who were "flying wing" on him or were part of his formation.'

Officially, the top speed of the F8F-1 ranged from 615km/h (383mph) at sea level to 677km/h (421mph) at 6,000m (19,700ft). However, as was the case with several other high-performance, propeller-driven fighter aircraft, the Bearcat had the potential to come uncomfortably close to the speed of sound. Recalling VF-18's appearance at an air show near Miami, Florida, Ean noted: 'We were about 15 miles outside of Miami, at roughly 12,000 feet. We had the airport in sight and went into a high-speed dive and crossed the spectator

Above: three views of the cockpit of an F8F-1. The Bearcat's cockpit was not large and even pilots of medium build found it a close fit. However, it was well-organised and all controls were within easy reach of the pilot, who was provided with a g-suit, operated by compressed air from a tube on the cockpit's right-hand wall. The bubble canopy offered a markedly improved field of vision over that of previous US Navy fighters and the view over the nose was excellent

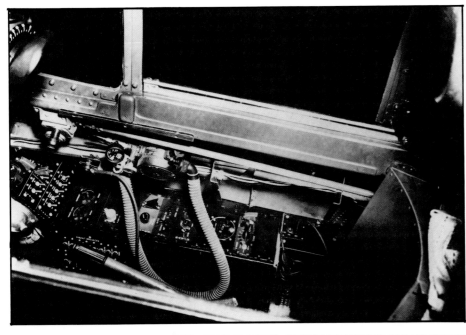

Above: a company test pilot takes a Grumman F8F-1 Bearcat on its first flight from the manufacturer's Bethpage works. An unusual safety feature of the design was the outer wing panels which broke away when the wing was overstressed and thus prevented the entire structure from collapsing

viewing area at about 75 feet. As we passed over the airport, we were doing close to 600 mph. Airport officials later told us they had never seen aeroplanes come in as swiftly and dramatically as we did.'

Grumman designers specified lightly-constructed wings as a means of minimising the F8F's weight, but they knew that the Bearcat's tremendous speed and power could put great stress on the wings. Hence, the outer 46 cm (18 in) of panel on both wings was designed with weak points which would break away if the wings were overstressed, thereby preventing the catastrophic failure of the whole wing structure. To ensure post-incident symmetry, early Bearcats were also fitted with explosive bolts which would automatically discard one wing tip if the other were taken off by stress.

The disposable wingtips were found only on the F8F-1 and, as James Ean notes, there was generally a smooth transition from the normal to the 'short' wing state: 'While practicing some dog-fight tactics, I made a particularly violent man-oeuvre to get away from my opponent and, at that

instant, both wing tips blew off. At first I wasn't exactly certain what had happened. The aircraft didn't have a different feel to it. The controls all responded much as they ordinarily would. I still had ailerons control on the remaining portions of the wings, but then I began to notice that I didn't have quite as much lift as I had prior to losing the wingtips. Since this was a new situation, however, I didn't want to push the aeroplane beyond the limits of my experience. I radioed the tower that I was coming in and made a nearly normal landing. Again, it was the loss of lift that most affected me, but I quickly determined how to compensate for it and make a smooth landing.

'It is interesting to note that I was not told that the wingtips were designed to separate from the aircraft. It was only after I had landed and expressed alarm at losing both tips that some of the main-tenance people told me that this was a design feature of the Bearcat. Even though the wingtips were a safety feature, it was so disconcerting to simply lose part of the aeroplane and, as a result of that one experience, I never again put that much stress on the aeroplane.'

VF-18's operations aboard USS *Ranger* were rather brief. Following the Navy Day air show in New Orleans, on 30 October 1945 the ship began heading north to Philadelphia, where she was decommissioned. Hence, Air Group 18, of which VF-18 was a component, spent nearly a year on shore duty while awaiting carrier assignment.

On 30 August 1946, Air Group 18 reported aboard the newly-commissioned *Essex*-class carrier USS *Leyte* (CV-32), operating from the US Naval Air Station at Quonset Point, Rhode Island. This was James Ean's first experience with the big, fast carriers which had provided such a decisive military presence during the war in the Pacific.

During carrier operations, he says, the F8F was 'strong and compact. The wings folded rather quickly and with a minimum of visibility restric-tions. Unless yours is the last aircraft to land aboard a carrier, it is very critical to be able to move your aircraft away from the arresting wires. Since there are other aircraft in the approach pattern–usually low on fuel after a long operation–timing is very important. After you have landed and the tailhook of your aeroplane has engaged an arresting wire, you have to disengage the tailhook, taxi forward of the crash barrier or be positioned on the flight deck in such a way that incoming aircraft won't run into you. Thus, you have to be doubly alert.

'Because there is so much noise on the flight deck, all communication with the flight deck crew is done by hand signals. They tell you when to disengage your tailhook, when to start taxying, when to fold your wings and which direction to go. All the time you are watching these signals, you are supposed to be working the cockpit controls. That is when the Bearcat's excellent visibility was most appreciated; you could really get a good view of the flight deck.'

What was no doubt James Ean's most memor-able experience with the F8F-1 occurred just prior to VF-18's move aboard USS *Leyte*. On 20 July 1946, Ean and three squadronmates departed from NAS Quonset Point on a cross-country hop which would have allowed them to have breakfast in

Cleveland, Ohio and lunch in Chicago, Illinois, with dinner to take place at some westward point.

'We left Quonset Point about 8.30 am and took a leisurely course down the east coast and then inland at New York to a route that would take us to Ohio. The weather forecast that day was not too promising, but we were sure it wouldn't affect us. As we began to go inland, however, before us was one of the worst-looking weather fronts I had ever seen. We decided to proceed in hopes we could find a clear path through it. We didn't and soon the last man in the formation – Tail-end Charlie – was lost. We circled for a while until we finally found him.

'In view of the worsening weather, we decided it would be foolish to push on to Cleveland. So we began looking for a clear place to land. As luck would have it, we did not come across any airports that could accommodate the F8F and, since we were getting low on fuel, we decided to land on the first good clearing we found. A short time later we spotted a big field outside of Cochranton, Pennsylvania and decided that's where we would land. I circled the field and maintained radio contact with each of the men in my flight as they made perfect wheels-up landings in this newly-ploughed field. The first landing went without incident, but as the other planes began preparing to land, our arrival became quite a local event.

'Circling the field, I could see people running from every direction to watch us land. They came right out onto the field to talk to my squadronmates and, of course, they were standing right where I wanted to land. Consequently, I had to find another field nearby and I had to come in under some high-tension wires to make a straight approach. As I neared the ground, I put the plane into the same nose-up attitude I would use when landing aboard ship. Just before impact I cut the throttle and came

across the soft muddy field, barely dragging my tail, and settled the nose down so the propeller blades bent under the cowl like skis and let me slide to a halt.

'Although I scratched up the undersurface of the aeroplane, it needed little repair. And the propeller had so nicely absorbed the punishment of the dirt landing that I didn't break the crankshaft. Later, the gear was lowered and a new prop was put on and the aeroplane was ready to go again.'

In 1948 the F8F-1 was replaced by an improved Bearcat, the F8F-2. However, despite the Bearcat's speed and manoeuvrability – and even the use of cannon in place of its four 0.5 in calibre machine guns – the day of the propeller-driven fighter had drawn to a close. In 1949 the front-line units began to pass on their F8Fs to the Reserve.

Below: the only combat the Bearcat saw was over the jungles of south-east Asia in the 1950s. Surplus US Navy Bearcats were supplied to the French Armée de l'Air and the Thai air force. An F8F of the latter is illustrated. They were used in various phases of the Indo-China war in the ground-support role, where their great speed and ability to absorb considerable punishment proved useful.
Bottom: a photographic F8F-2P of a Naval Air Reserve unit pictured over USS Midway. From 1949 F8Fs were withdrawn from US Navy front-line units and handed over to Air Reserve units, the last going in 1952

Douglas Skyraider

With landing gear, flaps and tailhook extended, an A-1 Skyraider of VA-25 approaches the flight deck of USS Midway in 1963. Five years later, in February 1968, a Skyraider of this squadron flew the type's last combat mission with the US Navy

The Douglas Skyraider series is a study in adaptability. Designed during World War II as the US Navy's first single-seat torpedo bomber, the Skyraider subsequently became an effective attack aircraft in both the Korean and Vietnam wars. During the latter conflict, in fact, Skyraiders successfully engaged and shot down jet-powered MiG fighters.

The Douglas Aircraft Company's long affiliation with the US Navy goes back to the torpedo-bearing DT-1 biplane of 1921. Just over two decades later, as the victorious Allies were advancing across the Pacific, a Douglas design team headed by chief engineer Ed Heinemann developed a totally new type of carrier-based aircraft to attack Japanese shipping.

During its long service life the aircraft was given three different designations. In 1944 it was called XBT2D-1 to denote that it was the experimental model of the first variant of the second torpedo bomber produced by Douglas for the US Navy. The

XBT2D-1 was intended to replace both the successful SBD Dauntless and the little-used BTD Destroyer. The single-seat configuration was used to maximise the weapons load.

The XBT2D was accepted by the US Navy while the war was still going on, but deliveries commenced after the war to newly-constituted attack squadrons VA-3B and VA-4B. For its new role, the aircraft was designated AD-1, indicating it was the first variant of the first attack aircraft produced by Douglas for the US Navy. The AD designation stuck until 1962, when the Navy's aircraft identification system was merged with the other US services for the sake of commonality; it then became the A-1.

The AD-1 was clearly bigger than other Navy single-seat aircraft of the immediate postwar period. It was 11·6m (38ft 2in) long, had a wingspan of 15m (50ft) and an empty weight of 4,790kg (10,550lb). The new aircraft–for which the names Dauntless II and Destroyer II were proposed before

Left: the cockpit of the XBT2D-1 was similar to that of the Skyraider, which was developed from this prototype. Flight instruments are at the centre of the panel, with engine instruments mounted to the right. An armament panel is mounted under the flight instruments

Above: a bomb-laden Skyraider of Attack Squadron 176 is readied for a catapult launch from USS Intrepid (CVS-11), when operating from 'Yankee Station' off North Vietnam. Below: a Skyraider returns to USS Constellation (CVA-64) after a mission over North Vietnam

the appellation Skyraider was accepted – was powered by the 250 hp Wright R-3350 engine.

Although the Skyraider did not see action during World War II, the type was used extensively during the conflict in Korea, which began on 25 June 1950. In fact AD-1 aircraft from VA-55 deployed aboard the aircraft carrier USS *Valley Forge* (CV-45) were among the first free world air elements to respond to the Communist invasion. VA-55's raids on 3 and 4 July 1950 resulted in the destruction of several North Korean targets.

Douglas Skyraiders of the Korean conflict are remembered by Vice Admiral George E. R. Kinnear II, USN, who is now Commander of the Naval Air Force of the US Atlantic Fleet. Early in his naval aviation career he flew a number of Skyraider variants with VA-45 following a tour of duty as a Vought F4U Corsair pilot with VF-173.

In comparing the two high-powered aircraft, Admiral Kinnear notes he made an easy transition from the F4U to the AD-2. 'You could hardly tell the difference,' he recalls, 'although I felt the AD was a more capable aircraft. Although the F4U was a smaller aeroplane, its propeller arc was the same as that of the AD, which made the Corsair more subject to torque. The F4U did some unusual things if you jammed on a lot of power at low speed: the propeller would try to hold still and the aeroplane would turn – or make what we called a "torque roll". The AD, however, was a much more stable aeroplane and easier to fly than the F4U.'

Kinnear reported to VA-45 in October 1950 and began flying the AD-2. The Squadron subsequently received the AD-4 and, for its cruise to Korean waters, the AD-4B, which had provisions for carrying tactical nuclear weapons. 'Gus' Kinnear, then a lieutenant (junior grade), was at that time one of a handful of US Navy pilots qualified in the special flight manoeuvres used to deliver nuclear weapons with the AD-4B. There was no use of nuclear weapons by either side during the Korean conflict, but the so-called 'cold war' between the western powers and the Soviet Bloc nations required a high degree of readiness by all US forces. Hence, the specialised training provided to certain AD-4B pilots. Admiral Kinnear notes there were two methods by which Skyraiders could deliver tactical nuclear devices: dive bombing and 'loft' bombing. The differences, he explained, depend on the weapon to be used. 'If you have a ground-burst weapon, which has a time delay so you can get away from the explosion, you can deliver it with great accuracy by using dive tactics. However, an air-burst weapon gives an entirely different effect on the target and must be "lofted", which is the only way to get the separation between the aircraft and the bomb.

'To "loft" the bomb you have to do a "Cuban Eight" manoeuvre: run in "on the deck", low and as fast as you can, then bring the aeroplane back up over the top, as if you were doing a loop. An automatic device was supposed to release, or "loft", the bomb just as you started to go over, but you had to be ready to back it up with a manual release. Once you got over the top, you rolled your wings around you so you would come back . . . in a normal attitude, instead of inverted.' There were considerable gravitational forces at work during this manoeuvre. Kinnear states: 'The profile of the aircraft

with the bomb was such that this type of delivery had to be done with great precision in order to score an accurate bomb hit. The pilot was programmed for exactly four "g"s, which did not cause an adverse effect because pressurised flight suits were then in use. In fact, one of the changes we made when we transitioned from the AD-2 to the AD-4 was to use g-suits.'

Kinnear flew the Skyraider in combat during the final phase of the United Nations action to halt communist aggression in Korea. He was with VA-45 when it deployed aboard the aircraft carrier USS *Lake Champlain* (CVA-39) to the Far East on 26 April 1953. In addition to VA-45's AD-4B aircraft, detachments from two VC (composite) squadrons operated other Skyraider variants. VC-12 flew the airborne early warning AD-4W version and VC-33 supported combat operations with the night-capable AD-4N; in both types a radar operator accompanied the pilot on all missions. Other elements of Air Group 4 aboard USS *Lake Champlain* flew Vought F4U-4 Corsairs, McDonnell F2H-2 Banshees and the photo-reconnaissance F2H-2P. 'By the time we got to Korea, the war had stabilised essentially along the demarcation line now in use. So we were involved primarily in keeping the transportation system interdicted, both night and day. VC-33's AD-4Ns did most of the night work, as did a team of F4U-NL night fighters. We tried to keep the bridges down, the highways torn up and the railroads out of commission – all to impede the movement of enemy troops and supplies to the front lines. We also flew close air support missions . . .'

Despite the diversity of aircraft – including both propeller-driven and jet-powered fighters – assigned to Air Group 4 at this time, Admiral Kinnear recalls that *Lake Champlain*'s aircraft all performed the role generally assigned only to attack squadrons. He points out: 'The Navy had aircraft capable of combating MiG fighters, but the US Air Force had the role. The MiG airfields were on the side of the lines for which the Air Force was responsible, so the Navy had little contact with enemy fighters. In the absence of a traditional fighter squadron role, our fighters were assigned attack squadron missions.

'The two squadrons of F2H jets aboard USS *Lake Champlain* – VF-22 and VF-62 – carried bombs and rockets and used their four 20 mm cannon for strafing. They flew the same missions our Skyraiders did, but the F2Hs didn't do them as well as we did because they weren't designed for that role. The jet fighters couldn't carry the tonnage we could and the jet fighter pilots didn't have the training in air-to-ground work that we did.'

Although the jet-powered fighters and the propeller-driven Skyraiders performed essentially the same mission in Korea, Admiral Kinnear notes important operational differences: 'On each launch there would be a division from each squadron and they would proceed independently to check in with the people ashore who were going to control their activity over the beach. The F2Hs were on an hour-and-a-half cycle and the ADs were on a three-hour cycle. The jets didn't have the fuel to stay out longer, but with the speeds they could attain, they could go out, drop their bombs and get back to the ship within a relatively short time.

'The jets could effectively drop their bombs, but they couldn't do some of the other things our ADs could do. After we got rid of our bombs, we could spend some time over the beach looking for strafing targets which we could attack with our 20 mm cannon. When you're trying to keep vehicular traffic from moving, it's very effective simply to have aircraft in the air – and we had the time to devote to that activity.'

Admiral Kinnear recalls that he generally flew one mission per day while with VA-45 during the Korean conflict. On occasion, however, two missions – one in the morning and one in the late afternoon – were ordered. The normal schedule of events was begun when 'Flight Quarters' were sounded approximately one-and-a-half hours prior to commencing actual flight operations. While pilots were being briefed in their squadron ready rooms during that time, aircraft were being brought up to the flight deck and prepared for take-off along with other aircraft already spotted in position on the flight deck. The briefing included weather and other operational information, as well as the latest reports concerning the proposed targets and any additional intelligence material.

At the call of 'Pilots, man your aircraft' the crews went up to the flight deck to conduct a pre-flight check of their aircraft. In the case of AD-4 pilots, Kinnear remembers, 'you would inspect the ordnance, paying particular attention to the fuses and the lead-in on the ammunition to your guns. Then you would "suit up" and get into the aeroplane. 'About 20 minutes before launch time, the engines were started on the propeller-driven aircraft. The jets didn't start until ten minutes later because fuel was always a critical consideration with them

and they didn't need the warm-up time the prop planes did. Generally, the jets took off first, then it was our turn. After that, we rendezvoused and headed for the beach.

'It is easier to rendezvous in a jet than it is in a propeller-driven aeroplane. A jet doesn't have to make much of a turn to allow other aircraft to catch up with it. In a prop aircraft such as the AD, which didn't have the speed differential, you had to allow other planes to catch up with you by making a 180-degree turn somewhere. If they still hadn't caught up, then you had to go into a "rendezvous circle" – a 360-degree turn – until everyone was on board.'

All of the United Nations air activity was co-ordinated by controllers either on the ground or aboard ships off the coast, including vessels operating directly off the enemy coast. 'Ordinarily, the controllers would assign you a sector', Kinnear recalls. 'If they didn't give you a firm target – a particular bridge to hit or a tunnel to seal – they would give you a segment to check for "targets of opportunity". Then, before returning to the ship, you and your wingman or some other aeroplane in the vicinity would check each other over – perform a complete visual inspection – to make sure no one tried to land aboard ship with any "hung" ordnance. If there were some unreleased rockets or bombs, they were all jettisoned over the open sea.'

The former VA-45 pilot experienced one encounter with MiG fighters which clearly demonstrated the ever-present danger of operating even remotely near Soviet territory. He says: 'One time I accompanied an AD-4N from VC-33, which was equipped with electronic countermeasures capability that could take fixes on radar stations. We

were sent way up north, near the Russian border, to knock out a particular radar station. Once the other Skyraider found it, I was to go in and hit it. In the process of going up there, I guess we got the Russians excited, because that was the only time I saw MiGs. But we were so low on the water that they couldn't find us–or, if they did, they chose not to come down and play with us.'

Although the two Skyraiders from Air Group 4 managed to elude hostile aircraft on that mission, it was a more difficult matter to dodge the heavy anti-aircraft fire used by Communist troops against United Nations aircraft. During his Korean tour of duty in Skyraiders, Admiral Kinnear received the Air Medal and a Gold Star in lieu of a second award. The citation for the latter award reflects one of the tougher aspects of a pilot staying with his aeroplane after it has sustained serious damage from anti-aircraft fire.

The citation records that 'finding himself thrown into a steep diving turn by jammed aileron controls, [Kinnear] succeeded in completing a recovery at an altitude of less than a hundred feet above the terrain, and effected a climb to a safe parachuting altitude [where] he elected to save the aircraft and, by sustained physical force and the lashing of the control stick with his flight scarf to the side of the cockpit, proceeded over 100 miles to an emergency airstrip . . . With the stick still lashed as securely as possible against the locked controls, [he] executed a successful wheels-down landing with no damage to

the aircraft, on an extremely narrow landing strip . . .'

What the citation neglected to mention, however, is that once the AD-4B pilot made the decision to attempt a flight back to friendly territory, he literally entrusted his life to the sturdiness of the aircraft. With the control column lashed to the cockpit side for stability, Admiral Kinnear in effect tied himself into his seat, thereby eliminating the option of jumping out of the damaged Skyraider. That he managed to reach an advance emergency airfield speaks well of both the ruggedness of the AD-4B and his own ability as a pilot.

While navigational aids of the 1950s were not as sophisticated as the devices available to today's pilots, a little resourcefulness could often fill the technology gap. On one occasion Kinnear was sent from USS *Lake Champlain* to Japan to bring back a replacement aircraft. The weather began to turn bad as he prepared to leave Japan, but the Skyraider pilot was confident that he could find the carrier before the weather conditions worsened. 'By the time I got near the ship', he recalls, 'it was socked in by fog and when I radioed in for clearance to land, the ship's air controllers knew I didn't have much in the way of navigational aids and they asked if I could fly back to Japan. That wasn't part of my plan, so I milled around for a while to figure out what I was going to do. Just then along came an AD-4W flown by a friend of mine, Charlie Haskell of VC-12. I got him on my radio and he said:

Above: A-1H Skyraiders of VA-52 were flying from USS Ticonderoga (CVA-14) in 1964. They took part in raids on North Vietnamese torpedo-boat bases following the Tonkin Gulf Incident. Left: flight-deck crewmen attach the catapult cable to an EA-1F of tactical electronic warfare squadron VAQ-33 aboard USS John F. Kennedy (CVA-67)

DOUGLAS A-1 SKYRAIDER

"Don't pay any attention to the ship. They're confused now. We'll back off about 20 miles and my radar operator and I will bring you in. And they did. They flew all the way in on my starboard side and lined me up perfectly with the centreline of the flight deck and I came aboard out of that fog just as if it were a bright, sunny day. Charlie then went around in the landing pattern and came aboard about ten minutes later.'

From initial production in 1945 until the last Skyraider, an AD-7, rolled off the Douglas production line in 1957, the series went through a number of modifications to fill various roles with units of the United States and its allies. Admiral Kinnear notes that: 'the AD-5 was a two-place, side-by-side version, that was pretty heavy and didn't fly as well as the others. There were a number of improvements in each succeeding version, but they all had one thing in common: the higher the series number, the heavier the aeroplane and the less "pizzazz" it had. All ADs were equipped with essentially the same engine, which was uprated, but not in proportion to the added fuselage weight.'

One of the more unusual Skyraider missions in Korea was the attack on the Hwachon Dam. The attack became necessary when the Chinese Communists, who controlled the dam, used its sluice gates to lower the level of the Pukhan and Han Rivers for their own advances and cause flooding conditions to impede the advance of UN forces. The mission of knocking out the dam was assigned to the AD-4s of VA-195 deployed aboard USS *Princeton* (CVA-37). On 30 April 1951, six ADs each carrying two 2,000lb bombs attacked the dam and put a hole in it, but did not damage the sluice gates. The following day, however, eight ADs led by Commander R. C. Merrick, commander of Air Group 19 aboard *Princeton*, and Lieutenant Commander Harold G. Carlson, commanding officer of VA-195, went in with aerial torpedoes. They were accompanied by Vought Corsairs carrying flak suppression bombs. Six of the eight torpedoes hit the dam and knocked out two flood gates.

Following the Korean conflict, as jet-powered attack aircraft were phased into Fleet operations, the US Navy's primary use of Skyraiders was for airborne early warning missions. The AD-5W, instantly recognisable by the large ventral radome covering, was assigned to two large Airborne Early Warning (VAW) squadrons which assigned detachments to each aircraft carrier. VAW-11 detachments deployed aboard Pacific Fleet ships and VAW-12 aircraft went to Atlantic Fleet carriers.

The US Navy and US Air Force each had different aircraft designation systems until the systems were combined in September 1962. At that time the Skyraiders in service became redesignated the A-1 series. AD-4NAs became A-1Ds, AD-5s became A-1Es, and AD-6 and AD-7 aircraft became A-1H and A-1J, respectively. With stepped-up American involvement in Vietnam in the mid-1960s, the A-1 series proved to be an outstanding counter-insurgency (COIN) aircraft and a number of former US Navy aircraft were acquired by the US Air Force and the Air Force of the Republic of Vietnam.

The loyalty of 'Spad' pilots was certainly deserved. During the Vietnam conflict, the first airman to receive the Medal of Honour, America's highest combat decoration for valour, flew the Skyraider. On 10 March 1966, US Air Force Major Bernard F. Fisher was flying an A-1E against a concentration of North Vietnamese regular infantry when his wingman, Major D. Wayne Myers, was forced down near advancing enemy troops. Major Fisher landed on the rubble-strewn runway where his wingman had landed and taxied the full length of the strip to where Major Myers was crouched near his stricken aircraft. Myers climbed aboard Fisher's A-1E, which took off amid a hail of fire.

The Skyraider continued to give good service up until the end of the Vietnam War. There is even reason to believe that former South Vietnamese A-1s captured by the communists are still in use in the internecine warfare in south-east Asia.

Below: the Hwachon Dam in North Korea was breached by aerial torpedoes dropped by the Skyraiders of VA-195 in April 1951. Previous attempts to bomb the Dam had been unsuccessful. Bottom: this colourfully-marked Skyraider is preserved in the markings of Attack Squadron 176

Gloster Meteor

The design of the Meteor was begun in 1940 to take advantage of the jet engine being developed by Frank Whittle. Eight prototypes were built, the first of which is illustrated; the fifth became the first Meteor to fly on 5 March 1943. No 616 Squadron converted to the Meteor in July and August 1944, becoming the RAF's first and only operational jet squadron in World War II. Its Meteors, the RAF's fastest fighters, took a leading part in the defence against the V-1 flying bomb

To a whole generation of RAF pilots the Gloster Meteor represented a transition in the concept of flight. True, the diminutive Vampire was its contemporary at a time when British aviation technology was in the world forefront, yet the 'Meatbox' was the only Allied jet fighter to see operational service during World War II and thereafter equipped 59 RAF squadrons.

To a pilot, accustomed to the noise and clatter of a Spitfire, Tempest or Mustang, the dawn of silent, vibration-free flight was exhilarating, not to say a trifle breath-taking. However, to offset the speed with which cockpit checks had now to be performed, particularly in the circuit prior to landing, the simplification of engine controls reduced the work of the pilot considerably. Gone were the aggravating propeller pitch controls and the torque-induced swing on take-off and landing. Landing was no longer the delicate balance between flare-out and stall and it was no longer necessary to take care to avoid nose-over through too-harsh braking. It was little wonder that during that twilight period between 1945 and 1952, when jet aircraft were replacing the old propeller aircraft, Mosquito and Tempest pilots looked disdainfully upon the new generation and talked disparagingly of the older

aircraft still 'sorting the men from the boys'.

The first impression of the cockpit of the Meteor was of its unprecedented field of view. Moreover, relatively few RAF fighter pilots had ever experienced the benefit of a tricycle undercarriage. On the other hand, the avid thirst of the jet engine was indelibly imposed on the mind of the new jet pilot, so that, once the Rolls-Royce Derwent turbojets had been started, all activity on the ground had to be accelerated so as not to waste time and fuel prior to take-off. Not surprisingly the Meteor very quickly acquired a large belly fuel tank.

Compared to the piston engine, starting the Derwent was simplicity itself; throttles closed, high-pressure and low-pressure fuel cocks on, ground/flight switch to 'ground', low-pressure fuel pump on, and then depress the starter button for a couple of seconds, thereby initiating the automatic starting cycle, during which the engine accelerated to idling speed of about 3,300 rpm. It was necessary to keep an eye on the jet pipe temperature to ensure it did not exceed about 500 degrees centigrade and also counter any jet pipe resonance which, if allowed to continue unchecked, might cause the loss of turbine blades.

A fairly common phenomenon during those

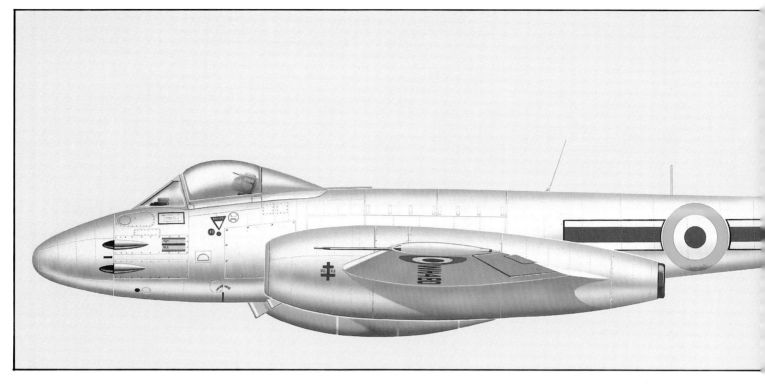

Above: a Meteor F Mk 8 of No 41 Squadron, flown by the CO. Developed from the F Mark 4, the F Mark 8 had a lengthened nose section to compensate for increased weight, additional fuel tankage and a new tail which overcame the control difficulties experienced with earlier marks. It had uprated engines, a modified canopy and an ejector seat as standard – the first RAF aircraft to be so equipped. The F Mark 8 retained the short-span wings of the F Mark 4, which improved the rate of roll. Handling was especially improved at high speeds

early days of jet engines was the 'wet start' when the igniters failed to function, and the engine became flooded with fuel. Owing to the very high flash point of the kerosene fuel this did not itself constitute a hazard. However, it was necessary to repeat the starting cycle with the high-pressure cock switched off so as to drain the engine of excess fuel, while the groundcrew sponged out loose fuel in the nacelle. Starting the engines in darkness was often an awe-inspiring sight for the uninitiated as the 'torching' effect from the jet pipes could light the night sky over a wide area.

A quick check round the cockpit before taxying included fire warning lights out, flaps up, remote-

indicating compass on and direction-indicator co-ordinated with it and uncaged, radio channel selected, altimeter set to airfield height and a check that brake pressure was building. After waving away the chocks, the brakes were momentarily applied and released, and a quick check round the instruments was made to ensure readings in the correct sense, and the pitot heater switched on.

Lining up on the runway, the final pre-take-off checks were elevator and rudder trim neutral, high-pressure and low-pressure fuel cocks on, low-pressure pumps on, flaps one-third down, pneumatic pressure 450 psi airbrakes in and hood closed and locked. Not quite the apocryphal 'fire and fuel OK,

then let's away' of the traditional seat-of-the-pants fighter pilot, but a marked lack of fuss compared with a previous fighter generation!

After moving forward a few yards to straighten the nosewheel, the brakes were applied and the throttles opened smoothly to the take-off revs of 14,550. On releasing the brakes the Meteor surged forward with unaccustomed acceleration. At about 80 knots the nosewheel could be eased off the ground, being careful not to raise it too high so as not to scrape the tail bumper on the runway. Owing to a blanking of the tailplane in the nose-up attitude, the Meteor did not unstick cleanly and had to be flown off positively at about 125 knots

Gloster Meteor cockpit

1: *Gyro gunsight* 2: *Airspeed indicator* 3: *Rate of climb indicator* 4: *Altimeter* 5: Direction indicator* 6: *Turn and bank indicator* 7: *Engine speed indicators* 8: *Dual jet pipe temperature gauge* 9: *Fuel pressure gauges* 10: *Oil temperature gauges* 11: *Oil pressure gauges* 12: *Compass indicator* 13: *Undercarriage warning light* 14: *Flap position indicator* 15: *Undercarriage lever* 16: *Undercarriage position indicator* 17: *Rudder pedals adjuster release* 18: *Instrument panel lights* 19: *Hood jettison handle* 20: *Fuel contents gauges* 21: *Oxygen regulator panel* 22: *IFF demolition switches* 23: *Emergency hydraulic handpump* 24: *Flaps lever* 25: *Floodlight* 26: Relighting switches* 27: *Landing*

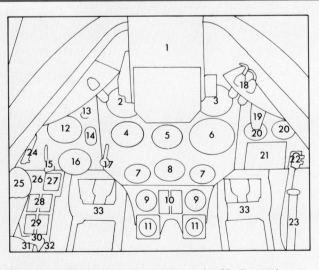

light switch 28: *Low pressure pump switches* 29: *Starter buttons* 30: *Airbrakes control* 31: *Throttle levers* 32: *Gun rounds counter* 33: *Rudder pedals*

Above: the instrumentation of an NF Mark 14's front cockpit, typical of later Meteors, shows differences in style to that of the earlier Mark illustrated in the artwork (left). However, it remained generally similar to that of late-war single-seat piston-engined RAF fighters. One factor pilots appreciated was the disappearance of the awkward fuel mixture and propeller speed controls, there being only throttle controls on the left cockpit wall for the engines. However, the speed of a jet fighter meant that instrument checks in flight had to be done very rapidly, and the engines' heavy fuel consumption made it necessary to make pre-take-off checks in minimum time

indicated, and then held fairly level to allow the speed to build up to the safety speed of 165 knots. The undercarriage was raised immediately on becoming airborne and flaps raised on reaching safety speed. Fuel used thus far would be about 40 gallons.

The speed built up very quickly and on reaching about 290 knots the nose could be raised for the climb to altitude, leaving the throttles open at take-off setting. A governor on the fuel pumps restricted the engine revs to 14,550 at sea level but these increased progressively to a maximum of 14,700 at 3,000 m (10,000 ft). The climb to 10,700 m (35,000 ft) occupied about seven minutes, the indicated air-speed being gradually reduced to 200 knots.

The Meteor, though never recognised as a 'pilot's aeroplane', was a fairly comfortable aircraft to fly, with well-balanced and quite effective controls up to a height of 11,000 m (36,000 ft). However, as speed was increased above about Mach 0·72 the controls became progressively heavier, particularly the ailerons, while the trimmers had to be used very coarsely to produce any appreciable effect. Fortunately operation of the flaps, undercarriage and airbrakes produced little change of trim.

To carry out what was euphemistically termed a Mach run at above 9,000 m (30,000 ft) the aircraft was simply flown straight and level with the throttles fully open. Speed built up on the Mach-meter to 0·76, by which time strong nose-up trim change would require a powerful stick force to counter it. The elevator trimmer could be used to assist up to this speed, but as speed increased beyond 0·76 the force had to be entirely manual. It was just possible to reach 0·82 by which time the Meteor would be shaking and snaking, and the pilot had difficulty in holding the stick against the nose-up force. Recovery was by throttling back slowly and opening the airbrakes. Deceleration was extremely rapid and the pilot would be forced quite sharply against his straps. The author recalls that a fellow pilot absent-mindedly recovered from a Mach run by throttling back and lowering the undercarriage! The Meteor certainly decelerated, but performed an enormous bunt, and the pilot eventually recovered consciousness flying inverted some 6,000 m (20,000 ft) lower. He soon discovered that all the wheel doors had been torn off.

Aerobatics in the Meteor, by the standards of the day, were delightful, there being plenty of power available to perform a concentrated sequence of manoeuvres with little time lost in regaining speed and height. Rolling was best done in the middle speed range owing to the heavy aileron stick forces needed at higher speeds. A succession of rolls could be carried out at an initial entry speed of about 290–300 knots, although upward rolls required a pull-up speed of 400 knots. A loop starting at 380 knots was comfortable, maintaining a smooth backward pressure on the stick, although speed built up very quickly on the way down and airbrakes were needed so as not to lose too much height. A roll off the top required about 20 knots higher entry speed, but speed remained perfectly adequate to avoid mushing out of the roll.

Firing the four 20 mm Hispano guns produced no appreciable trim change, and to pilots accustomed to fighters with wing-mounted armament

Above: converted from the NF Mark 14 night fighter and with armament deleted, the NF (T) Mark 14 was employed by the RAF Air Navigation schools until superseded by the Hawker Siddeley Dominie in 1965.
Left: the view from the rear cockpit of a Meteor trainer in flight.
Below left: a Meteor T Mark 7 preserved by the RAF. Entering Flying Training Command late in 1948, the mark became the RAF's first jet trainer, serving with several Advanced Flying Training Schools.
Above right: the T Mark 7 differed from its fighter counterparts by virtue of its two-seat cockpit in a lengthened nose section. The trainer even had a better rate of climb than the Meteor fighters

the Meteor's guns seemed very close indeed – more so than in the Mosquito or Vampire. However, once again the Meteor was handicapped by the high aileron stick forces as speed increased, and it was fairly hard to carry out a steady curve of pursuit attack at above 400 knots, especially in a diving attack when speed built up quickly. Bearing this in mind, the achievement by some Meteor pilots of downing MiG-15s over Korea was all the more praiseworthy.

The Meteor was an excellent ground-attack aeroplane, although, despite efforts by the manufacturers to promote it as such, its primary role remained in the interception mode. The care needed to launch the old solid-shot three-inch rockets without induced skid was scarcely a problem in the Meteor owing to the precision with which it could be flown at between 300 and 350 knots. However, as with all jet aircraft during the decade following World War II, rocket attacks could only be performed from very shallow dives owing to speed build-up and rapid loss of height; owing to maximum gravity drop by the rockets in this style of attack, good results were only achieved after a great deal of practice.

One of the common minor 'panics' likely to be encountered in the Meteor was the flaming-out of one or both engines, particularly during dogfighting practice, usually caused by inadvertent coarse use of throttle. Unlike the Vampire, which possessed no re-light facility – hence allowing the pilot only two choices: bail out or force land – the Meteor's Derwents could be restarted simply, preferably below 4,600m (15,000ft). Single-engined flying presented no problems at all provided the speed was maintained above 160 knots until the

wheels and flaps were lowered for landing, when a standard circuit and approach could be made. Indeed, when flying for maximum endurance it was fairly common practice to shut down one engine.

On a normal training flight one seemed to have consumed the fuel allowance all too soon. Roughly 1,800 litres (400 gallons) were used during an hour's applied flying, excluding the 40 gallons used in starting and take-off, and leaving 60 for re-joining the circuit and landing. The latter was just sufficient for one baulked landing and overshoot. Thus there was seldom time for an elaborate circuit, and final checks were accordingly brief: wheelbrakes off, brake pressure 120psi, wheels locked down and flaps one-third down – increased to full flap on the final approach. Speed in the circuit was reduced using the airbrakes to about 160 knots, decreasing to about 140 knots on the turn into wind and, as the remaining flap was selected down, one aimed to cross the boundary at slightly over 100 knots at average landing weights, maintaining at least 7,500rpm until a landing was certain, so as to be assured of quick thrust response in the event of having to overshoot. Unlike the previous generations of fighters, the Meteor was simply flown on to its mainwheels at fractionally under 100 knots and the nosewheel allowed to settle of its own accord – unless heavy braking was necessary.

There is no denying that towards the end of its Service life, the Meteor attracted some ridicule as being archaic in an environment of transonic F-86 Sabres and MiG-15s. Yet the absence of a British counterpart – until the advent of the Hawker Hunter meant that the Meteor was required to remain in service long after supersonic flight had become a reality elsewhere.

Grumman Panther

The Grumman F9F-2 Panther was the first US Navy jet fighter to be used in combat and to shoot down an enemy jet-powered aircraft. Initially proposed as a two-seat jet-powered night fighter, the XF9F-1 would have required no less than four Westinghouse J30 engines which were then available. That concept soon proved unworkable and was scrapped in favour of the less encumbered XF9F-2 design. The XF9F-2 was designed to be powered by a single Rolls-Royce Nene axial-flow jet engine producing 2,270 kg (5,000 lb) static thrust. That engine was subsequently built under licence by Pratt & Whitney.

The US Navy ordered 47 examples of the F9F-2 with the Pratt & Whitney power plant and 54 F9F-3s powered by the Allison J33-A-8 engine, developing 2,040 kg (4,600 lb). The former variant soon proved superior and all of the latter were converted to F9F-2 standard. Fighter squadron VF-51 was the first unit to receive the F9F-2, with deliveries beginning in May 1949. When North Korean troops invaded South Korea before daybreak on 25 June 1950, VF-51 and VF-52 were deployed aboard the attack aircraft carrier USS *Valley Forge* (CVA-45), then at anchor off Hong Kong. That carrier was one of the first American units to respond to the communist invasion which initiated the Korean conflict.

In August the American carrier force was reinforced by the arrival of USS *Philippine Sea* (CVA-47) with two F9F-2 squadrons aboard, VF-111 and VF-112. On 9 November the commanding officer of VF-111, Lieutenant Commander W. T. Amen, shot down a Russian-built MiG-15 defending North Korean emplacements along the Yalu River.

During the three years American forces supported the United Nations effort in Korea, the Grumman Panther flew a variety of missions. Both major variants of the Panther series are keenly recalled by retired Admiral James L. Holloway III, whose distinguished naval career was capped by a tour of duty as Chief of Naval Operations, the highest uniformed post in the US Navy.

'As the first officer assigned to Air Task Unit 1, I was in the position of organising the unit and the concept for the organisation of similar units in the Pacific. One of the first things I did was have the designation changed from ATU-1, which sounded

Above: after being succeeded in service by the swept-wing Grumman Cougar, the surviving Panthers were adapted for special duties, including service as target drones and drone controllers with the designations F9F-5KD and DF-9E. One such aircraft is pictured.
Below left: an F9F-2 Panther of composite squadron VC-61 leads two similar machines from VF-71 on an offensive patrol over North Korea in 1952. The Panther's four nose-mounted 20mm cannon were more often used against ground targets than enemy aircraft, as MiG activity over the east coast was comparatively rare.
Below: flown by a pilot of US Navy reserve squadron VF-781, a Panther prepares to hit the crash barrier aboard USS Bon Homme Richard during Korean cruise flight operations in 1951. On 9 November the previous year, a Panther of VF-111 had registered the US Navy's first jet-versus-jet kill

like a training unit, to Air Task Group 1. That way the terminology would be consistent with the air groups already deployed. Since none of the ATG-1 personnel had primary duty to the staff itself, because it was not a commissioned unit but was a task unit, they were assigned to the various squadrons that made up the unit. In my case, I was assigned to VF-111.'

Prior to ATG-1's deployment to the Korean combat zone aboard USS *Valley Forge*, the unit's operations officer increased his knowledge of jets, and particularly his familiarity with the F9F-2. He logged time in aircraft assigned to both of the pioneer naval jet combat squadrons, VF-52 and VF-111.

Admiral Holloway notes that these practice missions were primarily tactics flights. He recalls: 'We flew very few actual fighter missions, that is, gunnery shoots, because the role of the F9F-2 was almost exclusively one of interdiction and close support. North Korean MiG aircraft were not coming down on the eastern side of the country, where the Navy was operating. Rather, they were being engaged up in the north-east by the USAF.

'We did not have an opportunity to use the F9F-2 as a pure fighter aircraft, but I felt it did serve as a very fine attack aircraft. The Panther normally operated at altitudes above the turbulence and, during the high-speed bombing runs, it gave us an extremely stable platform from which to put our ordnance right on the target.'

In addition to being the first American aircraft carrier to enter the Korean conflict, USS *Valley Forge* was also the first to make three deployments with Task Force 77 operating in the Sea of Japan. ATG-1 was deployed aboard the carrier during that third cruise and, as Admiral Holloway relates, there were some operational restrictions placed on the early Grumman F9F-2 aircraft: 'We deployed for Korea just before stall fences were placed on the wings, just outboard of the engine intakes, which permitted the F9F-2s to carry considerably heavier loads off the catapults. So when the winds were light during our first cruise aboard *Valley Forge*, we flew with very small bombing loads.'

ATG-1's first operational period 'on the line' off Korea lasted from 12 December 1951 to 13 June 1952. During that time, Holloway notes, 'a pilot would fly one Combat Air Patrol and then usually two or three air-to-ground missions before he drew another CAP. CAP was considered fairly dull, because there was no enemy activity in the vicinity of the carrier operating area. But of course the precautionary patrols had to be flown.

'The air-to-ground missions were almost equally divided between close-support and interdiction missions. During close-support missions, we were assigned to forward observers on the ground to provide bomb and rocket support for ground forces in the field actually engaged with the enemy. Interdiction missions were either strikes on rail yards or strong points, or what we called "road recces", which were armed reconnaissance missions against targets of opportunity on the main North Korean lines of communication. We also flew special missions, such as coastal armed reconnaissance, looking for waterborne logistics craft and any kind of military or logistic activity.

'The "road recces" were usually considered to be the most interesting and were flown in an unusual formation. The low man would fly between 30 and 90 metres off the deck, over the road, usually weaving to provide a moving target in case he suddenly came upon an anti-aircraft emplacement on the ground. Above him would be the two so-called

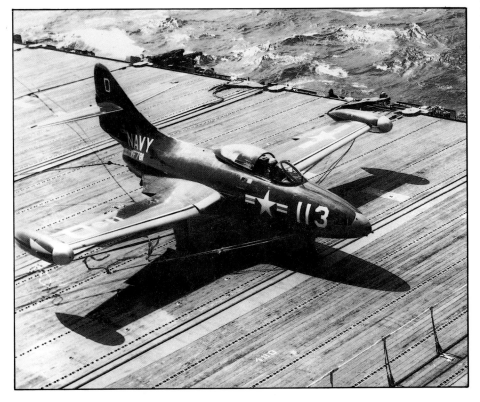

GRUMMAN F9F PANTHER

A line-up of F9F-2 aircraft of VF-112, one of the earliest Panther-equipped units to appear on the Korean battlefront in 1950. Together with sister squadron VF-112, VF-111 was then embarked aboard USS Philippine Sea. Carrier operation of the F9F-2 was eventually facilitated by the retrospective addition of aluminium 'fences' on the wing, which lowered the stalling speed and permitted a greater payload

"pouncers" flying at 300 to 900 metres, ready to deliver an attack by rockets or bombs on any target called out by the low man.

'In a typical "group grope", as we called co-ordinated attacks involving all squadrons of the air task group, we would hit the enemy with one division (or section) of F9F-2s for fighter cover, one division of four Panthers to use their 20 mm cannon and 260 lb VT-fuse fragmentation bombs for flak suppression, and perhaps a third division of jet fighters would carry 250 lb bombs to be used on the target itself. The ADs would come in with 500 lb, 1,000 lb or occasionally 2,000 lb bombs, and the Corsairs would have 500 lb bombs.

'These co-ordinated attacks required very careful timing because the jet fighters had to get their bombs on the target just as the propeller-driven aircraft rolled in for their runs. If the jets got in and out too soon, the ground gunners would have time to get back to their weapons and open up on the prop planes as they came down relatively slowly in their bombing runs. Conversely, if the jets were slow, we would find ourselves in a pretty wild *mêlée*, with the F9Fs flying through the formations of ADs and F4Us, us trying to drop our frag bombs and fire our 20 mm guns while the Skyraiders and Corsairs were trying to settle down on an accurate bombing run.'

ATG-1 had a respite of almost eleven months before it returned to combat in Korea. During that time its three Panther squadrons became familiar with their new aircraft. In the case of the F9F-5 it meant getting used to faster, more powerful aircraft, powered by the improved Pratt & Whitney J48-P-6A, which developed 2,830 kg (6,250 lb) static thrust. Admiral Holloway recalls that the difference in performance between the two Panther variants was 'quite noticeable' as the F9F-5 'had that additional power that was so useful when you needed it.'

In view of Holloway's more prominent squadron role as second in command of VF-52 during ATG-1's second Korean deployment, he flew more combat missions than during the first tour with Task Force 77. Since ATG-1's period 'on the line' from 12 May to 27 July 1953 was at a time when both sides in the conflict were trying to gain territory in anticipation of fixing an armistice line, combat activity was particularly heavy.

The Grumman F9F-2 brought Holloway through numerous hazardous missions, earning his

high regard: 'I thought the world of the Panther. On two occasions my aircraft was hit by flak, the first time by a 40 mm projectile, a weapon designed to bring down an aircraft with a single hit. I took this hit in the wingtip, which knocked off the tip-tank and end of the starboard wing, and brought the plane safely back to a friendly airfield. On another occasion I was hit by a 20 mm shell, which ripped off the starboard side of the horizontal stabiliser, about two feet out from the vertical fin. Again, I was able to recover from the attack and fly the aeroplane to an airfield in just below the armistice line on the east coast of South Korea.

'VF-52 suffered a lot of battle damage during that cruise. Eight pilots received hits by 40 mm shells and survived. In every case the F9F-2 was sturdy enough to absorb the hit and get the pilot back to the front lines, where he was able to "dead stick" it in, eject or land at an emergency airfield. I attribute this survival factor to the fact that, first, the Panther was a very sturdy aircraft; the skin was thick and the construction was strong. Secondly, in those days we didn't realise the high degree of volumetric density that we do in today's aircraft, in which even a 0.5 in bullet is likely to strike a critical control line or vital system. The old Panther had room to absorb some punishment and keep going.'

The ruggedness of the Grumman F9F-2 Panther can also be seen in the combat experiences of other members of VF-52. Beginning with an account concerning the squadron commanding officer, Lieutenant James J. Kinsella, Admiral Holloway relates: 'He was hit while flying at well over 400 knots and at an altitude of about 100 feet. The aeroplane caught fire, but he managed to turn it south to friendly territory, where it went out of control and crashed into a rice paddy and exploded. Yet, the cockpit area remained intact to the extent that he was able to walk away from the wreckage.

'Another time, Lieutenant (junior grade) John Chambers was with me on a mission up north and, rolling in to his bombing run, his aeroplane was hit right under the cockpit, in the dive brake area. The 40 mm shell exploded and blew up right through the cockpit and, although Chambers was severely wounded in the legs and both arms, his parachute and his seat protected his body from most of the force of the explosion. He was able to fly the plane with me – I'd also been hit on that run – 40 miles to the south, where we took it in to an advance emergency airfield.

Although he later flew the F9F-5, Holloway found that Panther variant to have certain drawbacks. He notes that, although the -5 had a more powerful engine than its predecessor, it 'also had a somewhat thinner wing and, if you weren't very careful, it could get you into trouble coming aboard ship. If you got a little low in your final approach to the ramp at the aft end of the flight deck, even if you jammed on power, it became very difficult to gain the lift necessary to get yourself up on the deck. As a result, the F9F-5 experienced a number of ramp strikes before the pilots got used to that aircraft. Instead of landing on the flight deck, the planes would hit the round-down, or back edge of the landing platform, and the plane would break in half and hurtle down the flight deck in a fireball.'

'Flying the Sabre presented no difficulties, but it was unforgiving of the slightest lapse of care.'

North American F-86 Sabre

Below: one of the Royal Australian Air Force's Commonwealth Sabres serving with No 2 Operational Training Unit. The aircraft is armed with two 20mm cannon instead of the six 0·5 in machine guns carried by most Sabres.
Bottom: Canadair Sabres of No 434 Squadron Royal Canadian Air Force were based at Zweibrucken in Germany during the 1950s

Remarkable as being the first transonic, swept-wing jet fighter to enter service in the West, the North American F-86 Sabre first joined the USAF's 1st Fighter Group at March Air Force Base in California, in March 1949, five years before the RAF received its first Hawker Hunter. Yet unlike so many another 'first of the breed', the Sabre was an instant success, became a popular aeroplane among its pilots and acquitted itself very well during the Korean War, when it became the principal weapon in the air arsenal of the United Nations' constituent air forces.

Smaller and lighter than the Hunter, the Sabre perpetuated the use of 0·5 in machine guns. Six

of these were mounted on the sides of the nose, resulting in a rather cramped cockpit, although in the tradition of American fighters the instrument layout was neat and logical in presentation. The big T-14E-1 ejector seat further restricted the pilot's freedom of movement. Many pilots will, however, proclaim a preference for a 'compact' cockpit, pointing to the ease with which various controls, instruments and switches may be reached. Cockpit conditioning, pressurisation, screen de-icing and pilot's g-suit utilised hot air bled from the engine compressor. Armour protection was afforded by alloy and steel plates behind the ejector seat and forward of the instrument panel. Gun aiming on the early Sabres was by a Mark 18 lead-computing gunsight coupled with an AN/APG-30 radar in the upper lip of the nose air intake. Navigation equipment included an AN/ARN-6 radio compass, communication by an AN/ARC-3 VHF command radio, and identification by AN/APX-6 IFF radar.

Flying the Sabre presented no difficulties, but it was unforgiving of the slightest lapse of care. The aircraft was fairly slow to accelerate on take-off and the nosewheel lifted at the unusually high speed of 185 km/h (115 mph) at normal weights; unstick occurred at slightly over 210 km/h (130 mph). About 640 m (700 yards) ground run was required in a 15 knot headwind at sea level. It was essential to hold the nose up to maintain at least a 13-degree angle of attack otherwise the aircraft would sink, the wing slats remaining open throughout the

take-off and closing at about 354km/h (220mph). After allowing the speed to build up to about 530km/h (330mph) the nose could be raised to the climbing attitude. The climb performance was roughly mid-way between that of the Meteor and Hunter, and a service ceiling of 14,600m (48,000ft) could be reached in 24 minutes.

Maximum level speed of Mach 0·91 could be achieved in early Sabres after a lengthy acceleration at the tropopause, at which speed the controls had become very heavy. The Sabre would reach supersonic speed in a dive, it being normal practice to roll over and pull through into a steep dive above about 11,000m (36,000ft); speed built up quickly and Mach 1 would be exceeded by the time the aircraft had dropped about 1,500m (5,000ft). At transonic speed, however, the Sabre tended to nose up with moderate buffet, and if the dive was continued below 7,600m (25,000ft) it would start to roll, a difficult tendency to check owing to the onset of aileron reversal.

These shortcomings were much-reduced in the

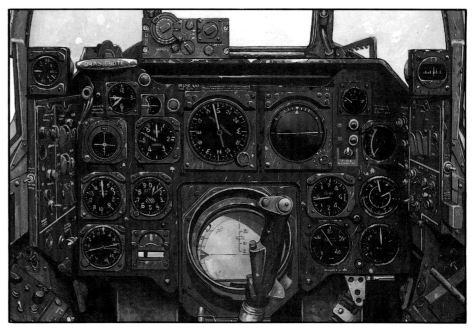

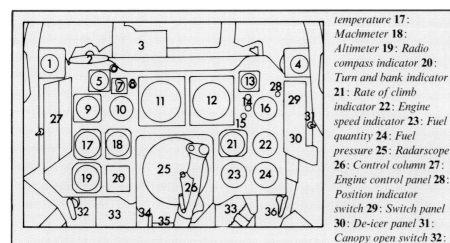

temperature **17**:
Machmeter **18**:
Altimeter **19**: Radio
compass indicator **20**:
Turn and bank indicator
21: Rate of climb
indicator **22**: Engine
speed indicator **23**: Fuel
quantity **24**: Fuel
pressure **25**: Radarscope
26: Control column **27**:
Engine control panel **28**:
Position indicator
switch **29**: Switch panel
30: De-icer panel **31**:
Canopy open switch **32**:
Emergency steering
handle **33**: Rudder
pedals **34**: Drop tank
release **35**: Oil pressure
36: Canopy lock

1: Accelerometer **2**: Chute release **3**: UHF radio **4**: Compass
5: Clock **6**: Undercarriage warning **7**: Pitch/trim indicator
8: Oxygen warning **9**: ILS indicator **10**: Airspeed indicator
11: Position indicator **12**: Artificial horizon **13**: Fuel
pressure **14**: Fire warning **15**: Arming switch **16**: Exhaust

F-86E which introduced power-operated controls and all-moving tailplane linked to the elevator. By introducing hydraulic operation of the ailerons and tailplane/elevator, the customary stick loads were eliminated and so a bungee artificial feel system was introduced.

Later still the wing leading-edge slats were eliminated and the whole leading edge extended forward; introduced at the same time as the 2,700 kg (5,910 lb) thrust 'dash-27' General Electric J47 engine, this larger-chord wing raised the top speed to Mach 0·92 but – more important in combat – also allowed the pilot to fly much closer to the limit without the onset of compressibility effects. Early Sabre pilots in Korea complained that intermittent opening of the wing· slats during combat made gun-aiming very difficult, but the F-86E was found to be infinitely superior.

In common with all the early generation of jet fighters, the Sabre carried relatively little internal fuel and thus possessed a very short endurance. By the time it reached Korea, however, it was normally

Left: the Sabre's swept wings and tail surfaces are shown to advantage in this picture. It was these design features, derived from German wartime research, which gave the Sabre its transonic performance capability.
Below left: the F-86D variant of the Sabre was an all-weather fighter with the nose reconfigured to incorporate a radar scanner above the intake

SABRE VERSUS MiG-15

The first encounter between the Sabre and the MiG-15 was described thus by Lt Col Bruce Hinton: 'The MiGs went across to our right and starting a climbing turn back to us. No time to lose! I punched off the tanks and went to full military on the throttle. A hard pull into their turn brought me in at their 5 o'clock and closing. They were climbing to meet us; we were diving slightly on them. I picked the MiG leader to attack. Baker 3 and 4 were taking on MiGs 3 and 4. As I closed to within 4,000 feet, the MiGs suddenly cleaned their external tanks. The tanks separated, twisting sideways and flipping end over end, trailing a plume of white spray.

'As I moved to the 6 o'clock position on the MiG leader, I started checking my airspeed. The F-86A is redlined at .95 mach and my machmeter was well beyond the redline. At this point, the MiG flight began to spread. Out of the corner of my eye, the element (MiG 3 and 4) seemed to be breaking away from the lead aircraft. MiG 1 and 2 slowly rolled from a climbing turn into a level left bank with the lead MiG going slightly high. That settled it and I picked up the closest MiG, the leader's wingman, put my pipper on his left fuselage about where the fuel tank should be and closed the range. The gunsight had stadiametric ranging and I set the sight for a 30 foot span . . .

'The lead MiG had drifted higher, sitting about 45° to the right and about 200 feet higher than No 2 and myself. Thinking "Could the MiG leader position himself to hit me from where he was or where he was going?" He could be about to work a defensive split (as a US pilot would do) to draw my attention away, or to pull off a high attack on my wingman and myself. Wingman? Baker 2 was not with me! Then I knew. When we had initiated the

break into the MiGs, I had momentarily straightened out to work with my radio. Baker 2, 3 and 4 had continued the break coming around on the MiG element that had been crossing. My Pause had caused our separation. I was alone!

'I decided to watch the MiG leader but work on No 2, who suddenly popped his speed brakes then retracted them immediately. That momentary drag increased my closure rate and I put my pipper on his tailpipe. My airplane abruptly began a violent twisting and bouncing in his jet wash, so I slid off to the inside slightly, clearing the turbulence. Rangedown to about 800 feet. I pressed the trigger for a good long burst into his engine. Pieces flew out, smoke filled the tailpipe, and the flame lengthened out the opening. He lost airspeed at once and I put out my speed brakes, throttled to idle and moved in closer to him. We hung there in the sky, turning left, with my airplane tight against his underside in a show formation. We were about 5 feet apart and I got a good close view of his MiG. It was a beautiful, sports car of a fighter. The silver aluminium of pure metal was clean and gleaming . . .

'After hanging there for what seemed like a long time, I moved out and over him looking for other MiGs. None in sight we were all alone. The MiG was losing altitude very fast in a 45° left bank at low airspeed. I moved farther to his inside, now about 2,000 feet above and thought, "Why doesn't he blow?" His airplane was smoking out of several places and fire was still coming out of his tailpipe. "OK! I'll finish him!" In a diving left turn, I put the pipper on his forward fuselage and fired a long, long burst. The API flashed and twinkled on the left and right wing roots and in the cockpit area. He rolled on his back and dived, trailing smoke and flame, crashing into the snow covered earth below. There was no parachute.'

NORTH AMERICAN F-86 SABRE

fitted with a pair of underwing drop tanks which bestowed a radius of action of about 400 km (250 miles) with normal reserves. When these were replaced by a couple of 1,000 lb bombs, the F-86A was capable of a radius of only 80 km (50 miles). Later on the number of wing strong points was increased to four, but with external stores on all these the Sabre was very sluggish indeed, and demanded operation from 2,700 m (3,000 yard) runways, restricting its deployment.

In any retrospective analysis it is perhaps invidious to exaggerate an aeroplane's weaknesses. The truth indeed remains that for five years the F-86 was the only fighter in the world capable of matching the Communist-built MiG-15 and, in so doing, pioneered combat tactics at transonic speeds. It was extremely popular with its pilots and survived in service for many years, not only in the USAF but also with countless other Western air forces, not forgetting the RAF – still fretting in the absence of the Hunter and Swift – in which Sabres equipped 12 squadrons in England and Germany.

Above right: after retiring from front-line service, the Sabre was used in a number of experimental test programmes as a chase plane.
Right: the USAF's last production version of the Sabre, the F-86H had wings of increased span, a lengthened and deepened fuselage and a new tailplane without the dihedral of former marks.
Below: Sabres of No 112 Squadron RAF fly in formation over the German countryside

'The facility with which the G91 operated equally well from fields or partly-constructed runways was quite incredible.'

Fiat G 91

The G 91's cockpit layout follows standard practice, with flight instruments mounted centrally and engine instruments on the right of the panel. Armament controls are at the bottom left of the main panel. Engine starting, fuel management, radio and camera controls are on the left side console, together with the throttle. On the right are oxygen, navigation, air conditioning and lighting panels

'When I held the stick of the G 91 and opened the throttle,' said Major Vittorio Sanseverino, 'only one pilot before me, Bignamini, also a Fiat test pilot, had ever handled the new light fighter. I was immediately astonished by its manoeuvrability: it was extraordinarily easy to fly!' Sanseverino, flying the G 91, was the winner of the NATO competition which in September 1957 brought the Italian fighter and its French rivals together on the Bretigny airfield in France. The competition, organised by Supreme Headquarters Allied Powers in Europe (SHAPE) was the logical outcome of two equally important issues: first, the lessons learned from the Korean War, which had emphasised the importance of the fighter's role in tactical support

of ground forces; and the other, the result of discussions at the Lisbon Conference where a meeting of the Atlantic Council was held in February 1952. At that conference the decision was taken to proceed with the rearmament of the West European Powers, and from subsequent studies there emerged the need for a light fighter, for which various specifications were laid down.

'We had only two months in which to finalise, on paper, the design and characteristics of the new fighter', recalled Giulio Ciampolini who was at that time a member of the team under Gabrielli, Fiat's chief designer. Professor Gabrielli had the common sense to draw upon the experience of the Turin company in licence-production of the F86K;

subsequently, deliberate rumours were circulating to the effect that the G 91 was a smaller version of the popular North American F-86 Sabre. However, this was obviously not so. It is sufficient to point out the advanced characteristics and the ingenuity with which the new aircraft had been designed and which initially provided for an empty weight of under 2,200 kg (4,800 lb) – only twice the weight of an average-size car of that period.

By March 1954 something like ten projects had been submitted for the light fighter: among these were the Italian Sagittarius II, the British Folland Gnat and various French projects, the Taon and the Mystère XXVI being the most notable. The preliminary examination of the projects resulted in the French Taon coming first, while Gabrielli's fighter was second. In accordance with the rules of the competition it was recommended that three prototypes of each projected aircraft be built, to which was later added the Mystère XXVI project, re-named Etendard. However, as soon as the prototypes were built the position of the winners was reversed and the G 91 placed first.

The Italian fighter benefited especially from its advanced design and also from the various concepts of the Italian armed forces as to their requirements in any future conflict. Being more exposed, in the Veneto area, to any advance by ground forces from the East, Italy was considered to be fairly vulnerable on the ground in the event of an enemy attack as its airfields were within range of enemy fighter-bombers and light bombers. Standard runways 2,000–3,000 m (6,600–9,800 ft) long would become bomber targets and their length would be reduced by a third or a half, thereby compelling friendly aircraft to take off in limited space and to run over hastily filled-in holes or to take off direct from fields adjacent to runways. The G 91 was therefore designed with this possibility in mind. As a result, the very satisfactory operational demon-

Above: a G 91R1 of 5° Aerobrigata, Italian air force. The R1 was an early version of the G 91, a total of 23 production examples being built.
Left: in addition to aircraft overhaul and periodic inspections every 100 hours, minor replacements and repairs can be carried out with the equipment and tools available at the flight line.
Above right: the G 91Y was designed to fulfil Italian air force requirements for an aircraft able to carry out close support to ground troops, interdiction against defended targets, photographic and armed reconnaissance and with a secondary capability for combat.
Below right: basic armament of the G 91Y consists of two 30mm DEFA guns installed on either side of the armoured pilot cockpit

stration given by the G 91 on grassy fields eventually gave victory to the Italian fighter. 'The facility with which the G 91 operated, equally well from fields or partly-constructed runways', recalled Major Sanseverino, 'was quite incredible; furthermore, Fiat had perfected supply and control machinery and equipment which facilitated the execution of these tasks. And then, when I took off! Let me tell you: the finest propeller-driven fighter aircraft which I had ever flown previously had been the Lockheed P-38, in my view an excellent fighter which, fitted with two engines with propellers rotating in opposite direction, did not have the asymmetry of single-engined fighters. Well, while I was testing the G 91 I found it had the stability, the symmetrical manoeuvrability and the lightness of the P-38, with the advantage of greater power, high speed and excellent stability, whether firing the four 12·7mm guns or releasing bombs or rockets.'

The G 91's first flight took place at Turin on

9 August 1956; Fiat's chief test pilot, Major Bignamini, was at the controls. The second prototype took to the air on 26 July 1957 and, compared with the first, which had been destroyed during a flying accident on 20 February, had a more powerful engine and increased area of the vertical fin. It was powered by the excellent Bristol Orpheus engine, which had been tried out experimentally with the Gnat, the British aircraft entered for the NATO competition. The more powerful Orpheus engine was subsequently built by Fiat under licence and fitted to all single-engined G 91s.

After the first prototype was destroyed a further three were built for the Italian air force, followed by a pre-series of 27 aircraft. Mass production was effected in two separate batches, the first bearing the designation R1, of which there were 23, and the second R1A–25 aircraft. The R1A version differed only in its instruments. The last series for the Italian air force, designated R1B, consisted of

50 aircraft, powered by Orpheus engines of greater power and had a slightly greater take-off weight and modifications to its armament, which now consisted of two DEFA 30mm guns in addition to the usual racks for bombs and rockets.

The R3, destined for the Luftwaffe, was similar to the R1B: 394 aircraft were built of which 50 were constructed in Italy and 344 in Germany. The later R4 version, of which there were 50, initially intended for Greece, was later taken up by the Luftwaffe. In all, 167 aircraft of the modified version of the two-seater were subsequently built for training and bore the suffix letter T. Twenty-four aircraft from the pre-series and the single R1A were modified to G 91PAN standard for the aerobatic team of the Italian air force. Major Sanseverino observed: 'this choice shows the manoeuvrability of the G 91. The aerobatic team found it an ideal aircraft for the more daring manoeuvres, even though some of them were often quite difficult'. In fact, it suffices to give this one example: the specifications of the NATO competition required that the rate of roll (a sure indication of manoeuvrability) of the G 91 should be at least 100 degrees in one second. In practice the G 91 showed that it was capable of accomplishing a roll of 250 degrees in that time.

Meanwhile, studies had begun at Fiat on a series of modified G 91s for various other tasks, among these a supersonic version. This latter project was later abandoned in favour of a more advanced type with greater engine power and therefore offering the possibility of a greater weapons payload and a greater range. The final design resulted in an aircraft with two engines—two General Electric J85s with a single air intake. This variation was designated by the suffix letter Y, which indicated the path of the airflow which later separated to flow to the respective engines. The first flight of the new prototype took place towards the end of 1966 with Major Sanseverino at the controls. The aircraft's power had been increased by a good 63 per cent with a weapons payload increased by 25 per cent, therefore giving an abundant reserve of thrust. At the beginning of 1970 the aircraft came into service with the 8th CB Group of the Italian air force.

In spite of some criticisms, relating specifically to the single ventral air intake for the two engines, the G 91Y soon found great favour among pilots and evoked the interest of several foreign air forces. No contracts were concluded, however, chiefly on account of a political embargo on the sale of armaments. The G 91Y, the production of which has now ceased, is still the main aircraft in service with units used for the tactical support of the Italian air force; several aircraft of the R1 version are still giving honourable service, as are the T and T1 two-seaters for training purposes. In 1978 the G 91 completed 20 years of active service, a more than satisfactory career when it is remembered that it has flown in the skies of over half of Europe.

The G 91Y differs from the G 91R in having two engines—the 'Y' signifies the flow of air from the single intake—and their small size leaves more room for fuel in the fuselage. The engines are particularly suited for achieving a compromise between take-off performance and combat radius at low altitude, this depending upon the high percentage of thrust supplied by employment of the afterburner

'Once strapped into the small but compact cockpit of the A-4, the pilot had the illusion that the aircraft was built around him.'

Douglas A-4 Skyhawk

The first TA-4F two-seat training version of the Skyhawk pictured on take-off with an underwing load of Sidewinder air-to-air missiles. Nicknamed Heinemann's Hot Rod in honour of its designer, the Skyhawk light attack aircraft entered US Navy service in 1956 and the last of 2,960 aircraft of this type was delivered to US Marine Corps Attack Squadron 331 in February 1979. Although superseded in front-line Navy attack squadrons, the A-4 serves on with training and reserve units and for practice in air combat manoeuvres

Edward H. Heinemann, chief engineer of Douglas Aircraft Company's El Segundo Division, enjoys the enviable reputation of being the developer of two of the US Navy's most successful single-seat attack aircraft. His Douglas AD Skyraider series, which first flew in the closing days of World War II, served with distinction during both the Korean and Vietnam conflicts and went on to wider use beyond that required by the US Navy. Although his turbo-prop-powered XA2D-1 Skyshark did not reach production as the successor to the Skyraider, his A4D Skyhawk series has remained in front-line service since the mid-1950s.

The XA2D-1 bore a close family resemblance to

the propellor-driven Skyraider which it was intended to succeed as a carrier-based, single-seat attack aircraft. However, the A4D-1 proposed to the US Navy in February 1952 was completely different from the AD series, which was supposed to be phased out of service. Naval planners did not anticipate that the AD and the twin-jet A3D Skywarrior would fit into operational requirements of the late 1960s and early 1970s.

Thus, Douglas' fourth attack aircraft built for the US Navy (hence, the designation A4D) was extremely practical and designed for the future. The Heinemann design team made sure the overall dimensions of the Skyhawk would fit the elevators

DOUGLAS A-4 SKYHAWK

of the *Essex*-class aircraft carriers then primarily deployed by the US Navy. Those specifications eliminated the otherwise standard use of folding wings and/or tail surfaces to enable naval aircraft to be stowed or maintained on the aircraft carrier's hangar deck (within the confines of the ship). In turn, that development resulted in the weight of the folding mechanism being saved, as well as the efficiency derived from an aircraft which could be readied for launch with less preparation. Further weight savings were achieved by having the landing gear retract forward; in the event of a hydraulic system failure, the tricycle gear could fall freely and be locked by airstream pressure, thereby eliminating the need for a back-up system.

The US Navy was so impressed by the A4D, which was soon nicknamed 'Heinemann's Hot Rod', that on 21 June 1952 a contract was awarded to Douglas for pre-production aircraft designated A4D-1. Two years and a day later the first of the series, officially named 'Skyhawk', made its first flight. On 15 October 1955 one of the pre-production A4D-1s established a new FAI Class 'C' world record by flying an average 695·127 mph over a 500-kilometer closed-circuit course.

On 27 September 1956, the first production Skyhawks were assigned to attack squadron VA-72 with the US Atlantic Fleet. Other squadron assignments followed. The A4D-1 was powered by the 3,500 kg (7,700 lb) static thrust Wright J65-W-4 or J65-W-4B, derived from the Armstrong Siddeley Sapphire engine. There were 165 production A4D-1s and they were subsequently augmented by 542 A4D-2 aircraft with various improvements including an in-flight refuelling probe. The -2s remained in service with the US Navy and Marine Corps until 1965, when many were converted to trainers.

The first armed conflict in which A4Ds were used was during the Lebanon crisis beginning on 15 July 1958. To stabilise the civil war then racking that Middle East nation, US President Dwight D. Eisenhower ordered a landing of American troops. Those troops were supported by armed aircraft launched from the first US aircraft carrier to reach the scene, USS *Essex* (CVA-9). Among the aircraft from Air Task Group 201 launched from *Essex* were A4D-2s of VA-83 led by the squadron commanding officer, Commander (later Admiral and Chief of Naval Operations) James L. Holloway.

The Skyhawk series underwent continuous improvement during the late 1950s and early 1960s. Radar equipment in the nose and other new features marked the A4D-2N, which first flew on 21 August 1959 and the improved J52-P-6A engine of the A4D-5 was so efficient as to extend the aircraft's range about 27 per cent. When the US Navy and Air Force converted to a common aircraft designation system in September 1962, the Skyhawk retained the designation A-4 and noted its variants as follows: A4D-1 became A-4A, A4D-2 became A-4B, A4D-2N became A-4C and A4D-5 became A-4E. There was no A-4D to avoid confusion with the previous designation. Some 499 A-4Es were built and the first operational unit to receive them was VA-23.

At this point American aid was being expanded to South Vietnamese forces fending off guerilla attacks by communist-led forces from North Vietnam. As US involvement was stepped up, the A-4 Skyhawk gained prominence as the Navy's primary jet-powered attack aircraft.

A-4 operations are recalled by Rear Admiral Robert E. Kirksey, USN, who is now Commander of Carrier Group Three in the US Pacific Fleet. A onetime fighter pilot in Grumman F9F-6 and -7 Cougars, as well as North American FJ-3 Fury aircraft, Admiral Kirksey was assigned to Skyhawks in 1962. His transition to the Skyhawk was achieved during an assignment with VA-125, the Readiness Training Squadron (RTS) which qualified A-4 pilots for the Pacific Fleet. He subsequently served with VA-195 deployed aboard USS *Bon Homme*

Inset below: USS Hancock's emergency crash barrier is utilised by an A-4E Skyhawk of VA-212 during operations off the coast of Vietnam. Designer Ed Heinemann's decision to confine the type's size to the maximum acceptable by US carrier lifts made the A-4 one of the Navy's smallest attack aircraft. Incorporating the lessons learned by ground attack units in Korea, the design proved a potent weapon of war in the Vietnam conflict. Some 30 US Navy and Marine Corps attack units flew the type in 1968 at the height of the war

Richard (CVA-31) and participated in the early air strikes over Vietnam. During later tours of duty as executive officer and then commanding officer of VA-55, he flew from USS *Constellation* (CVA-64) and USS *Hancock* (CVA-19).

'I started out in VA-195 with the A-4C, the first Skyhawk to have radar and an automatic flight control system. Once strapped into the small but compact cockpit of the A-4, the pilot had the illusion that the aircraft was built around him. Instantaneous response to stick pressure coupled with what I call "honest" flying characteristics allowed the pilot to concentrate more completely on his weapons delivery technique and mission

profile. The later models of the A-4 – the A-4E and A-4F – were even more responsive and handled even better than the A-4C; it was like making the transition from driving the family station wagon to driving a sports car.'

'I particularly liked the responsiveness of the A-4, as well as the configuration of the instrumentation within the cockpit. You had all essential flight instruments within clear view. The pilots external vision was also unobstructed by the wing surface because the cockpit sits so far forward on the fuselage. It was as if you were being thrust through the air with your hand on the controls and when you started to do rolls or other aerobatic

Below: a lone A-4F of VA-55 overflies USS Hancock (CVA-19). Principal recognition feature of the variant, which first flew in August 1966, was the large dorsal 'hump' or fairing, clearly visible in this picture, which contained new avionics equipment. Other innovations included a zero-zero ejection seat, wing spoilers and nosewheel steering. Certain previous marks of Skyhawk have been retrospectively updated to A-4F standard, while the humpless but similar TA-4F trainer, which preceded the former into service, was also ordered in quantity

Top: an A-4E from the carrier USS Bon Homme Richard (CVA-31) pictured on a mission over Vietnam in 1969.
Above: two unofficial, but much-prized badges awarded to US Navy aircrews who operated from carriers in the Gulf of Tonkin against North Vietnam

manoeuvres, it was almost as if you were outside of the aircraft doing it all yourself. The aircraft had a tremendous roll rate. It was also very responsive to power, even though it was a subsonic aircraft.'

As a product of the 'cold war' of the 1950s, the A-4 was envisaged as a carrier-based nuclear weapons delivery system. Toward that end, the nose of the aircraft was designed to set particularly high to enable the A-4 to accommodate a large nuclear device beneath the fuselage. That configuration puts the A-4 into a unique landing attitude, particularly when returning to an aircraft carrier.

'You had to get used to being so high off the ground.' recalls Admiral Kirksey. 'In the Grumman Cougar that I'd flown before, it was a matter of pulling down one step and climbing into the cockpit. You have to use a ladder–going up seven or eight steps–to get into the cockpit of the A-4. But once you get used to the feel of the A-4, you don't really think that much about it.

'The A-4 was also a good aircraft to operate around the carrier. Forward visibility was reduced some because of the nose-high attitude during slow approach speeds for landing; however, the aircraft's responsiveness and manoeuvrability were definite advantages over some others I flew. Once the attitude and airspeed were in control, you flew a constant rate of descent all the way to touchdown. Your primary visual reference outside the cockpit was through the left-forward portion of the canopy. If you could see too much of the landing area aboard the carrier, you were too "flat" or "fast" and not flying a good approach.'

Although the compactness of the A-4 cockpit gives the pilot an interesting relationship to the aircraft, there are also some problems with that snug fit. Admiral Kirksey notes: 'There is hardly any room for the pilots shoulders–and I'm not a hefty person! By the time you put some survival equipment on the torso harness, an extra flashlight

and a 0·38 caliber revolver–you wonder how you are going to get into the cockpit. People larger than I have done it, but I still have the feeling that it almost takes a shoehorn to squeeze the pilot into an A-4.'

Admiral Kirksey's assignment to A-4s came just as that aircraft was in transition from a conventional weapons delivery system to one using sophisticated computer technology. Bomb delivery by the traditional method, he recalls, involved lining up the target with a fixed gunsight and then calculating various wind factors. 'At the right moment you pressed the "pickle"–the bomb release button on the control column–dropped the bomb and hoped for a hit near the target. But in the more sophisticated Skyhawks–such as the A-4F–you would hit the "pickle" and start your recovery, pulling the nose of the aircraft up and through the horizon. When you reached the angular rate desired, the bomb would release automatically and with much greater accuracy.

'It was also very exciting flying the nuclear weapons loft manoeuvre profile–that is a half-cuban right. The run-in was at 50 to 100 feet at a speed of 500 knots. When you hit the target area, you would pull up into a four 'g' loop and the automatic release computed for the bomb would "pickle off" at a predetermined angle. Of course, you would recover in the opposite direction. It took skill to do this just right and we practiced frequently.'

Most A-4 missions over Vietnam were devoted to interdiction. Admiral Kirksey remembers: 'We dropped 500lb bombs on targets such as bridges, infrastructure, trucks, and tanks. We were doing air-to-ground strikes and, within both Carrier Air Wing 14 and 21, we were the "dedicated" squadron to carry out "Iron Hand" missions–strikes aimed at destroying or neutralising North Vietnamese SA-2 surface-to-air missile (SAM) sites. To perform that mission, VA-55 carried the Shrike, an anti-radiation missile that could knock out the radar complexes.

'We were also equipped to carry Bullpup missiles, which could be guided from the aircraft. Later, with the A-4E, we had the television-controlled Walleye "smart" bombs. The A-4F also carried the Sidewinder air-to-air missile – not to go out hunting for MiG fighters, but if we got into an encounter with a MiG, we had two Sidewinders to use in our own defense.'

A veteran of over 200 combat missions over North Vietnam, Admiral Kirksey considers the Douglas A-4 Skyhawk series to have been the yeoman aircraft of that war. 'The A-4 was assigned many tough missions and did them well. We did mostly 45-degree dive bombing, which is more accurate than bombing at lower angles. When equipped with the CP-741 bombing computer, the A-4F automatically released the bombs when the correct lead angle was reached.

'With the A-4F we could take out bridges on a "surgical" basis. We proved that around Haiphong, where we took out every bridge there, without damaging the city. We had good bombers [pilots adept at bombing], who had a lot of practice and who did a good job with the A-4.'

Rear Admiral Robert Kirksey has a unique insight into the broad spectrum of operations throughout the Vietnam conflict. He flew combat missions at the very beginning of hostilities and then went on to become commanding officer of the Pacific Fleet's first multi-purpose aircraft carrier, USS *Kitty Hawk* (CV-63), which was involved in the final postwar operations off Vietnam. From that broad perspective, Admiral Kirksey has formulated some lessons learned from A-4 operations over Vietnam.

'The first lesson we learned was don't go in low to the target. For a while we used Snakeye fin-retarded bombs which could be delivered at low altitude and would not detonate until the aircraft was clear of the area. But enemy small-arms fire and barrages of anti-aircraft artillery (AAA) fire were very intense and taking a heavy toll of our aircraft. The enemy used considerable 37 and 57mm ammunition and later, 100mm shells.

'Of course, the surface-to-air missile threat was the argument against coming in too high, which would put the attack aircraft within the greatest danger of the SAM envelope. Eventually, we wound up at a medium altitude, at which we could fight a SAM just as we could defend ourselves against another aeroplane.

'A medium altitude also kept us out of the AAA

Below: '*Yankee Air Pirates*' *was a form of abuse much-used by the North Vietnamese when referring to American airmen. Hence it was adopted by US Navy aircrews as one of their badges.*
Bottom: pictured during carrier qualifications aboard USS America (CVA-66), this Skyhawk of Carrier Air Wing 6 is about to be catapulted. Despite its small size, the A-4 packed a hefty punch. Built-in armament was two 20mm cannon in the wing roots. External stores on later versions totalled over 4,000 kg (9,000 lb) in weight and bombs, rockets or air-to-surface missiles could be carried

environment, except for the 100 mm shells which, from time-to-time, gave us fits. But there were enough Radar Homing and Warning (RHAW) devices in use to alert us when ground-based fire control radar was locking on our aircraft. Hence, the main point was to stay out of an unsophisticated environment–too close to the ground–where a young boy with a rifle might get lucky and bring down an aeroplane.

'Another lesson was never fly over an undercast in SAM territory. If a SAM popped up out of the clouds, you simply didn't have time to evade it. You almost had to see it lifting off and be able to track it for at least a short time. Then you could lower the nose of the aircraft and get some energy to out-manoeuvre the SAM. We lost some pilots who flew over undercast areas and didn't return from their mission. They were probably brought down by SAMs. We also believed never fly directly under an overcast. The enemy measured the base of the overcast and set their AAA fuses for that altitude in hopes of catching someone flying in at the base of the clouds. From our bombing missions we learned that the lowest point of pull-out from a dive should be at about 3,000 feet above the target area. Any lower than that exposed us to small and medium arms fire.

'We approached the coast of Vietnam about 12,000 to 13,000 feet altitude. As soon as we "went feet dry"–were over land–we would come down to about 9,000 feet. Heavily laden with bombs, the A-4 could go 300 to 330 knots, so we would use that descent from altitude to build up energy and increase our airspeed to around 350 knots. We would try to arrive over the target at about 8,000 to 9,000 feet and from there roll into a 45-degree dive. We would begin the pull-out at 4,500 to 5,000 feet and bottom-out around 3,000 feet.

'Another lesson of A-4 operations was don't make multiple bomb runs. If you were carrying six bombs, you set all of your bomb release stations so they would drop during one run. The North Vietnamese had a lot of mobile AAA equipment and could hold you in cross-fire. They would start getting your range and fire when you pulled up the first time. They would continue to track you and as soon as you started in for another attack, you more than doubled your chances of being tagged. They were getting better and better at determining just how much of a lead each weapon required for various types of aircraft. That's why we said don't make repeat runs.

'In keeping with that, we also tried never to set a predictable pattern around a target. That wasn't always possible, however, because we attempted to recover from our runs so that we were pointed toward the Tonkin Gulf. That way, if we were hit, our chances of survival, once we got over the water, went up by an order of magnitude. Conversely, if you went down over land, chances were that you would be captured.

'Another lesson was don't let one missile hit two aircraft. Initially, we were flying too close together, almost in formation. In one case, one missile did get two of our A-4s. After that we figured about 700 feet between aircraft was a good loose combat spread. It was based on the projected distribution of particles when a SAM detonated.

'A really important lesson was never get slow. We learned that if you lost your energy–got the nose of the aircraft too high in any condition where your airspeed was around 250 knots–the only thing you could do to get away from a SAM was to point your aircraft to the earth and go. Once you recovered your energy, you pulled a 'g' [high speed turn] because the SAM couldn't turn as fast as you could.'

As Admiral Kirksey subsequently learned, however, there were times when SAMs could not be evaded. His own first-hand experience with SAM hits took place during an "Iron Hand" mission over Hanoi. 'Our mission was to hit the SAM sites located around the target area to prepare the way for our main body of strike and fighter aircraft. As we approached Hanoi we were met by a barrage firing of SAMs from the missile sites surrounding the target complex. My wingman reported a SAM tracking for me, but I could not sort out which one due to the density of SAMs in the air. Shortly thereafter I was hit as a SAM detonated under my aircraft. The best I could tell was the left wing took the brunt of the hit. All cockpit indications read

Above: the Skyhawk's cockpit is small and compact, but nevertheless contains a bewildering array of flight, engine and armament systems displays. Two-seat operational Skyhawks had a second, similar cockpit which reduced fuel capacity by restricting tank size.
Above right: an A-4 pilot keeps station with his colleagues. The A-4M featured an enlarged canopy which improved pilot visibility, although forward view during approach and on the ground was still limited.
Right: a formation of A-4 Skyhawks from the aircraft carrier USS Hancock. Ed Heinemann's Skyraider replacement enjoyed nearly 26 years of production before the line closed in early 1979

with electrical cable shot away and the hydraulics gone – the aircraft held together and got me back in one piece. Any other aircraft would not have survived that kind of punishment.' Admiral Kirksey's performance during that mission, particularly the fact that he remained over the combat area after receiving the first SAM hit, was recognised when he was awarded the Silver Star Medal, one of the highest American combat decorations.

Admiral Kirksey notes that his squadron of A-4s received continual protection from fighter aircraft in the air wing. The MiG combat air patrol was generally quite effective in keeping the enemy fighters away from the attack aircraft. During a mission south of Haiphong, however, VA-55 literally stumbled onto a MiG. 'Just as I was getting ready to roll in, I looked down and I saw what we all later agreed was a MiG-17. He was right in our pattern. Just ahead of us. He was so perfectly positioned that I almost expected him to roll in on the target! Of course, we called the fighters and they went down after him. He then headed for the deck and took off in the direction of Kep Airfield, outside of Hanoi, and got away from us.'

In addition to the A-4's ruggedness, dependability, and stability, that aircraft is also something of a fighter. On 31 May 1967, Lieutenant Ted Swartz, an A-4C pilot with VA-76 deployed aboard USS *Bon Homme Richard*, was attacking two MiG fighters on the ground at Kep airfield when two MiG-17s that were in the air got on his tail. He out-manoeuvred the two swept-wing supersonic fighters and, armed with only Zuni air-to-surface missiles, Lieutenant Swartz scored a direct hit on one MiG-17, which plunged in flames to the ground.

During the 1967 Middle East War, at least two Israeli A-4s are known to have earned the distinction of becoming MiG killers. Indeed, the A-4 is still one of the most important aircraft in the Israeli inventory and, when the supply of ex-US Navy A-4s was exhausted, Douglas began a new production run of the venerable attack aircraft to meet further demand. Other US allies have also received A-4s

normal. Shortly after firing my last Shrike missile, another volley of SAMs were called away.

'When the second SAM hit, my wingman reported that I was on fire and called for me to eject. I was also losing the hydraulic flight control system along with everything electrically operated or controlled. I found that I was able to fly the aircraft by interlocking my hands and legs around the control stick. I decided to stay with the aircraft – fire or no fire – and head for the water to eject near friendly forces. As I crossed the coastline, the fire extinguished itself and the engine continued to operate. I decided to stay with the plane and attempt a straight-in approach at Danang airfield.

'After I landed in the emergency arresting gear at Danang, I found out that there were 40 major holes in the aeroplane. The holes averaged three to eight inches in diameter. Part of the nose gear wheel had been completely distorted. There were over 200 other measurable holes in the aircraft and the whole undercarriage was . . . nearly burned through.

'Although the engine was fine and was subsequently used in another aircraft, the rest of my A-4 was struck from the rolls. But as bad off as it was –

Above: A-4E Skyhawks of VA-45 aboard the anti-submarine warfare aircraft carrier USS Intrepid in 1972. Grumman S-2 Tracker ASW aircraft are parked in the background.
Right: an A-4E of VA-23 salvoes a load of 3 in rockets into a Vietcong position. During the Vietnam War the Skyhawk was extensively used in support of friendly troops and in attacking ground targets in the North

'The noise level is high and most pilots are initially very conscious of the fact that they are being suspended by four columns of hot air.'
Wg Cdr G.R. Profit RAF

British Aerospace Harrier

The year 1979 marks the tenth anniversary of the Hawker Harrier's entry into service with the RAF. However, the lineage of this unique V/STOL fighter goes a good way further back than that, the Harrier's grandfather being the Hawker P1127 which first flew in October 1960. In conventional flight the Harrier handles like any other fast ground-attack fighter; it is its V/STOL capabilities which hold the fascination from the handling point of view. V/STOL handling cannot be directly compared with flying a helicopter–indeed it is easier to master in many ways–but before describing the flying techniques, it is of interest to consider the history of the Hawker Siddeley/Rolls-Royce solution to the problem of giving a fighter aircraft independence from vulnerable airfields.

When the P1127 first flew nearly 20 years ago, Hawkers investigated the unknowns of hovering flight before flying the aircraft conventionally. Hawker's design centered around the Rolls-Royce Pegasus, a large bypass engine with four inter-connected exhaust nozzles which could be swivelled from fully aft for conventional flight to the vertical hovering position. The front or 'cold' nozzles as they are called exhaust bypass air from the low pressure fan, while the rear or hot nozzles exhaust the remaining airflow from the turbine. The nozzles are rotated by a motor powered by air bled from the engine compressor and the air motor is controlled by a nozzle selector lever positioned next to the throttle in the cockpit. The nozzle lever is the only extra cockpit control associated with V/STOL flight. Moving the nozzle lever fully forward swivels the nozzles fully aft, while moving the nozzle lever back swivels the nozzles down.

When in hovering flight there are obviously no aerodynamic forces present to enable the normal flying control surfaces–the tailplane, ailerons and rudder–to control the aircraft. Control is achieved by ducting high-pressure air from the engine to reaction controls in the nose, tail and wingtips of the aircraft. The reaction controls are inter-connected with the associated flying controls and are supplied with high-pressure air as soon as the nozzles are lowered. To understand this simple principle, consider a Harrier hovering steadily; the pilot wishes to bank to the right and he moves the control column to the right. This raises the right aileron which causes the top reaction control in the right wing to open and deflect bleed-air upwards. Simultaneously the left aileron is lowered causing the bottom reaction control in the left wing to open and deflect bleed air downwards. The end result is a roll to the right. To the pilot, the control response is similar to that experienced in conventional flight. Control in the pitch and yaw axes is achieved in a similar manner.

The initial hovers were flown by Bill Bedford, Hawkers' chief test pilot at Dunsfold in 1961. The P1127 was restrained by tethers; it was marginal on thrust, and even after 317kg (700lb) of airframe components had been stripped, the aircraft was only able to carry about three minutes' worth of fuel. Nevertheless, it worked. After twenty-one hovering flights the P1127 made its first conventional flight in March 1961. Six P1127s were built and between 1962 and 1964 many changes were made to improve both the V/STOL and conventional handling characteristics of the aircraft. During this period, the thrust of the Pegasus engine was increased from its previous 6,100kg (13,500lb) to 7,000kg (15,500lb).

Among the offensive loads which may be carried on the Harrier's four wing and single fuselage hardpoints is the Matra rocket pack seen here in action. The twin ventral bulges accommodate 30mm Aden cannon and are non-detachable

The final development aircraft was called the Kestrel. Resulting from an agreement between the United Kingdom, the United States and the Federal Republic of Germany, nine Kestrels were built and their performance was assessed by the Tripartite Evaluation Squadron commanded by Wing Commander David Scrimgeour. The Kestrel was the first jet V/STOL aircraft to be granted a Release to Service, and the results of the Tripartite Squadron showed that it had enormous development potential. Throughout this period, Hawkers had been working on the design of a supersonic V/STOL aircraft, the P1154. The BS 100 engine for this aircraft had been run on a test-bed demonstrating the feasibility of plenum chamber burning, a form of reheat essential for supersonic flight. However, this project was cancelled by the government in late 1964, and at the same time an advanced version of the Kestrel was announced for production as a ground-attack fighter for the RAF; this aircraft – the P1127 (RAF) – became the Harrier.

Although similar in appearance to the Kestrel, the Harrier was a new aircraft from the engineering point of view, with only five per cent of parts common to both aircraft. The Pegasus was further developed to produce 8,600 kg (19,000 lb) of thrust for the Harrier GR Mk 1 and a water-injection system was added to sustain V/STOL thrust in high ambient temperatures. The reaction controls were improved, and a new pitch and roll autostabilisation system was fitted to lower the pilot workload in V/STOL flight. The undercarriage was completely redesigned to overcome the crosswind landing problems encountered earlier. The wing design was extensively modified to enable higher 'g' to be pulled, while the centre of gravity was moved forward to improve handling with underwing stores fitted.

Consider a simple sortie consisting of a vertical

Far left and left: the first carrier trial of a VTOL aircraft was conducted aboard HMS Ark Royal in February 1963 with a P1127. The two pictured Harriers were successfully used to prove the concept of carrier deck operations on HMS Eagle in March 1970.
Below: the launch is signalled of a US Marine Corps AV-8A Harrier of Marine Attack Squadron VMA-513, flying from USS Guam in the Atlantic. Helicopter carriers such as the Guam assumed a new tactical importance with the advent of the Harrier in 1971

Insets: the cockpit of the Harrier's experimental predecessor, the P1127. The main instrument display (inset far left) differs little from conventional fighters, with the 'Basic Six' in the centre and engine indicators to the right. Further right, however, is found the nozzle lever (inset left), which serves to deflect the jet efflux, transferring from horizontal to vertical flight or vice versa. Below: first flown in April 1969, the Harrier T Mark 2 trainer has a lengthened forward fuselage and extended tail 'puffer' pipe. Right: the trainer's cockpit canopy folds over for access

take-off into the hover, a circuit and a vertical landing. Before walking out to the aircraft the pilot will have performed a number of calculations on a simple V/STOL computer. Having taken into account the ambient temperature, pressure and individual engine performance, he will know the maximum fuel weights at which it will be possible to take off vertically and hover. After strapping into the Martin Baker ejection seat, a glance round the cockpit shows it to be small but comfortable and all controls come easily to hand.

After completion of the appropriate checks, the engine is started using the integral gas turbine starter. The Pegasus is a powerful engine and the steady vibration after start-up, not dissimilar to that of a large piston engine, is immediately obvious. Taxying is simple; the powerful hydraulic nosewheel steering system is engaged by a trigger on the control column and the parking brake is released. Idling thrust is high and on a hard surface the Harrier will immediately start to move without an increase in engine revs. While taxying towards the VTOL pad, the take-off checks are completed. The VTOL pad can be anything from an area of concrete to a 4·6 sq m (50 sq ft) planked aluminium pad. The aircraft is lined up pointing into wind on the pad and the final engine checks are carried out. Engine acceleration times are within limits, bleed air pressure from the engine to the reaction controls is correct, and permission to take off has been given. The nozzles are lowered rapidly to the hover position, the hand is moved to the throttle and full power applied–'slammed' is perhaps a more appropriate description, because it is important to lift off as rapidly as possible before the engine starts to ingest its own hot exhaust gases.

Despite the rapid engine acceleration and sudden increase in noise level, the take-off is a gentle affair and the aircraft rises slowly from the ground. With assistance from the autostabilisers the aircraft is controlled using the control column and rudders in exactly the same manner as in conventional flight: stick back, nose up, pick up a wing drop with ailerons, prevent the nose yawing with rudder. Once clear of the turbulent ground effect, a small reduction in power can be made to reduce the rate of climb and, as normal hovering height is reached, final adjustments to the throttle will settle the aircraft in a steady hover. Position over the pad is maintained by gentle adjustments to the aircraft's

attitude. The noise level is high and most pilots are initially very conscious of the fact that they are being supported by four columns of hot air, but that is all there is to hovering the Harrier.

Acceleration to wingborne flight is the next step. Having settled in a steady hover, power is increased by a couple of per cent, the nozzle lever is firmly grasped and slowly edged forward from the hover position. The aircraft starts to accelerate and, as speed increases and the wings generate lift, the nozzle lever can be moved progressively forward until conventional flying speeds are reached with the nozzles fully aft. Providing sideslip is minimised and the nozzles are not moved so rapidly that sink develops, the transition to wingborne flight is simple. It is essential to minimise sideslip between 30 and 90 knots because at these low airspeeds there is insufficient airflow over the fin to maintain directional stability. Intake momentum drag will cause any sideslip angle to increase, and if uncorrected with rudder the nose will continue to yaw out of wind. Because of wing sweepback and other design features contributing to lateral stability, the aircraft will roll away from the direction of sideslip. The aileron reaction controls may not be powerful enough to counteract this roll and control of the aircraft will be lost with disastrous results. However, the problem is minimised in the present Harrier by a sideforce indicator in the head-up display, rudder pedal shakers and an excellent yaw autostabiliser system.

Once fully wingborne, a normal circuit is flown at similar speeds to most jet fighter aircraft. The turn onto the landing approach is started at about 200 knots and the nozzles are lowered to 40 degrees. At this stage the pilot loses interest in airspeed and concentrates on maintaining a specific angle of attack by adjusting the throttle as necessary. Having descended to about 45 m (150 ft) about one mile out from the landing pad, the nozzles are moved to the hover position. The aircraft is flown in a conventional manner, again minimising sideslip in the critical airspeed band, and the throttle is used to control height. With the nozzles in the hover position, speed decreases rapidly with a matching loss of wing lift which, if the aircraft is not to lose height, must be matched by an increase in engine power to provide vertical thrust.

Towards the end of a well-judged decelerating transition the aircraft drifts gently towards the

Top: the Harrier GR Mark 3 introduced a laser rangefinder in a longer nose-cone and uprated engines.
Centre: a mixed formation of aircraft, comprising the AV-8A (nearest camera), the Harrier GR Mark 1 and the two-seat operational trainer (background).
Above: British Aerospace's company-owned demonstrator climbs from the 'ski jump', which will facilitate shipboard take-offs at higher weights

landing pad at 30 to 40 knots and height is controlled at 20–30 m (70–100 ft). Forward motion is stopped by raising the nose to deflect thrust forwards, or a more elegant way is to move the nozzle lever momentarily into the braking stop position to provide reverse thrust. Once a stable hover is achieved directly over the pad, a small power reduction initiates a rate of descent and it is then necessary to control the descent with small throttle adjustments. As soon as the mainwheels touch the landing pad the throttle is closed.

Partially jetborne short take-offs and landings are the normal method of operating when the Harrier's weight, including fuel and weapons load, is too high for VTOL. Having mastered the skills of the latter it is a simple step to progress to STOL. After carrying out the pre-take-off checks the aircraft is taxied on to the take-off strip. As before, the engine acceleration times are checked and the throttle is fully opened, but this time with the nozzles pointing aft. The acceleration is fierce and the airspeed indicator rapidly winds towards 110 knots, a typical precomputed take-off speed at high all-up weights. As 110 knots is reached, the nozzle lever is rotated smartly to the adjustable nozzle stop. This has been set to 50 degrees to enable selection without having to check the angle on the nozzle gauge in the cockpit. The aircraft leaps into the air and the nozzle lever is smoothly moved forward to accelerate to wingborne flight.

For the slow landing, a normal conventional circuit is flown to position for the start of the turn onto finals. The landing approach speed depends on the weight of the aircraft and the engine rpm used. The higher the revs the lower the airspeed, but the landing techniques used obviate the necessity to perform any approach speed calculations before take-off. The turn onto finals is started with the nozzles set at 20 degrees and revs are adjusted to maintain the optimum angle of attack. During the turn the nozzles are progressively lowered to 70 degrees, with appropriate throttle increases to maintain the angle of attack.

The hand is then moved from the throttle to the nozzle lever and the nozzles are used to control the angle of attack, and therefore the approach speed. If the angle of attack starts to rise above the optimum, which means the airspeed is decreasing, the nozzle lever is edged forward to increase airspeed and therefore wing lift. The nozzle lever is being used in exactly the same sense as a throttle during a landing approach in a conventional aircraft, but more anticipation is required. This technique is used throughout the remainder of the approach until the aircraft is just short of the point of touchdown. The hand is then transferred back to the throttle and a small power adjustment settles the aircraft on the ground. The throttle is closed immediately and the nozzles are moved to the braking position. The hand moves back to the throttle again to increase rpm to provide reverse thrust braking. The speed quickly reduces to 60 knots when the throttle is closed and the aircraft is brought to a stop using the toe brakes.

'I went up knowing a MiG-17 couldn't climb with a Phantom and I knew that their missiles wouldn't be effective.'
Lt Cdr R. Cunningham USN

McDonnell F-4 Phantom

Lieutenant Randall H. Cunningham was the only US Navy fighter pilot to achieve ace status in the Vietnam War, sharing this honour with his Radar Intercept Officer Lieutenant (junior grade) William P. Driscoll. Cunningham (centre) is pictured aboard the carrier USS Constellation (CVA-64), while describing his combats of 10 May 1972 to his squadronmates in VF-96, the Fighting Falcons. On that day Cunningham and Driscoll downed three North Vietnamese fighters and thus achieved the five victories needed to qualify as aces. All Randy Cunningham's kills were scored while flying the McDonnell Douglas F-4J Phantom and all were shared with Willie Driscoll

The McDonnell Douglas F-4 Phantom II is 'one of the most honest aeroplanes in the world,' according to Lieutenant Commander Randall 'Duke' Cunningham. The 37-year-old US Navy pilot draws his authority on the subject from over 2,000 flight hours and over 500 aircraft carrier landings in the F-4 series–in addition to the fact that he became the first American to shoot down five enemy MiG fighters during the Vietnam War.

Commander Cunningham noted that 'the F-4 will almost "talk" to a pilot. She will tell you every move she's going to make. During high-speed aerial combat you encounter tremendous positive and negative gravitational forces, especially when pulling up or around to get into a firing position. In the F-4, when you pull behind your adversary at five, six or seven 'g's, she will buffet as a way of telling you that if you pull any harder, she will

"depart" into a spin, which puts you at a great disadvantage.

'You might need just half a g more to pull to a shot solution and if you ignore the warning signs and chance it, she will "depart" on you. But the F-4 is as forgiving as she is honest. She won't throw you into a violent spin that makes the aeroplane completely uncontrollable. All you have to do is neutralise the controls and she will come right out of the spin. In fact, you have to hold pro-spin controls in to get the F-4 to spin. A lot of aeroplanes won't do that, however. They will spin you right into the ground. The MiG-19, for example, gets into a spin and it just doesn't come out.

'The F-4 is good at fast speeds, but she also handles well in the low-speed range. Of course, in combat it's not a good idea to slow down on your opponent, because even though you're beating him,

283

his wingman–or wingmen–will come in and blow your smoke away. So you want to be careful about keeping your energy [speed] up. But the F-4 will stay slow and be very controllable at slow airspeeds, if you know how to handle it. You have to move the stick around with a feather-light touch and just barely use the rudders. At slow speeds you use mostly the "back" stick and no ailerons, because if you pop a spoiler up on one side, you'll depart that wing and go into a spin. And if you're slow, that's what your opponent is waiting for. When your nose is down, you increase your speed and go out in front–and the guy in front loses in a slow-speed fight.'

The McDonnell Douglas F-4 Phantom II series did not lose many dogfights during almost eight years of aerial conflict over Vietnam. The first MiG kills of the war took place on 17 June 1965, when two F-4Bs from Navy fighter squadron VF-21 deployed aboard USS *Midway* (CVA-41) bagged two MiG-17s near Gen Phu in North Vietnam. Navy F-4 aircrews, including 'Duke' Cunningham and his radar intercept officer (RIO), Lieutenant William Driscoll, accounted for a total of 38 MiG

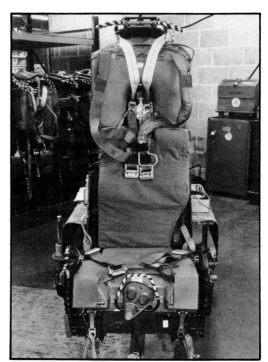

Above right: both the pilot's and RIO's cockpits in the Phantom were fitted with rocket-assisted ejection seats. Thus a crew could successfully eject from a crippled aircraft at sea level, for example, if the F-4 crashed during a catapult launch. Ejection was initiated by pulling the two handles at the top of the seat, which ensured that the crew member was in the correct posture and so likely to escape injury. An emergency lever between the crewman's legs, at the base of the seat, could be used for the same purpose, but the airman could suffer spinal injury during the ejection. Cunningham and Driscoll were forced to eject at the end of their successful sortie on 10 May, when their Phantom was severely damaged by a surface-to-air missile.
Right: an artist's impression of Randy Cunningham and Willie Driscoll's F-4J on 10 May 1972

fighters. US Air Force F-4 crews shot down 108 enemy MiGs.

Although the F-4 became the 'MiG Killer' of Vietnam, it began its service life not as a fighter but as an attack aircraft. On 18 October 1954, the US Navy authorised the McDonnell Aircraft Company to begin work on a single-seat, twin-engined attack aircraft. It was to be designated the AH-1, which, under the Navy identification system then in use, denoted it was to be the first variant of the first attack aircraft produced for McDonnell for the Navy.

A year later, however, the role was changed from that of cannon-firing attack aircraft to missile-equipped, long-range, high-altitude interceptor. The projected Soviet threat at that time was a fleet of conventional bombers protected by fighter escorts. The McDonnell-designed Navy interceptor was to be developed as a non-dogfighting, missile-

carrying weapons platform capable of encountering and destroying the Soviet bombers and their escorts.

By the time the prototype made its first flight, on 27 May 1958, the aircraft's primary mission had become all-weather fleet air defence. It was designated F4H-1–the first variant of the fourth fighter aircraft produced by McDonnell for the Navy. The new aircraft was named Phantom II, marking it as the supersonic successor to McDonnell's first carrier-based jet fighter, the FH-1 Phantom of the mid-1940s. The F4H-1 was selected instead of its competitor, the Chance Vought F8U-3, an improved version of the single-seat Crusader.

Since the Phantom II also retained its attack capability, it was a logical choice for subsequent selection by the US Air Force's Tactical Air Command (TAC). In 1962, the Air Force initiated orders for two variants: the F-110A fighter and the RF-110A reconnaissance version of the Phantom

Above left: the pilot's instrument display in the Phantom includes a radar scope mounted centrally at the top of the panel, with flight instruments below it. Fuel and engine gauges are to the right, while on the left is a missile status panel, with missile controls beneath it. The F-4 can carry four Sparrow radar-guided missiles and four infra-red Sidewinders. It is necessary for the RIO to lock the radar onto a target before the Sparrow can be fired, whereas the Sidewinder is released when a sound signal warns the pilot that the missile has acquired a heat source on which to home.
Above far left and left: the view forward from the F-4's rear cockpit is minimal, as its occupant's primary duties are navigation and operating the radar. However, during close-range, air-to-air combats in Vietnam, the radar intercept officer often acted as rear lookout

II. However, with the integration of US Navy and Air Force designation systems in September 1962, both services' Phantoms were known as F-4 aircraft.

By the time of the Tonkin Gulf incident on 2 August 1964, when US warships were attacked by North Vietnamese surface craft, both the Navy and Air Force were completely operational with the F-4. Thus, when American involvement in Vietnam was stepped up, the Phantom II became an important part of US air superiority.

Early in the Vietnam conflict, the F-4 series was most effective as a weapons delivery system. F-4 pilots had been trained in the interceptor role, with little attention to air combat manoeuvres. The air war in Vietnam did not, however, become a 'push-button war', as the purely missile advocates proposed. Instead, individual air combat over southeast Asia developed along the lines of the encounters experienced during World War I, one aeroplane versus another, with victory going to the pilot who made the best use of his aircraft and weapons.

In this environment, the 1950s-vintage MiG-17 could become a formidable opponent of the F-4, as could the MiG-19, which was also older and less sophisticated than the F-4. Cunningham said: 'The MiG drivers were out-manoeuvring our missiles and our aeroplanes. A study of those early encounters revealed that the F-4 was heavier and less man-oeuvrable than the MiG series. The Phantom wouldn't out-turn the MiG series at speeds below 420 knots and its weapons just wouldn't hack the turns and the g-loads that the MiG could pull to defeat them. As a result of that study, the Navy established its Fighter Weapons School to train pilots in air-to-air combat. There we were taught how to fight and survive in the air, much of which was based on the 'dicta' set down by Oswald Boelcke, the German ace of World War I.

'At the Navy Fighter Weapons School, we would "fight" dissimilar aircraft. Thus, we would be sent up in Phantoms to engage the Douglas A-4 Skyhawk, which could simulate the MiG-17. It was small, difficult to see, could out-turn the Phantom and had a lot of energy. Even though the Phantom was considered vastly superior to the A-4 in that one-on-one scenario, it took a lot of practice to score a kill.

'We flew the F-4 against the Northrop F-5E, which simulated the MiG-21. The F-5E is highly manoeuvrable and, in fact, at lower speeds it's better than the MiG-21. Aerial tactics is strictly a game of relative motion and time distance problems. The question is: "Can I get to a certain position to

the McDonnell Douglas F-4J, powered by two General Electric J79-GE-10 engines each developing 8,100 kg (17,900 lb) static thrust, here's how he rated his opponents. MiG-17: 'Easily the best-turning of the Soviet-built jet fighters used in Vietnam, the MiG-17 was supposed to be a 'guns only' aeroplane. It was armed with a 23 mm and a 37 mm gun and sometimes an Atoll heat-seeking missile. The MiG-17 can turn at 19 degrees per second, versus a rate of 11·5 degrees per second for the F-4. The MiG-17 pilots were trained to stay down near the treetops and to turn and fight on their own terms. By staying low, against the clutter of the trees, they were difficult to pick up on the pulse-only radar used by the F-4B; it took the pulse-doppler radar in the F-4J to pick them up. If I were an enemy pilot and I wanted to survive against an F-4, I would fly the MiG-17. I'd also use a MiG-17 if I wanted to fight a Phantom with a fairly inexperienced pilot who would try to stay in on the turns. One good tight turn and he'd be dead.'

MiG-19: 'It's also a good aeroplane and it, too, will out-turn a Phantom at slower speeds. It has afterburning engines which give it a lot of energy and it has good firepower, but the MiG-19 has very limited fuel and at low speeds it is very hard to control. However, I understand that the Chinese-built version is supposed to manoeuvre well at slow airspeeds.'

MiG-21: 'The MiG-21 pilots were primarily trained for interceptor missions. They were directed by ground controllers to come in at supersonic speeds – often Mach 1·6 or 1·7 – behind our forces. After they fired their heat-seeking missiles, the MiG-21 drivers would dive for the deck and run. That was their tactic and that's the way they knocked down a lot of our aeroplanes. They wouldn't engage in dogfighting. Although the MiG-21 was a newer aeroplane, it did not see much air-to-air combat because of the tactical restrictions imposed on it. Quite often, in fact, the MiG-21s were lost if we jammed their communications and broke the link to their ground controllers.

'In air-to-air combat, the MiG-21's delta wing configuration allows it to turn very well, but the induced drag of that form "bleeds" energy rapidly. When a MiG-21 pilot turns his aeroplane, it costs him. So the trick is to try to manoeuvre the MiG-21 down to an altitude more favourable to the F-4 – usually below 20,000 feet. That's where the Phantom really performs well with its wing; it will turn and accelerate well. But if you get above 20,000 feet and tangle with a MiG-21, he'll chew you to pieces because of the advantages of his wing and his speed.'

US Air Force F-4 pilots have conceded that one of the weak points of their air combat training was the use of other F-4 aircraft to simulate enemy fighters. Such training did not adequately prepare them for encounters with the older, but slower and tighter-turning MiG series aircraft. As Lieutenant Commander Randy Cunningham points out, the Navy's policy of using various types of aircraft for air combat manoeuvring prepared carrier-based F-4 pilots for a wider range of circumstances which could occur in aerial engagements with the enemy. The Air Force has since begun to train its fighter pilots to engage a variety of aircraft types.

'I've flamed out both engines a couple of times,'

Above: the F-4J flown by Randy Cunningham on 10 May was in fact assigned to the commander of Air Wing 9. This is denoted by the '00' marking at the top of the rudder and by the coloured stars on the fuselage side.
Left: Cunningham and Driscoll disembark from a Boeing-Vertol CH-46 after their rescue from the Gulf of Tonkin on 10 May.
Below: a MiG-21 identified as the mount of Colonel Toon, the North Vietnamese ace who became Cunningham's fifth victim. Toon was flying a MiG-17 when he was shot down

kill the enemy before his wingman can get to me?" In learning to apply this rule to our encounters with the F-5E, we were better-prepared to meet the MiG-21 in combat. It becomes especially important in multiple tactics, when you've got someone shooting at you and you have to take someone else off your wingman's tail; you look to see whether his relative motion can bring him into range faster than you can get into a range to shoot at your opponent.'

'Duke' Cunningham is quick to point out that 'nothing is true in tactics, because there are too many variables.' However, by and large, his F-4 experiences in combat qualify him to make certain judgements about his adversaries. Compared to

McDONNELL F-4 PHANTOM

Cunningham noted as an example of the ways he learned to cope with different air combat situations, 'but it was because I put the aeroplane in a vertical climb and reduced power to the extent that I achieved zero airspeed. I could do that because I had forced the F-5E chasing me to bleed energy to the point where he couldn't zoom with me in the vertical.'

The Navy pilot explained that an aircraft in flight has one g of gravity on it, 'but as you begin to turn and manoeuvre, the aircraft bleeds off energy due to induced drag. When you "unload" or "zero g" an aeroplane, you lose all of the induced drag. If you 'unload' it and go purely ballistic, the aircraft accelerates efficiently. The point to remember in combat is that you can unload the aeroplane by going up vertically, as well as horizontally.

'Many people didn't realize that flying an aeroplane is three-dimensional. I could force my opponent to over-speed in a purely vertical plane, just as I can in a horizontal plane. Or, I can unload the aeroplane and go straight up, like a rocket and gain the advantage. If I stand the aeroplane on its tail and unload it, I can top-out a lot higher than if I pulled a lot of g going vertical.

'When I'm going vertically and my opponent drops off, I'll kick rudder and drop down on him. But before you can go vertical, you have to judge his energy level. If you go pure vertical, thinking he's going to drop off, and you misjudge his energy level, you increase his kill probability as airspeeds dissipate . . . he can either top-out above you and come down, or he can use his airspeed to manoeuvre below you.'

Cunningham's first victory marked the end of a long period of security for North Vietnamese fighter pilots. That period began after 28 March 1970, when Lieutenants Jerry Beaulier and Steve Barkley in an F-4J of VF-142, then deployed aboard USS *Constellation*, shot down a MiG-21. Ironically, the same type of enemy jet fighter was destroyed when the 'safe period' ended on 19 January 1972, when Randy Cunningham and Willie Driscoll shot down their first MiG.

At that time US President Johnson's bombing halt was in effect and American combat aircraft were expressly ordered not to hit targets in North Vietnam. As time wore on, however, and as American aircraft operating near North Vietnam continued to draw enemy fire, that policy was relaxed slightly. US aircraft could return fire at specific enemy anti-aircraft or missile sites that had opened up on them during their missions. To give effect to such 'protective reaction' strikes, American commanders ensured that there were enough combat-ready aircraft in the air to deal adequately with any hostile fire originating in North Vietnam.

Left: with braking parachute deployed, this F-4J of VX-4 completes its landing run. This unit is a test squadron, which is based at Naval Air Station Point Mugu, California, and undertakes missile development work.
Below: a United States Air Force F-4D tucks up its undercarriage on take-off. This version of the Phantom is specially equipped for ground attack

McDONNELL F-4 PHANTOM

On 19 January 1972, Carrier Air Wing 9 aircraft formed part of a large strike force over Laos, while unarmed reconnaissance aircraft, which were allowed to overfly North Vietnam, performed a mission over the MiG-21 airfield at Quang Lang. Earlier, US Boeing B-52s over Laos had been attacked by fighters from Quang Lang, which was heavily fortified. The extent of that defence was evident some distance from the airfield, as noted by Randy Cunningham and his wingman, Lieutenant Brian Grant and his RIO, Lieutenant Jerry Sullivan.

After drawing considerable automatic anti-aircraft (AAA) and surface-to-air missile (SAM) fire from the Quang Lang area, Cunningham and Grant were ordered to fly a MiG Combat Air Patrol (MiG CAP) in that region. 'Our job was to keep any MiGs off the strike force,' Cunningham recalls, 'but on our way into and over the airfield, 17 SAMs were fired at us – in pairs. You can't do much in the way of looking for MiGs when you're dodging all of those SAMs.

'I was just coming out of my third SAM break, going down almost purely vertical, trying to get energy, when I looked up and saw a couple of glints. I knew there weren't supposed to be any aeroplanes up there, north of Quang Lang, because all of the strike force was behind me. I thought they might have been [Vought] A-7s, off-target and going after some SAM sites. But I saw a glow at their tailpipes and A-7s don't have afterburners. You never think you're going to see a MiG because everyone has told you that you won't. So I put my nose toward the glint and pressed on.

'Two days before that, our sister squadron, VF-92, had sounded a MiG call for what turned out

Left: operating high-performance jets from an aircraft carrier is a potentially-hazardous business. The F-4J pictured has missed engaging the arrestor wires with its tailhook and has been brought to a halt in the crash barrier of USS America (CVA-66) during 1970 combat operations in the Gulf of Tonkin. Below left: an F-4J of VF-151 is directed forward to the port catapult of USS Midway (CVA-41). Below: three of VF-96's sister units in Carrier Air Wing 9 are represented in this photograph taken aboard USS Constellation on 9 May 1972. The F-4J leaving the catapult is from VF-92, while the LTV A-7E light attack aircraft in the foreground belong to VA-146 and VA-147

to be one of our own RA-5 Vigilantes . . . There was no way that I was going to send a false MiG call and endure the torment those two went through. So I pressed on until I got within visual range of the aircraft I had spotted. Coming down on them, I had a perfect plan view of the two aircraft. I saw two of the prettiest silver delta-wing aircraft I had ever seen. I pressed down on them. One was 700 to 800 feet above the trees and his wingman was on his starboard side, slightly stepped up. I came down behind the one on the port side . . .'

The MiG-21 pilot must have seen the American F-4 just as the Sidewinder missile fired because he executed a very hard 'break' turn to the right. The missile was unable to sustain the hard turn and exploded beneath the MiG. As the MiG pilot continued his roll to the right, Randy Cunningham started a lag pursuit roll to the left, half expecting the other MiG-21 to come after him. But, he recalled, at the first sign of trouble the second MiG 'just ran off and left his wingman'.

Cunningham and Driscoll then came out of the roll and were back behind the first delta-wing MiG. They fired a second Sidewinder, which, Cunningham noted, 'just took off his whole tail. The aeroplane pitched, head over heels, and came down near a village.' The Navy F-4J went after the second MiG-21 and got a radar lock-on. The pilot fired a Sparrow missile, but a malfunction in the firing mechanism prevented the missile from going after its intended target. However, that did not prevent nearly the entire crew of the aircraft carrier from creating a mob scene after Cunningham and Driscoll returned to USS *Constellation*.

Following USS *Constellation*'s unexpected return to the combat zone, Randy Cunningham and his wingman, Brian Grant, were on a MiG CAP mission on 8 May when the North Vietnamese opened up with SAMs. Cunningham and Grant were to precede a strike group, clear the area of MiGs and let the Force CAP protect the bombers. However, they remained in the area as the strike group approached and were soon informed by their controllers that enemy fighters were quickly approaching them.

On the controller's signal Grant called for a turn in place, which he and 'Duke' Cunningham quickly executed. As they came out of the manoeuvre, however, Cunningham was horrified to see a MiG-17 appear at the 7 o'clock position, slightly to the left of Grant's tail. Cunningham informed Grant of his predicament and told him to jettison his centreline fuel tank to eliminate drag during the necessary evasive manoeuvres to follow. 'The MiG driver must have been last in his class in aerial gunnery', Cunningham recalls.

The Navy had developed several special disengagement manoeuvres, details of which are still classified by the US Government. Hence, Cunningham instructed his wingman: 'Use the MiG-17 disengagement manoeuvre, but don't use negative 'g's because you'll push into his line of fire.'

Grant successfully completed the disengagement manoeuvre. Meanwhile, Cunningham came in on the swept-wing MiG-17 for a high-angle attack and saw the North Vietnamese pilot launch an Atoll heat-seeking missile toward Grant's F-4. Cunningham ordered Grant to break to the left to avoid

the missile and subsequently fired one of his Sidewinders at the MiG, which was forced to turn into the missile to keep from being hit.

As Cunningham began the next attack, his RIO, Willie Driscoll, warned him of two additional MiG-17s passing overhead in the opposite direction. The two bandits were initially thought to be well out of range, but they turned sharply and began making a run from behind the Cunningham-Driscoll F-4. Although slightly out of range, one MiG-17 began firing at the Americans.

Cunningham now faced the tough decision of whether to take evasive action to save himself or to press on and try to get the MiG still hanging onto Brian Grant's tail. The MiG pilot abruptly made the decision easier. He broke off and turned his tail to Cunningham and Driscoll. 'I couldn't believe it', Cunningham remembers. 'At first I thought he had turned toward me, because first I saw a perfect plan view, then I saw just a dot, which at that distance could have been either his nose or his tail. And he had guns, so he could have made a run at me. In an instant I realised what had happened, so I fired a second Sidewinder, which went right up his tailpipe and blew his tail off.'

Having eliminated the danger to his wingman, Cunningham then executed the MiG-17 disengagement manoeuvre, rolled and unloaded his F-4. In the process, he instructed Brian Grant to go vertical, as he hoped to entice the two remaining MiG-17s into following him into a prearranged manoeuvre that allowed Grant to shoot at least one of his pursuers down.

Unfortunately, the MiGs managed to get back on his tail and begin closing in on Cunningham, as he had lost considerable energy in his turns. In desperation, the American rolled his aeroplane 120 degrees, and pulled back on the control column with all his might. He put a 12-g strain on the F-4 that broke the wing panels and came back so close to one of his adversaries that he almost hit him. Then, miraculously, Cunningham flew into a cloud bank. The two F-4s agreed to rendezvous above the clouds and both went into vertical climbs. 'I went up knowing a MiG-17 couldn't climb with a Phantom,' Cunningham recollects, 'and I knew that their missiles wouldn't be effective. I was heading right for the sun and if they fired a missile at me, it would seek the greatest heat source, which is the sun. Sure enough, they did come up after me out of the clouds. But then Brian rolled in on them and when they saw him they did a cross turn and went right back down into the clouds. We went back into the clouds to try to find them, but our radar didn't pick them up.'

US Navy fighter squadron VF-96 has an illustrious history which goes back to the Korean War of the early 1950s, when it was the activated Reserve squadron VF-791. However, there is no doubt that the most memorable day in the squadron's nearly three decades of service was 10 May 1972. During some of the heaviest air fighting of the Vietnam War, VF-96 brought down a total of six MiG fighters on that day alone. Lieutenants Matt Connelly and Tom Blonski in one F-4J nailed two MiG-17s, Lieutenants Steve Shoemaker and Keith Crenshaw in another F-4J shot down a MiG-17 and, in one of the hardest-fought aerial encounters

Randy Cunningham and Willie Driscoll pose jubilantly with an F-4 Phantom. Cunningham and his fellow fighter pilots in the US Navy had the advantage of a thorough training in air combat manoeuvres at the Navy Fighter Weapons School before meeting the North Vietnamese in combat. This training pitted the F-4 against aircraft of similar characteristics to those flown by the North Vietnamese

of the war, Randy Cunningham and Willie Driscoll bagged three MiG-17s.

Cunningham and Driscoll were part of the Force CAP that day, escorting a strike mission against the railyards at Haiphong, south-east of Hanoi. All of the Navy aircraft were equipped with bombs and the entire North Vietnamese air defence command was ready for them. Cunningham and his wingman, Brian Grant, unloaded their bombs and began evading SAMs when they received word that all of the fighter bases surrounding the enemy capital were sending up everything they had: MiG-17s, MiG-19s and MiG-21s.

As in the engagement two days before, Cunningham soon found himself trailed by two MiG-17s. He took a chance and 'broke' into them, which caused one North Vietnamese jet to overshoot. Cunningham seized the advantage and set a Sidewinder streaking after him; the MIG blew up, becoming victory number three.

Victory number four came a short time later when Cunningham and Driscoll were being chased by four MiGs while they went after a MiG-17 that was closing in on the squadron executive officer, Commander Dwight Timm, and his RIO, Jim Fox. Intent on saving his superior's life, 'Duke' Cunningham disregarded the four MiG-17s firing at him—and a pair of MiG-19s diving from directly overhead—and called for Commander Timm to manoeuvre his opponent so as to place the MiG's tail toward Cunningham's F-4. That done, Cunningham fired a Sidewinder, which destroyed the enemy fighter. For that action, Cunningham was nominated for the Medal of Honour, America's highest award for valour. Fierce inter-service rivalry for such awards, however, edged Cunningham out of the top honour. He received the Navy Cross, the second highest award.

By the end of that encounter, all of the other MiG activity was off to the east. Cunningham headed in that direction, but on the way he saw a MiG-17 heading directly toward him. Wanting to come as close as possible, to keep the more manoeuvrable adversary from out-turning him, Cunningham headed right for the MiG-17, but the North Vietnamese pilot did not break away as expected. Instead, he opened fire, forcing Cunningham to pull up. This MiG pilot's unusual skill and daring soon made it apparent that he was no average 'gomer', the pejorative label applied to all North Vietnamese. Indeed, it was subsequently learned that 'Duke'

Cunningham's final opponent was Colonel Toon, the highest-scoring North Vietnamese fighter ace, who was hoping to make the Cunningham-Driscoll F-4J his 14th kill.

The American ace remembers. 'I went pure vertical and looked over the corner of my ejection seat, expecting to see him two miles away and running. I was going to chase him and kill him. Instead, there looking at me—canopy to canopy—was a figure wearing little gomer goggles, a gomer cloth helmet and a white scarf. He stayed right with me, but I had more speed than he did, so I out-zoomed him.'

However, the North Vietnamese ace quickly manoeuvred onto Cunningham's six o'clock position, directly behind the F-4. Now all of Cunnigham's long hours of air combat manoeuvre training would come into play, as he and his adversary jockeyed for position. Cunningham used the F-4's speed and Colonel Toon used the MiG-17's manoeuvrability and tight-turning capability. Each was looking for the other to make the one fatal mistake which would allow a decisive shot.

At one point, Cunningham notes, 'I got my nose on his tailpipe and started to come down. I could see him sitting in the cockpit, just looking back at me and waiting. But he was smart. He waited until I committed my nose, then he broke up and in to me and came right around to my seven o'clock position.' The battle continued in a series of rolling scissors manoeuvres, in which the advantage shifted from the American to the North Vietnamese and back several times. Finally, the two aircraft were making another canopy-to-canopy pass, with Toon's nose pointed just ahead of Cunningham's F-4. The Navy ace then disregarded the basic rule of not trying to fight a MiG-17 at slow speed. He idled the engine and put out his speed brakes to pull down behind, as the MiG-17 went right out in front of him.

Cunningham had a clear view of his opponent's tailpipe but was too close to fire a missile. It was only when both aircraft struggled to unload that Colonel Toon pulled up too hard and departed his aircraft. 'I stood on the port rudder, at very slow air speed', Cunningham remembers, 'I put my nose on him and eased the trigger. A missile went off—whoosh!—and it looked like it blew up alongside him. I followed him down and noticed that a fire erupted in his aeroplane.'

Four additional MiG-17s came down on Cunningham and Driscoll, and they had to fight their way out of North Vietnam. On the way to the coast, however, their F-4J was hit by a SAM and caught fire. Vowing never to be taken prisoner, 'Duke' Cunningham managed to ride the stricken Phantom until the Gulf of Tonkin was in sight. Finally, when the aircraft was virtually uncontrollable—the entire tail had burned away—Cunningham and Driscoll ejected and parachuted into the murky waters below them.

The rest of Carrier Air Wing 9 fought off North Vietnamese torpedo boats and other craft attempting to seize the downed Phantom crew. Finally a rescue helicopter brought them to safety. Randy Cunningham and Willie Driscoll survived to become legendary characters of the Vietnam air war—thanks to superior airmanship and the McDonnell Douglas F-4J Phantom II.

'After 11 minutes cruising, the surface temperature stabilises between 280 and 300 degrees centigrade . . . causing the aircraft to stretch by 11 inches.'

Lockheed SR-71

Taxying in after another mission in the stratosphere, the SR-71 is literally 'too hot to handle', having endured temperatures of around 300 degrees centigrade during its flight. The intense heat causes the aircraft to stretch, as well as being responsible for other changes to the aircraft's surface

'I offered any employee fifty dollars if he could find anything simple about that project,' says Clarence L. 'Kelly' Johnson, 'and I still have that fifty dollars.' The 'project' was the Lockheed SR-71 Blackbird, which Kelly Johnson's Burbank-based 'Skunk Works' design team created in such secrecy that few people outside the team of 137 – not even equipment and materials suppliers – knew anything about the CIA-funded aircraft.

The original contract was placed in 1959 for the development of a surveillance aircraft capable of overflying Communist countries at great height and at speeds of not less than Mach 3. This meant that components and materials had first to be developed which could operate in temperatures in excess of 300 degrees centigrade. Scarcely a single part of the A-11, as the SR-71 was then designated, could be bought 'off the shelf', hence Kelly Johnson's less-than-generous offer. Special titanium alloys were developed with tensile strengths of up to 200,000 psi. The Pratt & Whitney J58 engines, which were developed especially for the A-11, needed special fuel which would serve as a heat-sink for excess heat in electronics and other systems.

All this innovation resulted in an aeroplane quite unlike any other, both in appearance and performance. The SR-71 two-seater is as long as a Boeing 727 airliner, with a needle-nosed fuselage

shaped like a power boat's hull, of convex, diamond-shaped cross section, a delta wing, and two massive engine nacelles topped off with inward-canted fins. The Blackbird, which is actually painted a very dark blue, is arguably a most menacing-looking aircraft, and yet it fulfills a totally non-aggressive role.

If designing and building the SR-71 was a demanding and unique task, then flying the aircraft is even more so. The Blackbirds, of which 24 are believed to have been built, are operated by the United States Air Force 9th Strategic Reconnaissance Wing from Beale Air Force Base, near Marysville in California's Sacramento Valley. Flight crews consist of the pilot and a reconnaissance systems officer (RSO). They are volunteers, mostly captains, majors and colonels, each with a minimum of 1,500 command hours on jets and 2,500–3,500 hours total time, and aged between 27 and 33 years. The 9th SRW is an elitist outfit; aspiring crew members undergo a stringent screening process during which their professional and medical records are reviewed and the men are given the same demanding physical examinations used for astronauts. Medical and personnel evaluation boards pass on their recommendations to the 9th's commander, who personally interviews each man. Once selected, potential SR-71 crewmen begin training on Northrop T 38s, whose handling characteristics are basically similar to the Blackbird's. After simulator training a pilot makes five transition flights in a unique two-pilot training SR-71B before soloing with his RSO. After a further five flights together the pilot/RSO team are certified 'mission ready'.

A typical mission from Beale AFB begins two days before take-off time, when pilot and RSO begin pre-flight briefings and planning. On actual flight day they report to the unit's Physiological Support Division – much as manned space pro-gramme personnel do – for a specially-formulated, high-protein, low-residue meal, usually steak and eggs, as some flights last ten hours or more. Then it is time for a one-hour physical check before a final briefing on the expected weather and mission characteristics.

Another 20 minutes is set aside for donning their 'silver tuxedos' – the astronaut-style suits and hel-mets which require three helpers apiece to get into, and which provide life support should a de-compression occur or ejection become necessary at the Blackbird's stratospheric operating altitudes. Once kitted out, the suits are checked for leaks by blowing up, and the crew plug into their portable

air-conditioning units for the van ride out to the flight line. 'We don't do a walkround check. These aeroplanes are the best maintained in the world; it's all done before we get there', explained Major Jim Sullivan. He was the SR-71 pilot who flew nonstop from California to the Farnborough Air Show in 1974, covering the 5,600 km (3,490 mile) New York-London sector in 115 minutes and 42 seconds at an average speed of 2,924 km/h (1,817 mph), reaching Amsterdam before the Black-bird had slowed down sufficiently to turn around for the let-down to Farnborough.

Once aboard the SR-71 the pilot and his RSO sit high atop the fuselage, every inch of which is packed with systems and fuel – 36,000 kg (80,000 lb) of a special, low-vapour-pressure hydrocarbon derivative called JP-7 which only the Blackbird uses to feed its two 13,600 kg (30,000 lb) thrust J58s designed to operate constantly on full afterburner. When it sits in the California sunshine, the SR-71 continually 'bleeds' fuel, for its tanks are porous when unheated and unpressurised. Thus take-off delays are kept to a minimum. Once internal checks have been completed, the J58s are turned over by a directly-coupled bank of three Chrysler V8 automobile engines.

Once on Beale's runway, power is brought up to full afterburner thrust; the Blackbird rolls for a mile and passes 200 knots before lifting off. Its radar-vectored climb through special corridors approved by the Federal Aviation Administration to keep its supersonic 'footprint' clear of areas of dense population finishes at a standard operational altitude of 24,000 m (80,000 ft) – nearly six miles above the highest flying commercial jet airliners. At that altitude the SR-71 zips along at Mach 3+ or 3,200 km/h (2,000 mph).

After 11 minutes' cruising, the surface tempera-ture stabilises between 280 and 300 degrees centi-grade, hotter than a domestic oven, imposing thermal stresses on the structure and causing the aircraft to 'stretch' by 11 inches. The wing skins crinkle with the intense heat, forming intentional chordwise corrugations specifically devised by Lockheed to stay exactly aligned with the airflow. The blue-black paint, which adds about 27 kg (60 lb) to the Blackbird's weight, helps reduce skin temperatures by about 50 degrees fahrenheit, and

Above: four elevons on the SR-71's wing trailing edge, two inboard and two outboard of the engine nacelles, control pitch and roll.

Left: an SR-71, flown from Beale AFB, California by Major J. Sullivan, lets down at Farnborough, England.

Below left: advanced in every respect of its design, the SR-71 is the most sophisticated aircraft to have flown, yet it is aerodynamically simple. The fuselage has a convex diamond cross-section into which the leading edges of the delta wing are merged, extending to needle nose. These features provide as much lift and as little drag as possible at Mach 3.

Below: the Pratt & Whitney J58 turbojets of the SR-71 each develop 13,835 kg (32,500 lb) static thrust with afterburner; optimum performance is maintained by computer

must be protected on the ground from scuffing or marking which could destroy its heat-absorbing qualities. Special mats are placed over the structure during servicing and ground crews wear foot-muffs when walking on the aeroplane.

Thirty yards behind the cockpit, the J58 engines blast the SR-71's tailpipes not to red, or even orange heat, but literally white hot. Stability is monitored and constantly adjusted by automatic on-board Control Configured Vehicle (CCV) systems, with astro-inertial navigation for precise positioning – absolutely vital in an aircraft travelling more than half a mile every second.

After one hour's flight at over Mach 3, the Blackbird's fuel is almost gone, and the aircraft must meet up with one of the special JP-7-carrying Boeing KC-135Q tankers which the Strategic Air Command deploys along routes used by the SR-71s. A night refuelling is especially dramatic, 'filling your fishbowl visor with so many disco-show coloured lights that some pilots have had to fight strong sensations of vertigo', one crewman

reported. With frequent air-to-air refuelling the Blackbird has truly global range, and is known to have made flights over Communist China, the Middle East and Japan from California.

At an altitude of 24km (15 miles) the SR-71's flight is calm and undisturbed. It reigns supreme at that altitude, save for meteorological balloons, for which crews must constantly be vigilant. Optimum performance from the J58 engines is maintained by computer, which adjusts the inlet 'shock spikes' which protrude from the nacelles, gradually retracting them from the fully-forwarded position at Mach 1.6 to the fully-retracted position at Mach 3. The intakes are very sensitive to exact alignment of airflow, so that high-speed manoeuvres particularly in yaw must be very smooth to prevent an 'inlet unstart' which causes the engine to flame-out and suddenly expel its shock-wave. Then, said one SR-71 pilot, 'the aircraft attempts to swap ends at high supersonic speeds. This violent, mind-boggling experience has been described as like having a mid-air collision. Until the inlet is restarted, the

pilot's head is sometimes bounced from one side of the canopy to the other and his eyeballs touch all their limit switches.'

Aerodynamically the otherwise-complex SR-71 is simple. The leading edge of the wing extends right to the nose, forming a chine which acts like a canard surface and gives little drag and much lift at Mach 3, while contributing to directional stability. Four elevons command all pitch and roll movements via hydraulic power units, with no separate elevators and ailerons, and the canted fins deflect through 20 degrees left or right – either individually or together – to act as rudders.

While the pilot is flying the systems, his RSO is busy behind him with his equipment – astro-inertial navigation, optical cameras, infra-red Linescan and SLAR (sideways-looking airborne radar), which can survey an incredible 260,000 sq km (100,000 square miles) of the earth's surface each hour and see things the human eye might miss from 15 m (50 ft). All the time the Blackbird is unseen and unheard, for above 15,000 m (50,000 ft) they hardly ever leave contrails.

At the end of the flight there is one last idiosyncrasy peculiar to the Blackbird – after landing, groundcrews must be careful not to touch the aircraft's surfaces for at least half an hour while the intense heat dissipates. The SR-71 is a 'hot ship' indeed and looks set to retain the honour of being the USAF's fastest aircraft for some time to come.

Above: an SR-71 leaves the ground after a take-off run of around one mile. Delays on the ground are kept to a minimum, as the Blackbird's tanks bleed JP-7 fuel when unheated and unpressurised. A specially-equipped squadron of JP-7-carrying Boeing KC-135 Stratotankers serves the 9th SRW's refuelling needs.
Below: developed from the projected YF-12A interceptor, the SR-71 entered USAF service in early 1966. The type succeeded such diverse types as the Boeing RB-47 Stratojets and sailplane-like Lockheed U-2

'At airshows the crowds are often treated to the spectacle of an Eagle pointing its nose vertically upwards and climbing away until out of sight even in a clear blue sky.'

McDonnell Douglas F-15 Eagle

An F-15 Eagle in service with the Israeli air force pulls up into a climb with its afterburner lit. Each of the Eagle's F-100 turbofans can develop 11,349 kg (25,000 lb) of thrust with afterburning. This gives the fighter tremendous reserves of power, which can be used either to sustain high G manoeuvres, or to accelerate away from an opponent

The F-15 Eagle is the US Air Force's standard air superiority fighter and was first developed to deal with the Soviet high-performance MiG-25. A typical mission in the F-15 begins two hours before take-off, with a briefing on the flight. This covers such routine matters as the radio callsigns to be used, the radio frequencies, co-ordinates to be fed into the inertial navigation system (INS), restrictions to be observed during combat manoeuvres and contingency plans in the event of unexpected bad weather or unserviceability problems with an aircraft. There is also a weather briefing. After the drive to the flightline, the fighter must undergo its pre-flight inspection. In Europe the F-15s of the US 36th Tactical Fighter Wing are dispersed among hardened aircraft shelters (HAS), which will provide protection against anything but a direct hit from a heavy bomb, whereas in the United States the Eagles are generally lined up on their squadron's ramp area.

First impressions of the Eagle are of its size, as the aircraft's wing spans 13 m (42.8 ft) and length overall is 19.4 m (63.8 ft), making it somewhat larger than the two-seat F-4 Phantom. Another difference is its height, as the twin tails stand 5.6 m

(18.5 ft) off the ground and the wing is mounted high on the fuselage. This makes the pilot's walk-around inspection an easier job than on the low-wing Phantom. Starting at the nose, the pilot walks round in a clockwise direction, checking for hydraulic or fuel leaks, seeing that maintenance access panels have been properly fastened and confirming that the air-to-air missiles (which may be dummy or live rounds, according to the mission) have been properly mounted and that their safety pins are in place. When satisfied with this check, the pilot mounts the ladder hooked to the Eagle's cockpit canopy rail, pausing to glance over the wing and fuselage upper surfaces, which are impossible to check during the walk-around. The Eagle also has a built-in access ladder, but this is only used when operating away from base. The last item of equipment to be checked is the ejection seat, which is capable of blasting a pilot clear of the Eagle in all conditions of flight and even while the aircraft is standing on the runway.

Stepping down into the cockpit, four straps attach the pilot's harness to the ejection seat with its parachute and survival pack. The cockpit is roomy by fighter standards, but inevitably as the flight progresses muscles begin to ache and the seat pack grows harder. The layout of instruments and controls is excellent, and much thought and design effort has ensured that all controls come readily to hand. The result is a fighter that can be flown 'hands on', with no need to look down into the cockpit to change radio frequencies or to check an essential instrument. One of the keys to this capability is the head-up display (HUD), which is mounted behind the windscreen above the main instruments and has the appearance of a reflector gunsight. All essential flight, navigation and weapons' aiming data is projected onto its screen, so that there is no need to look down into the cockpit during combat.

Similarly radar, communications and armament switches are mounted on the control stick and throttles, so that they can be used at the same time that the fighter is being manoeuvred. This does call for some dexterity and mental agility, but with training it soon becomes second nature. Of course it is only essential data that is displayed on the HUD, and so the Eagle also has a conventional instrument panel; this is well laid out, with the main flight instruments in the centre, engine instruments

Above: An Eagle pilot's view through his head-up display as an AIM-9 Sidewinder missile is fired. The target designator box can be clearly seen on the left of the display, while the numerals at the top give the aircraft's magnetic heading. The 'W' symbol in the centre of the circles indicates the aircraft's attitude and can also be seen on the central dial of the flight instrument panel in the cockpit (left). Left: The cockpit of the F-15 Eagle with all panel lights illuminated. The head-up display is mounted on top of the main instrument panel, with communications and HUD controls immediately beneath it. The main flight instruments are in the centre of the panel, with armament controls to the left and engine instruments to the right. Note the caution lights panel in the extreme right corner of the main instrument panel and the built-in test equipment panel in the foreground on the left console

to the right and the armament control panel to the left. Radar and navigation data are displayed on a computer terminal above the armament panel. Other controls such as the oxygen regulator, lights, ECM (electronic countermeasures) controls, fuel and engine starting switches are mounted on side consoles. Each of these has different-shaped handles and switches, so that they can be operated by touch with less chance of mistakes being made.

After a twelve-point cockpit checklist has been run through the engines can be started. The procedure is simple, thanks to the built-in Jet Fuel Starter (JFS), and no external power source is needed. Once the starter has been run up, it is engaged to the right-hand engine. As the F100 main engine begins to turn, the engine instruments come to life with rpm and turbine inlet temperature readings. The airframe begins to tremble and a muffled thump comes from the igniting fuel. At 50 per cent rpm the JFS disengages from the main engine, which then spins up to around 70 per cent rpm in idle thrust. After checking that the hydraulic pump driven by the right F100 is operating properly, the left engine is started.

With both engines running, the aircraft's avionics and hydraulic systems can be switched on and checked. A built-in test system comprises a control panel on the left console and a caution lights panel to the right of the engine instruments. Each system, including radar, HUD and INS, is marked on a dial on the control panel, and when the test button is pressed a light on the panel goes on to show that the system is being automatically checked. If all is well, the light goes out when the check is completed. If there is a fault the light remains on. At the same time that these checks are run, the inertial navigation system is aligned. This involves feeding in the aircraft's present position (which will have been very precisely surveyed) and the local magnetic variation. A full alignment cycle will take nearly ten

minutes, but after three minutes the INS will produce sufficiently accurate results for most flights. If the F-15 is on alert with a Fighter-Interceptor Squadron and liable to be scrambled at a moment's notice, the shorter alignment period may have to be used. The INS can then be fed with up to twelve navigational 'waypoints' (selected points along the aircraft's route), after which it will not only provide a read-out of the Eagle's position at any time, but will also give instructions to steer to any of the pre-selected waypoints.

At last the Eagle is ready to taxi and, with the wheel chocks waved away, power is advanced to slightly above idle thrust. Unless checked by the brakes, the Eagle will soon be moving at some 50 knots. Half this speed is all that is necessary for taxying, with manoeuvring on the ground being achieved by the use of brakes and nose wheel steering. Care must be exercised to allow sufficient clearance for the wingtips, especially when operating from an HAS, and the exhaust from the twin-F100 engines is another potential hazard. Before turning onto the runway, a maintenance team performs a last-minute external check of the aircraft, looking for damaged tyres or hydraulic leaks. They also remove safety pins from the missiles. The pilot then confirms that the ejection seat is live, that his seat harness is secure and that the canopy is down and locked. Flaps are set for take-off, the operation of the flight controls are checked and the radar switched to its operating mode. The Eagle moves onto the runway and lines up for take-off. While the fighter is held on its brakes, each engine is run up to military power (i.e. the maximum power obtainable without using the afterburner), and rpm, turbine inlet temperature, oil pressure and fuel flow are checked. The rpm reading should be just over 90 per cent and inlet temperature 322°C (900°F).

Once the Eagle has passed all these checks satisfactorily, it is clear to take off. Brakes are released and the throttles advanced to military power. Acceleration is rapid and is felt as a firm pressure on the pilot's back. When the Eagle reaches 120 knots a gentle backward pressure on the stick 'rotates' (pulls up) the nose to an angle of 10 degrees. At 150 knots, with the Eagle some 915 m (3,000 ft) down the runway, the fighter lifts off. Under normal conditions, the Eagle will leave the ground in under half of the available take-off run. However, if the fighter is operating from a short runway in high temperatures, it may be necessary to take off in full afterburner. In this case the throttles are pushed forward to the full afterburner position after brake release. As each of the afterburners' five stages ignites, the pilot feels a jolt in the back. Accelerating rapidly down the runway, the Eagle reaches rotation speed in seconds and take-off speed shortly thereafter. Within 460 m (1,500 ft) the fighter is airborne and flaps and landing gear have to be retracted quickly to 'clean up' the aircraft before it accelerates past the gear's 250-knot limiting speed. One thing that the Eagle pilot does not have to worry about, however, is retrimming the aircraft once flaps and gear are up. This is done automatically by a pitch trim compensator, which is also able to cope with retrimming necessitated by changes in speed, extension of the airbrake and the release of weapons.

After lift-off the Eagle climbs at a speed of 350 knots, its angle of pitch increasing from 10 degrees to around 45 degrees. Accelerating up to Mach 0.95, the fighter reaches an altitude of 9,150 m (30,000 ft) in 1.25 minutes. If a shallower angle of climb is selected, the Eagle will quickly go super-sonic. Alternatively, because of the fighter's out-standing thrust-to-weight ratio (1.4 to 1), it is able to accelerate in a vertical climb. At airshows the crowds are often treated to the spectacle of an Eagle pointing its nose vertically upwards after lift-off and climbing away until out of sight even in a clear blue sky. For normal operations, though, the sedater departure is preferred. Once airborne the pilot immediately appreciates the excellent visi-bility from the Eagle's cockpit. Turning his head he can see both the tailfins, with only a small blindspot to the rear created by the ejector seat rails. Similarly, in a 60-degree bank, the airspace beneath the fighter's belly can be checked. Even in the age of the missile a fighter pilot needs to keep a sharp look-out for enemy aircraft. Another pleas-ing feature of the Eagle is its highly effective pressurization and air conditioning system, which makes a great contribution to pilot comfort and therefore efficiency.

The Eagle's manoeuvrability and general hand-ling qualities are outstanding by any standard. The fighter's high thrust-to-weight ratio allows it to retain its energy (or even accelerate) during turning manoeuvres in which most fighters bleed energy. Similarly, the Eagle's low (by fighter standards) wing loading of 56 lb per square foot also con-tributes to its manoeuvrability and good handling qualities. If an Eagle is put into a 6G turn (6G is a force equal to six times that of gravity) it will continue to accelerate. This means that the in-creased energy can be used to climb while maintain-ing the turn, or that the turn can be further tightened until just over 7Gs are pulled. At lighter weights the aircraft can be flown to limits of plus 9Gs or minus 3Gs, although at these extremes the fighter's G-tolerance is greater than that of the average fighter pilot. At low speed the Eagle remains controllable at high angles of attack (nose-up pitch), a condition in which its prede-cessor the F-4 Phantom would depart controlled flight in a vicious stall/spin. The Eagle is virtually unspinnable.

The Eagle's control response is excellent, with the fairly heavy 'stick forces' giving the feeling of positive control in all phases of flight. A control augmentation system also helps to achieve sta-bility. The Eagle's rate of roll is especially high, thanks to the combined use of conventional ailerons and stabilitors. The latter surfaces com-bine the functions of elevators (operating in con-cert) and ailerons (operating differentially) for additional control during rolling manoeuvres. The twin rudders are also most effective, as there is less tendency for them to be 'blanketed' by the airframe in high angle-of-attack manoeuvres, than there is for a single fin-and-rudder assembly. A large airbrake mounted on top of the fuselage behind the cockpit canopy provides efficient aerodynamic braking when it is fully extended to a 45 degree angle. This can be a very effective move in air combat, as if it takes the opponent by surprise he will be forced to overshoot. The decrease in speed is so abrupt that the Eagle's pilot is likely to be thrown forward in his harness.

During low-speed, high angle-of-attack man-oeuvres the automatic operation of the variable-geometry engine-intake ramps is very noticeable. Their up-and-down movement ensures that each

An F-15A Eagle of the 49th Tactical Fighter Squadron, based at Holloman AFB, New Mexico, is pictured with its dorsal airbrake fully extended. When used in combat the airbrake enables the Eagle to decelerate rapidly, perhaps forcing an opponent to overshoot

An AIM-7 Sparrow medium-range missile is launched by an F-15. The missile is first ejected from its semi-recessed mounting in the Eagle's underside and then its rocket motor ignites. It is a semi-active radar homing missile and so requires its target to be illuminated by the launch aircraft's radar

engine receives the optimum flow of air at whatever angle of pitch the intake is to the airflow. Fuel management is fully automatic, and so the pilot does not have to switch from external tanks (up to three of which can be carried) to fuselage or wing tanks as they are emptied, in order to maintain a flow of fuel to the engines. A warning light comes on when 'bingo' fuel level is reached. This is a pre-calculated fuel state, which will give the pilot sufficient flight time to return to base and land – with a reserve allowance for emergencies added in. The Eagle can, of course, be refuelled in flight from a tanker aircraft.

Route flying in the F-15 is pleasant and relatively simple. As Tactical Air Command's Eagles may be called on to deploy at a moment's notice from their bases in the United States to Europe, the Middle East or Northeast Asia, this is an important aspect of their operations. Flying at altitudes above 12,200 m (40,000 ft) airline traffic is avoided, as is most of the bad weather. Cruising speed is around Mach 0.9 and fuel is consumed at the rate of some 1,000 kg (2,200 lb) per hour. As an F-15C's total internal fuel load is 6,103 kg (13,455 lb), and this can be increased by three 2,725-litre (600-gallon) capacity external fuel tanks or conformal fuel pallets (with less drag than external tanks), the Eagle's ferry range is considerable (6,000 km/3,700 miles). The primary navigation aid is the INS, which will automatically steer the aircraft to the selected waypoint or destination. Its accuracy can be determined and if necessary updated by cross-checking its reading with that obtained from a TACAN (tactical air navigation) radio navigation beacon. Once on course the pilot can engage the autopilot and relax a little.

In combat the Eagle's APG-63 radar can detect targets at ranges of nearly 160 km (100 miles), but the radar's greatest attribute is its ability to pick out low-flying targets against ground clutter. As the radar data is computer-processed it is displayed clearly in symbol form on the radar scope. This is a great improvement over the unprocessed radar information displayed in earlier fighters. Furthermore, once the radar has locked onto a target, information also appears on the HUD. The data available includes the target's range, its altitude and speed, its heading and the rate of closure. A box symbol on the HUD indicates the target's position and if a rifle-scope is fitted alongside the HUD, it is possible to pick up the enemy aircraft beyond normal visual range, identify it and then launch an AIM-7 Sparrow missile in the confidence that it will knock down an enemy and not a friend. The 'hands-on' radar controls on the control stick and throttles allow both the radar to be operated and various weapons to be selected and fired. The Eagle's air-to-air armament comprises four medium-range AIM-7 Sparrow missiles, four short-range AIM-9 Sidewinder missiles and a built-in 20 mm Vulcan multi-barrel cannon with 940 rounds of ammunition. If for example the gun armament is selected, the HUD will display an aiming reticle and aiming point cross, a box indicating the target's position and the number of rounds of ammunition remaining. It will also indicate when the target is within range.

The Eagle pilot has the option of engaging the target before closing to visual range, using his AIM-7 missiles at a range of typically 40 km (25 miles). If he elects to close to dogfighting range, the Eagle's outstanding ability to pull tight turns will be a great advantage. Even if the opponent looks as though he is gaining the upper hand, the Eagle's tremendous acceleration allows it to disengage. This is done by pulling up into a near vertical climb in full afterburner. Once above the fight, the Eagle pilot can then re-engage with the inestimable advantages of superior speed and altitude, which have won pilots dogfights since the days of Bishop and Richthofen.

With the mission completed and the bingo fuel light burning, it is time for the Eagle to return to its airfield. In clear weather the TACAN will bring it to within sight of the runway, although the INS or automatic direction finding beacon will do the job as well. Once overhead, typically with fuel down to 1,360 kg (3,000 lb), the Eagle flies a standard 360-degree landing pattern. On the initial approach the speed is 325 knots, decreasing to 220 knots as the Eagle is pulled through 180 degrees onto the downwind leg. Landing gear and flaps are lowered and the panel lights confirm that the wheels are down and locked. The speed decreases again during the turn from base onto the final approach. The Eagle is now flying at around 140 knots and touches down at a speed of 110 knots. Once the mainwheels are on the runway, the nose is pulled up at an angle of 12 degrees or so, to achieve aerodynamic breaking during the landing run. At 80 knots the nose drops onto the runway and the Eagle is braked to a stop. The airbrake may be used during the final approach and touchdown, but a good landing is possible without it. Neither breaking parachute nor engine thrust reversers are fitted. However, the Eagle does have a tail hook for emergency arrested landings. In poor visibility the Eagle's pilot can either be talked down to a landing by a radar controller during a ground controlled approach, or he can make use of the instrument landing system, with instructions projected onto the HUD.

Usually the Eagle will have come to a stop well before the midfield point, where it can turn off the main runway and taxi back to its parking ramp or HAS. All equipment is then turned off and the radar and INS are checked. Then the engines can be shut down. After dismounting, the pilot makes a quick post-flight walk-around check and discusses any serviceability problems with the crew chief.

Boeing 747

The flight deck of a Lufthansa Boeing 747. It is manned by the flight engineer (foreground), the airliner's captain (rear left) and co-pilot. Note that the engine instruments in the centre of the pilots' control panel are duplicated by the display in the bottom left hand corner of the engineer's panel

The Boeing 747 airliner is an aircraft of considerable significance in the history of civil air transport operations, as it was the first of the wide-bodied, long-haul airliners – a capability neatly summed up by its popular name of 'Jumbo Jet'. The airliner is operated by a crew of three, comprising the captain, his co-pilot and the flight engineer. Their flight deck occupies a bubble-shaped cabin mounted on top of the fuselage, some 9 m (29.5 ft) above the ground. This unusually high position makes taxiing the Boeing 747 a rather alarming experience for a new pilot more used to a lower viewpoint. However, this strangeness soon wears off with experience.

The aircraft's captain by time-honoured convention sits in the left-hand seat, with his co-pilot to his right. Both pilots are faced with their primary flight instruments and horn-shaped control columns. Between them on the control panel is a bank of engine instruments, and on the roof above there is a mass of warning lights and switches for the aircraft's systems, plus radio controls. Conveniently located between the two pilots' seats are

the four throttle levers, which are within comfortable reach of either crew member. Normally, they are operated in concert and so the levers are spaced close enough together for all four to be operated by a single hand movement. However, should a single engine need to be throttled back, for example while practising flying the airliner with one engine lost during a crew training sortie, the four throttles can be operated individually. Incidentally, it is more usual for emergency procedures such as coping with engine failure to be practised on the flight simulator than on the real aircraft. The flap control lever is beside the throttle quadrant and behind them are the engine start levers, inertial navigation system and autopilot controls.

The third crew member, the flight engineer, sits behind the two pilots. He normally faces his instrument panels, which are mounted on the right wall of the cabin, but his seat can swivel forwards to face the direction of flight for safety during take-off and landings. The flight engineer's responsibility is to monitor and manage the aircraft's numerous systems. He controls the fuel systems and maintains a check of the fuel consumed throughout the flight. He also monitors engine performance, cabin pressurization and air conditioning, electrical and hydraulic systems. The three crew members work as a team with the captain in overall control.

Although most airlines follow generally similar procedures, they will differ in the details of their flight operations. This account of flying the Boeing 747 is based on the experience of the West German national airline Lufthansa, one of the first carriers to operate the Boeing 747. Its current fleet comprises ten of these aircraft, including both the 747E, which can carry 410 passengers, plus 15 tons of baggage and general cargo in the underfloor holds, and the 747D which carries 278 passengers and 35 tons of cargo. Lufthansa was also the first airline to operate the Boeing 747F, a pure freighter version with a capacity of up to 108 tons, which began a service from Frankfurt to New York in 1972.

The captain of a Boeing 747 is a senior pilot with perhaps as much as twenty years' flying experience behind him. As well as needing to pass a rigorous medical examination twice every year, he is also subjected to regular flight checks by examiners to ensure that he maintains a high level of proficiency. Even the second pilot will have progressed from flying the Boeing 737 twin-jet or three-engined

Boeing 727 before graduating to the very much larger 747. In addition to airline route flying, the crews also regularly train in a flight simulator. It is essential for any airline to maintain a steady supply of trained aircrew, as for every airliner in service an average of eight crews is required if it is to be operated profitably.

As with any modern aircraft, a considerable amount of preparation and pre-flight planning is needed before the Boeing 747 can leave the ground. Two hours before take-off time the two pilots and the flight engineer assemble in the airline's Flight Crew Information Centre. Most of the planning has been done by a computer, which prints out an operational flight plan. The information includes payload, from which is calculated the zero fuel weight and then the allowable fuel load on take-off.

aids, restricted areas or changes to airfields along their route.

After the briefing session the flight deck crew join the cabin staff and then board their aircraft. The maintenance staff have fuelled the aircraft, cargo and luggage is loaded into the holds and in-flight meals are stored in the galleys. The flight engineer completes a walk-around inspection and checks the operation of all hydraulic, pneumatic and electrical systems. The captain also does a walk-around inspection to satisfy himself that the airliner is ready for flight and then climbs up to the flight deck to check out the navigation and communications systems. As the passengers board, the crew contact the control tower for a local weather report and then calculate take-off data. The co-pilot starts to read through the pre-flight checklist, with the

One of Air India's fleet of ten Boeing 747s taxies out for take-off. The exceptionally high position of the flight deck above the taxi-way is shown to good advantage in this view

Fuel consumption is calculated for all stages of the flight, making allowances for possible diversions en route. However, the final decision as to how much fuel is loaded aboard the aircraft is not made by the computer, but by the aircraft captain. The operational flight plan will also show both the total flight time and a breakdown of the time taken to fly each segment of the route. It will give the course to be flown between each radio beacon along the route and the various flight levels to be followed (altitude is expressed in terms of flight levels, or FL, in civil aviation, for example FL 330 = 33,000 ft). The weather briefing is an important part of pre-flight preparations, as many vital calculations – notably that for fuel consumption – depend upon variables of wind and temperature. Lastly the flight crew checks NOTAMS (notices to airmen) which will warn them of any unserviceable navigation

captain and flight engineer performing the checks. The engines are then started one by one and when all four are running the control tower is radioed for clearance to taxi. The aircraft is pushed from its parking bay by a 70-ton diesel tractor, which develops some 600 hp and is low enough (1.5 m/ 4.9 ft high) to pass under the Boeing 747's belly. The aircraft then taxies under its own power to the runway assigned by control. The pre-take-off checks are completed. Then the captain radioes the tower for permission to take-off. When he receives the reply 'clear to take-off', the throttles are pushed forward and the Boeing 747 accelerates down the runway. The four JT9D turbofans are soon developing full power. At a pre-calculated speed, which varies with aircraft weight and atmospheric conditions, the aircraft is 'rotated', (the nose lifts high off the runway) and then it takes to the air.

Once it is airborne the undercarriage is retracted. The first consideration during take-off – one of the most potentially hazardous phases of the flight – is safety, but a close second in importance are noise abatement considerations. In order to reduce the nuisance to people living in the vicinity of the airport, the aircraft maintains a steep climb after lift-off. Engine thrust is therefore used to gain height rather than speed. For this reason the aircraft's flaps, which increase the wing's lift, are not retracted until after the airliner has reached 915 m (3,000 ft) altitude. The aircraft is then instructed by Air Traffic Control to follow a specific flight path, which will take it clear of the congested air space around the airport and onto its outbound route. It is in following complicated departure procedures that much of the skill in airline flying is displayed, for as one senior Lufthansa pilot said of the actual handling of the aircraft: 'Its superior technology doesn't make it any less easy to fly.'

Once the Boeing 747 has reached its initial cruising altitude, typically FL 330, it will be flying at a speed of about 940 km/h (585 mph). The aircraft's inertial navigation system, backed up by radio navigation receivers, are relied on to follow a pre-determined route. With the autopilot engaged, the aircraft will fly where its navigation equipment tells it to go. The job of the crew is to monitor the efficient operation of this automatic process. They may notice, for example, by reference to the artificial horizon on the main instrument panel that the autopilot is flying the aircraft in a 5-degree bank rather than as it should with wings level. The remedy is to switch on the second autopilot system and radio to the destination airfield so that the faulty system can be swiftly replaced after landing. The cross-checking process is not only carried out by the crew, but also by the equipment itself.

As the flight progresses, fuel is burned off, the aircraft becomes lighter and so its cruising altitude increases from 10,100 m (33,000 ft) to perhaps 11,300 m (37,000 ft). The crew is in shortwave radio contact with Lufthansa's operations control centre, so that they can report technical faults requiring maintenance, or the crew can be told if their destination airfield becomes 'fogged in'. Should the aircraft's weather radar pick up storm clouds on the route, necessitating a diversion, the crew can radio for a new operational flight plan which will include revised fuel consumption and navigational calculations to account for the changes in course and flight time.

Some thirty minutes before it is due to land the Boeing 747 begins its descent from cruising altitude. The radio frequency is switched from that of route control to approach control. The aircraft is then directed in its descent by the controller until it picks up the ILS (instrument landing system) beam at a height of some 600 m (2,000 ft) and a distance of 12 km (8 miles) from the runway threshold. Flaps and landing gear are extended as the aircraft approaches the runway. The captain flies his approach by reference to his ILS indicator. This instrument consists of horizontal and vertical needles, which have to be centred over a central 'bullseye' for the aircraft to follow the ILS glide path. This system will bring the aircraft to within sight of the runway, following a descent angle of between 2.5 degrees and 3 degrees and passing over an outer marker, which warns the crew that they are nearing the runway. The captain then 'flares' the massive airliner down onto the runway (this involves pulling the nose up so that the main wheels touch first), puts the engines into reverse thrust, deploys the wing-mounted lift-dumpers to slow the landing run and finally brakes to a halt. He then calls the tower for instructions to taxi into a parking space and follows the yellow guidelines along the taxiway to the terminal area. The post-flight checks are completed and the engines shut down as the passenger loading bridges are extended to the aircraft's doors.

An Aer Lingus Boeing 747 is about to touch down at the end of its flight. The triple-slotted flaps on the wing trailing edge are fully extended, as are the variable-camber Krueger flaps on the leading edge

'As the passengers eat lunch we are now travelling at 2,170 km/h (1,350 mph) - a mile every 2.5 seconds and faster than a 0.303 in rifle bullet.'
Captain D. G. Ross

British Aerospace/ Aérospatiale Concorde

After several years of initial studies, the aerospace industries of Britain and France agreed in 1962 to go ahead with a joint project to develop an intercontinental supersonic transport. The challenge has been met by Concorde, an aircraft beautiful in her lines, exceedingly powerful and coveted by those privileged to fly her.

Approaching her on the ramp, the marked sweep and many curves of the slim delta wing are apparent. Instead of elevators and ailerons there are six 'elevons' which govern both pitch and roll, powerful hydraulic actuators being suspended beneath each control surface. There are no flaps or airbrakes, the droop snoot stretches 7·3 metres (24 feet) out in front of the pilot and the very tall undercarriage allows the pitching moment for the take-off rotation to take place.

The sharp, box-shaped engine intakes have hydraulic ramps which move in flight to keep the airflow on the compressor face at a constant 560 km/h (350 mph) while the aircraft is cruising at speeds some 1,600 km/h (1,000 mph) higher. Each Rolls-Royce Olympus engine produces over 17,250 kg thrust and the rear end, with reheat and nozzle assemblies, testifies that this is an air transport 'with a difference'.

The flight deck is small and every square inch

Below: the Anglo-French supersonic Concorde in flight. It was back in 1962 that the two companies signed the treaty 'regarding the development and production of a civil supersonic aircraft'.

utilised. Once in the seat everything is perfectly at hand. The visor/heat shield stretches out in front, and there are 303 dials to monitor, including the angle of attack indicator, skin temperature gauge, 'G' meter, reheat controls, centre of gravity indicators and a Machmeter reading up to Mach 2·5. The flight controls are 'fly by wire' and autostabilised in all axes. Mechanical signalling without 'autostab' is available to back this up and the relevant controls are on the overhead panel.

The aircraft has 13 fuel tanks and the 118,200 litres (26,000 gallons) of kerosene they contain are used as a 'heat sink' for the air-conditioning, hydraulic system and engine oil cooling. Pumps which supply each engine with fuel at a rate of 7 litres every second during the take-off are part of a system which also transfers fuel for longitudinal balance during transonic acceleration. A pressurisation system maintains a cabin altitude of 1,700 m (5,500 ft) with the aircraft cruising at up to 18,300 m (60,000 ft), while a Category IIIa autoland system allows flight down to a decision height of 4·5 metres (15 feet) and 200 metres (650 feet) visibility.

Concorde spent a record 5,000 hours of flight testing before certification, and pilot conversion takes almost six months. This includes ten weeks of lectures with the manufacturers at Filton,

Bristol, 64 hours of simulator, eight hours of local flying and fourteen route flights under supervision. Flight preparation starts with a check of the route weather, fuel and air traffic control (ATC) flight plans before proceeding to the aircraft. An hour is then spent with the pre-flight checks and engine starting, external power supplies being used for the latter.

In order to taxi, the visor and nose are lowered to the 5 degree position and the parking brakes released. The residual thrust of the four Olympus gas turbines when idling is more than sufficient to accelerate the aircraft to over 72 km/h (45 mph) along the taxiway if unchecked. This speed is too high around a busy airport and the carbon fibre brakes are therefore used against the residual thrust. An electric cooling fan is included in each wheel brake assembly, but a close eye must be kept on the brake temperature gauges.

The pilot's seat is 11·5 m (38 ft) in front of the nosewheel and 30 m (98 ft) ahead of the main-wheels. This has to be remembered when taxying because the nose must project well out over the grass at sharp bends in order to keep the wheels on the paved area. The 'taxi' and 'before take-off' check lists are being completed and the fuel balanced to give the correct centre of gravity for take-off. One of the final actions before take-off is to 'inhibit' the master warning–a device which monitors all

fully open are a sure sign that reheat has ignited. There follows a very confident surge of power. Fifteen seconds later at 185 km/h (115 mph) the engineer calls 'power checked' if he is satisfied with the parameters. The engines are now consuming fuel at a total rate of 80 tons per hour. Keeping straight with gentle use of rudder is all that is needed. V_1 is usually at 305 km/h (190 mph) and 'rotate' at 362 km/h (225 mph), depending on aircraft weight and airfield conditions.

The rotation is a precise instrument manoeuvre using the expanded scale on the artificial horizon (ADI). In 5·5 seconds the attitude is smoothly increased to a pitch attitude of 15 degrees but depending again on weight and ambient conditions. The electrical flight control signalling and auto-stabilisers help the precise control required in pitch and roll throughout the flight envelope, the artificial pitch feel maintaining a constant load factor and the roll feel a constant relationship between roll rate and control wheel force.

The mainwheels leave the ground at 402 km/h (250 mph) groundspeed and the pitch attitude maintained until power is reduced for noise abate-ment reasons. We are now flying at 480 km/h (300 mph) and less than a minute has passed since starting our roll. With the undercarriage 'tucked up' and provided we are clear of noise sensitive areas, full climb power is applied and the nose and

the aircraft's systems and presents them in 37 categories, drawing the crew's attention to a malfunction with a bell and a light. Clearly a master warning during the take-off for a very minor degradation would cause an unnecessary distraction, and all but seven categories are 'inhibited' until the aircraft is well away from the ground.

Timing is very important during the departure for power changes and noise abatement. The take-off begins with a countdown and as 'now' is called the throttles are advanced rapidly to full power and clocks started. Electronic sensors and the engine primary nozzle indicators swinging

visor raised, giving a very noticeable hush in the cockpit.

The climb is made at VMO (maximum permis-sible airspeed), staying hard against the maximum speed side of the flight envelope. This is 400 knots until an altitude of 9,750 m (32,000 ft) and then increases to 530 knots. However, while maintaining the IAS (indicated airspeed) at VMO, Mach number is increasing as we climb and at Mach 0·7 and 2,750 m (9,000 ft) the rearward movement of centre of pressure is well under way. The engineer begins the transfer of fuel from tanks 9 and 10 in the forward fuselage to tank 11 in the rear, thereby

Concorde, seen (right) in British Airways colours, entered service on 2 January 1976 after 20 years of design and development. The birdlike appearance on landing is due to the 'droop snoot' and slender delta wing shape, which was decided upon after hundreds of hours of wind-tunnel testing.

moving the centre of gravity aft to balance a nose-down trim change. Three computers help with the balancing and a C of G indicator, together with the flight control position, confirms the accuracy of the fuel transfer.

At Mach 0·93 and 7,600 m (25,000 ft) the reheats are again ignited and a small 'kick' felt as the power increases. We are now on our way through the sound barrier while climbing at the same time. At 8,840 m (29,000 ft) the pressure instruments oscillate as the shock wave crosses the static vents and we are supersonic; the 'auto-stab' counters the trim changes perfectly. By the

time 13,100 m (43,000 ft) is reached, the speed is Mach 1·7 (1,150 mph) and the transonic high drag zone is behind us. Reheats are switched off and the climb continued at 530 knots IAS. The aircraft skin temperature has been increasing rapidly during the acceleration due to kinetic heating and by Mach 2·0 will be up to 127 degrees centigrade. As the outside air is −56 degrees, a temperature rise of 183 degrees–almost twice boiling point–has been made and the airframe expanded over 3·5 cm (9 in) in length.

At 15,240 m (50,000 ft), 530 knots IAS equals Mach 2·0. The aircraft is still climbing and power

is reduced by electronically selecting 'cruise rating'. The throttles remain fully open. The outside air temperature particularly affects the climb perform- ance and in relatively colder atmospheres, rates of climb well over 300m (1,000ft) per minute are normal at higher flight levels.

As the passengers eat lunch we are now travelling at 2,170km/h (1,350mph)–a mile every $2\frac{1}{2}$ seconds and faster than a 0·303in rifle bullet. The three inertial navigation systems maintain the great circle track to the next way-point and, looking out, the sky has the dark blue of the upper atmosphere, the curvature of the earth is evident and wispy cirrus clouds are nine kilometres beneath us. The Concorde tracks are very carefully planned to avoid populated areas; a 'boom carpet' is being laid behind us on the earth twelve miles below and although the intensity is not enough to cause damage it might cause a little consternation.

The flight controls remain precise, but care must be taken for even a $\frac{1}{2}$ degree pitch change will give a considerable rate of climb or descent. Bank, however, is another story, for 20 degrees will need 208km (129 miles) turning diameter. Temperature and windshears are ironed out by the autopilot/ autothrottle combination and the flight is usually very smooth. All in all it is one of the finest experi- ences in the world—flying such a superb machine at her design point in the stratosphere, lively but very, very purposeful.

An engine failure in the Mach 2 cruise presents no problem, such is the refinement of the design. Yaw is in the traditional sense but bank is *towards* the live engine. This is due to a spill door under the dead engine opening to dump excess air from the intake and rolling the aircraft against the yaw. With or without 'autostab', even a double engine failure is easily contained with gentle rudder and elevon pressure. The aircraft response to an engine failure is conventional when flying subsonically.

As landfall approaches, a deceleration and descent have to be made; the deceleration is required to cross the coast at less than the speed of sound and a descent because the lowest authorised airspeed above 12,500m (41,000ft) is greater than

Mach 1. The throttles are initially retarded to halfway, keeping sufficient air supply for equipment cooling. This must be a gradual movement, for rapid closure is like hitting a brick wall as the extraordinary drag at Mach 2 'grabs you by the tail'. The aircraft descends, the airframe cools rapidly as the Mach number reduces and the engin- eer brings the fuel forward again. It takes about 265km (165 miles) to slow down from Mach 2 to Mach 1 and another 160km (100 miles) from Mach 1 to landing.

The slim delta will not stall. As high angles of attack are reached, vortices along the leading edge develop and the depression within the centre of these is positioned along the wing surface at the leading edge and lift created. However, the drag rise is enormous and the power available limits the minimum speed usable. At an angle of attack of about 21 degrees, an excessive nose-up pitch occurs but a 'safety flight control' system keeps the pilot well away from this point. The absence of flaps means that the high angle of attack lift characteristics have to be used for the approach and landing. The aircraft is well on the back of the drag curve, but the twin autothrottles give exact speed control.

Initial approach speed is 354km/h (220mph) and at maximum landing weight the threshold speed is 301km/h (187mph). The pitch attitude is 10·5 degrees and 'nose cone' lowered to the 12·5 degree position to improve forward visibility. The auto-throttles are disconnected at 12m (40ft), a slight back pressure applied on the control column at 6m (20ft)—not enough to change noticeably the aircraft's pitch attitude—and at 4·5m (15feet) the throttles are closed. A precise attitude of 10·5 degrees is maintained, allowing ground effect to flare the aircraft. The nose has a tendency to drop and a continuous back pressure is needed to keep the all-important attitude; one degree less will give too firm a landing and two degrees more brings the tail onto the runway—hence the tail- wheel. The nose is lowered, the engines are put into reverse and the carbon fibre brakes stop 110 tons from almost 305km/h (190mph) in just over a mile.

Above left: Concorde 02 at San Francisco International Airport after its record breaking flight from Mexico City. The flight, which took place in October 1974, took only 2 hours 19 minutes.
Above: The Concorde cockpit, showing pilot controls and instrumentation.

Panavia Tornado GR.1

'Tornado is not simply an aircraft, it is an integrated weapons system . . .'

The most significant aircraft within the NATO inventory is, without doubt, the superlative Panavia Tornado. Since its introduction to operational service in June 1982, the GR.1 (IDS – Interdictor Strike) variant has become the primary strike/attack aircraft of the RAF, German Air Force and Navy, Italian Air Force and the Saudi Arabian Air Force. To each of these air arms the aircraft brought a new dimension of capability with its 24-hour all-weather pinpoint first-run attack precision, claims which have been made by many aircraft but which none have been truly able to fulfil. For a few weeks in early 1991 the GR.1s of the RAF, Italian and Saudi Air Forces were heavily engaged in Operation Desert Storm, the allied air offensive against Iraq. Whilst the 'mud-moving' GR.1s were seeking out targets in Kuwait and Iraq, the RAF and Saudi F.3s (ADV – Air Defence Variant) flew Combat Air Patrols along the border. In a further demonstration of the multi-role capability of the Tornado, GR.1As flew reconnaissance missions.

Tornado is not simply an aircraft, it is an integrated weapons system designed in all respects for its designated NATO role of low level penetration of ultra-high-value targets. One major advantage over its 'rivals' is in having two crewmen to share the high workloads, and two sets of eyes to look out of the cockpit – the old saying that if you 'see it you have a chance of avoiding it' still holds good in the electronic age.

Whilst the pilot completes the external checks, the Nav straps in and winds up the aircraft systems. First to go on is the IN (intertial navigation) which provides the aircraft's basic positional data. The heart of the 'system' is the main computer and the radar. The cassette is slotted into the recorder and fed into the main computer. The route is checked on one of the two TV/TABS (visual display units) which, together with the combined radar/moving map display, dominate the rear-seat displays. Satisfied that the basic details are correct, the TV/TABS are set up to show ROUTE, traditionally on the left screen, and NAV, on the right screen, with additional details selected by use of the multi-function keys.

The RAF did not bring in laser-designation equipment to the Gulf until half-way through the conflict, but it proved a vital factor in pinpointing exact targets such as individual hardened aircraft shelters. Britain's TIALD (Therma) Imaging And Laser Designation) pod is attached to the left underfuselage pylon of the GR.1. (Paul Jackson)

Other nations that received Tornados are Germany (Luftwaffe and Marineflieger in IDS attack and ECR electronic combat and reconnaissance forms), Italy (in IDS form for attack, reconnaissance air superiority), and Saudi Arabia (IDS and ADV). Above are two Saudi IDSs.

Front cockpit of the Tornado GR.1.

Both strapped in, front-seat systems checked, including the all-important terrain-following radar (TFR) and autopilot control systems, engines running – the time has come to taxi.

At night the cockpits are a veritable maze of lights, from the panel of red and amber captions on the warning panel to the right of the front console, to an array of greens, reds and ambers in other areas of both cockpits. Radar, TV/TABS, TFR and HUD all display 'green spaghetti' for their numbers and symbols. As the aircraft moves out to the runway, further systems checks (including radar) confirm that all is GO. Line up, brakes on, full cold power . . . select min reheat . . . release the brakes . . . rolling . . . move the throttles to max reheat, and the acceleration

increases. Pull back on the stick and the Tornado leaves the runway . . . gear up . . . flap up . . . 300 knots take out the reheat to conserve fuel.

Wings back to 45 degrees sweep, the mid-speed cruise setting, (fully forward – 25 degrees sweep – being the low-speed, such as take-off and landing and slow-speed manoeuvring, and fully back – 67 degrees sweep – for high-speed/supersonic).

The airframe tends to let you know if the wings need sweeping and you've forgotten – a gentle buffet or a below average speed problem. The full range of underwing stores – EW on the outboard pylons, underwing fuel tanks and Sidewinder AAMs on the inboard pylons – make little difference to the handling characteristics of the aircraft or its performance. Likewise, a payload of up to eight 1000 lbs on the centre-line hardpoints has little effect other than to make the aircraft somewhat sluggish in tight turns. With the fly-by-wire electronic controls through a stability system, the Tornado is a very smooth performer even in severe low level turbulence.

Each engine makes the RB199 one of the best combat engines in service. Response is rapid and smooth, fuel consumption excellent, although still at a frightening rate when reheat is engaged. Furthermore, it is good at dealing with bird-strikes, an ever-present hazard during low level operations. A quick whiff of fried chicken permeates the cockpits but the engines keep producing the goods.

With the weather looking poor ahead, the TFR is brought into play to get the aircraft down through the cloud and into low level – set the required flying height, check all the indications, engage the system, and let go of the control column. You are now in the hands of the aircraft computer and autopilot as to where you go, and the TFR as to what height you level out at. Sharpens the mind wonderfully as the aircraft descends into cloud with mountains to left and right! This is the system which gives the Tornado its TRUE 24-hour all-weather flying capability; there is no need to see the ground, simply let the aircraft get on with it, pilot keeping a confidence check on the indications and being ready to take over should the need arise, the nav keeping the aircraft computer position accurate with radar fixes, both monitoring the EW suite just in case.

Bad weather persists as the target area approaches – no problem. A blind hands-off attack was one of the design concepts of the aircraft. Check the weapons selection on the weapons panel, select attack mode on the TV/TAB and look for the target on the radar. Use the hand control to move the target indicator over the radar response, press the insert button and the aircraft turns a few degrees to go for the updated position . . . press the weapons release button and wait for the computer to drop the weapons when all the parameters have been satisfied.

Bombs gone! The weather clears and the ground becomes visible, so out of TFR and push the nose down to hide in a tiny valley which is going roughly the right way. All that remains is to get back to base in one piece. With its EW suite of active jamming – flares and chaff – the Tornado is well placed to look after itself in most circumstances. An additional weapon was added to GR.1s in the Gulf, the ALARM missile, designed to take-out any AAA or SAM radar which might be taking too close an interest in the Tornado. Additional self-defence is provided by AiM-9L Sidewinder heat-seeking AAMs, a pair of which are carried, this all-aspect missile giving the Tornado a good anti-fighter capability although, like all 'bomber' crews, the aim is not to get involved in a fight. The pair of 27mm cannon add yet another dimension with air-to-air or air-to-ground capability.

The quickest way to get a fast-jet on the ground is to come into the circuit at speed and 'break' downwind to land, washing the speed off in the turn. Another trick which the Tornado has is to land in a very short space of runway – without the aid of a troublesome drogue parachute. By rocking the throttles to one side the pilot selects two elements which will deploy as soon as the wheels touch the ground – the spoilers on the wings to kill the lift, and the thrust-reverse buckets which will close over the engine exhausts. With the buckets deployed, the throttles are pushed forward and the aircraft comes to a rapid halt – pushing the throttles forward to stop is a strange experience!

Nose art became a new feature of RAF aircraft serving in the Gulf. Pin-ups were applied, together with graphics of the number of missions flown. The aircraft received names matching the two identification letters on their fins: ZA465 'FK' became Foxy Killer *and is seen here with one of the highest mission tallies (44 missions, two with JP233 anti-runway weapons, 28 with conventional 'dumb' bombs, and 14 with laser-guided bombs). (Paul Jackson)*

RAF Tornado GR.1s in desert colours at a Saudi air base, awaiting the next mission during the 1991 Gulf conflict. (Paul Jackson)

Lockheed F-117A Nighthawk

For several years the Lockheed 'stealth fighter' was not only secret, but the subject of official disinformation which even extended to its designation. Its correct designation leaves us none the wiser, as it is in no sense a fighter (having no air-to-air capability whatever) and US fighter numbers left off at 111. More importantly, once the 'black jet' was revealed, the truth was far stranger than any fiction.

Every part of the F-117A is unusual. For propulsion Lockheed picked the General Electric F404–F1D2, rated at about 11,000 lb thrust. The basic engine is a turbojet version of the familiar F404, but instead of discharging through an afterburner it exhausts through a large mixer, which combines the jet with a huge flow of cool air. The resulting mixed flow is squeezed out to exit through a two-dimensional nozzle forming the trailing edge of the wing, 6 in high and 65 in wide. The lower edge of the nozzle extends well aft and curves up, hiding all hot parts from the ground, and Shuttle-type tiles keep the lower edge cool so that it never distorts. Equally odd is the inlet, in the form of two giant square apertures side by side, leaning back in side elevation

and in plan. Each square is criss-crossed by a grill of sharp knife-wedge strips covered in RAM, closer together than enemy radar wavelengths. If any radar energy should somehow pass the grid, nothing can get out again. The grill has vital alcohol spray de-icing.

Approaching the F-117A for our familiarization flight we are struck by many facts. First, this is like no other flying machine in the world. Its shape has been dictated totally by the need to achieve near-zeros RCS (radar cross-section). Aerodynamic efficiency, and even handling, took a back seat, and stability in pitch and yaw are both negative. We are awed by the fact that every square inch of the dark grey exterior is very special. Nobody is allowed to walk on it, except for handpicked ground crew with special footwear who are allowed on top of the inlet only. As we get closer, though we know the 117 is the same size as an F-15, we are also awed by the fact that it looks bigger. We can walk under it without stooping, and we climb a ten-rung ladder (carefully protected against damaging the skin) to reach the cockpit. Gross weight is 52,500 lb.

We settle into the standard ACES II seat and

One of the 46 F-117As belonging to Nos 415 and 416 Tactical Fighter Squadrons, 37th TFW, USAF, all of which were operational during the 1991 Gulf conflict. Note the braking parachute is also dark.

One of the most interesting aspects of this view is the narrow-slot exhaust outlet showing between the wing and ruddervator. The slot is 5 ft 5 in long and just 4 in high, with an extended lower lip and ringed in Space Shuttle type heat tiles.

look around. With the canopy shut we can't see much. This is no F-16; you sit up high in solitary state and have no rear view at all. The canopy is as special as the rest, because the flat panes are treated to deflect all radar waves hitting it. The canopy is the heaviest ever fitted to a tactical aircraft. If we wish to eject and fail to jettison the canopy, we simply can't get out. We soon get the idea that we fly the mission mainly on the avionics, and the panel ahead is rather like an F/A-18. On each side are standard 5-in MFDs (multifunction displays), while in the middle is the big monochrome display fed by the main sensors. Twin power levers to the left and a conventional stick are quite normal, as is the big HUD (head-up display) through which we will look most of the time.

We switch on a lot of systems, including the quad-redundant FBW (fly by wire) flight control system, derived from that of the F-16. Then we can test for free movement. The system works off stick position, not stick force. We do almost all the flying with giant elevons, inboard and outboard on each wing from root to tip. To allow the flight-control computers to fight the yaw instability, we need the twin V-shaped rudders (there is no fin), which lean back at the same 67.5° angle as the wing. They were made 50 per cent larger during development. The wing-leading edge is fixed, and there is no airbrake.

With a steerable nosewheel taxiing is simple. At the runway, we are glad it was made so long. We have a thrust-weight ratio of 0.4, no flaps or drooping ailerons, and a wing nothing like any normal lifting aerofoil, with a unique pressure distribution generating lines of lift along the facet angles. We open up to 100 per cent and just let the speed build. We can't do anything more until we are nearing the 200 knot level, especially if this is high-altitude Tonopah on a hot day. Eventually we can haul back and at a large AOA (angle of attack) we at last leave the ground. Gear retraction is quick, and we get the idea that,

the faster this bird goes, the better it flies.

We navigate on INS (inertial navigation system) until we near the target. We don't have that much fuel, but as we are invisible (we hope) we stay very low. We switch on the sensors. Above the nose is a large ball housing a Flir (forward-looking infra-red) and laser designator. Obviously we cannot betray our presence by having a radar on board (apart from the tiny downward-pointing radar altimeters). We slew and depress the ball to point at the target, and lock on. We close quickly, and at the appropriate moment the left weapon door opens and the weapon, a GBU-10 smart bomb – a powerful weapon based on the 2,000 lb Mk 84 GP bomb – is dropped automatically. It falls into a hypothetical 'basket' above the target from where it can be picked up and guided. We start with the forward laser, but soon the target passes out of sight under the nose. No problem, the task is automatically switched to the second (identical) sensor, the DLIR (downward-looking IR] and its bore-sighted laser. This illuminates the target as we pass overhead and depart, ensuring a direct hit.

This is a serious and very expensive aircraft, and with limited fuel we want to get back on that runway. We are hardly likely to get lost, but we must remember that, unless we have bolted on large reflectors, no air traffic controller can see us, so we could present a threat to other traffic. We start our approach far out, like a B-52, and come in as if on rails, but fast! Holding off means stick hard back and the nose high. Then as soon as we feel the runway, we stream the drag chute. This is comfortably large, and very powerful. It is also usually black, like the rest of the aircraft.

As we taxi back to the ramp we feel rather superior. Sitting high up at the apex of this extraordinary arrowhead we suddenly realise that it all has one purpose in view: hitting a high-value point target and coming back. The inference is obvious: if ever we have to do this 'for real' then this is the delivery system to use.

Another view of the pyramidal cockpit area, showing the jagged edges for radar dispersion, and the forward-looking infra-red sensor recessed behind a mesh beneath the windscreen.

'I was amazed at just how agile that fighter really was, and at the ability to point the nose'
Major Bob Wade

Mikoyan MiG-29 'Fulcrum'

Approaching the MiG-29 on the ground it looks purposeful and it looks right, although the nose droops too much, the intakes are too raked and sharp, and the fins are too angular for the word beauty to be applied. It is a fighter aeroplane pure and simple, optimised for the role of bettering any other aircraft over the field of battle. Above all the aircraft looks right aerodynamically, and in fact the MiG's aerodynamic form is responsible for its remarkable performance. Western aircraft designers used sophisticated digital computers and fly-by-wire control systems to give acceptable handling to aircraft which were inherently too unstable to be flown by an unaided human pilot. Mikoyan went back into the wind tunnel and produced a shape which was a better compromise between the conflicting demands of agility and controllability, producing an agile shape which was not inherently unstable.

Furthermore, when designing flight control systems for their aircraft the Soviets chose to incorporate soft limits. They tested the real ultimate boundaries, exploring the post-stall area of the envelope, then came in from these to set inner, soft limits. These warned the pilot when he was approaching those parts of the envelope where he might risk departure if he stayed too long, or where he might overstress the aircraft, but they did not prevent him from making brief excursions into the 'tatty bits' of the envelope or from over-stressing the aircraft, to seize a tactical advantage, out-turn a missile, or avoid hitting a hill. Loss of control becomes progressively more likely, but will not be immediate. This gives great confidence when manoeuvring at the edges of the envelope. The soft limits of the MiG-29 are considerably greater than the hard limits of equivalent Western fighters. This means that the Soviet fighter pilot can fly slower, or at higher α, or at higher g than the F-16 pilot, even without reaching the soft limits of his flight control system, which are defined by stick stops.

Flying the MiG-29 would be certain to shatter many widely-held assumptions about Soviet technology and philosophy. Kitting up before flight the average Western fighter pilot would find Soviet g suits immediately familiar, while flying suits and flying boots are reportedly more com-

Under view of the MiG 29.

MiG 29s have been exported to ten or more foreign nations, the first going to India; this aircraft was photographed at Batajnica in Yugoslavia. (Jon Lake)

fortable. The helmet is light and comfortable and is cut well away from the face. An integral air bladder can be inflated to clamp it even more firmly to the head, and this is actuated on cabin depressurization. A more observant Western pilot might notice the mountings for a helmet-mounted sight, already in squadron service with MiG-29 export customers, and still years away from issue to most Western fighter pilots. This allows the MiG-29 to designate a target well off his centreline (or 'boresight') simply by looking at it, and gives a useful tactical advantage in some circumstances.

The start-up sequence is quick and simple, and can be achieved using standard NATO ground support equipment. If the Warsaw Pact had ever rolled forward, the MiG-29 squadrons would not have been forced to wait for their own starter trolleys, etc. to catch up. Extensive built-in test equipment is incorporated, and fault rectification can be extremely quick. Radios, for example can quickly be plugged in or removed, and pre-set channels re-programmed. Normal turn-around times are extremely short. In extremis, we are told, the MiG-29 can take off (and indeed complete a simulated mission) on one engine, allowing a slightly shorter elapsed time before the wheels leave the runway. Normally, of course, you use both, though unless a very short take off is necessary, max dry power is usually sufficient. With both of the Isotov RD-33 engines (manufactured by the Leningrad/Klimov Scientific and Technical Association) in full afterburner, however, (producing 18,300 lbs of thrust each) take off acceleration is blistering, and the aircraft can be off the ground within 240 metres.

Such is the efficiency of the intake system, that even with the main intakes shut off by huge doors on take off, to prevent FOD ingestion, there is no evidence in the cockpit that all the air is being sucked through louvres on the top surfaces of the wingroot. Acceleration and afterburner light up are extremely smooth, with no hint of the 'kick in the pants' familiar to Western fighter pilots.

As with all modern 'Superfighters' acceleration, rate of climb, and maximum speed are extremely impressive, but where the MiG-29 really comes into its own is in its remarkably well integrated weapons system and its sheer agility. Taking the weapons system first, the MiG-29 can broadly be compared with aircraft like the F-15 Eagle and F/A-18 Hornet, since its powerful multi-mode pulse Doppler radar gives it much better look-down, shootdown and BVR (Beyond Visual Range) capability than aircraft like the F-16. The radar is not, however, the MiG-29's only sensor. For detecting, tracking and engaging an enemy passively (that is to say without generating electromagnetic emissions) the MiG-29 can use its infra-red search and track system (IRST). This sensor is reportedly more accurate than radar in angular tracking, and has a collimated laser for ranging. When in use, the radar is slaved to the IRST, and will be activated only if the target flies into cloud, or if IR contact is lost for some other reason. When combined with an IR-homing version of the AA-10 'Alamo' missile, this gives the MiG-29 a formidable 'fire and forget', unde-tectable passive BVR kill capability, since the MiG-29 can turn away from the target after missile launch, and since the target aircraft will not be warned that an IR homing missile is 'on its way' by its RWR equipment. These sensors are backed up by an excellent onboard electronic warfare suite, which includes passive warning receivers and active jammers.

The MiG-29's comprehensive array of sensors are backed up by a formidable arsenal of weapons, carried on six underwing pylons. A centreline fuel tank can also be carried, but underwing fuel tanks are for ferrying only. Two R.27R (AKU-470) missiles (known to NATO as the AA-10 'Alamo') can be carried inboard, consisting of semi-active radar homing and/or

IR-homing versions of this missile, which is broadly equivalent to the US AIM-7 Sparrow. For closer range work, the MiG-29 can carry four R.60 (AA-8 'Aphid') or four of the newer R.73 (AKU-72/AA-11 'Archer') IR-homing dogfight missiles. The latter, with its vectoring thrust rocket motor and front and rear moving control surfaces, has superb manoeuvrability, especially at launch, making it an ideal weapon for launching at 'off-axis' targets in conjunction with the helmet sight mentioned earlier. The MiG-29's missile armament is augmented by a 30mm cannon in the port wingroot leading edge extension.

In a long range, BVR engagement, the MiG-29 pilot relies on his aircraft's sensors to detect and engage an enemy aircraft before it can engage him. In a close-in engagement he relies on being able to out-turn and out-manoeuvre the enemy. He is able to do this because his aircraft has superior handling characteristics, especially at low speed and high α, a wider aerodynamic and structural envelope, and superior turn performance. The MiG-29 also enjoys an outstanding powerplant, which performs well throughout the envelope.

By tailoring vortex flows very carefully, the designers of the MiG-29 produced a fighter which can sustain 30 α without departing, and can achieve angles of up to 50 α for up to fifteen seconds. The 'Cobra' manoeuvre demonstrated at Farnborough showed an ability to reach angles of above 80 α momentarily. This 'pointability' could be devastating, allowing the MiG-29 pilot to get a firing solution from a position where he would not normally be a threat. The F-15 cannot emulate this, and no Western fighter can do it safely and predictably, day in, day out, at airshow altitudes.

While very high α manoeuvres do have their uses, the ability to sustain higher angles of attack is also an invaluable means of improving turn performance. Pitch rate is limited by the maximum usable Angle of Attack, and this is of crucial importance during the early phase of a turn. The turn performance is governed chiefly by the ability of the wing to generate lift since excess lift (beyond that required to 'balance' gravity) provides the turning force. Lift is directly proportional to angle of attack (α) (up until just before the wing stalls), so the MiG-29's high α capability allows it to generate more lift than equivalent Western fighters at a given airspeed, and to turn more tightly.

The MiG-29's higher *g* limit (9½ *g* in service, 10½ *g* for airshows, 14 *g* as a combat 'never exceed' absolute structural limit) can also be important because, all other factors being equal, higher *g* will give a smaller turn radius. A smaller radius could be achieved by flying more slowly, at lower *g*, but here too the MiG-29's low speed handling characteristics and high α capability give it the edge.

The last word should go to Bob Wade. "The Mikoyan Design Bureau used a different design approach to what we in the West have gone towards. They've gone to great lengths to keep everything very simple, with a very high mean time between failures, and without needing expensive and complicated systems to maintain the airplane. They've achieved the same type of flight performance and handling to Western fighters through better thrust-to-weight ratio and better aerodynamic design."

Picture Acknowledgments

API, Aeritalia, Aer India, Aer Lingus, Air Portraits, W.D. Askham/ Courtesy of Deutsches Museum Munich, Boeing, British Aerospace, British Airways, Bundesarchiv, E.F. Cheesman, H.W. Cowin, Crown Copyright, V. Cook, E. Denny, P. Endsleigh Castle, Eshel GmbH, Flight, Fairey Holdings, Fokker-VFW International, Ford Archives/ Henry Ford Museum Michigan, J. Frost Newspaper Collection, J. Gilbert, J. Gilbert/Leisuresport, J. Goulding, Grumman, M. Hooks, Robert Hunt Library, S. Howe, I.W.M., M. Jerram, J.K. Kerr, P. Kilduff, Lufthansa, Messerschmitt-Bölkow-Blohn GmbH, McDonnell Douglas, Military Aircraft Photographs, MoD, Musée de l'Air, National Defence HQ Canada, D. Oliver, Orbis, M.B. Passingham, L. Peacock, Popperfoto, B. Robertson, Peter Sarson/Tony Bryan, F. Selinger, Shorts/H.W. Cowin, E. Stuart, Michael Turner, United Press International, US Air Force, US Navy, L. Valoušek, Westland.

Index

aerobatics, 52, *55*, 84, *101*, 102, 111, 190, 194, 244, 268
Aérospatiale Concorde, 297
afterburner, 294, *297*, 299
Airborne Cigar (ABC), *174*
airbrake, 300, *300*
air combat, 122, 124, *133*, 136–137, 184, 190, 291, 292
air combat tactics, 69, 285
Aircraft Manufacturing Company (Airco), 61
Air Fighting Development Unit, 219
airline flying, 97–98
Albatros DVa, 42
Alquines aerodrome, 74
Amen, W.T., 258
America USS, 273, *291*
American Airlines, 95
Amiens Gaol raid, 168
Amm, Lt E.O., 44
Antoinette, 2–4, *2–4*
 Antoinette II, *3*
 Antoinette IV, *3*, *4*
 Antoinette V, *4*
 Antoinette VI, *4*
Ark Royal, HMS, 144, 146, *278*
Armstrong, Capt D.V., 52
Atlantic Council, 265
Atoll missile, 291
Auffarth, Oblt Harald, 65
Avro
 504K, *76*, 77–80, *77–80*
 Lancaster, 171–180, *171–180*
 Triplane, 5–7, *5–7*

Bader, Grp Capt Sir Douglas, *124*, *133*, 133, 134, 135
'Balbo' formation, 138
Bär, Obslt Heinz, 238
Barber, Anthony, 156
Barkhorn, Gen Gerhard, 238
Barkley, Steve, 288
barnstorming, *21*, *22*, 24–25, 80
Barraca, Maj Francesco, 60
Beale, AFB, Ca., 293, 294
Beaulier, Jerry, 288
Bechereau, Louis, 60
Bedford, Bill, 277, *277*
Bellamy, V.L., *112*
Bell P-39 Airacobra, *200*
'Bent-Wing Bastard', 200
Berthold, Hptm Rudolf, 45
Bethpage, Long Island NY, 242
Bicknell, Flt Lt Leslie, 111
Bignamini, Maj, 265
Bird, Lt A.F., 38
Bismarck, 146
Blackburn, Robert, 18, 19, 20
Blackburn
 1912 Monoplane, 17–20, *17–20*
 Type E, *20*
Blackpool Aviation Meeting (1909), 3
Blériot, Louis, 9, 10, 11, 12, *12*
Blériot
 Type XI monoplane, 8–12, *8–12*
 Type XXVII, *8*
Block, Hyman C., 62
'Blockbuster' bomb, 168, 171, 174

Blonski, Tom, 291
'Bloody April' (1917), 37
Blue Angels, 244
Board, Gregory, 183
Boeing
 B-17 Flying Fortress, 201–212, *201–212*
 KC-135Q, 295
 P-26, 118–120, *118–120*
 727, 303
 737, 302
 747 'Jumbo Jet', 302–4, *302–4*
 747D, 302
 747E, 302
 747F, 302
Boeing-Vertol CH-46, *287*
Boelcke, Hptm Oswald, 26, *27*, 30, 31, 285
Bon Homme Richard, USS, *259*, 270, 271, 275
Boxer, USS, *194*, 198, 200
Boyington, Gregory 'Pappy', 183
braking parachute, *288*
Brancker, Sir Sefton, 13, *81*, 83
Brest, 147
Brewster F2A Buffalo, 183, 185
Bristol
 Boxkite, 13–17, *13–17*
 Bulldog, 101–103, *101–103*
 F2B Fighter, *66*, 67–71, *67–71*
Bristol & Colonial Aeroplane Company, 13
British Aerospace
 Harrier, and AV-8, 277–282, *277–282*
 AV-8A, *278*, 282
 GR Mk 1, 278, 282

Index

British Aerospace (cont.)
  GR Mk 3, *282*
  T Mk 2, *281*
  Concorde, 305–8, *305–8*
Brooklands, 5, 6, 15
Brothers, Flt Lt Peter, 121, 122
Brown, Lt Ben E., 60
Brown, Capt Eric, 90, 93
Browne, Ross, 11, 12
Buffum, Cpl Thomas A., 38–39, 57
Bulman, W.P.S. 'George', 107
Bullpup missile, 273
Burns, Richard, 214, 218
Burton, Sqn Ldr H.F. 'Billy', 135

Cameron, Ian, 144, 146
Camm, Sir Sydney, 107, 126
Canadian Aeroplanes Limited (CAL), 21
'Canucks', 21
Capon, Carl, 122, 123, 124
Carlson, Harold G., 252
Castle, Capt Vernon, 24
catapult (aircraft carrier), 188, 198, 200
Chabera, Flt, Cdr, *229*
Chambers, John, 260
Chance Vought F4U Corsair, 183, 192–200,
  192–200
'Charlie', 187
'Charlie pattern' formation, 188
Chicago, 95
Chichester, Sir Francis, 83
Child, Lt, 30, 31
China National Airlines, 100
Ciampolini, Giulio, 265
Cobham, Sir Alan, 84
Coke, David, 122
Coltishall, Norfolk, 132
Combat Air Patrol (CAP), 191, 259
Compton, Wg Cdr Bill, 138
Concorde, 305–8, *305–8*
condensation trails, *202*
Connelly, Matt, 291
Constantinesco interrupter gear, 51, *67*, 115
Constellation, USS, *249*, 271, *283*, 288, 291, *291*
Control Configured Vehicle (CCV), 295
Cooper, Capt Merian C., 63
Copenhagen raid (March 1945), 168
'Corrugated Coffin', 89
counter-insurgency (COIN) aircraft, 252
counter-insurgency missions, 191
Cousins, Lt William S., 59
Cowpens, USS, 188, 189, 190, 243
Creagh, 'South', 137
Crenshaw, Keith, 291
Crowley-Milling, AVM Sir Denis, 136
'Cuban Eight' manoeuvre, 249
Cubitt Ltd, 65
Cunningham, Lt Randall 'Duke', 283, *283*,
  284, 287, *287*, 288, 290, 291, 292, *292*
Curtiss
  JN-4 Jenny, 21–26, *21–25*
  P-40, 181, 183, *216*

Danang airfield, 275
'deck launch' technique, 188
Deere, Air Commodore Sir Alan 'Al', 138
Degelow, Lt Carl, 45
de Havilland, Sir Geoffrey, 61, 81, 84
de Havilland
  DH4, 61, *61*, 62, 63, *63*, 65
  DH9, *61*, 62, 63, 64, *64*, 65, *65*
  DH9A, *64*
  DH60 Gipsy Moth, 81, 83, 84
  Tiger Moth, *81*, 83, *83*, 84, *84*
  Mosquito, 161–169, *161–169*
  B Mk IV, *166*
  B Mk IX, 166
  B Mk XVI, *163*, 168
  B Mk XVIII, *169*
  B Mk 35, *161*, 168
  FB Mk XI, *165*, 166
  NF Mk 36, *163*

T Mk 3, *164*
TT Mk 39, *163*
Dieppe raid (August 1942), 136–137
disengagement manoeuvres, 291
dive bombing, 249
Dixon, Carl, 24, 42, 72, 74, 75
Doolittle, Lt Gen Jimmy, 157
Dorand AR1, 62
Dornier Do 17, *122*
Dougan, 2nd Lt W.L., 44
Dougherty, Earl, *21*, 22
Douglas, Lt, 30, 31
Douglas
  A-1 Skyraider, 247–252, *247–252*
  A-1D (AD-4NA), 249, 251
  A-1E (AD-5), 252
  A-1H (AD-6), *251*
  A-1J (AD-7), 252
  AD-1, 247, 249
  AD-2, 249
  EA-1F, *251*
  XBT2D-1, 247, *248*
  A-4 Skyhawk, 269–276, *269–276*
  A-4A (A4D-1), 269
  A-4B (A4D-2), 270
  A-4C (A4D-2N), 270
  A-4E (A4D-5), 270, *270*, 271, *272*, 273, *276*
  A-4F, 271, *271*, 272, 273
  A-4M, 274
  TA-4F, *269*
  XA2D-1, 269
  DC-2, 95
  DC-3, C-47, 95–100, *95–100*
  DST, 95
  Dakota *see* DC-3
  SBD Dauntless, 186
Driscoll, Lt (jg) William P., 283, 284, *287*,
  288, 291, 292, *292*
Dun-sur-Meuse raid (1918), 63
Dutch Harbour, Aleutians, 181
Dams raid (1943), 178

Eagle, HMS, *278*
Eaker, Lt Gen Ira C., 118
Ean, Lt James, 186–191 *passim*, 241, 242,
  243, 244, 245
Eisenhower, Gen Dwight D., 270
Eilijah, 83
Emperor, HMS, 191,
Enemy Coast Ahead, 178
'Ensign Eliminator', 200
Esmonde, Lt Cdr Eugene, 147
Essen raid (March 1945), *178*
Essex, USS, 186, 270
Essex-class carriers (CVs), 186, 188, *189*, 197,
  198

Fairey Swordfish, 141–147, *141–147*
Fajtl, Col František, 225, 229
Farman biplane 16, *16*
Farmer, 122, 123, 124
Fazan, Tom, 213
Fiat
  G 91, 265–268, *265–268*
  G 91PAN, 268
  G 91R1, 267, *267*
  G 91R1A, 267
  G 91R1B, 267
  G 91R3, 268
  G 91R4, 268
  G 91T, 268
  G 91Y, *267*, 268
Field Carrier Landing Practice (FCLP), 187,
  188
Fighter Weapons School, 285
Filton, Bristol, 297
'finger four' formation, *134*
First and The Last, The, 231
Fisher, Maj Bernard F., 252
'flaming onions', *54*, 57
Fliegende Stachelschwein, 148
flight procedure, 97–98
flight simulator, 302, 303

flying clubs, 83
'Flying Porcupine', 148
'Flying Washboard', 85
Focke Wulfe Fw 190, 136, 137
Foggin, Cyril, 19
Fokker, Anthony, 29, 41, 47
Fokker
  DVI, 41
  DVII, 41–47, *41–47*
  Dr I Triplane, 37–40, *37–40*
  E-Type Eindecker, 26–31, *26–31*
  EI, 27, 29, *29*, 30
  EII, *29*, 30
  EIII, *27*, 30, *31*
  EIV, 31
'Fokker scourge'. (1915), 30
Fonck, Capt René, 60
Ford
  2-AT Air Pullman, 85
  3-AT, 85–86
  4-AT Tri-Motor, 85–88, *85–88*
  5-AT Tri-Motor, 88, *88*
  C-9, *87*
Fox, Jim, 292
Frantz, Sgt Joseph, 27
Frazer-Nash turret, 172
Friedrichs, Lt Fritz, 93

Gabrielli, Prof, 265, 266
Galland, Gen Adolf, 231, 238, *240*
Galland hood, 235
Gann, Ernest K., 86, 87, 88, 95, 98, 100
Garnett, David, 83
Garros, Roland, 11, 29
Gaskell, Sgt Geoffrey, 112–113
Gates Air Circus, 24–25
Gen Phu, 284
GH airborne radar, 177
Gibson, Wg Cdr Guy, VC, 178
Glen, Lt., 30, 31
Glenview, Ill., 187
Gloster
  Gladiator, 109–113, *109–113*
  Sea Gladiator, *112*
  Gauntlet, 109
  Meteor, 253–257, *253–257*
  F Mk 8, *254*
  NF Mk 14, *255*, *257*
  T Mk 7, *257*
Gneisenau, 147
Gollob, Gen Gordon, 238
Goodyear, Harry, 20
Gosport, Hampshire, 77
Gosport speaking tube, 77
Gosport training system, 15
Gould Lee, AVM Sir Arthur, 36, 50, 53, 54,
  55
Grand Central Terminal, Glendale, L.A.,
'Grand Slam' bomb, 171, *176*
Grant, Lt Brian, 290, 291, 292
Grant, Sqn Ldr Reg, 137
Gray, Bob, 158
'group grope', 260
Grumman, Leroy, 185
Grumman
  F4F Wildcat, 181, 182, 185
  FM-2 (General Motors), 186
  F6F Hellcat, 183, 185–191, *185–191*
  -3, *185*, 186, *186*, *187*, 189, 242
  -3N, 191
  -5, 191, *191*
  -5N, 191
  XF6F-1, 186
  XF6F-2, 186
  XF6F-3, 186
  F8F Bearcat, 241–246, *241–246*
  -1, *242*, 244, *244*, 245
  -2, *241*, 246
  -2P, *241*, 246
  F9F Panther, 200, 258–60, *258–60*
  -2, 258, 259, *259*, 260, *260*
  -3, 258
  -5, 260

-5KD, *259*
-9E Cougar, 259
XF9F-1, *258*
XF9F-2, 258
S-2 Tracker A8W, *276*
'Grumman Iron Works', 186, 189
g-suits, 244
Guadalcanal, 183, 192
Guam, uss, 278
Gutknecht, Oblt, 43

H2S radar, 172, 176, 177
Hagg, Arthur, 83
Haiphong, 273, 292
Hale, George, 202
Halford, Frank, 81, 83
Hampton, H.N., 107
Hancock, uss, 270, 271, *271*
Handley Page
  O/100, 72, *72*
  O/400, 72–75, *72–75*
Hanoi, 274
hardened aircraft shelters (HAS), 298, 299
Harpon, 4
Harries, Wg Cdr Ray, 139
Harris, MRAF Sir Arthur, 171
Harris, Flt Lt George H.G., *174*
Haskell, Charlie, 251
Hawker
  Fury, 114–117, *114–117*
  Hart, 105–108, *105–108*
  Harrier *see* British Aerospace
  Hurricane, 121–127, *121–127*
  P1083, *274*
  P1127 Kestrel F(GA) Mk 1, 277, 278, *278,*
    281
  P1154, 278
Hawkinge, Kent, 115
head-up display (HUD), 298, *299,* 301
Heber, Fritz, 29
'Heinemann's Hot Rod', *269,* 270
Hendon School (Blériot), 11
Hendon air display, *10*
Heppell, Plt Off Whaley, 134
Herrmann, Obst Hajo, 238
Heuval, George Van der, 212
Hill, ACM Sir Roderick, 52
Hispano HA1112-M1L, *237*
'Hog', 200
Holloway, Admiral James L., III, 258, 259,
  260, 270
Hope-Boyd, Adrian, 112
Horikoshi, Jiro, 181
Hornchurch, 109, 111
Hornet, uss, 157, 159, *159,* 186
Horsley, Terence, 142, 147
'Hose Nose', 193, *199*
Houser, Vice-Admiral William D., 192–200
  passim
Hoy, Capt E.C., 44
Hucks, B.C., 20
Hucks starter, 222
Hunter, John, 137
Hwachon Dam, 252, *252*

Immelmann, Oblt Max, *27,* 30, 31
Immelman turn, *27*
Indomitable, hms, 191
inertial navigation system (INS), 298, 299,
  301, 304
instrument land system (ILS), 301, 304
Interruptor gear, 29, 51 *see also*
  Constantinesco
Intrepid, uss, 188, *249, 276*
'Iron Annie', 89
'Iron Hand' missions (Vietnam War), 272,
  274
Island Airways, 88
Isübbe, Heinrich, 29
Ivanovo, 221, 225

Jacobs, Josef, 39, 40, *40*
Jameson, Wg Cdr 'Jamie', 136

John F. Kennedy, uss, *251*
Johnson, Clarence L. 'Kelly', 293
Johnson, AVM J.E. 'Johnnie', 129, *139*
Johnson Lyndon B., 288
Johnson, Scott, 90, 91
'Johnson Bar', 87
Jones, Sgt, 30
Jullerot, Maj Henri, 13
'Jumbo Jet' *see* Boeing 747
Junkers, Prof Hugo, 89
Junkers Ju 52/3m, 89–93, *89–93*

kamikaze (suicide attacks), *184*
Kansas City, 97, 98
Kazakov, Staff-Capt Alexander, 29
Kearsage, uss, 242
Kenley, Surrey, 137
Kep Airfield, Hanoi, 275
Kinnear, Vice-Admiral George E.R., II, 249,
  250, 251, 252
Kinsella, Lt James J., 260
Kirksey, Rear-Admiral Robert E., 270–276
  passim
Kitty Hawk, uss 273
Kleizkamp raid (April 1944), 168
Knight, Lt Clayton, 64, 65
Korean War, 192, 193–194, *194, 195,* 198,
  200, 249, 251, 252, *252,* 258–261, *259, 260,*
  265
Kostrba, Hpt, *30*
Kraut, Lt der R. Richard, *45*

Lagesse, Cpt C.H.R., 44
Lake Champlain, uss, 195, 198, 200, 249, 251
Landing Signal Officer (LSO), 187, 192, 193,
  197
Lamb, Cdr Charles, 142, 143, 144
Langley AFB, Va., *120*
Laos, 294
Larkhill, Wilts, 15
Latham, Hubert, 2, 3, 4
Lavochkin
  La-5, 225–229, *225–229*
  La-7, 229
Lawrence, T.E., 75
Lawson, Capt Ted, 157, 159
Lazoryk, 122
Lebanon crisis (1958), 270
Leffers, Lt Gustav, 30, 31
Lend-Lease, 191
Leonard, 1st Lt Edmond C., Jnr, 63
Levavasseur, Léon, 2, *3*
Lewis, Sqn Ldr John, 35
Leyte, uss, 245
'Liberty Plane', 62
Ling-Temco-Vought (LTV) A-7E Corsair II,
  291
Lisbon Conference (1952), 265
Lockheed, SR-71 Blackbird, 293–296,
  293–296
Locklear, Ormer, 22
Loerzer, Oblt Bruno, 41
'loft' bombing technique, 249
Los Angeles, 95
Love Field, Texas, 22
Lufthansa, 302, 304
Luke, 2nd Lt Frank, Jnr, 59
Lützow, Obst Günther, 238

McClung, Lt, 60
McCudden, Maj James, VC, 33
McDonnell Douglas
  F-4 Phantom II, 283–292, *283–292*
  F-4B, 284
  F-4D, *288*
  F-4J, *284,* 287, *288, 291,* 292
  F-15 Eagle, 297–301, *297–301*
Macmillan, Norman, 53
MAC-ship, 142
Malcolm hood, 220
March AFB, Ca., 261
March Field, Ca., 118
Marcus Island attack (1943), 186

'Marianas Turkey Shoot' (19 June 1944), *183,*
  189
Marske, Yorkshire, 18
Martin Baker ejection seat, 281
Martindale, Capt Stanley, 74, 75
Martlesham Heath, Suffolk, 121
Matušek, *229*
May, Wesley, *22*
Merrick, R.C., 252
Messerschmitt
  Bf 109, 230–237, *230–237*
  -109E Emil, 133, *133, 230,* 231, *231,* 233,
    235, *235,* 237
  -109F Friedrich, 133, 233
  -109G Gustav, *233,* 235, 237
  Me 262 Schwalbe, 238–240, *238–240*
Midway, uss, 246, 247, 284, *291*
Midway, Battle of, 183
Midway-class carriers, 197
MiG
  -15: 198
  -17: 287, 292
  -19: 287, 292
  -21: 287, *287,* 292
  -25: 297
'MiG Alley', 198
MiG Combat Air Patrol (MiG CAP), 290
Miles, Geoff, 124
Mitsubishi
  A5M Claude, 181
  A6M Zero-Sen (Zeke), 181–184, *181–184*
  -3, 183
  -5b, *181*
  -5c, *183*
  -11, *181*
  -52, *181*
Möhne Dam, 178
Mölders, General der Jagdflieger Werner, 233
'Monica' tail warning radar, 172
Montgomery-Moore, Maj Cecil, 21, 22, 23
Moore, Maj W.G., 55
Morris, Lt, 22
Myers, D. Wayne, 252

National Slovak Uprising, 229
Nesbitt-Dufort, Wg Cdr John, 108, 114, 115,
  153
Netheravon, Wiltshire, 72
Nettleton, Sqn Ldr J.D., VC, *172*
Newark Airport, Notts, 95
New York, 95, 97, 98
night fighting, 221
Nivelles, Belgium, 42
No Parachute, 36, 55
Norden bombsight, *204*
Normandie-Niemen regiment, 221, 223, 224,
  224
North American
  B-25 Mitchell, 157–60, *157–160*
  -25C, *159*
  -25J, *159*
  F-86 Sabre, 261–264, *261–264*
  -86A, 264
  -86D, *263*
  -86E, 263
  -86H, *264*
  P-51 Mustang, *200,* 213–220, *213–220*
  -51D, 213, *214, 216,* 218, 219, *219, 220*
  -51K, 218
  Mk III, 219, 220
  SNJ Texan, 187
Northrop F-5E, 286
Norwegian Campaign (1940), 143
Nowotny, Maj Walter, 238

Okiyama, Masatake, 183
Old Rhinebeck airfield, New York, *39,* 57

Palen, Cole, *39,* 57
parachutes, 43, *43*
Paris Air Show (1932), 107
Pau School (Blériot), 11
PB-1a gunsight, 225

Index

Pearl Harbour, 181, 185
Pégoud, Adolphe, 12
'Penguins', 10
Perring, 2nd Lt J.H. 'Bert', 65
Petter, W.E., 152
Pfalz D XII, 43
Philippine Sea, USS, *195*, *199*, 258, *260*
Pickard, Grp Capt Percy, 168
Pippart, Lt Hans, 59
Platz, Reinhold, 41
Plinston, Sqn Ldr G.H., 114, 115
Point Mugu, Ca., *288*
Polikarpov I-16, 181
Potter, Charles, 148
Prince, Lt, 75
Princeton, USS, 252
Prinz Eugen, 147
Put-in-Bay Island, Ohio, 88

Quang Lang, 290
Quenault, Caporal, 27
Quill, Jeffrey, 134
Quonset Point, Rhode Island, 245

Raesch, Lt Josef, 43, *43*
RAF (Royal Aircraft Factory) SE5, 43
RAF Museum, Hendon, 107
Ranger, USS, 243, 244, 245
Rathbun, Camp, 22
Reid, Stuart, *75*
Reims Aviation Meeting (1909), 4
Renown, HMS, 146
'Rhubarb' operations, 136, 138
Richthofen, Manfred von, 33, *37*, 38, *40*
Rickenbacker, Capt Eddie, 60
Risso, Gen J.M., 221
Roberts, 1st Lt, 40
Roe, Alliott Verdon, 5–7
Rohozná, *226*
Rolls Royce Olympus, 297
Ross. D.G., Capt, 297

Sable, USS, 187
St Louis, 97, 98
Sakai, Saburo, 181, 182, 183, 184
SAM (surface-to-air missile), 272, 274, 275, 290, 291
Sanseverino, Vittorio, 265, 267, 268
Saunders, ACM Sir Hugh 'Ding Bat', 138
'scarecrow', 178
Scharnhorst, 147
Schenk, Fw Wolfgang, *238*
Schmidt, Lt, *43*
Schneider, Franz, 29
School of Special Flying, Gosport, 77
Schorlemer, Freiherr von, 27, 29
Schwendler, William T., 185
Scrimgeour, Wg Cmdr David, 279
Shikoku Island, *183*
Shoemaker, Steve, 291
Short Sunderland, 148–151, *148–151*
Shrike missile, 272

Shuttleworth Trust, Old Warden, 15, 19
Sidewinder missile, 273, *285*, *299*, 301, *301*
Simpson, Duncan, 105, *108*
Sinanju, 198
Six Day War (1967), 275
'ski jump' launching technique, *282*
'Skunk Works', 293
Smith, Capt, 97–98
Smith-Barry, Col Robert, 15, 77
Snakeye fin-retarded bomb, 273
Sopwith
  Camel, 48–55, *48–55*
  Scout (Pup), 32–36, *32–36*
Southall, Ivan, 149
Sparrow missile, 301, *301*
SPAD (Societé Pour Aviation et ses
   Dérivés), 56
  SVII, *56*
  SXIII, 56–60, *56–60*
Spanish Civil War, *117*
Sparrow missile, *285*
Spratt, Lt, 75
Squantum Naval Air Station, 241
Steinhoff, Gen Johannes, 238
Stenthes, Lt, 60
'stepped down' formation, 119
'stepped up' formation, 119
Stevenson, Lt, 73
Stewart, Maj Oliver, 35, 36, 51, 52, 55, 67, 71
Stout, Bill, 85
'Sto-Wing', *189*
Strähle, Paul, 45, 46
strategic bombing, 201
'Stringbag', 141, *141*
Stringer, Patrick, 144
Sullivan, Maj Jim, 294
Sullivan, Lt Jerry, 290
Supermarine
  Spitfire, *126*, 129–140, *129–140*
  Mk 1, 132, 133, *134*
  Mk V, *133*, 134
  Mk IX, *133*, 136, 137, *139*, 140
  Mk XII, 139
  Mk XIV, *138*, 140, *140*
  Mk XVI, 140
  PR Mk XIX, *137*
supersonic speed, 262
Surma, Franik, 122
Sutton, Oliver, 36, 52
Sutton Harness, 36, 52
Swartz, Ted, 275
Sykes, Capt Ronald, 51, 52

'tail-chase' formation, 194
'Tallboy' bomb, 171, *176*
Tallman, Frank, 85, 87, 88, 158, *160*
Tangmere, Sussex, 137
'Tante Ju', 89
They Shall Not Pass Unseen, 149
Thomas, B. Douglas, 21
*Those Magnificent Men in their Flying
   Machines*, 6, 15

Thousand Bomber Raid, *178*
Ticonderoga, USS, *251*
Timm, Cdr Dwight, 292
'Tin Goose', 85
'Tiny Tim' rocket projectile, 196
Tonkin Gulf incident (2 August 1964), 284
Toon, Col, *287*, 292
torpedo, aerial, 144–146
Traill, 146
transcontinental airline flights (USA), 95
Transcontinental Air Transport, 88
Trans-Continental and Western Air (TWA), 97
Trans World Airlines (TWA), 88, 97
transonic flight, 261, 264
Tripartite Evaluation Squadron, 278
Tuck, Wg Cdr R.R. Stanford, 109, 121, *122*, *126*, 133, 231
'Turbinlite', 221
Turner, Michael, *54*, *101*, *156*
Turner-Hughes, C., 84
Tweer, Gustav, 27, 29

Udet, Gen Obst Ernst, 43, 233

Valley Forge, USS, 249, 258, 259
Valoušek, Ladislav, 225, *226*, 229, *229*
Verity, Wg Cmdr H.S., 153
'vic' formation, *134*
Vietnam War, *249*, *251*, 252, 270–276 *passim*, 283–292 *passim*
Vicksburg, USS, 184
Victorious, HMS, *196*
'V/STOL, 277

Walleye 'smart' bombs, 273
Wallis, Wg Cdr Ken, 156
Wembley Park, Middlesex, 7
Westland Lysander, 152–156, *152–156*
Wheeler, Air Commodore Allen, 69, 71, 78, 80
Whittle, Air Commodore Sir Frank, *253*
Williams, Bertram, 11, 12
Williams, Neil, 6, 15, 16, 19, 20, 35
Wilmot, Chester, 137
Window, 172, 174, 177, *178*
Winter War, 102
Wolverine, USS 187
Woollett, Capt Henry, 53
Wootton, Frank, *107*, *133*

Yakovlev
  Yak-1: 222, *224*
  Yak-3: *221*, *223*, 224
  Yak-7: 222
  Yak-9: *221*, 222, 223, 224
Yorktown, USS, 186, *191*

Zindel, Dipl Ing Ernst, 93
Zolná, *226*, 229
Zuni missile, 275